A "mosquito" came buzzing up today and sucked my "blood," then made good his escape. He didn't even say thanks! If Dracula sucks your blood I hear you turn into a vampire, so when a mosquito sucks your blood does that mean you turn into a mosquito? Yeeargh! Nooo! I don't wanna turn into a mosquito! I like normal food.

—Akira Toriyama, 1981

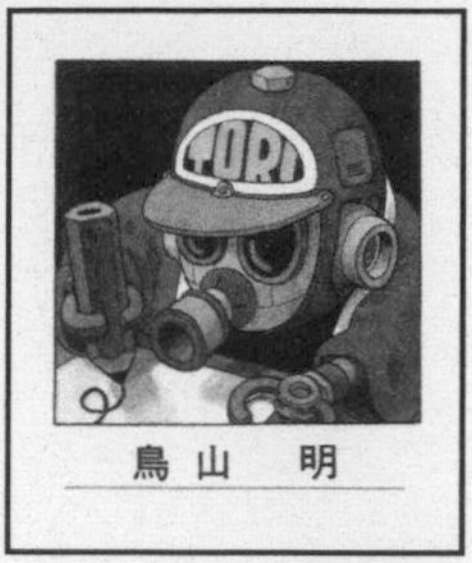
TORI
鳥山 明

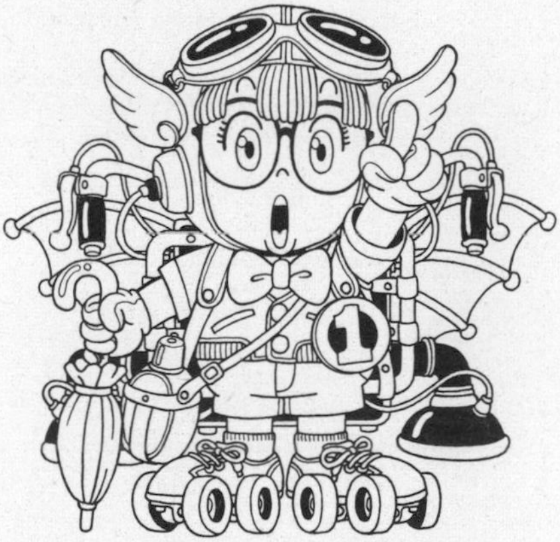

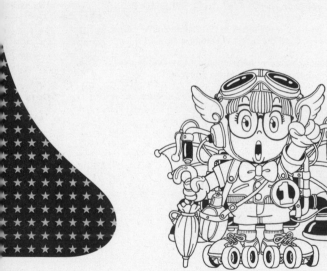

Akira Toriyama's first weekly series, **Dr. Slump**, has entertained generations of readers in Japan since it was introduced in Shueisha's **Weekly Shonen Jump** magazine in 1980. A few years later, he created his wildly popular **Dragon Ball** series, which brought him international success. Toriyama is also known for his character designs for video games, including **Dragon Warrior, Chrono Trigger** and **Tobal No. 1**. He lives with his family in Japan.

DR. SLUMP VOL. 5
SHONEN JUMP Manga Edition

STORY AND ART BY
AKIRA TORIYAMA

English Adaptation & Translation/Alexander O. Smith
Touch-up Art & Lettering/Walden Wong
Cover & Interior Design/Hidemi Sahara
Editor/Yuki Takagaki

Published by VIZ Media, LLC
P.O. Box 77010
San Francisco, CA 94107

10 9 8 7 6 5 4 3 2
First printing, December 2005
Second printing, August 2014

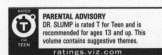

PARENTAL ADVISORY
DR. SLUMP is rated T for Teen and is
recommended for ages 13 and up. This
volume contains suggestive themes.
ratings.viz.com

SHONEN JUMP MANGA

Dr. SLUMP

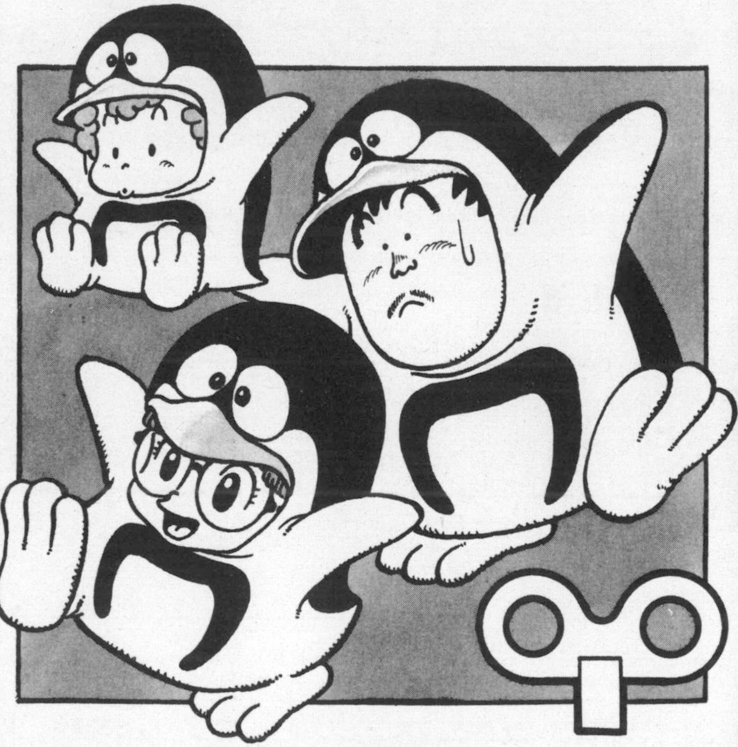

Story & Art by

Akira Toriyama

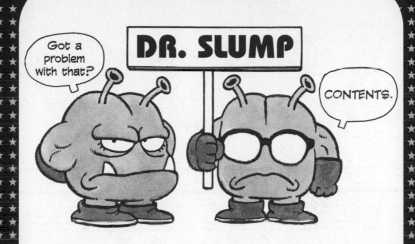

Got a problem with that?

DR. SLUMP

CONTENTS.

Vol. 5

Super Slump Police Special
Untouchable Arale

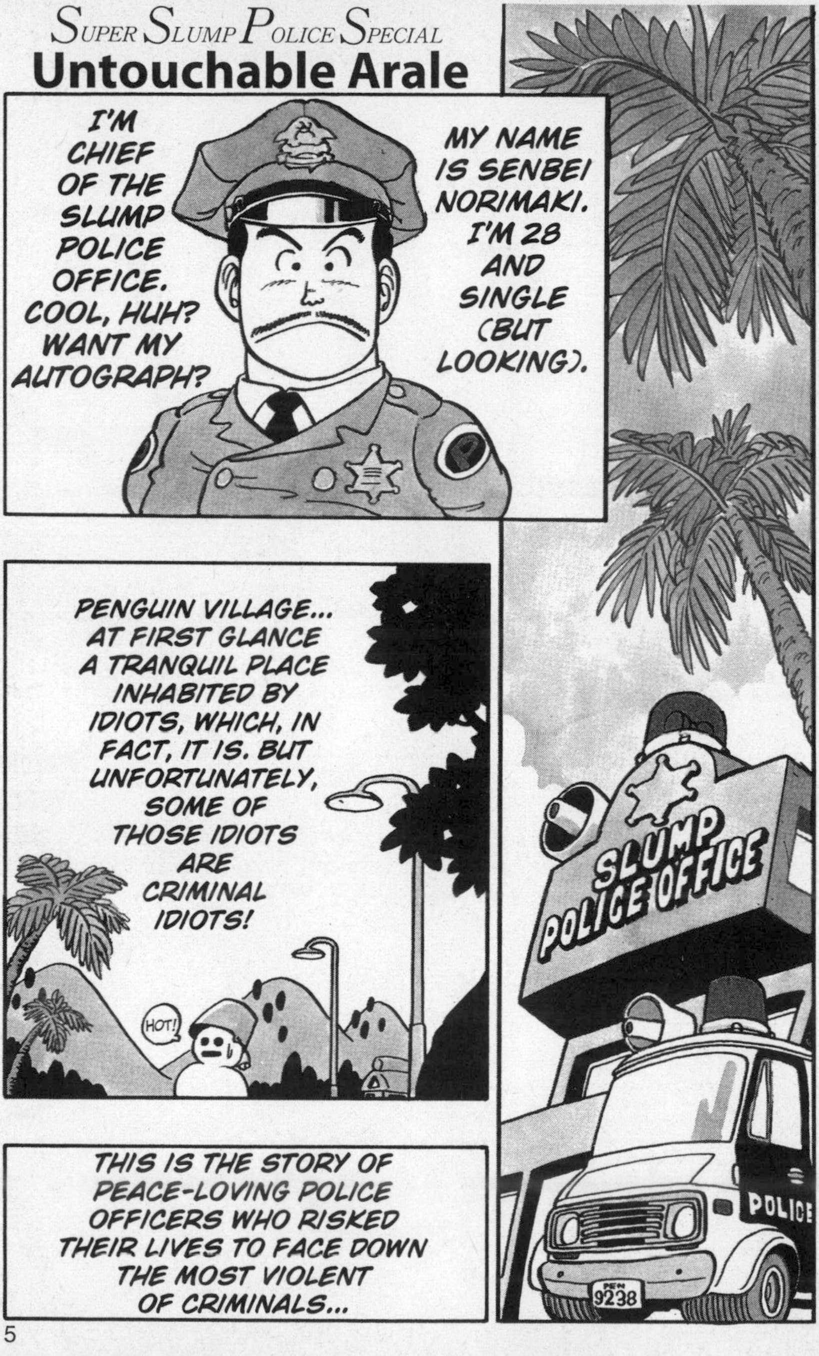
SLUMP POLICE OFFICE
POLICE
PEN 9238
MY NAME IS SENBEI NORIMAKI. I'M 28 AND SINGLE (BUT LOOKING).
I'M CHIEF OF THE SLUMP POLICE OFFICE. COOL, HUH? WANT MY AUTOGRAPH?
PENGUIN VILLAGE... AT FIRST GLANCE A TRANQUIL PLACE INHABITED BY IDIOTS, WHICH, IN FACT, IT IS. BUT UNFORTUNATELY, SOME OF THOSE IDIOTS ARE CRIMINAL IDIOTS!
HOT!
THIS IS THE STORY OF PEACE-LOVING POLICE OFFICERS WHO RISKED THEIR LIVES TO FACE DOWN THE MOST VIOLENT OF CRIMINALS...

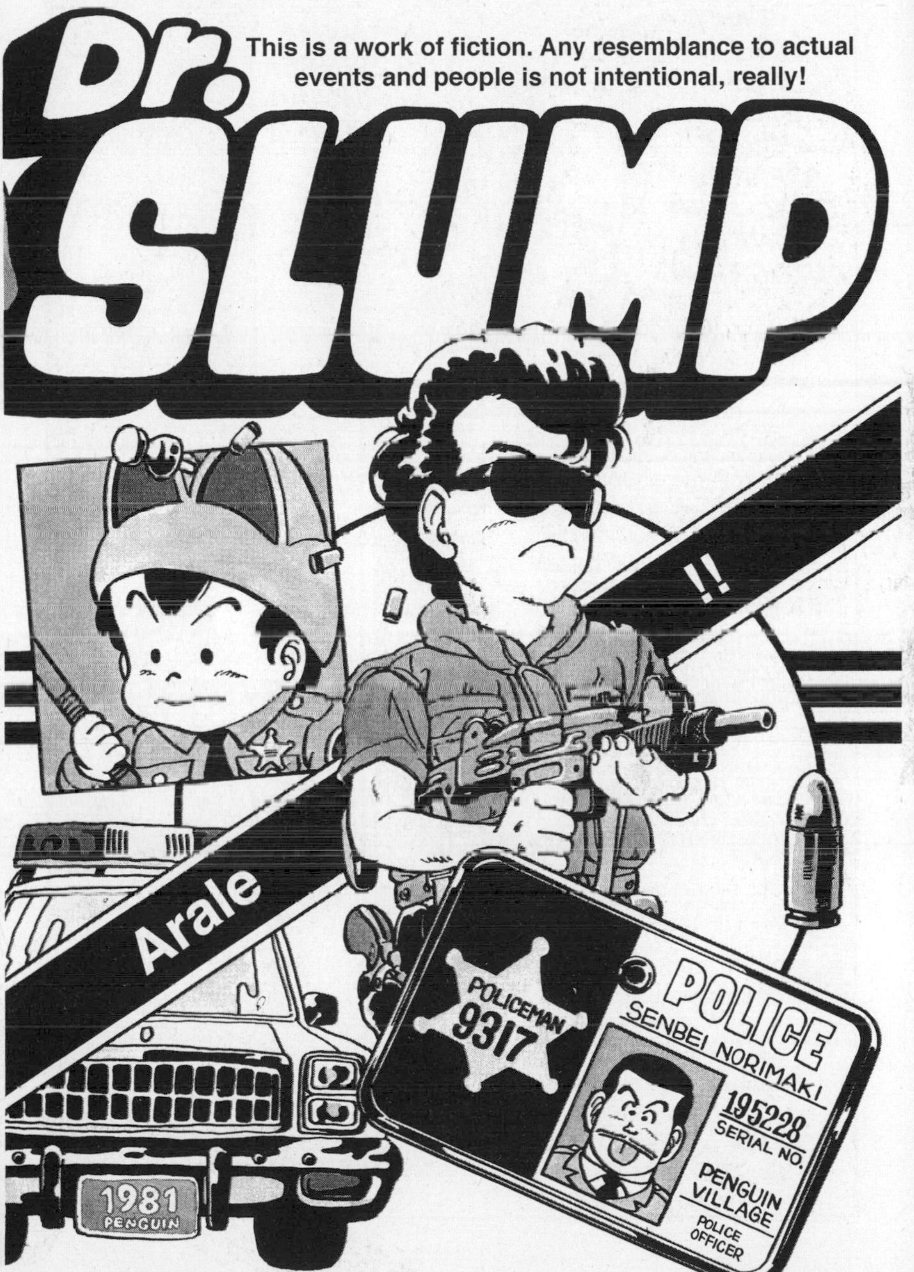
Dr. SLUMP
This is a work of fiction. Any resemblance to actual events and people is not intentional, really!
!!
Arale
POLICEMAN 9317
POLICE
SENBEI NORIMAKI
195228
SERIAL NO.
PENGUIN VILLAGE
POLICE OFFICER
1981
PENGUIN

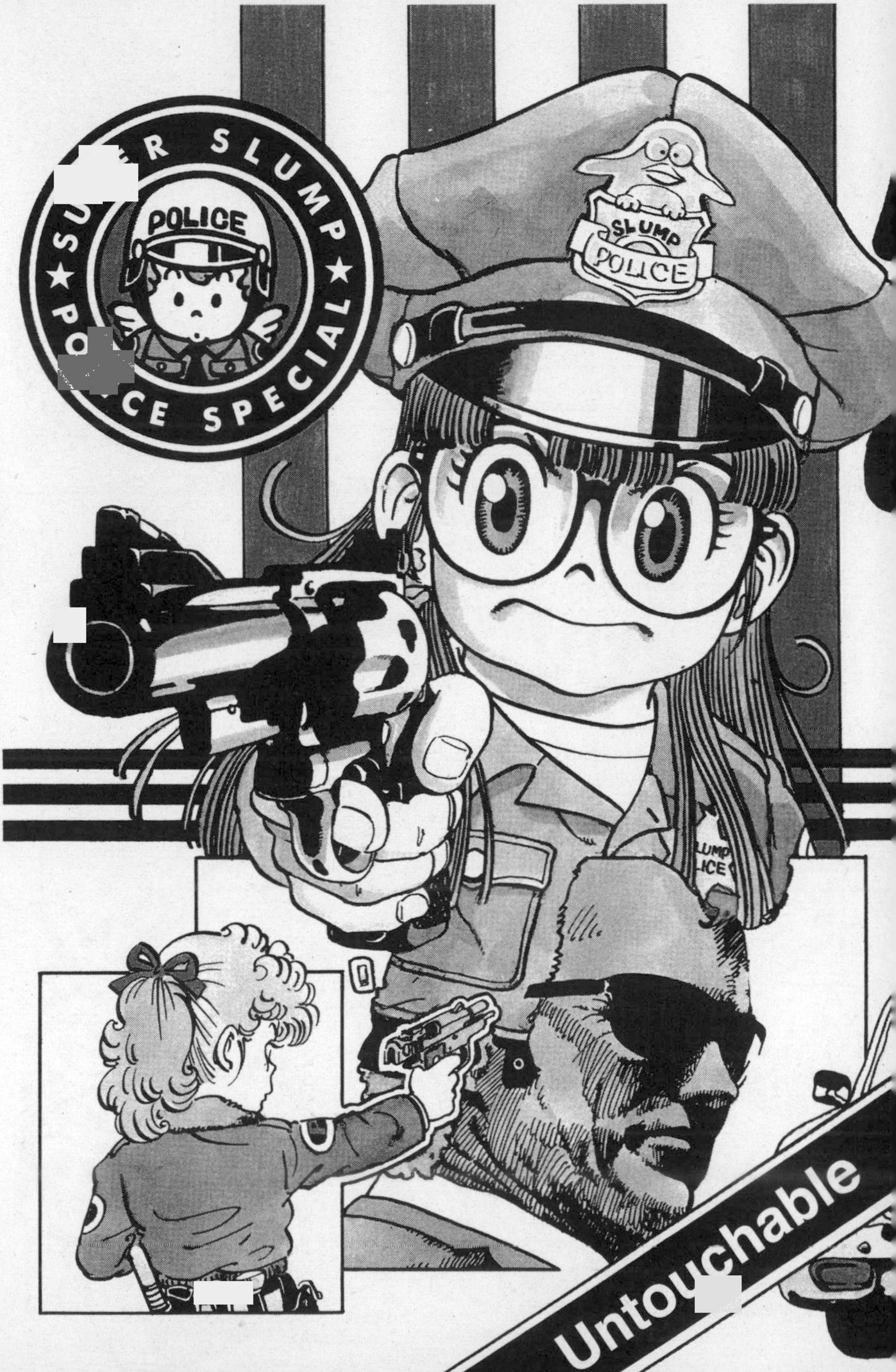
SLUMP
SPECIAL
POLICE
SLUMP
POLICE
Untouchable

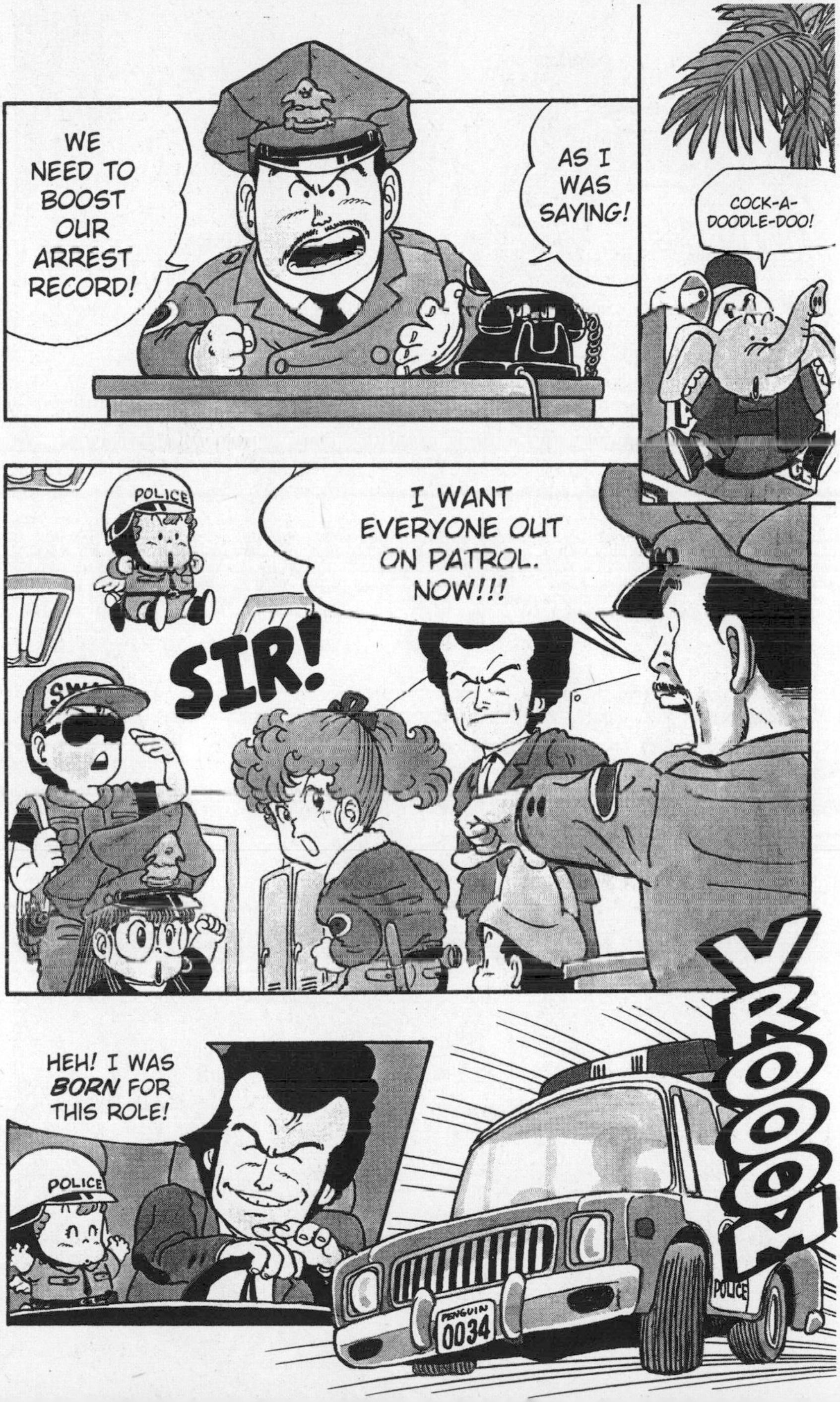
COCK-A-DOODLE-DOO!
AS I WAS SAYING!
WE NEED TO BOOST OUR ARREST RECORD!
I WANT EVERYONE OUT ON PATROL. NOW!!!
POLICE
SIR!
VROOOOM
POLICE
PENGUIN 0034
HEH! I WAS BORN FOR THIS ROLE!
POLICE

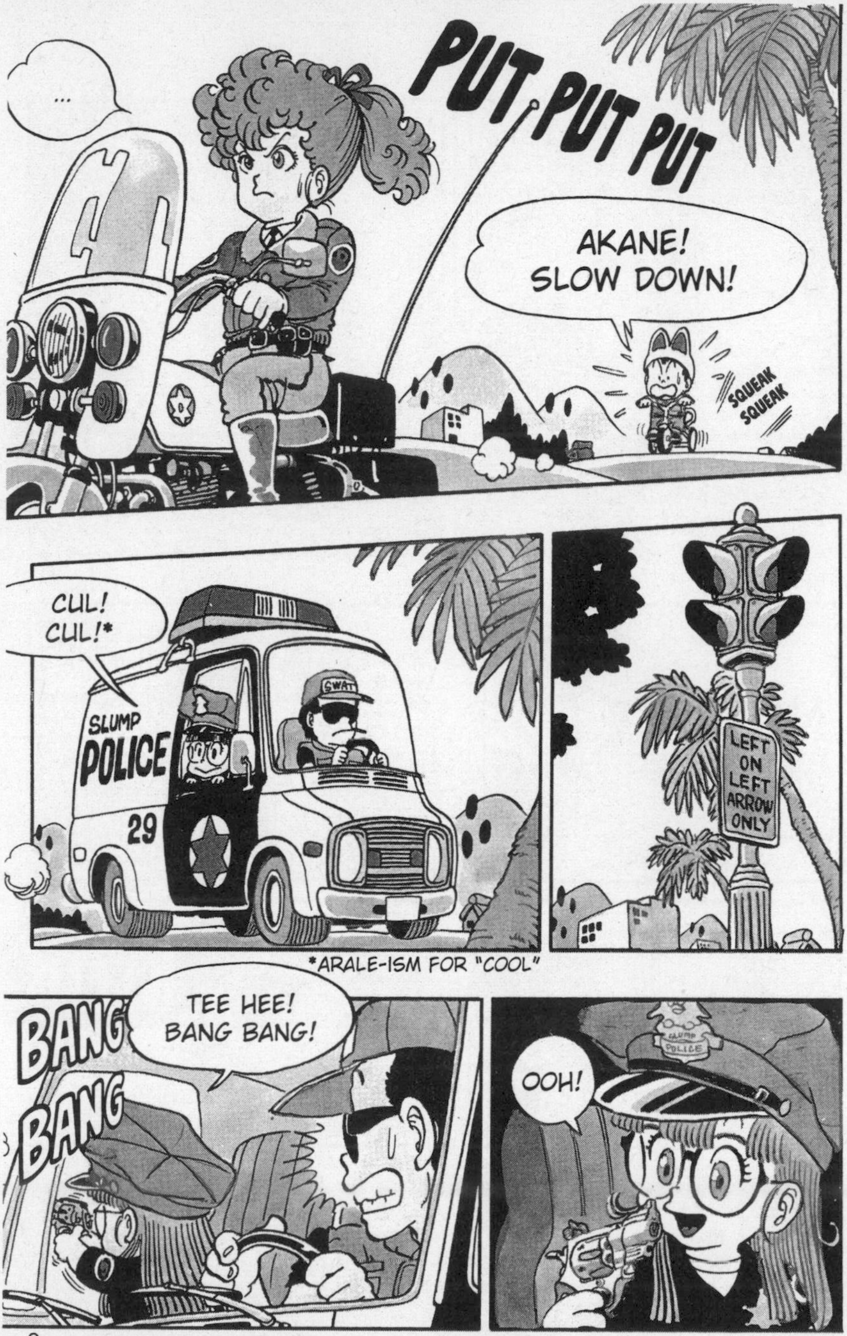
PUT PUT PUT
...
AKANE! SLOW DOWN!
SQUEAK SQUEAK
LEFT ON LEFT ARROW ONLY
CUL! CUL!*
SWAT
SLUMP POLICE
29
*ARALE-ISM FOR "COOL"
SLUMP POLICE
OOH!
TEE HEE! BANG BANG!
BANG BANG

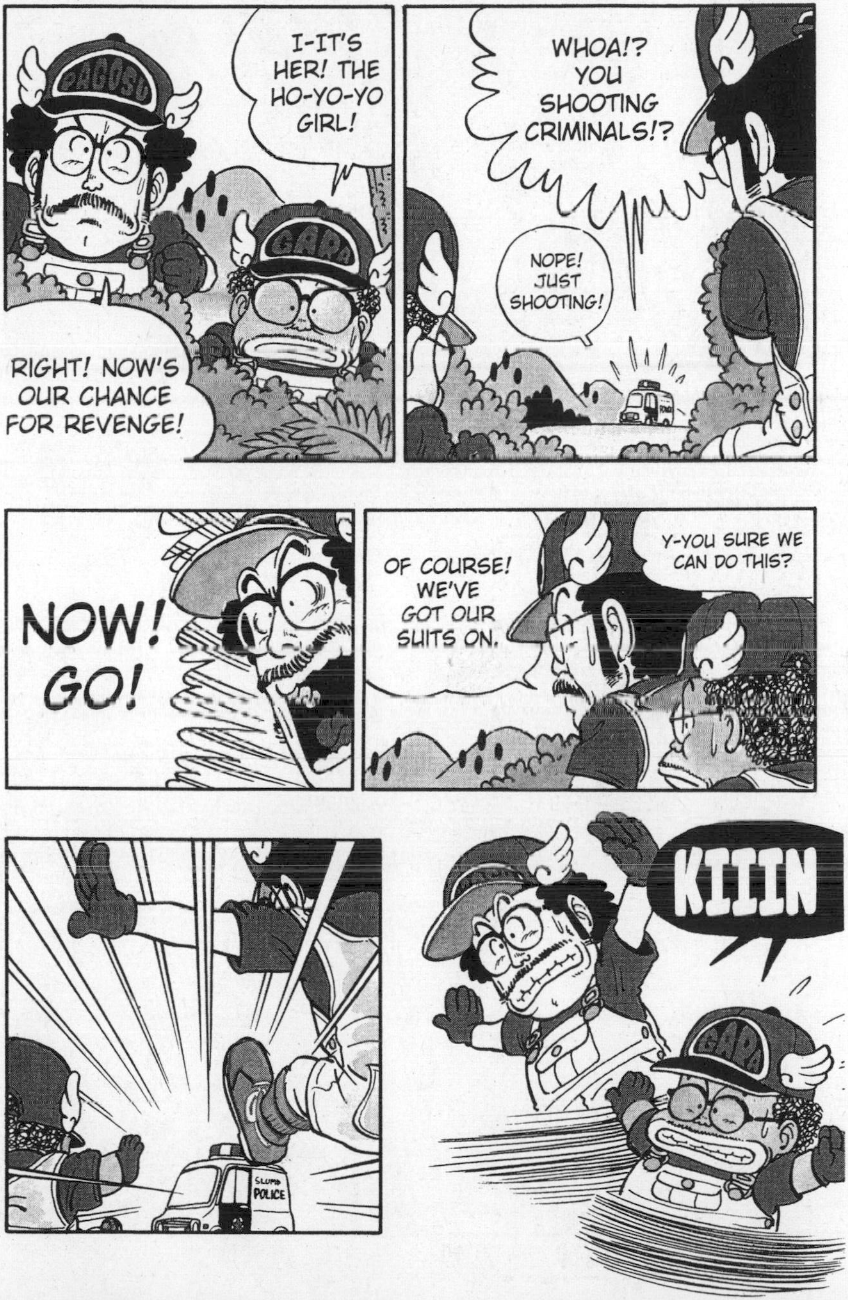
WHOA!? YOU SHOOTING CRIMINALS!?
NOPE! JUST SHOOTING!
I-IT'S HER! THE HO-YO-YO GIRL!
RIGHT! NOW'S OUR CHANCE FOR REVENGE!
Y-YOU SURE WE CAN DO THIS?
OF COURSE! WE'VE GOT OUR SUITS ON.
NOW! GO!
KIIIN
SLUMP POLICE

READ THIS WAY

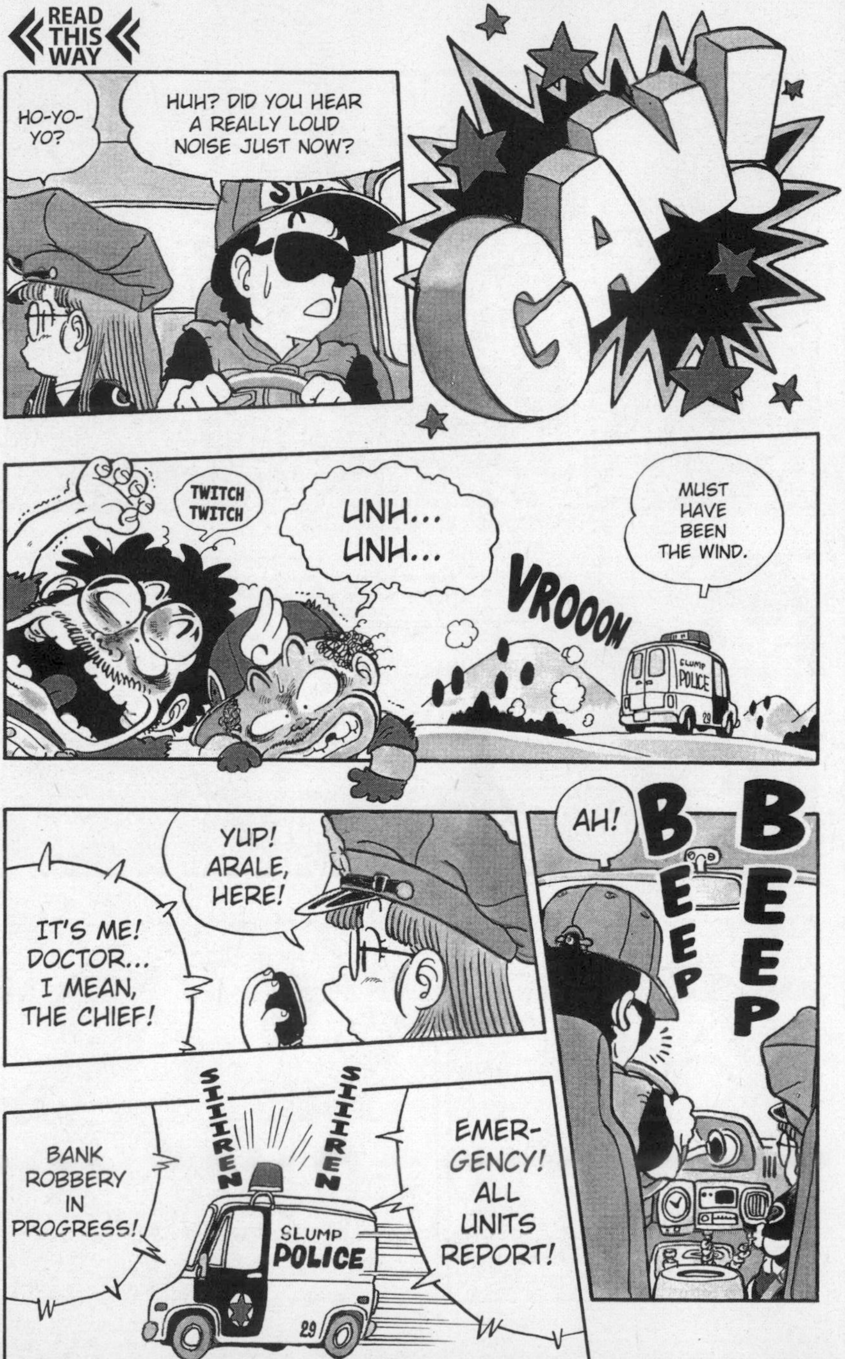
CAN!
HUH? DID YOU HEAR A REALLY LOUD NOISE JUST NOW?
HO-YO-YO?
MUST HAVE BEEN THE WIND.
VROOOM
SLUMP POLICE
UNH... UNH...
TWITCH TWITCH
AH!
BEEP BEEP
BEEP
YUP! ARALE, HERE!
IT'S ME! DOCTOR... I MEAN, THE CHIEF!
EMERGENCY! ALL UNITS REPORT!
SIIIREN
SIIIREN
BANK ROBBERY IN PROGRESS!
SLUMP POLICE

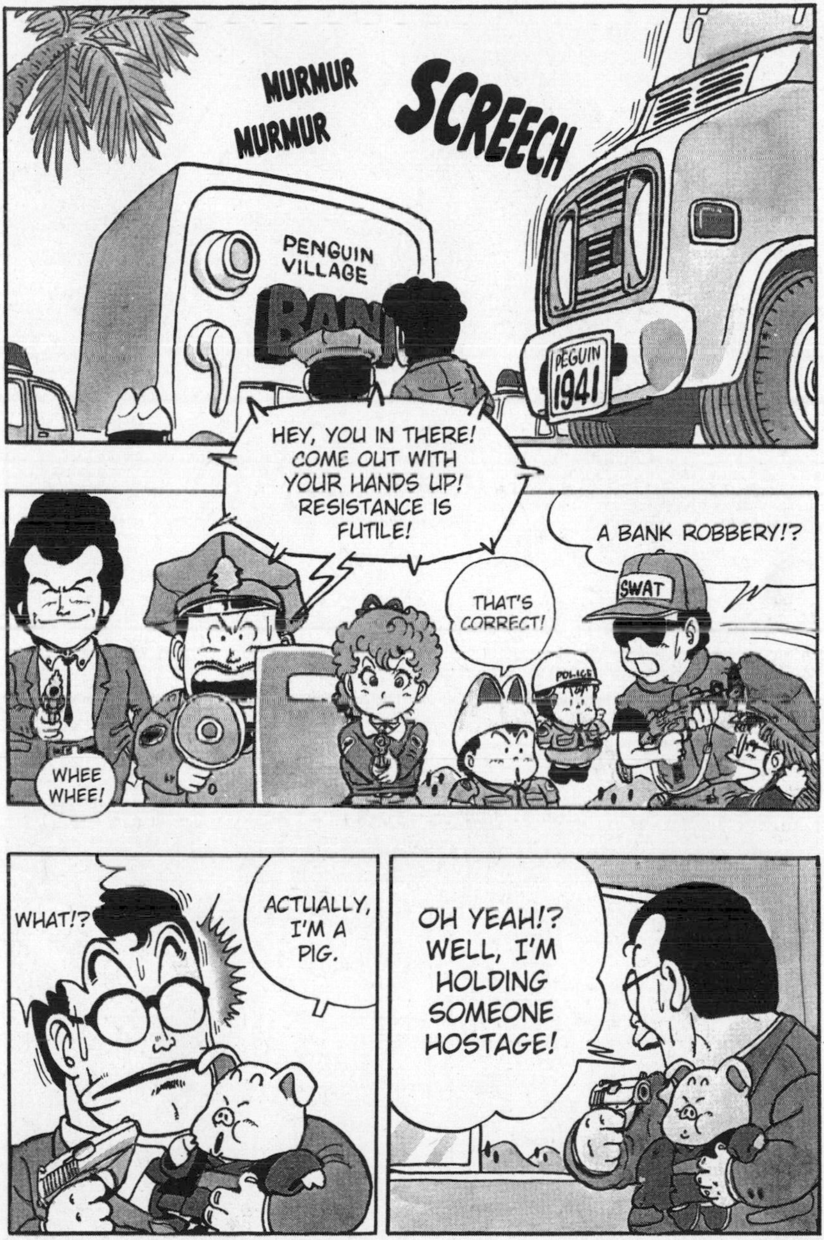
MURMUR
MURMUR
SCREECH
PENGUIN VILLAGE
PEGUIN 1941
HEY, YOU IN THERE! COME OUT WITH YOUR HANDS UP! RESISTANCE IS FUTILE!
A BANK ROBBERY!?
SWAT
THAT'S CORRECT!
POLICE
WHEE WHEE!
OH YEAH!? WELL, I'M HOLDING SOMEONE HOSTAGE!
ACTUALLY, I'M A PIG.
WHAT!?

READ THIS WAY

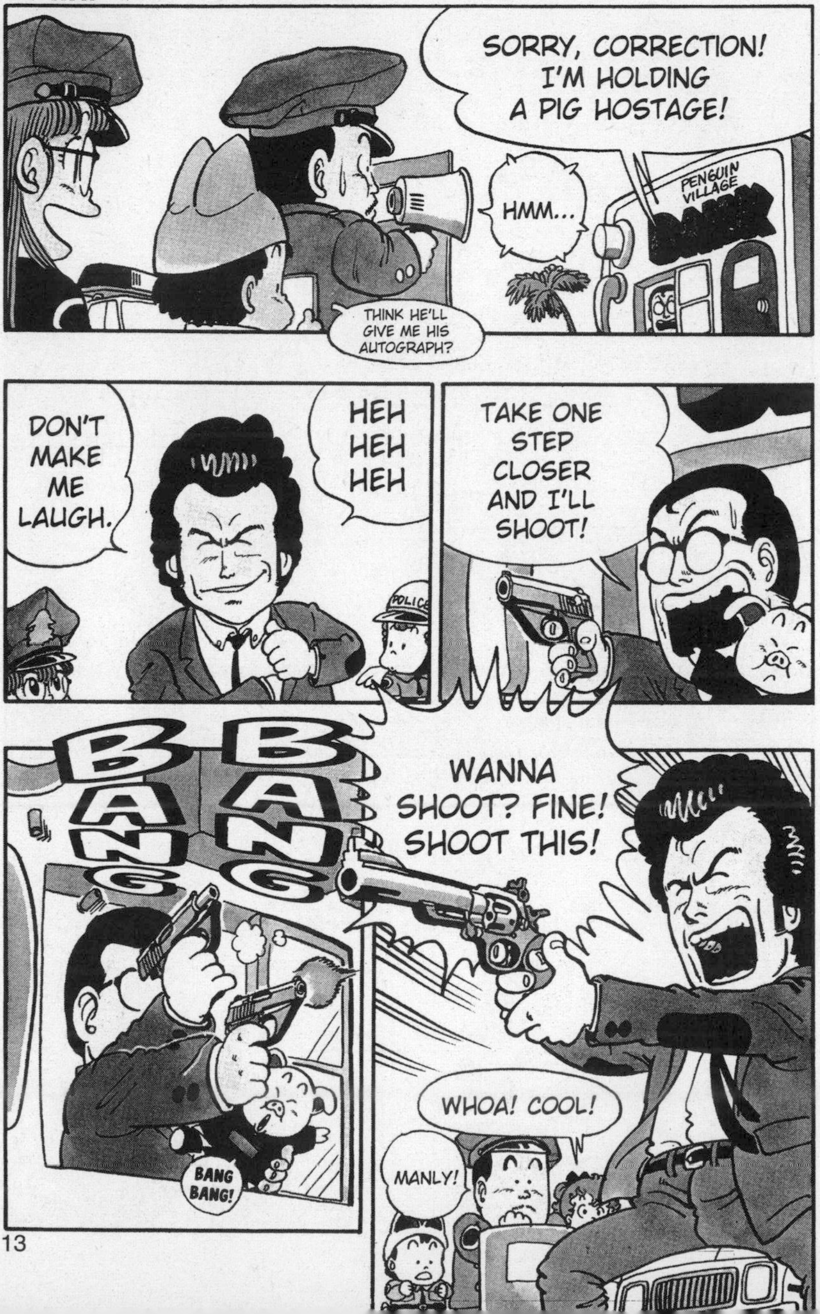
SORRY, CORRECTION! I'M HOLDING A PIG HOSTAGE!
PENGUIN VILLAGE
HMM...
THINK HE'LL GIVE ME HIS AUTOGRAPH?
TAKE ONE STEP CLOSER AND I'LL SHOOT!
HEH HEH HEH
DON'T MAKE ME LAUGH.
POLICE
WANNA SHOOT? FINE! SHOOT THIS!
WHOA! COOL!
MANLY!
BANG
BANG
BANG BANG!

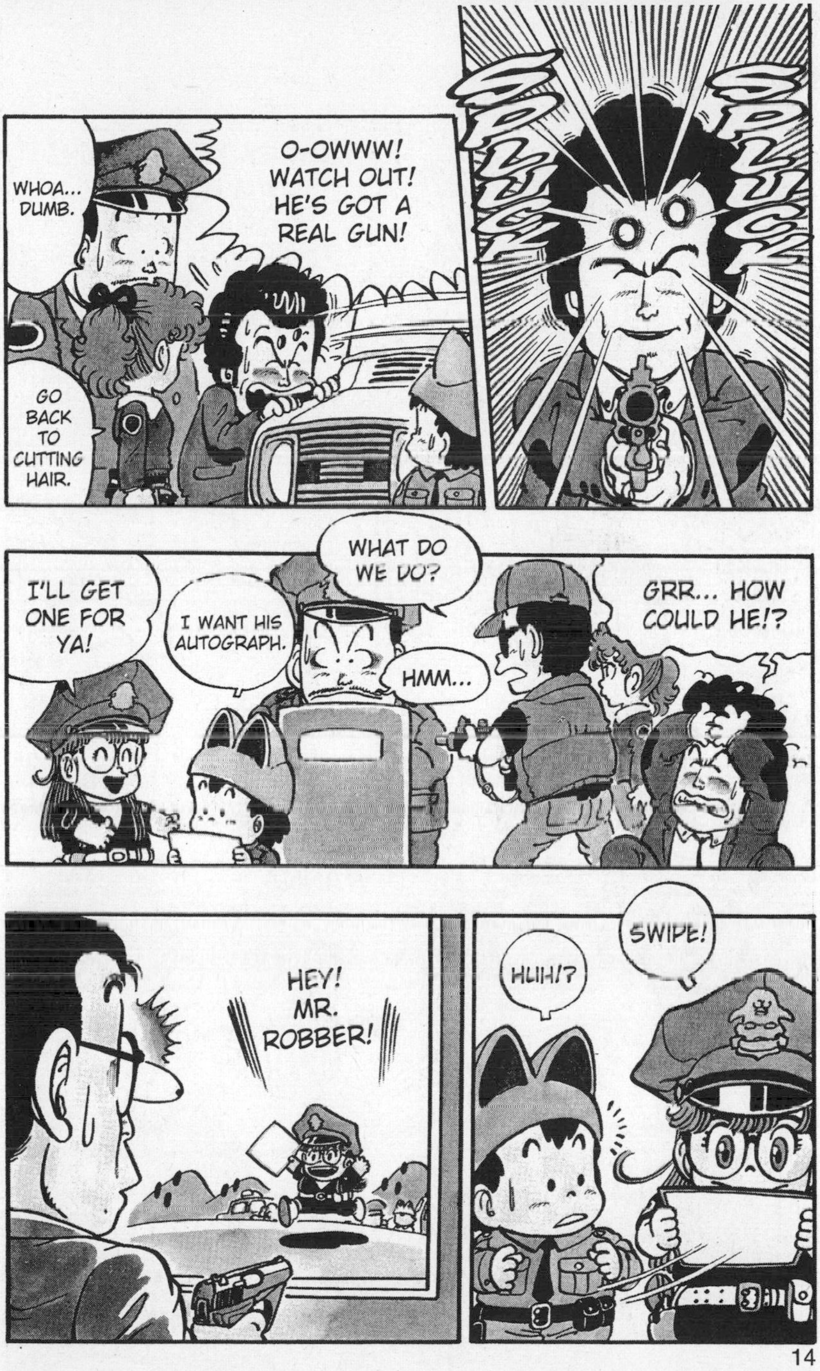
SPLUCH
O-OWWW! WATCH OUT! HE'S GOT A REAL GUN!
WHOA... DUMB.
GO BACK TO CUTTING HAIR.
GRR... HOW COULD HE!?
WHAT DO WE DO?
HMM...
I WANT HIS AUTOGRAPH.
I'LL GET ONE FOR YA!
SWIPE!
HUH!?
HEY! MR. ROBBER!

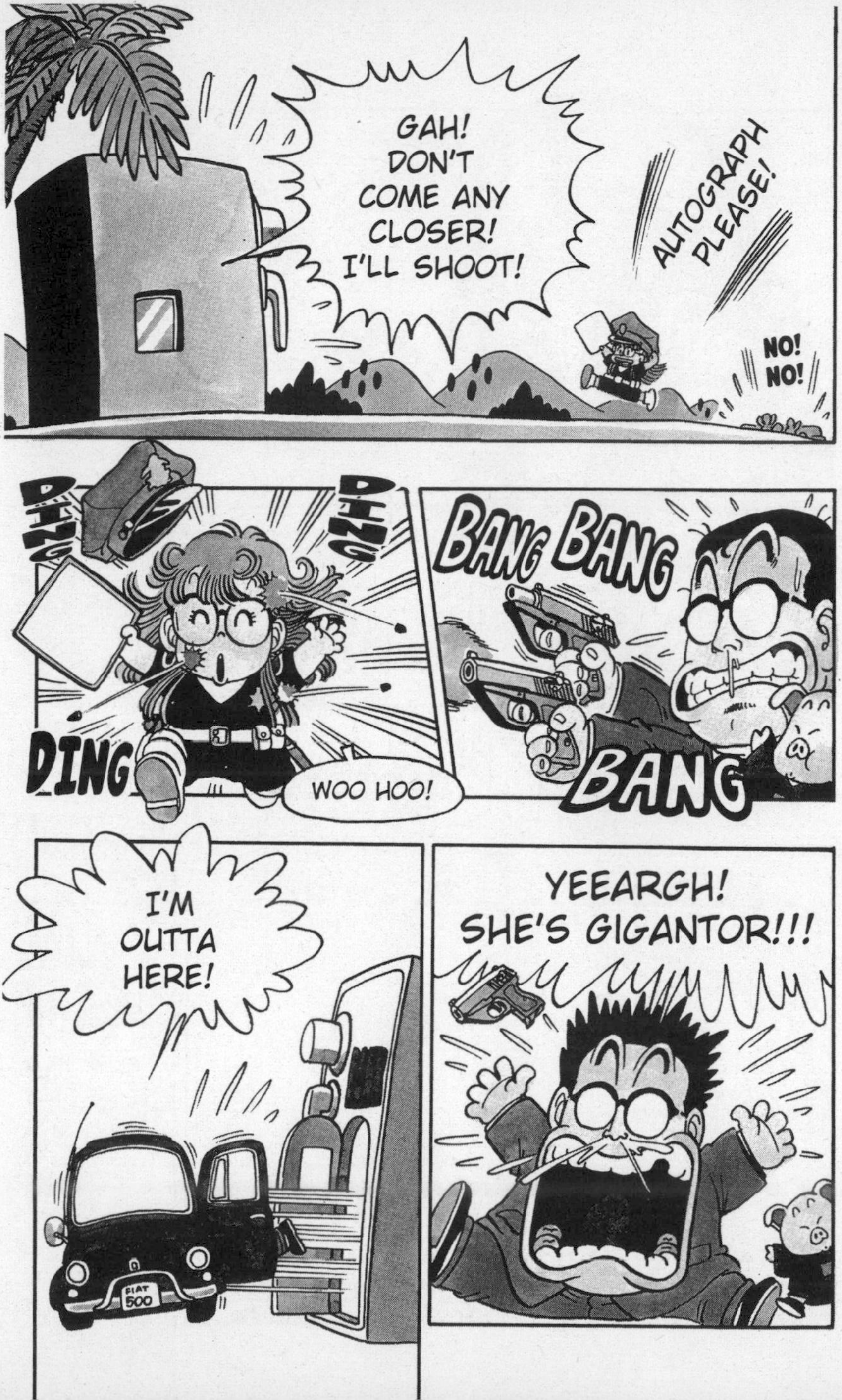
AUTOGRAPH PLEASE!
NO! NO!
GAH! DON'T COME ANY CLOSER! I'LL SHOOT!
BANG BANG
BANG
DING
DING
WOO HOO!
DING
YEEARGH! SHE'S GIGANTOR!!!
I'M OUTTA HERE!
FIAT 500

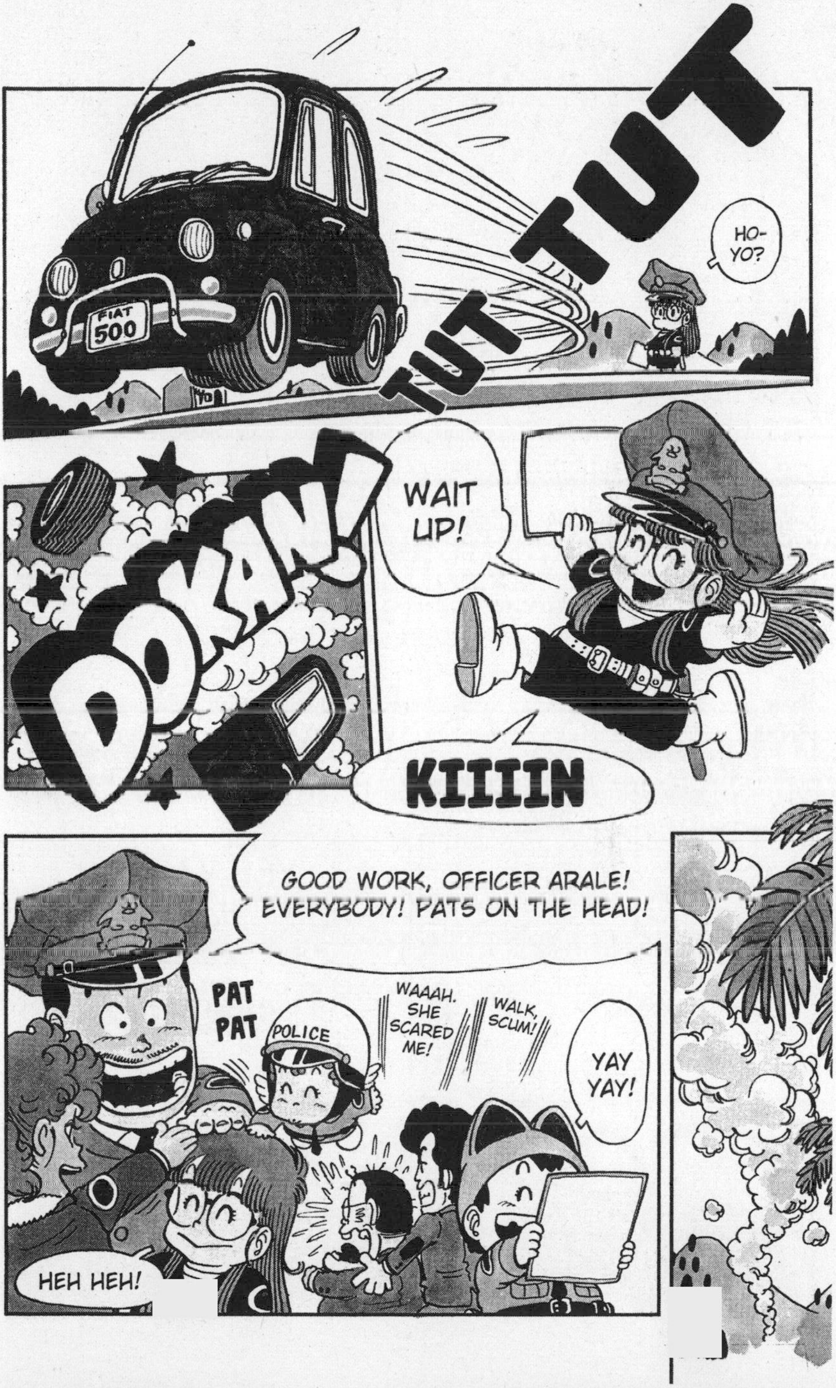
TUT TUT
HO-YO?
FIAT 500
WAIT UP!
KIIIIN
DOKAN!
GOOD WORK, OFFICER ARALE! EVERYBODY! PATS ON THE HEAD!
YAY YAY!
WALK, SCUM!
WAAAH. SHE SCARED ME!
PAT PAT
POLICE
HEH HEH!

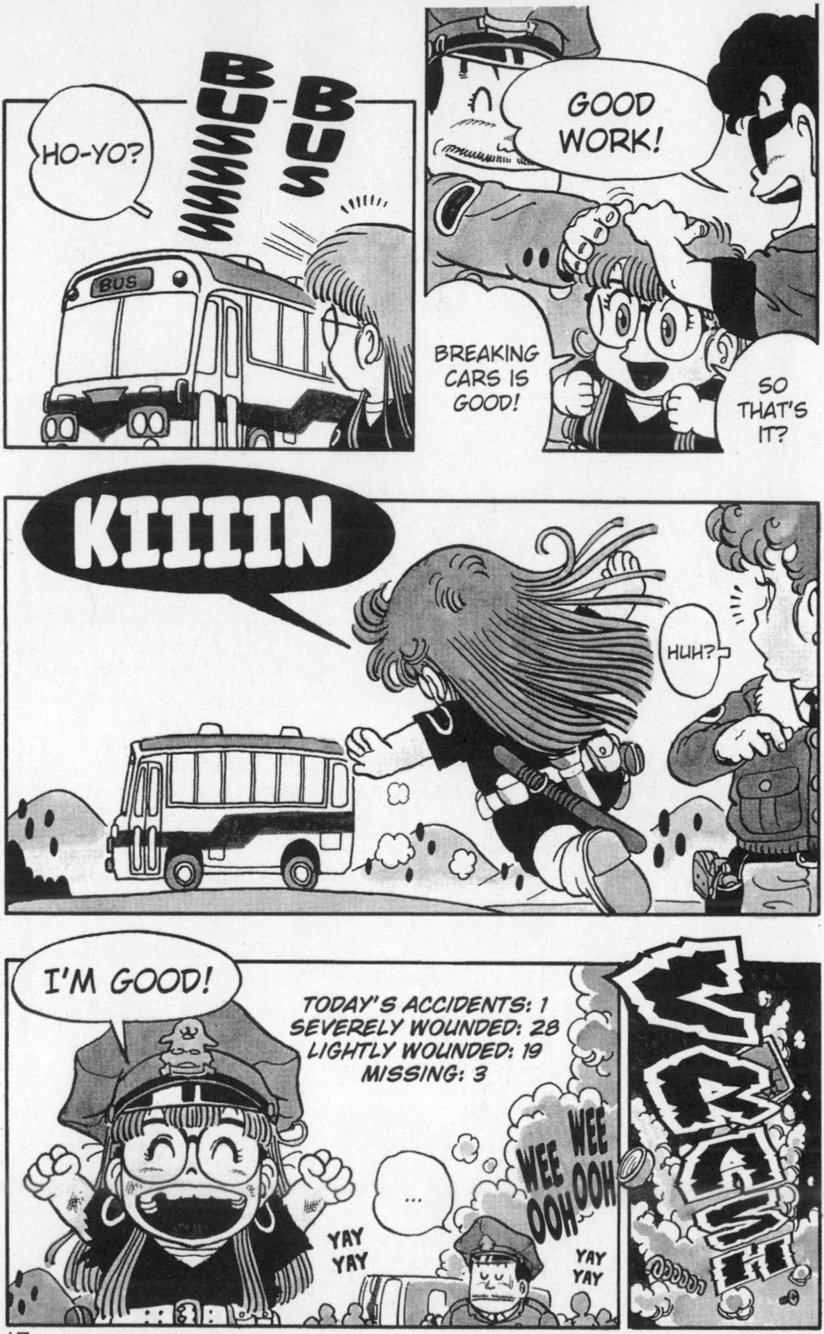
GOOD WORK!
BREAKING CARS IS GOOD!
SO THAT'S IT?
HO-YO?
BUSSSS-BUS
KIIIIN
HUH?
I'M GOOD!
TODAY'S ACCIDENTS: 1
SEVERELY WOUNDED: 28
LIGHTLY WOUNDED: 19
MISSING: 3
WEE OOH WEE OOH
...
YAY YAY
YAY YAY

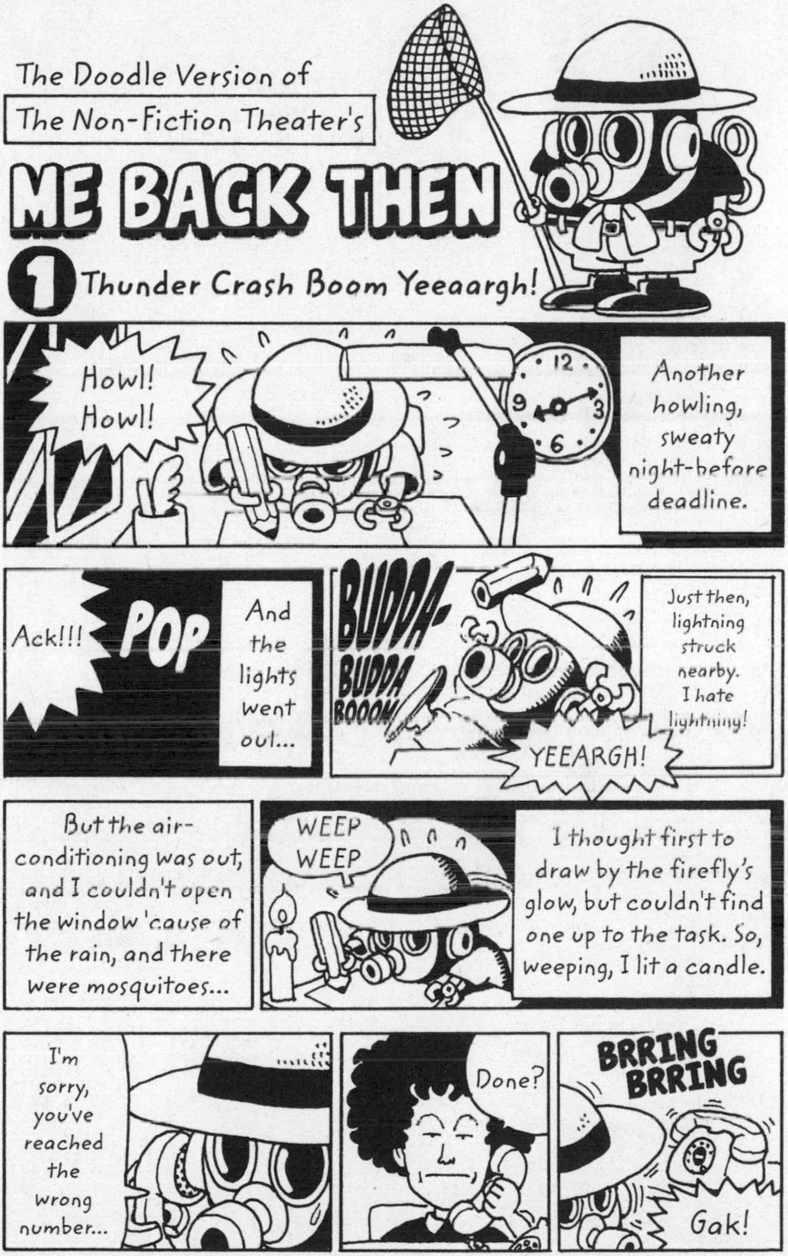
The Doodle Version of
The Non-Fiction Theater's
ME BACK THEN
1 Thunder Crash Boom Yeeaargh!
Another howling, sweaty night-before deadline.
Howl! Howl!
12 3 6 9
Just then, lightning struck nearby. I hate lightning!
BUDDA-BUDDA BOOOM
YEEARGH!
And the lights went out...
POP
Ack!!!
I thought first to draw by the firefly's glow, but couldn't find one up to the task. So, weeping, I lit a candle.
WEEP WEEP
But the air-conditioning was out, and I couldn't open the window 'cause of the rain, and there were mosquitoes...
BRRING BRRING
Gak!
Done?
I'm sorry, you've reached the wrong number...

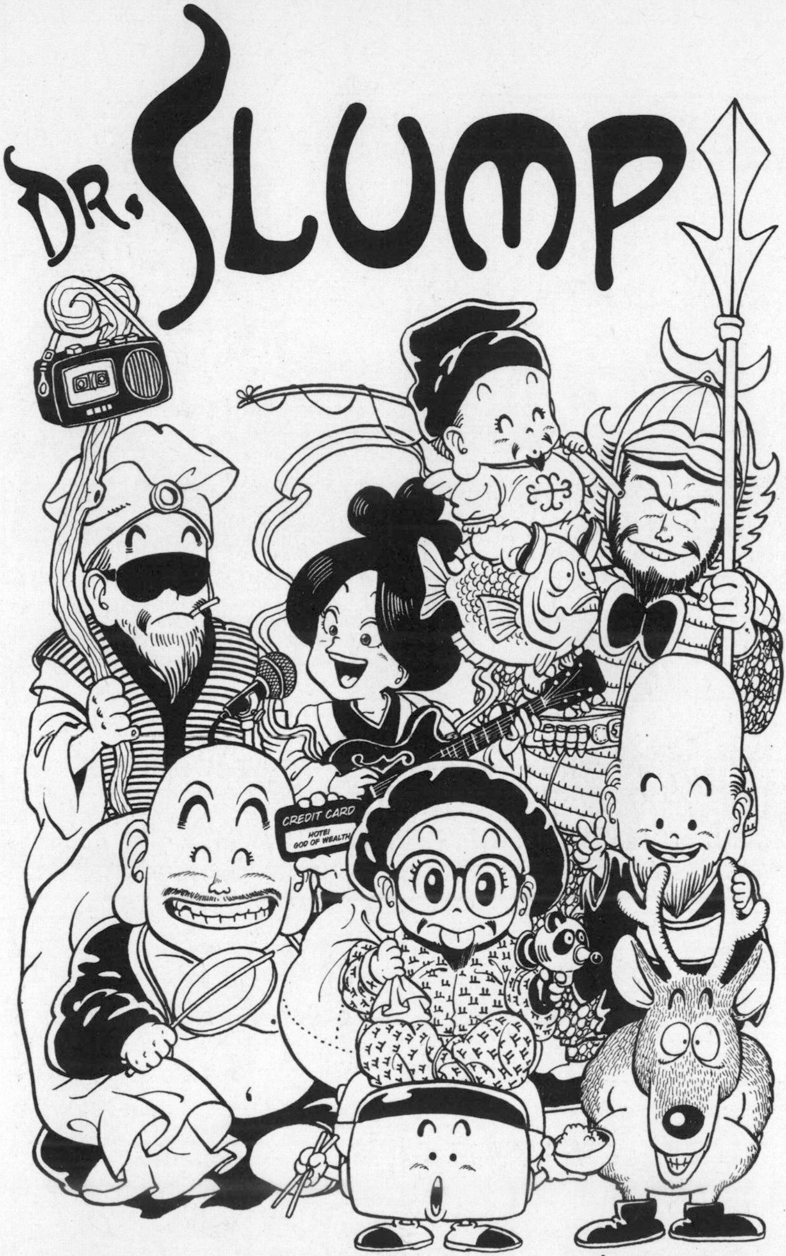
DR. SLUMP
CREDIT CARD
HOTEI
GOD OF WEALTH

♥ Affairs of the Heart!

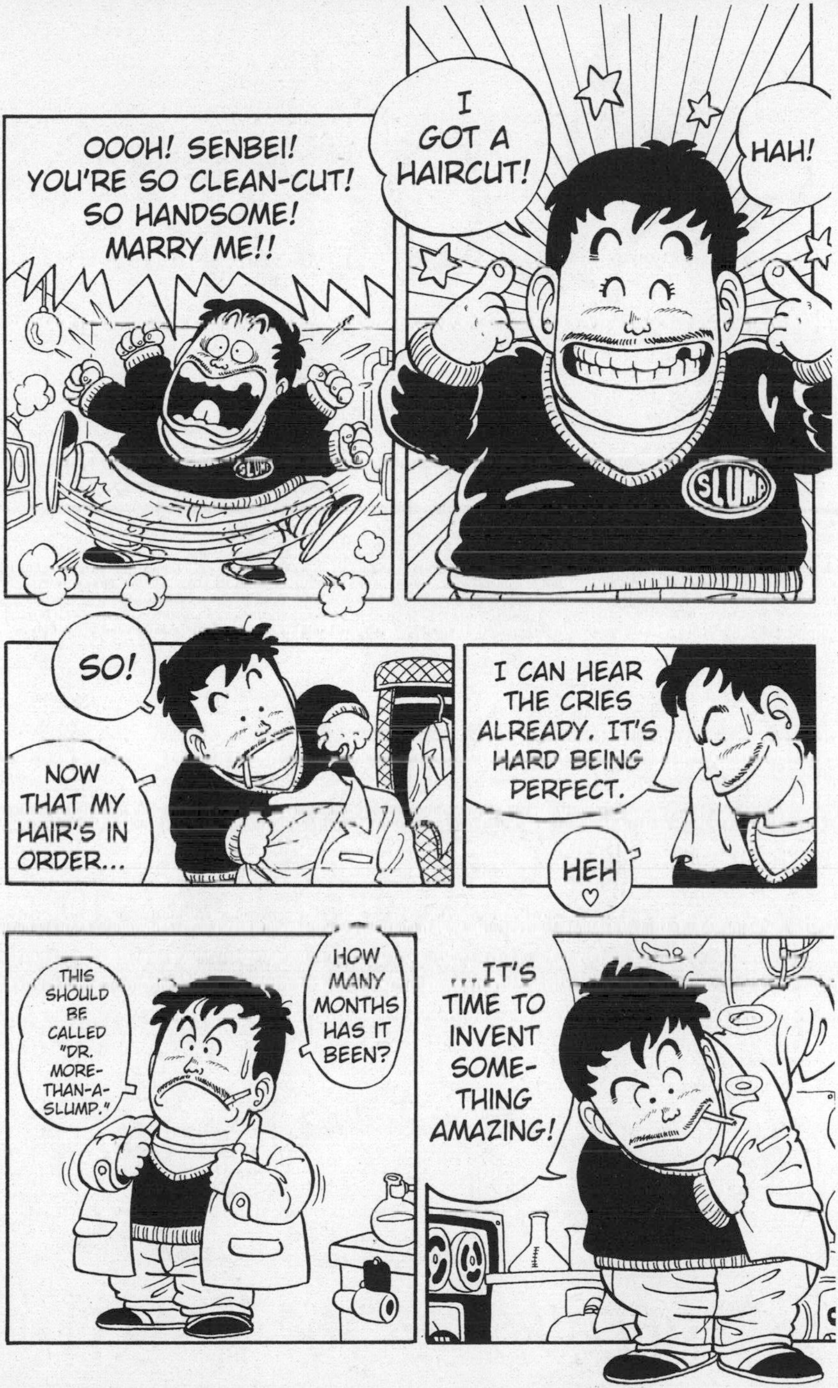
HAH!
I GOT A HAIRCUT!
OOOH! SENBEI! YOU'RE SO CLEAN-CUT! SO HANDSOME! MARRY ME!!
I CAN HEAR THE CRIES ALREADY. IT'S HARD BEING PERFECT.
HEH ♡
SO!
NOW THAT MY HAIR'S IN ORDER...
...IT'S TIME TO INVENT SOMETHING AMAZING!
HOW MANY MONTHS HAS IT BEEN?
THIS SHOULD BE CALLED "DR. MORE-THAN-A-SLUMP."

READ THIS WAY

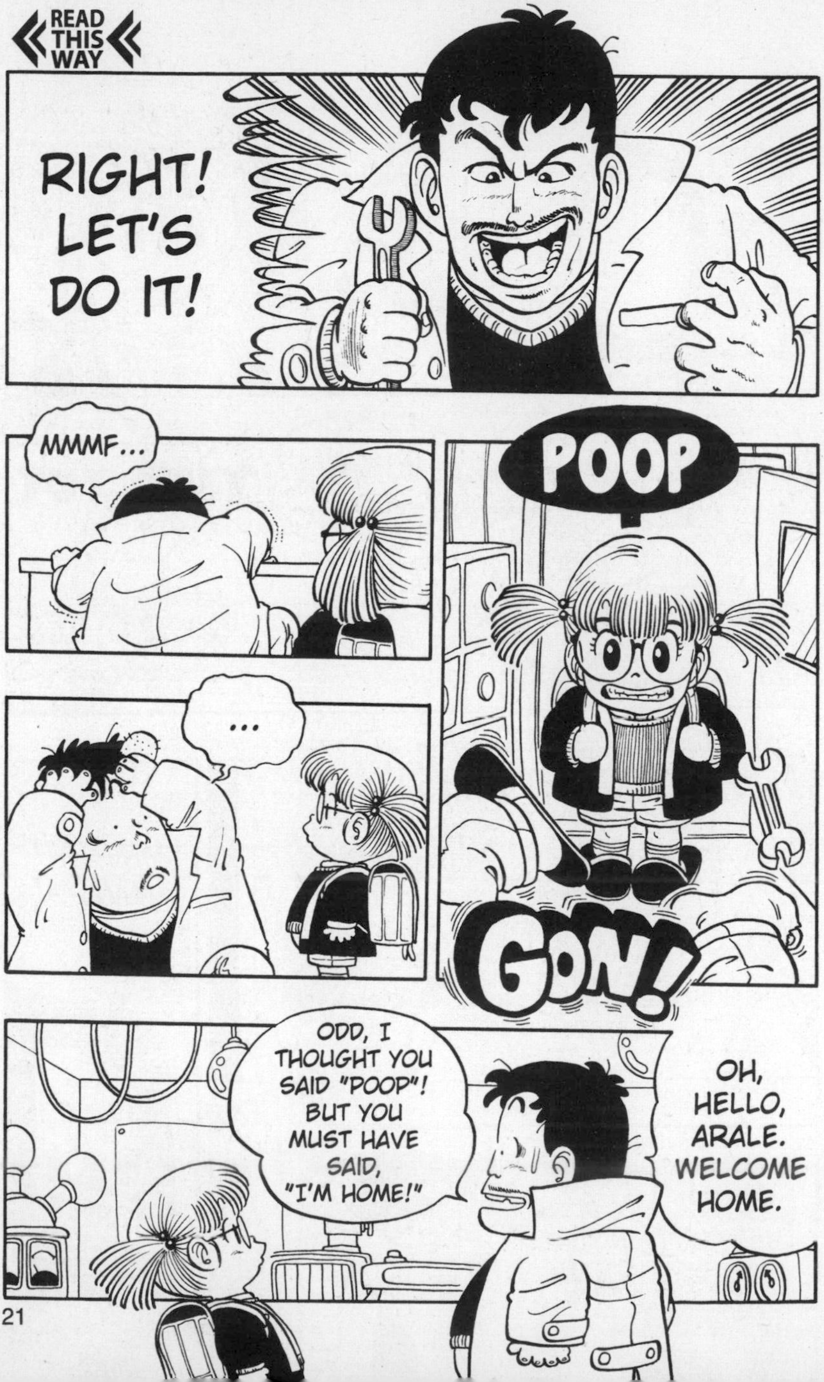
RIGHT! LET'S DO IT!
POOP
GON!
MMMF...
...
OH, HELLO, ARALE. WELCOME HOME.
ODD, I THOUGHT YOU SAID "POOP"! BUT YOU MUST HAVE SAID, "I'M HOME!"

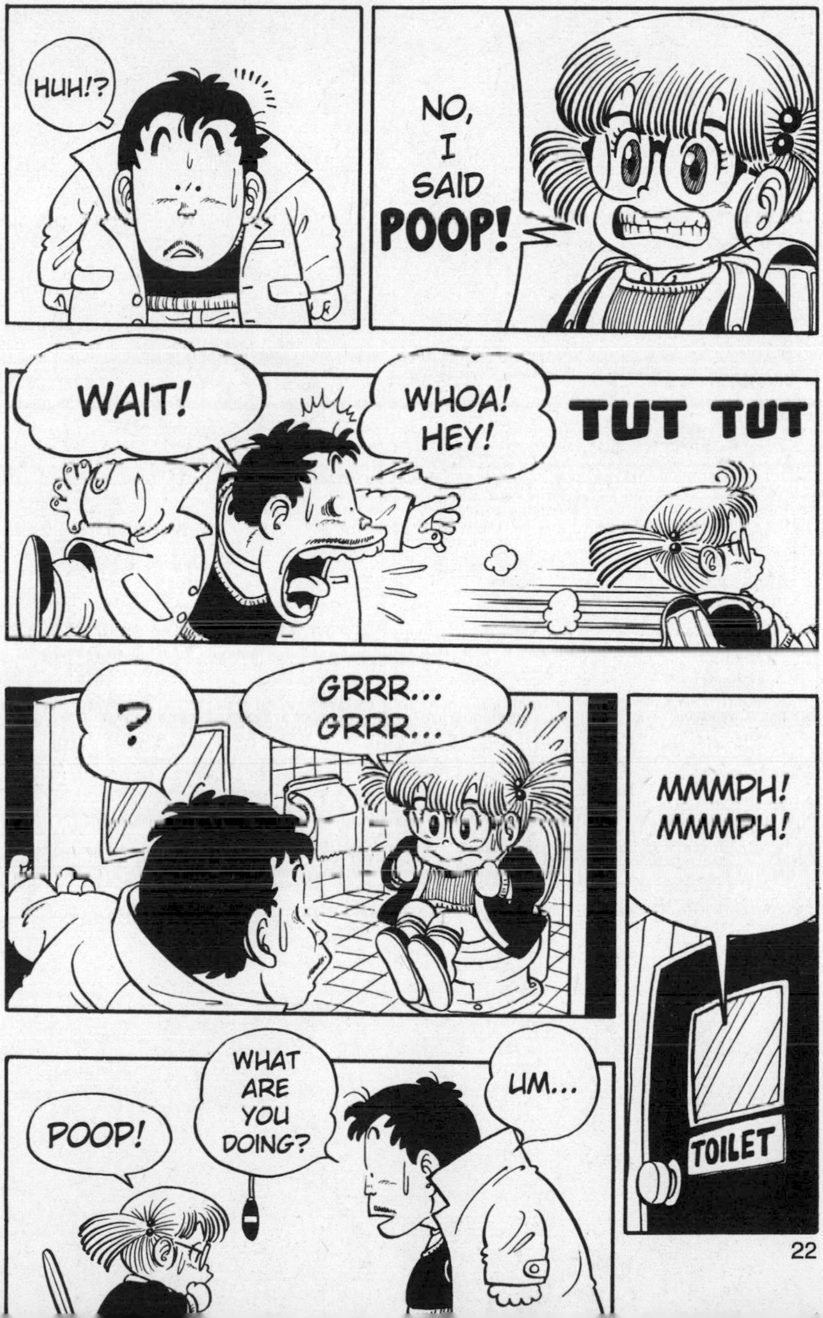
NO, I SAID POOP!
HUH!?
TUT TUT
WHOA! HEY!
WAIT!
MMMPH! MMMPH!
TOILET
GRRR... GRRR...
?
UM...
WHAT ARE YOU DOING?
POOP!

READ THIS WAY

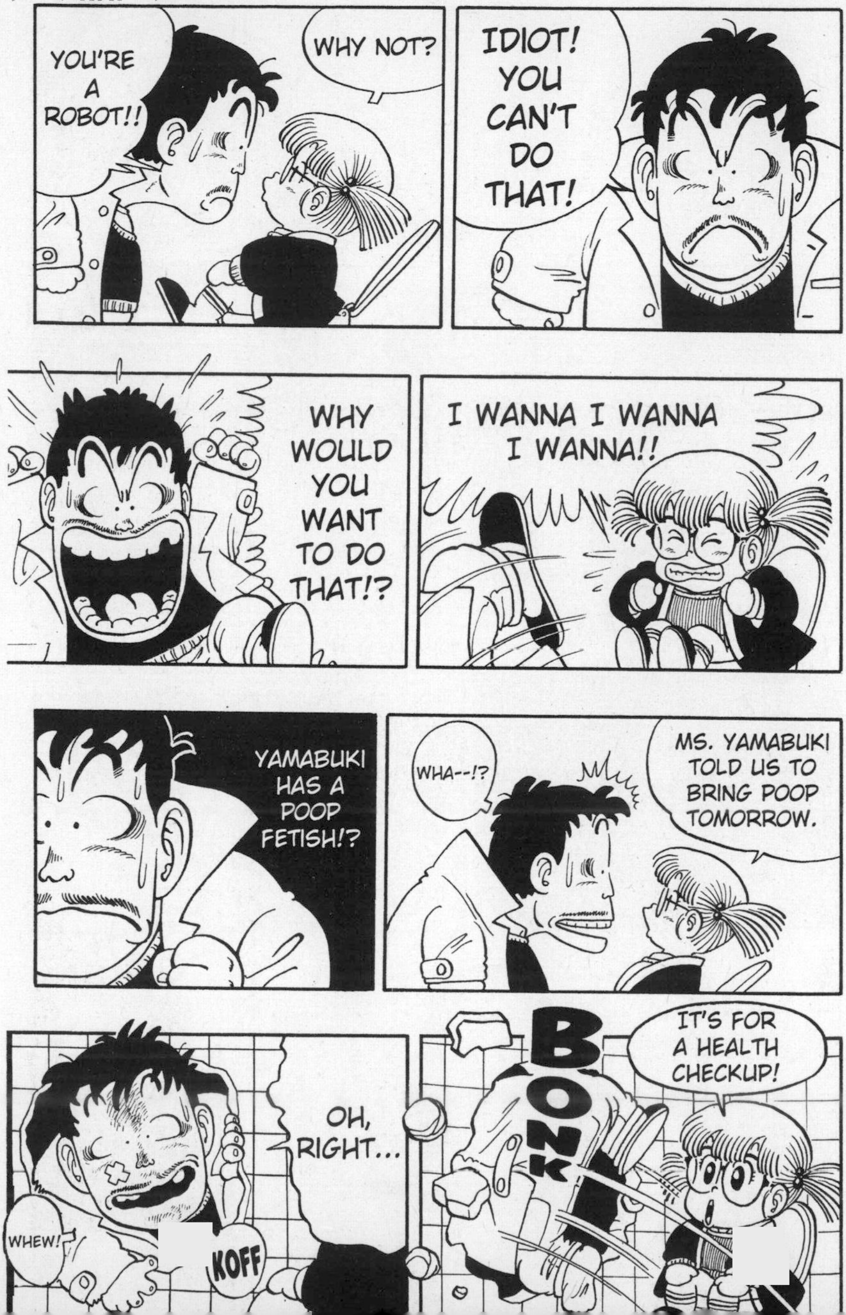
IDIOT! YOU CAN'T DO THAT!
WHY NOT?
YOU'RE A ROBOT!!
I WANNA I WANNA I WANNA!!
WHY WOULD YOU WANT TO DO THAT!?
MS. YAMABUKI TOLD US TO BRING POOP TOMORROW.
WHA--!?
YAMABUKI HAS A POOP FETISH!?
IT'S FOR A HEALTH CHECKUP!
BONK
OH, RIGHT...
WHEW!
KOFF

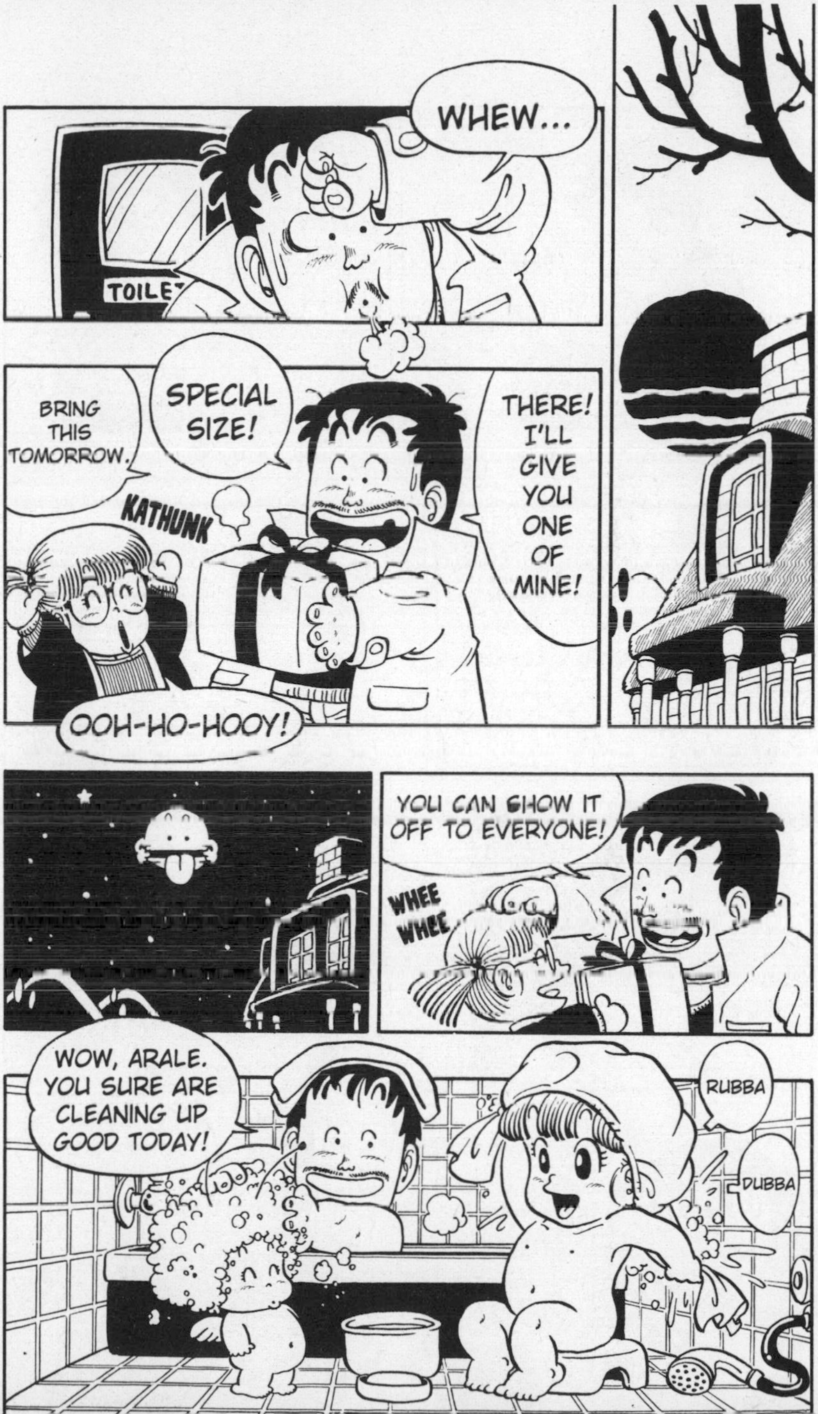
WHEW...
THERE! I'LL GIVE YOU ONE OF MINE!
SPECIAL SIZE!
BRING THIS TOMORROW.
KATHUNK
OOH-HO-HOOY!
YOU CAN SHOW IT OFF TO EVERYONE!
WHEE WHEE
RUBBA
DUBBA
WOW, ARALE. YOU SURE ARE CLEANING UP GOOD TODAY!

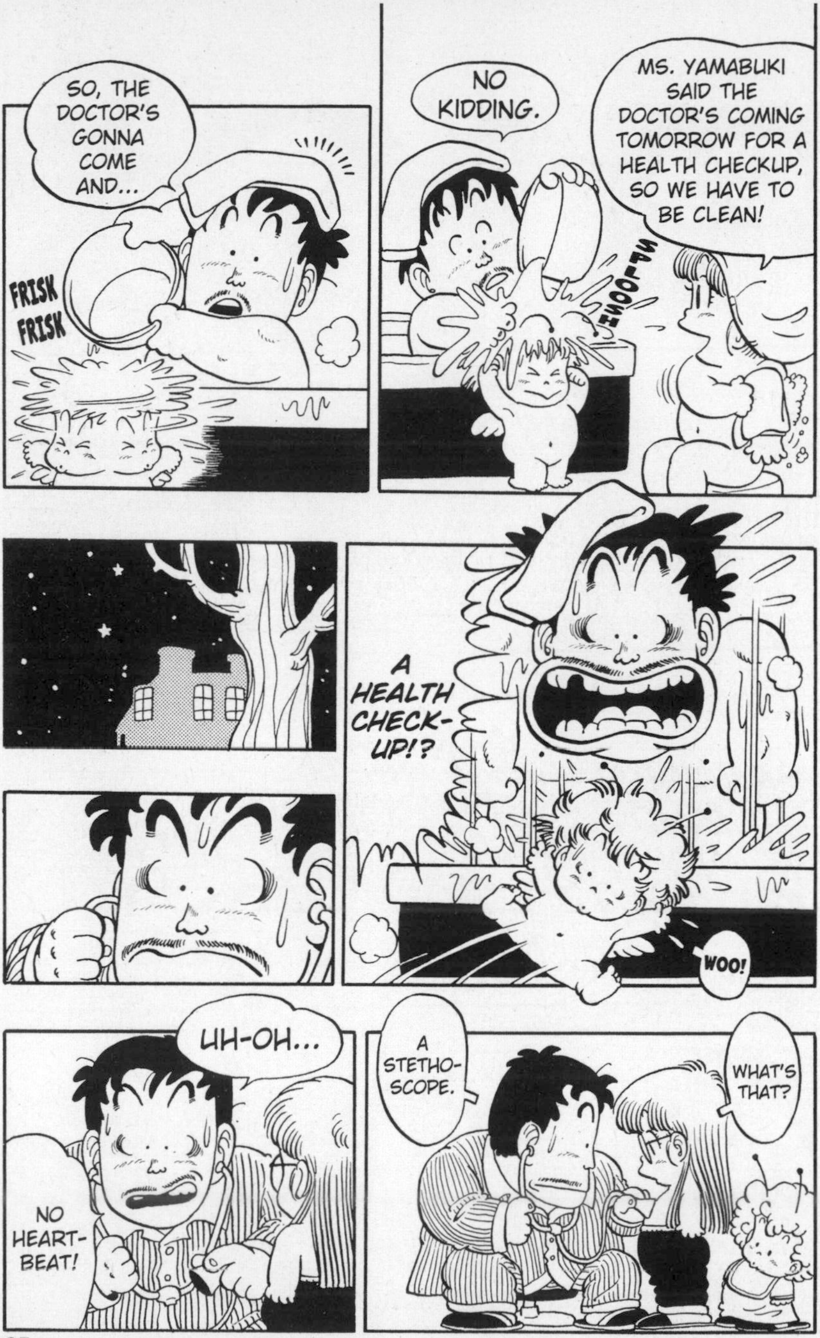

MS. YAMABUKI SAID THE DOCTOR'S COMING TOMORROW FOR A HEALTH CHECKUP, SO WE HAVE TO BE CLEAN!
NO KIDDING.
SPLOOSH
SO, THE DOCTOR'S GONNA COME AND...
FRISK FRISK
A HEALTH CHECK-UP!?
WOO!
WHAT'S THAT?
A STETHO-SCOPE.
UH-OH...
NO HEART-BEAT!

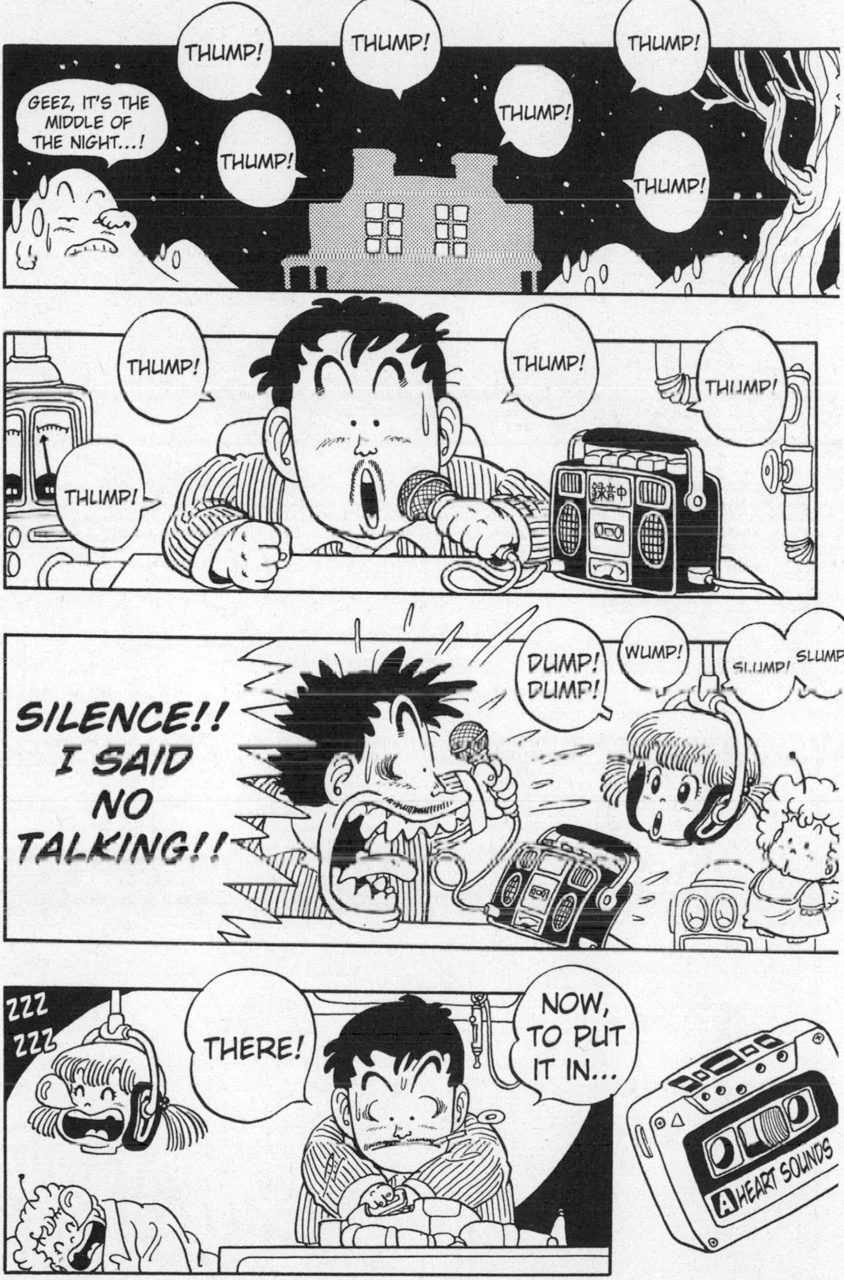
THUMP!
THUMP!
THUMP!
THUMP!
THUMP!
GEEZ, IT'S THE MIDDLE OF THE NIGHT...!
THUMP!
THUMP!
THUMP!
録音中
THUMP!
SLUMP! SLUMP!
WUMP!
DUMP! DUMP!
SILENCE!! I SAID NO TALKING!!
NOW, TO PUT IT IN...
THERE!
ZZZ ZZZ
A HEART SOUNDS

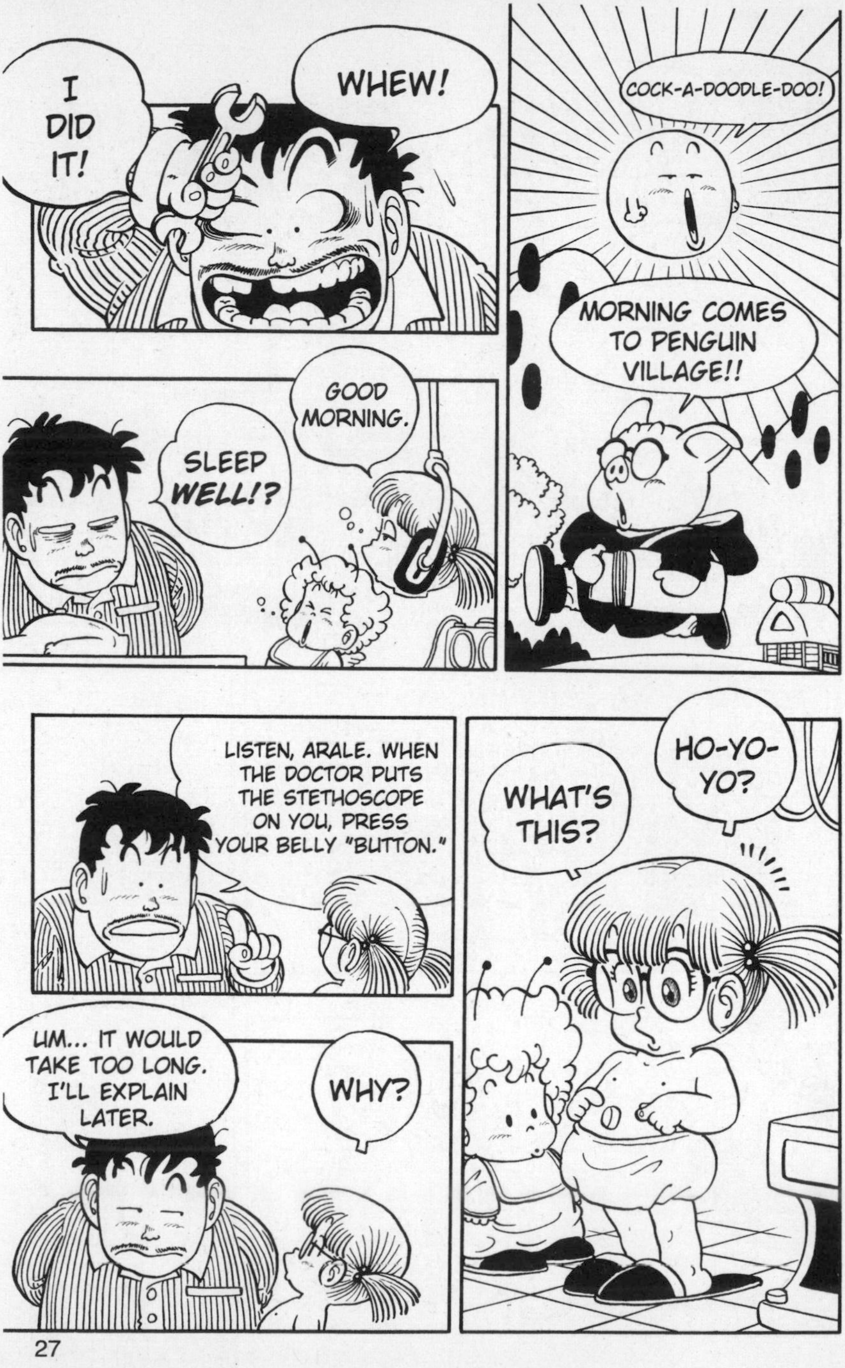
COCK-A-DOODLE-DOO!
MORNING COMES TO PENGUIN VILLAGE!!
WHEW!
I DID IT!
GOOD MORNING.
SLEEP WELL!?
HO-YO-YO?
WHAT'S THIS?
LISTEN, ARALE. WHEN THE DOCTOR PUTS THE STETHOSCOPE ON YOU, PRESS YOUR BELLY "BUTTON."
WHY?
UM... IT WOULD TAKE TOO LONG. I'LL EXPLAIN LATER.

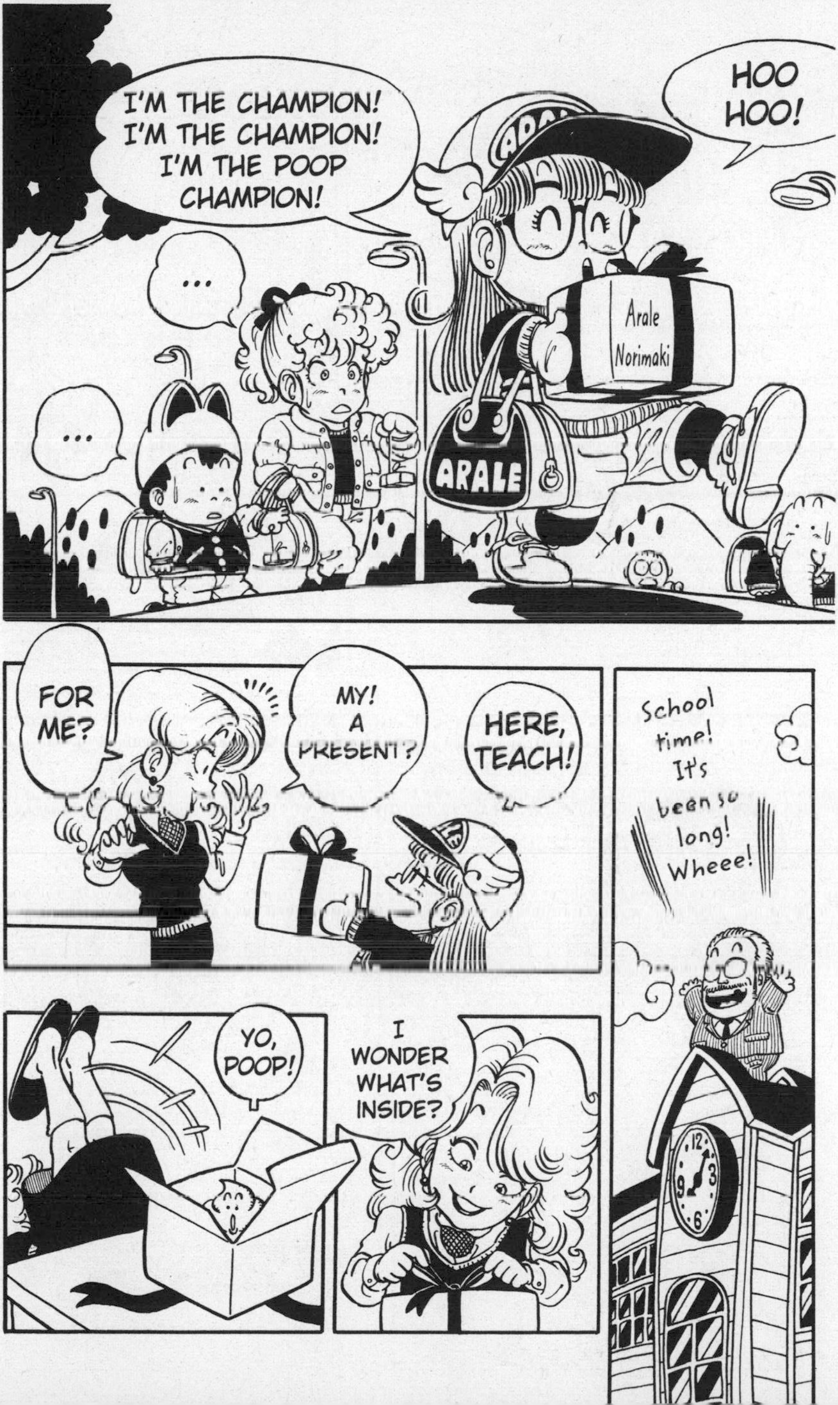
HOO HOO!
I'M THE CHAMPION! I'M THE CHAMPION! I'M THE POOP CHAMPION!
...
...
Arale Norimaki
ARALE
School time! It's been so long! Wheee!
HERE, TEACH!
MY! A PRESENT?
FOR ME?
I WONDER WHAT'S INSIDE?
YO, POOP!

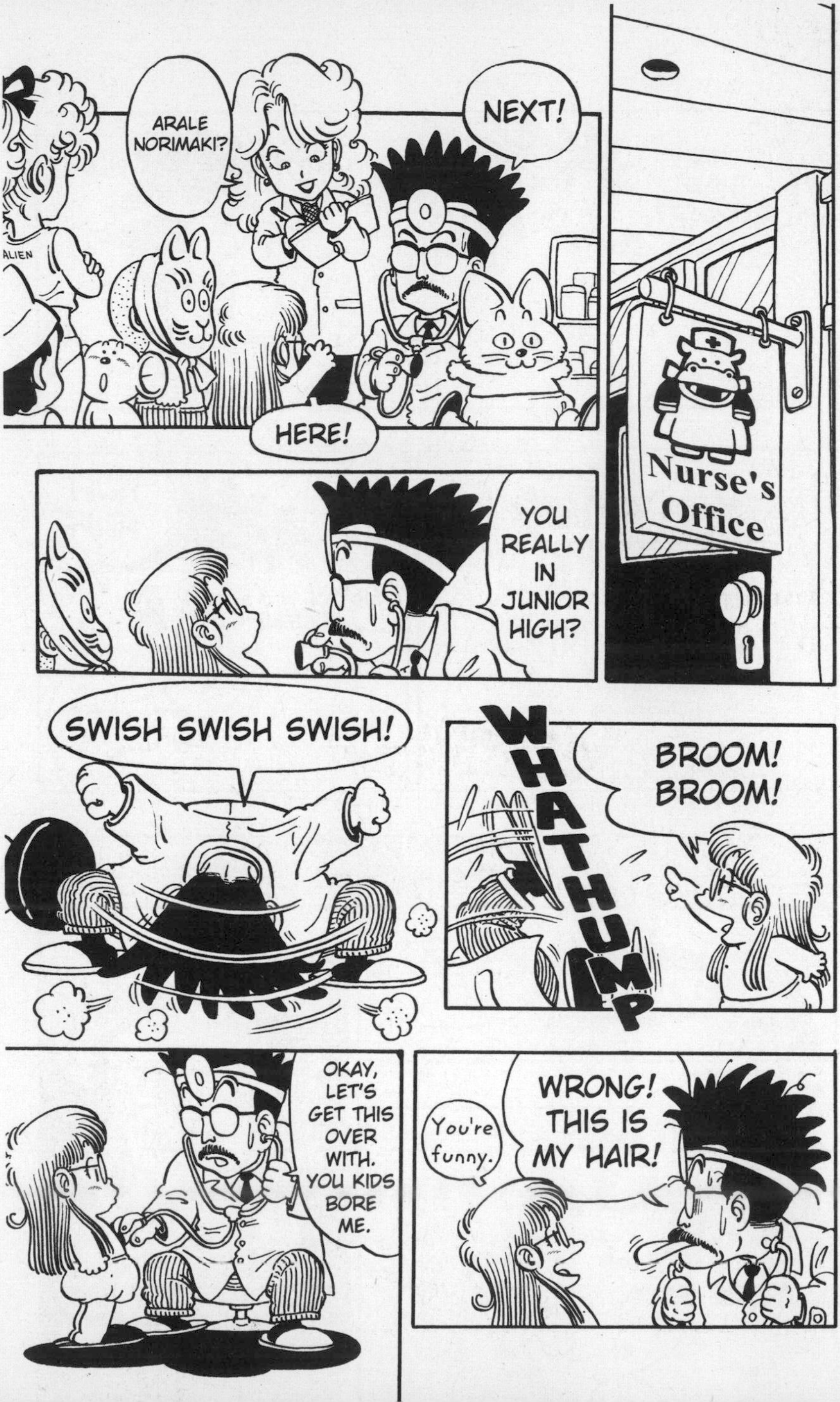
Nurse's Office
NEXT!
ARALE NORIMAKI?
HERE!
YOU REALLY IN JUNIOR HIGH?
WHATHUMP
BROOM! BROOM!
SWISH SWISH SWISH!
WRONG! THIS IS MY HAIR!
You're funny.
OKAY, LET'S GET THIS OVER WITH. YOU KIDS BORE ME.

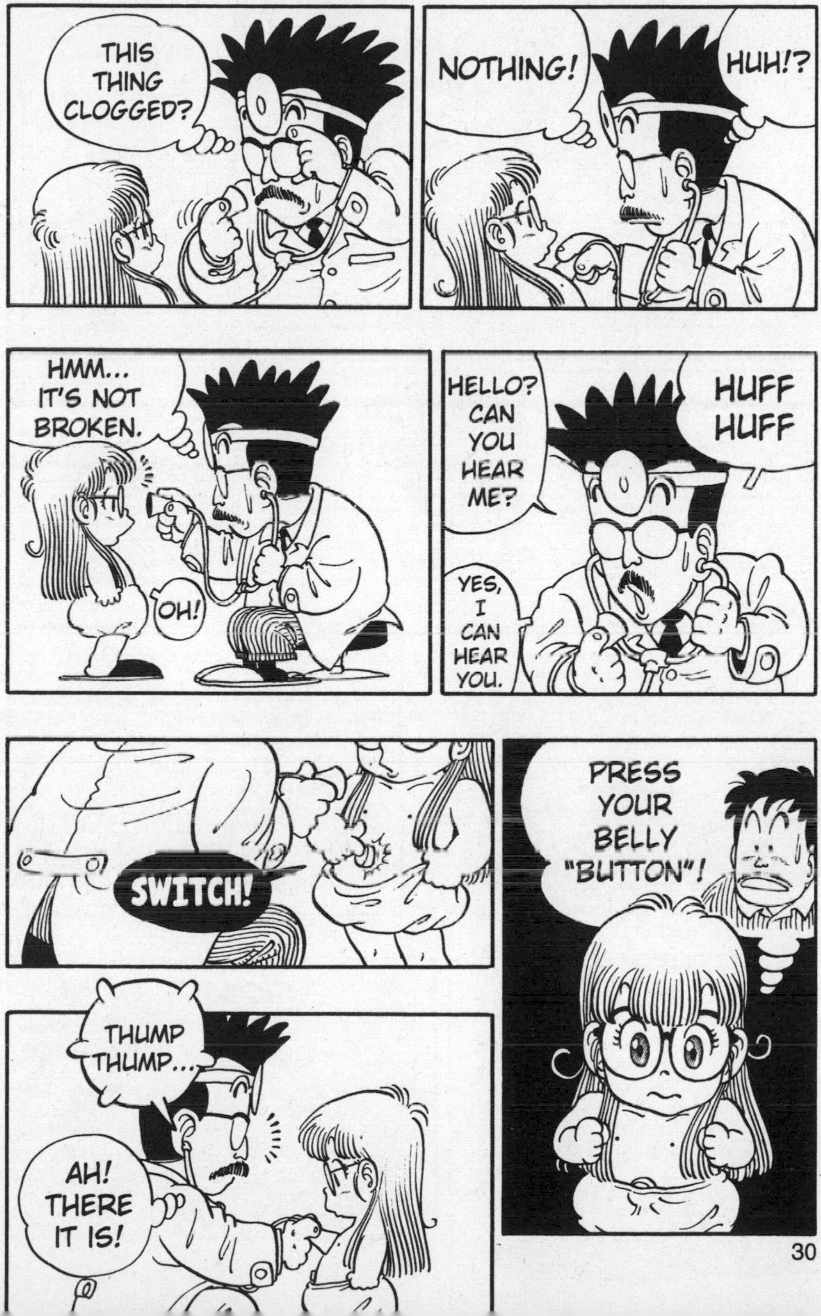
HUH!?
NOTHING!
THIS THING CLOGGED?
HUFF HUFF
HELLO? CAN YOU HEAR ME?
YES, I CAN HEAR YOU.
HMM... IT'S NOT BROKEN.
OH!
PRESS YOUR BELLY "BUTTON"!
SWITCH!
THUMP THUMP...
AH! THERE IT IS!

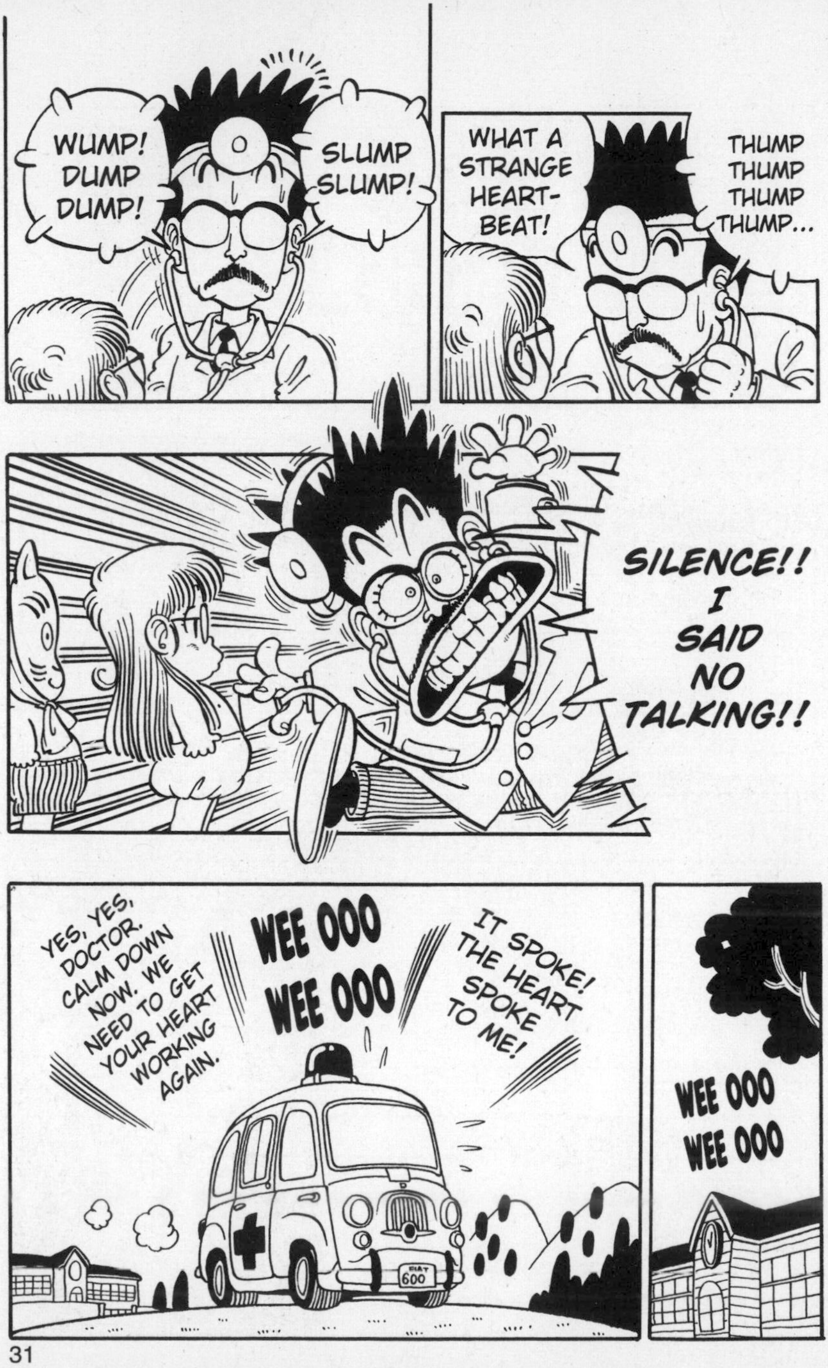
THUMP THUMP THUMP THUMP...
WHAT A STRANGE HEART-BEAT!
SLUMP SLUMP!
WUMP! DUMP DUMP!
SILENCE!! I SAID NO TALKING!!
WEE OOO WEE OOO
IT SPOKE! THE HEART SPOKE TO ME!
WEE OOO WEE OOO
YES, YES, DOCTOR. CALM DOWN NOW. WE NEED TO GET YOUR HEART WORKING AGAIN.
FIAT 600

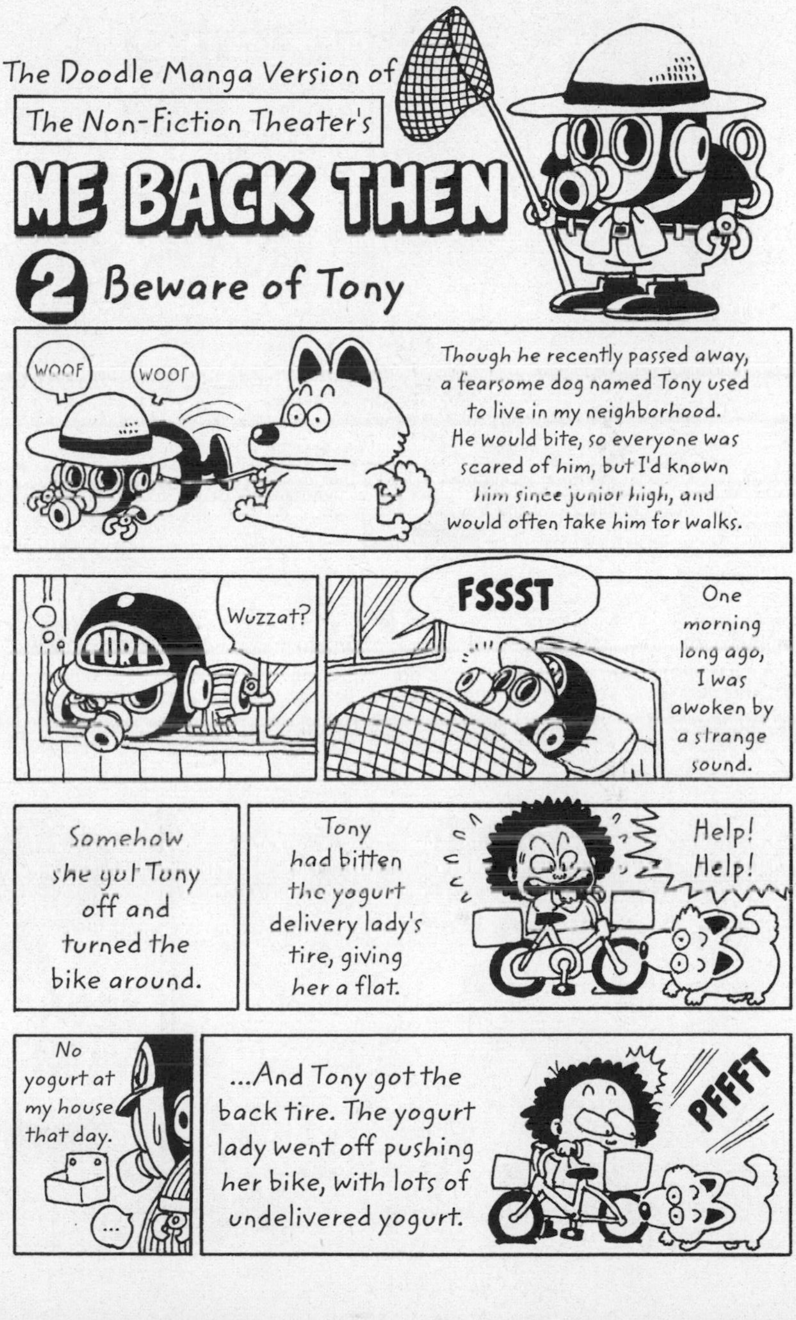
The Doodle Manga Version of
The Non-Fiction Theater's
ME BACK THEN
2 Beware of Tony
Though he recently passed away, a fearsome dog named Tony used to live in my neighborhood. He would bite, so everyone was scared of him, but I'd known him since junior high, and would often take him for walks.
WOOF
WOOF
One morning long ago, I was awoken by a strange sound.
FSSST
Wuzzat?
Help! Help!
Tony had bitten the yogurt delivery lady's tire, giving her a flat.
Somehow she got Tony off and turned the bike around.
PFFFT
...And Tony got the back tire. The yogurt lady went off pushing her bike, with lots of undelivered yogurt.
No yogurt at my house that day.
...

Monsters' Night

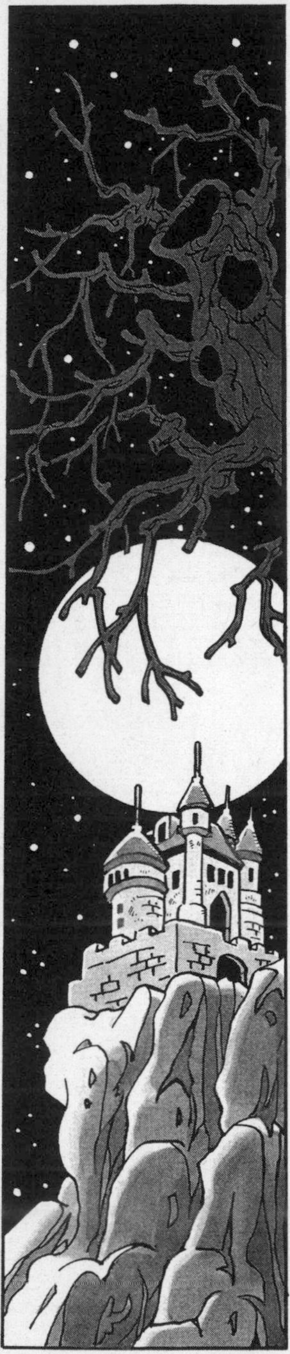

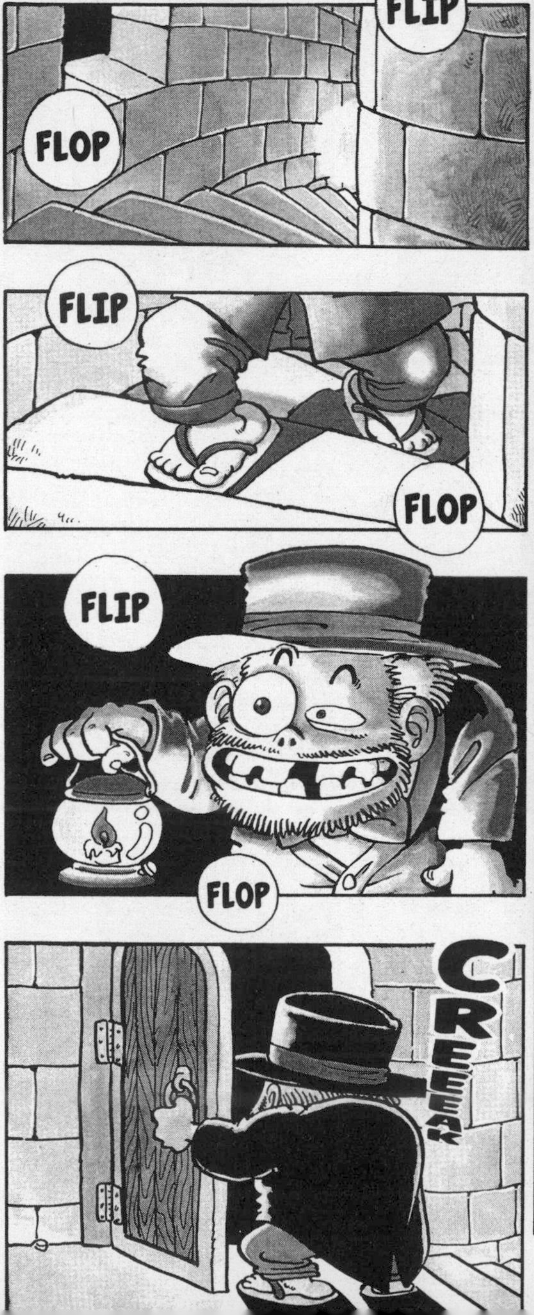
FLIP
FLOP
FLIP
FLOP
FLIP
FLOP
CREEEAK

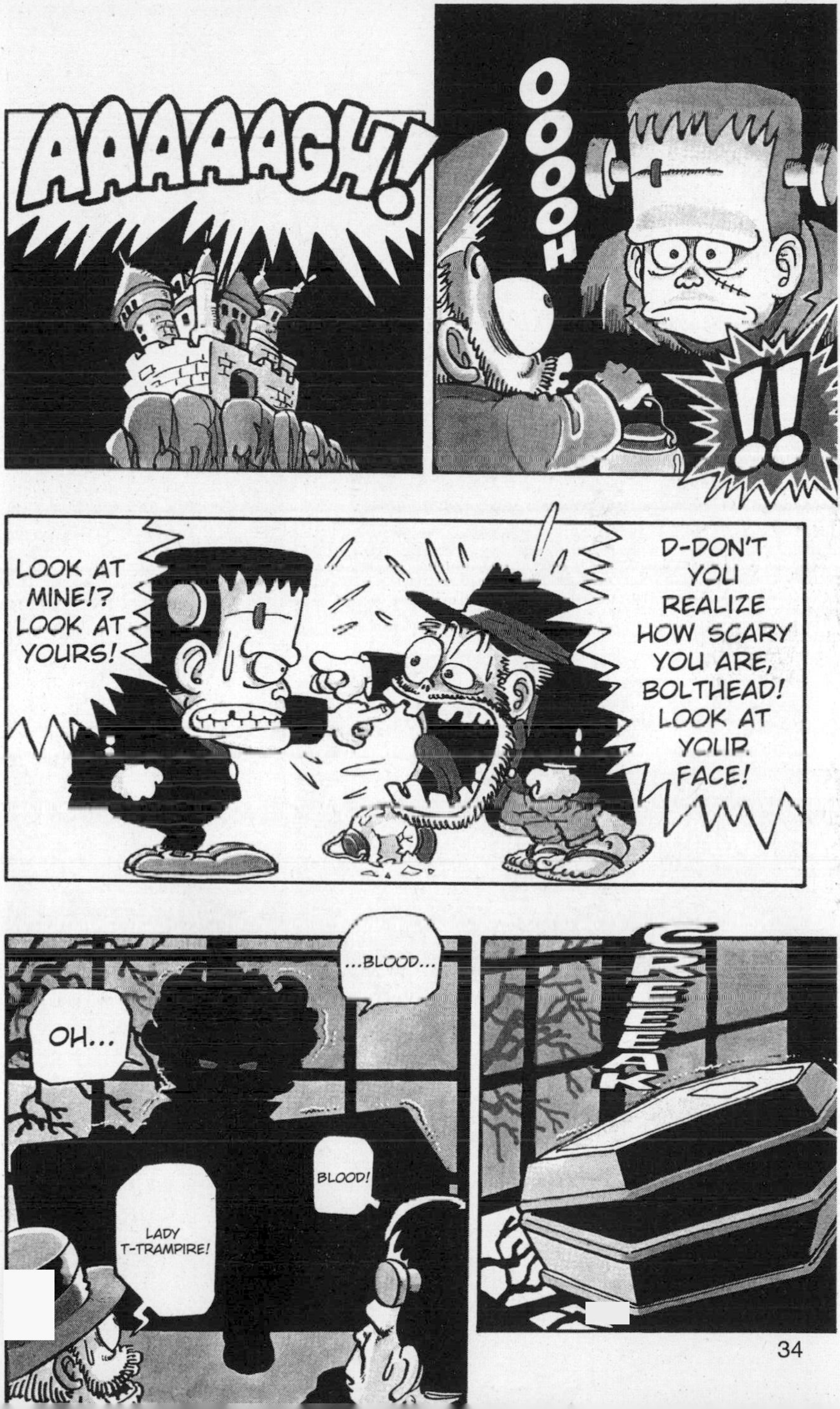
OOOOOH
!!
AAAAAGH!
D-DON'T YOU REALIZE HOW SCARY YOU ARE, BOLTHEAD! LOOK AT YOUR FACE!
LOOK AT MINE!? LOOK AT YOURS!
CREEEAK
...BLOOD...
OH...
BLOOD!
LADY T-TRAMPIRE!

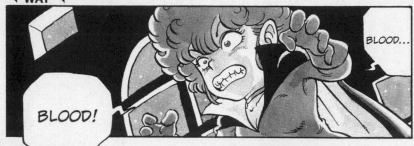

READ THIS WAY

BLOOD...
BLOOD!
I WANT BLOOD!
BUT MORE THAN THAT... I WANT MONEY!
KINDA TAKES THE GLAMOUR OUT OF IT.
BLOOD AND MONEY MAKE THE WORLD GO 'ROUND.
LET'S GO!
AGAIN, MILADY?
SUCKING BLOOD, STEALING CASH! YOU'RE EVIL!
WHAAAT!?

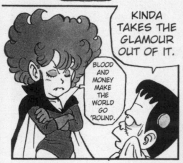

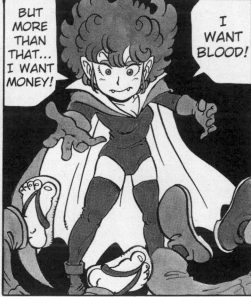

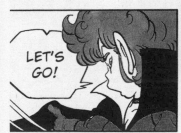

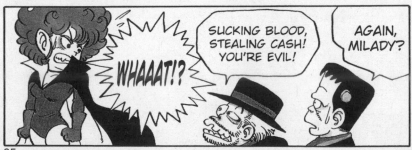

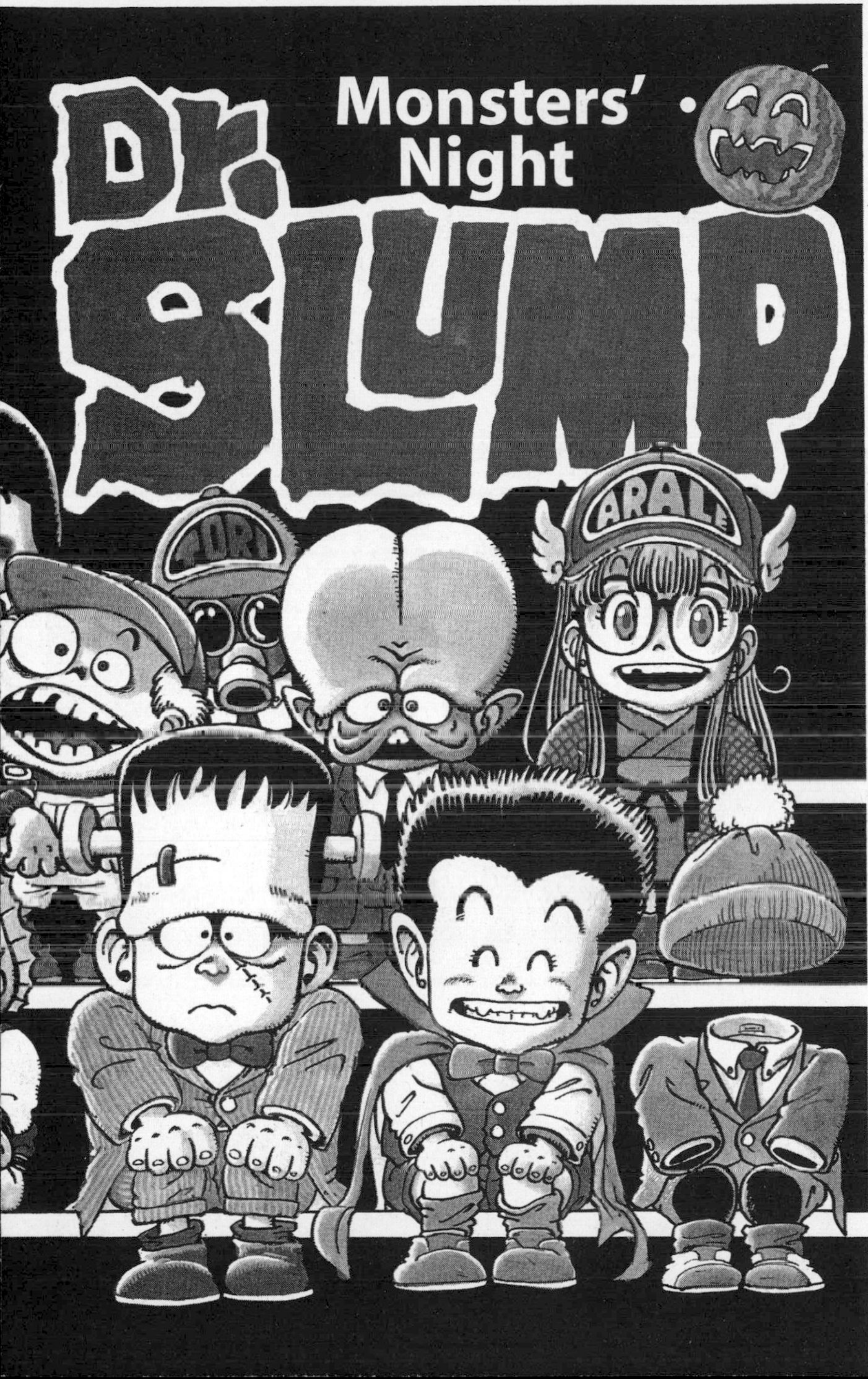
Dr. SLUMP
Monsters' Night
TORI
ARALE

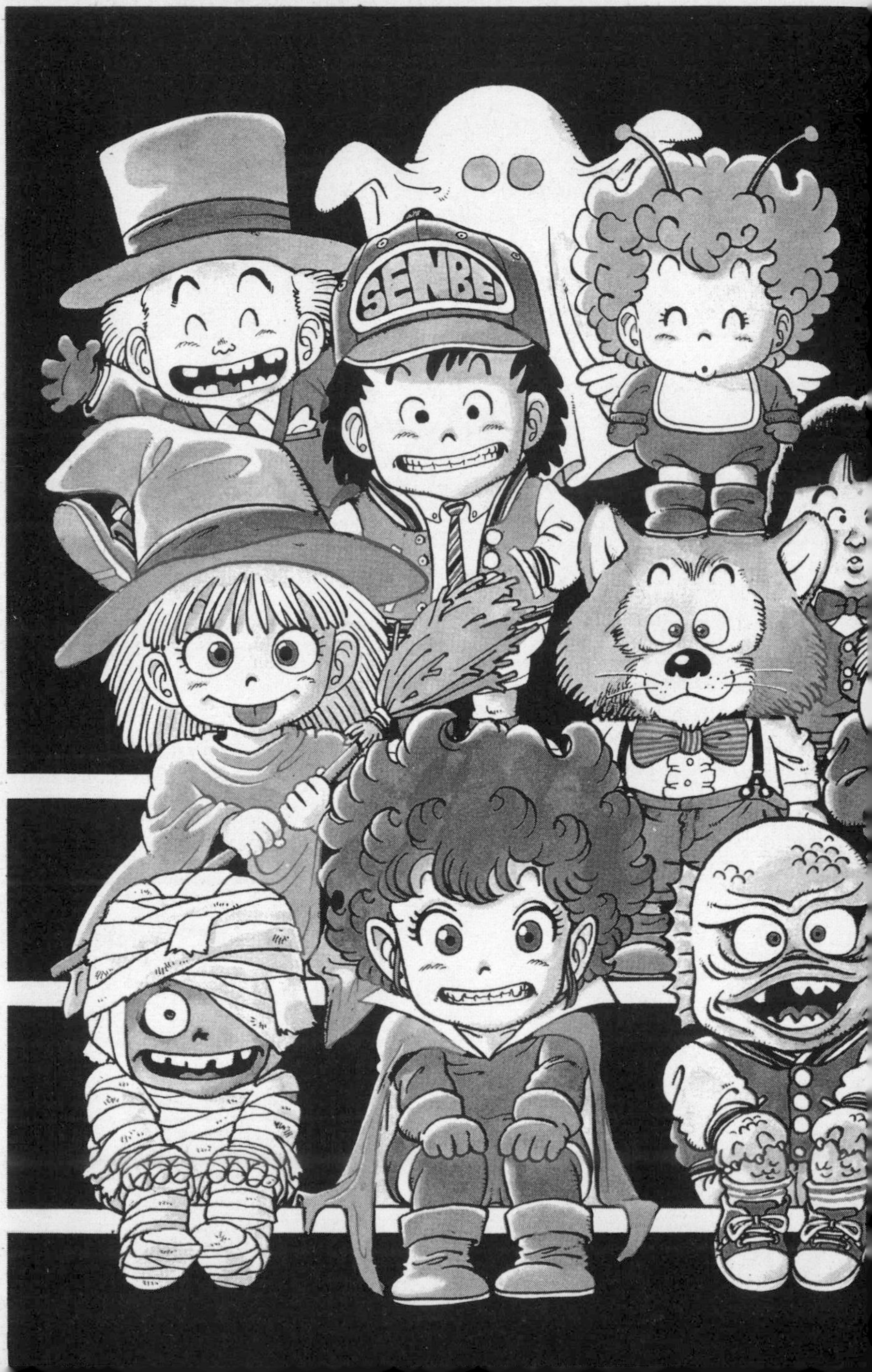

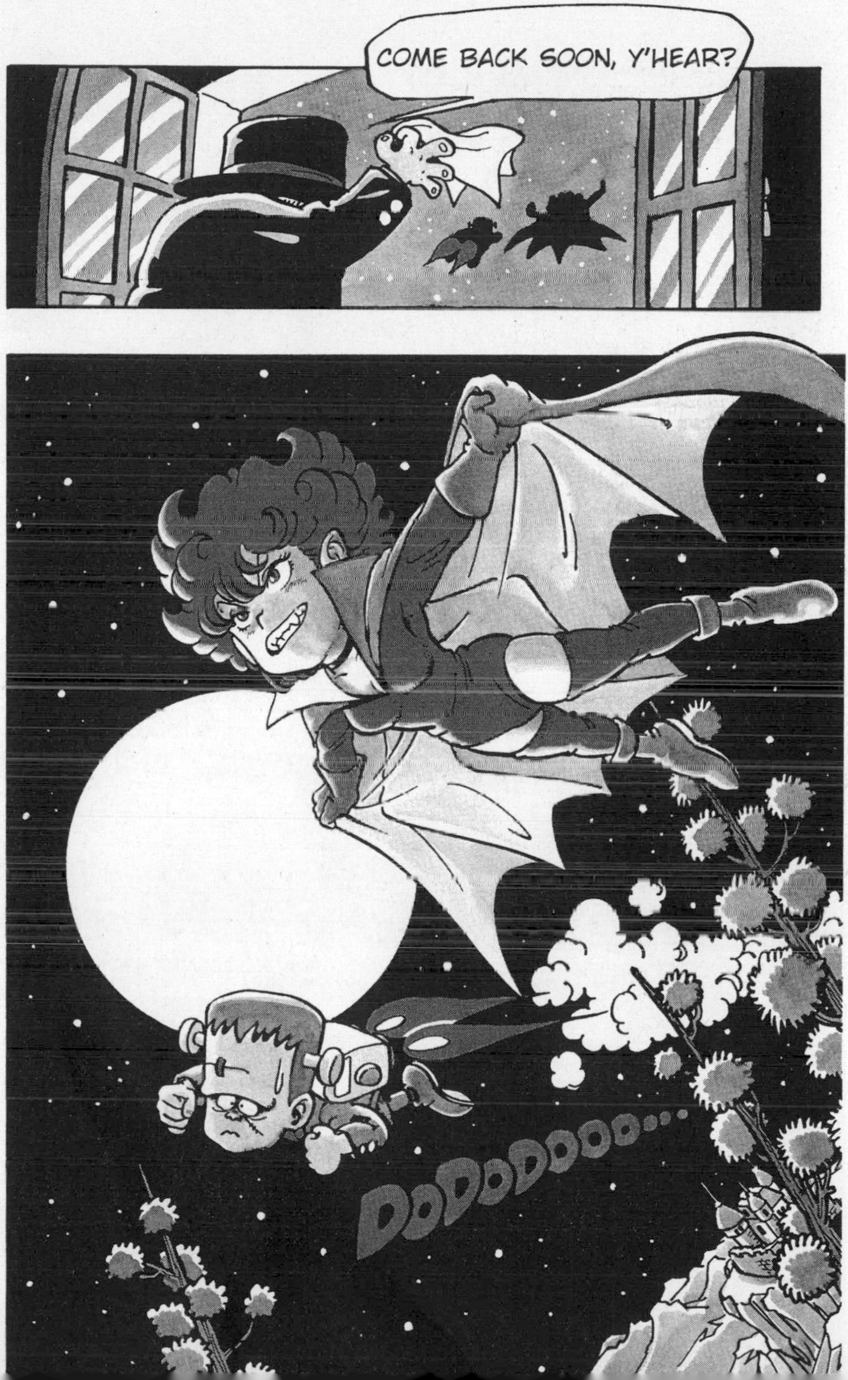
COME BACK SOON, Y'HEAR?
DODODOOO...

READ THIS WAY

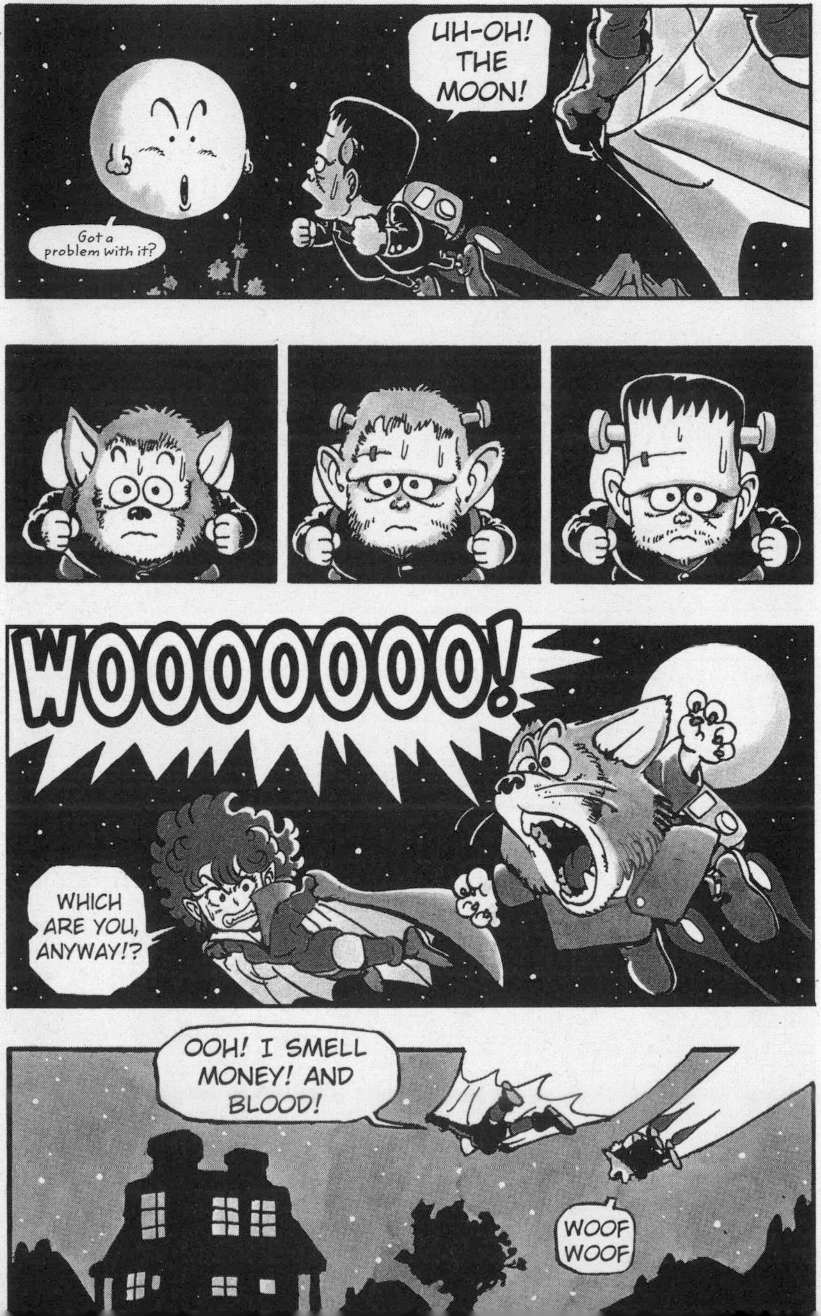

UH-OH! THE MOON!
Got a problem with it?
WOOOOOOO!
WHICH ARE YOU, ANYWAY!?
OOH! I SMELL MONEY! AND BLOOD!
WOOF WOOF

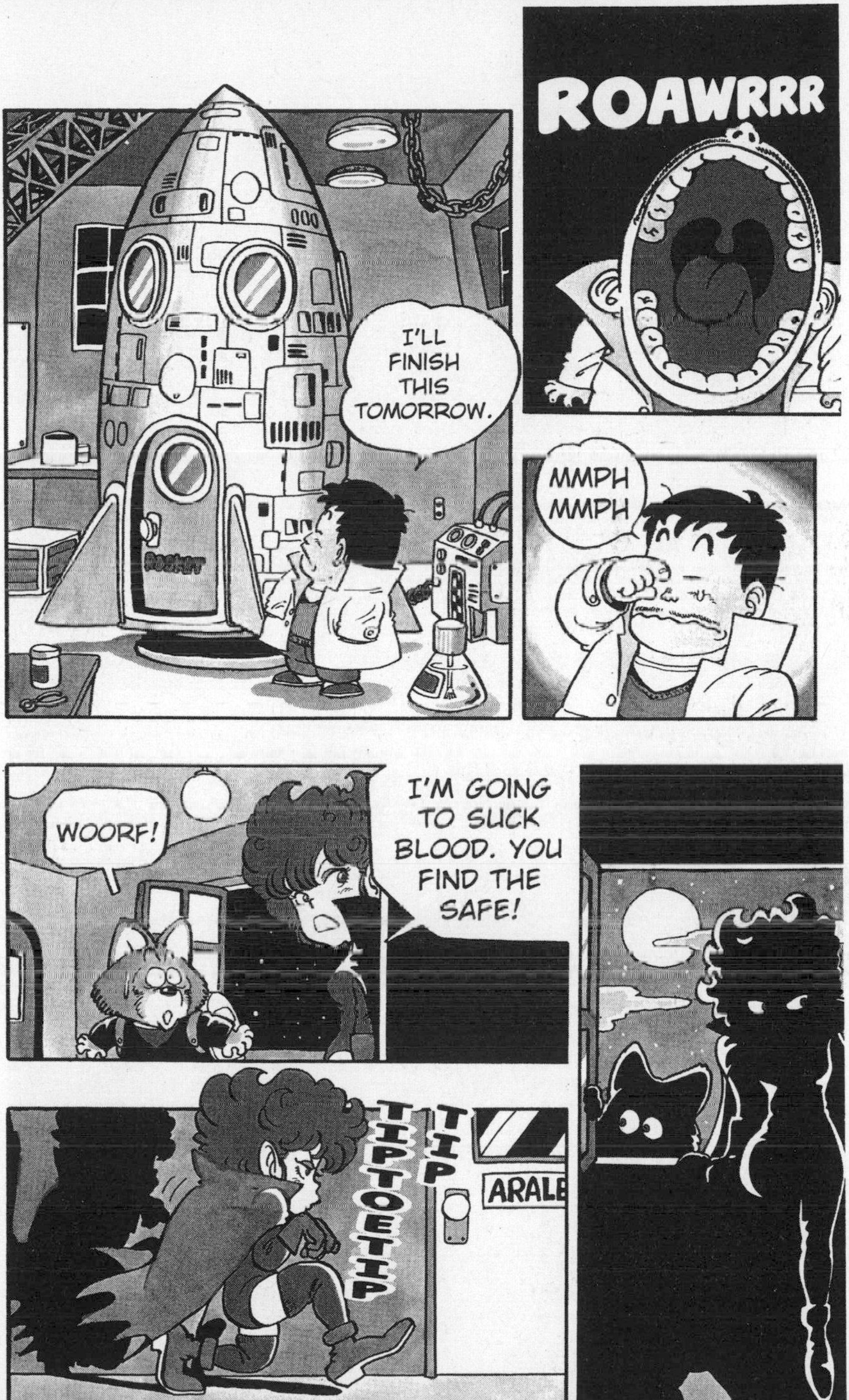
ROAWRRR
MMPH MMPH
I'LL FINISH THIS TOMORROW.
I'M GOING TO SUCK BLOOD. YOU FIND THE SAFE!
WOORF!
TIP
TIPTOETIP
ARALE

READ THIS WAY

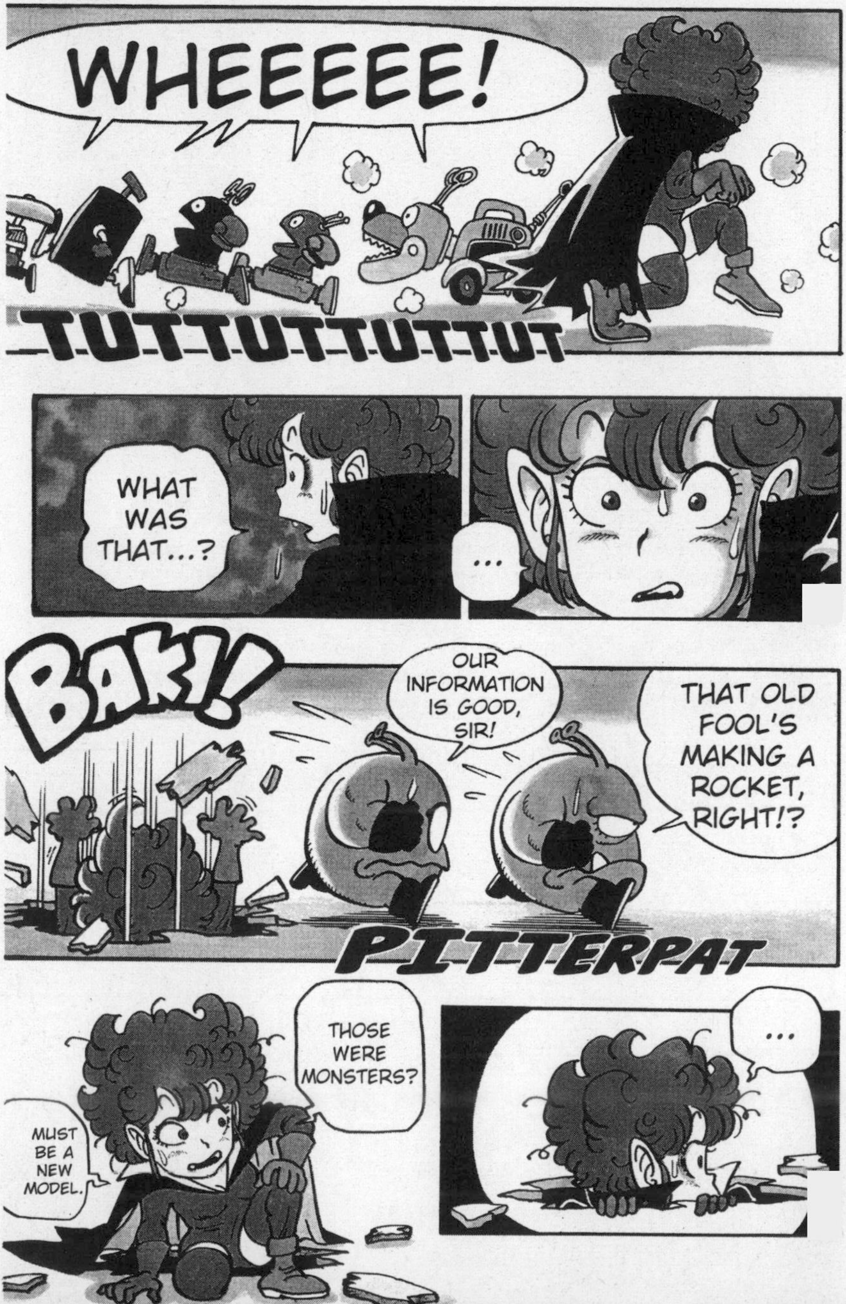
WHEEEEEE!
TUTTUTTUTTUT
...
WHAT WAS THAT...?
THAT OLD FOOL'S MAKING A ROCKET, RIGHT!?
OUR INFORMATION IS GOOD, SIR!
BAKI!
PITTERPAT
...
THOSE WERE MONSTERS?
MUST BE A NEW MODEL.

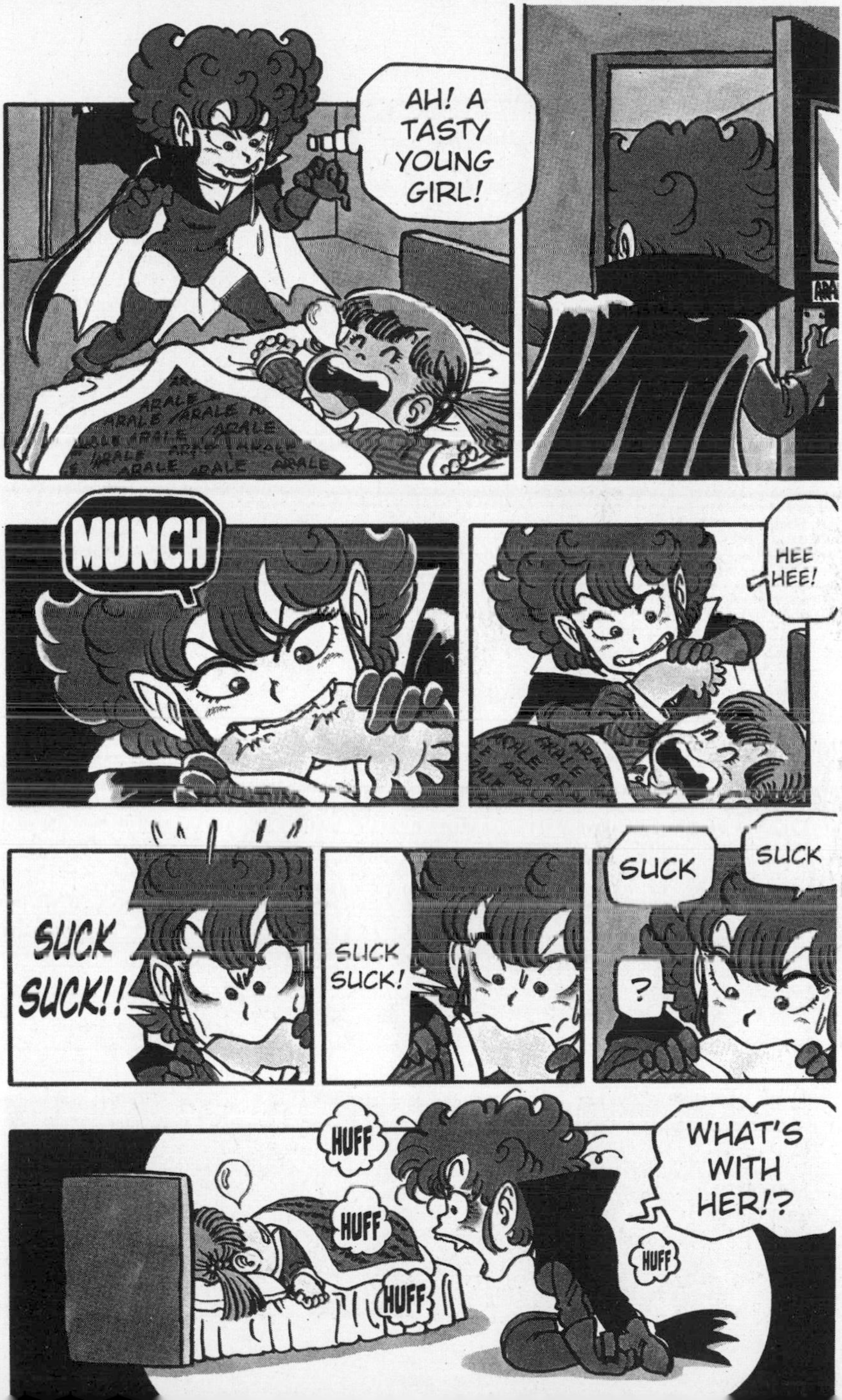
AH! A TASTY YOUNG GIRL!
HEE HEE!
MUNCH
SUCK
SUCK
?
SUCK SUCK!
SUCK SUCK!!
WHAT'S WITH HER!?
HUFF
HUFF
HUFF
HUFF

READ THIS WAY

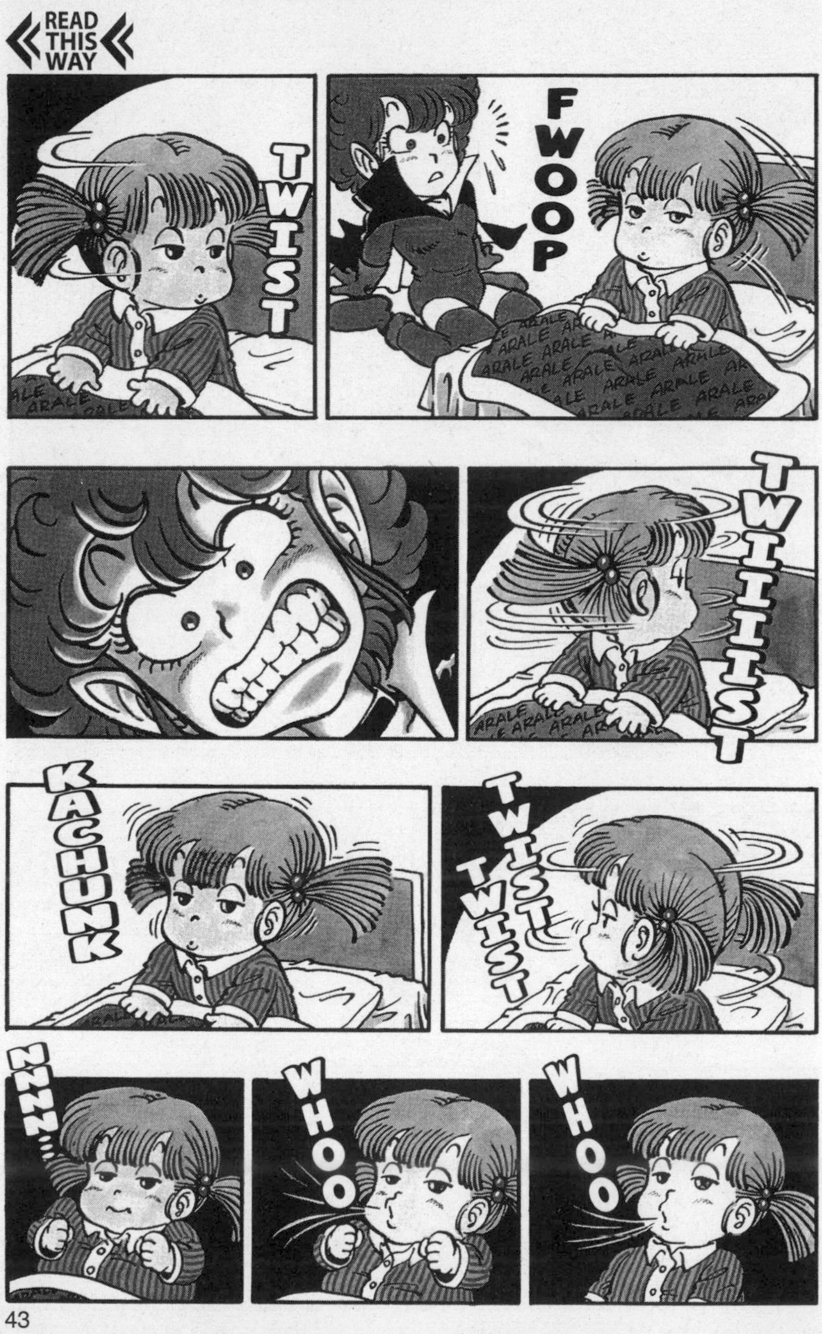

FWOOP
TWIST
TWIIIIIST
TWIST
TWIST
KACHUNK
WHOO
WHOO
NNNN...

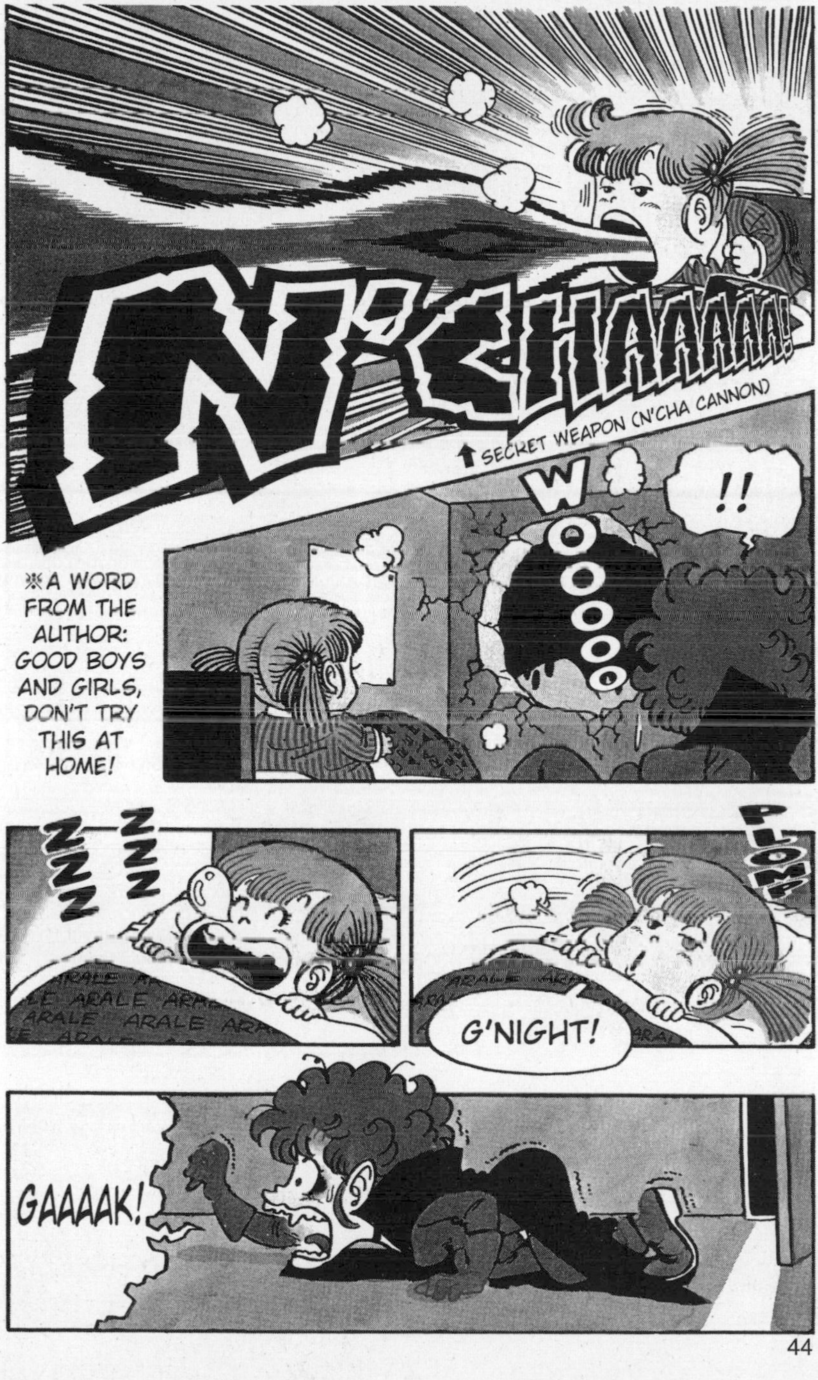
N'CHAAAAA!
⬆ SECRET WEAPON (N'CHA CANNON)
!!
WOOOOOO
※A WORD FROM THE AUTHOR: GOOD BOYS AND GIRLS, DON'T TRY THIS AT HOME!
PLOMP
G'NIGHT!
ZZZ ZZZ
GAAAAK!

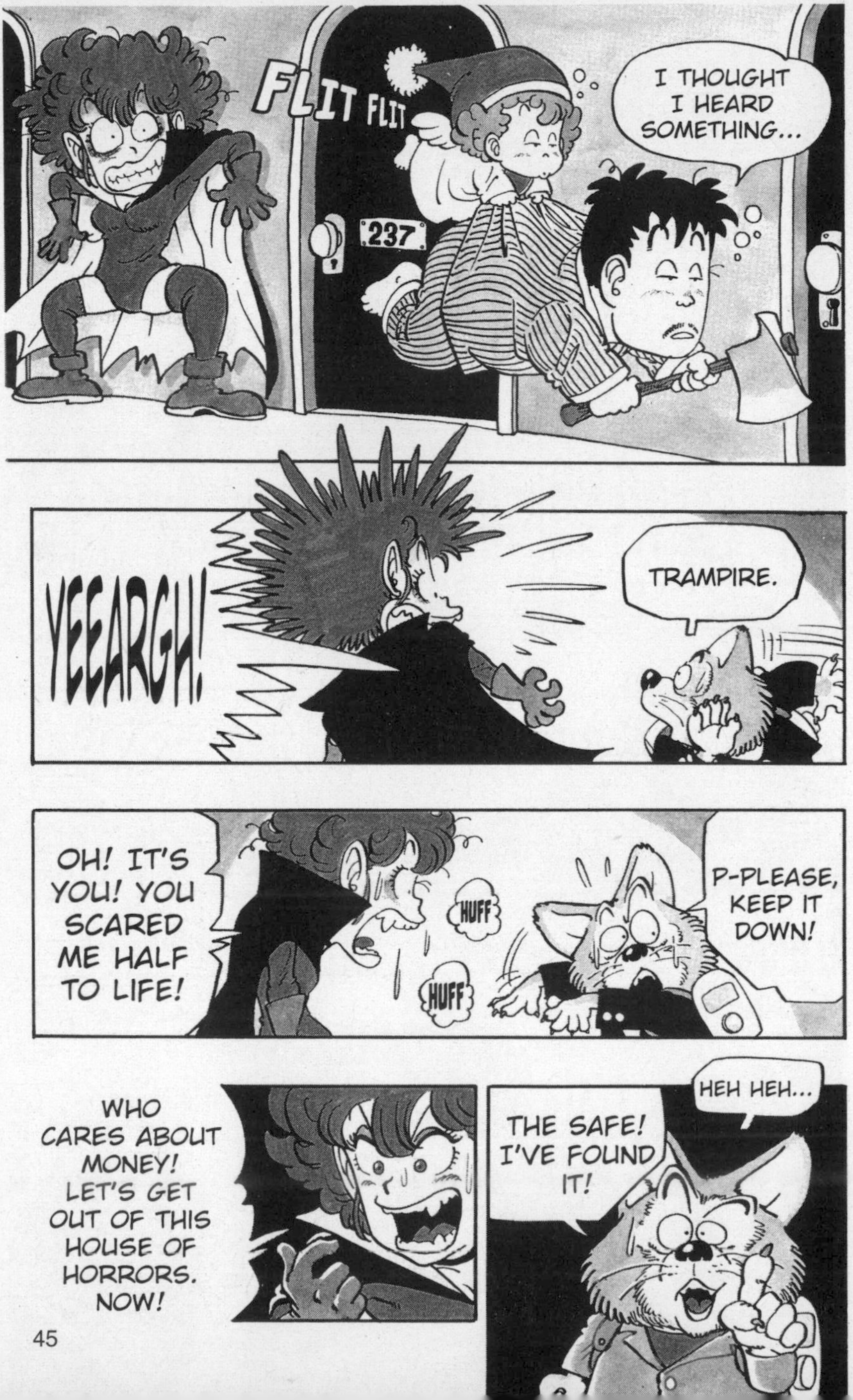
I THOUGHT I HEARD SOMETHING...
FLIT FLIT
TRAMPIRE.
YEEARGH!
P-PLEASE, KEEP IT DOWN!
OH! IT'S YOU! YOU SCARED ME HALF TO LIFE!
HUFF
HUFF
HEH HEH...
THE SAFE! I'VE FOUND IT!
WHO CARES ABOUT MONEY! LET'S GET OUT OF THIS HOUSE OF HORRORS. NOW!

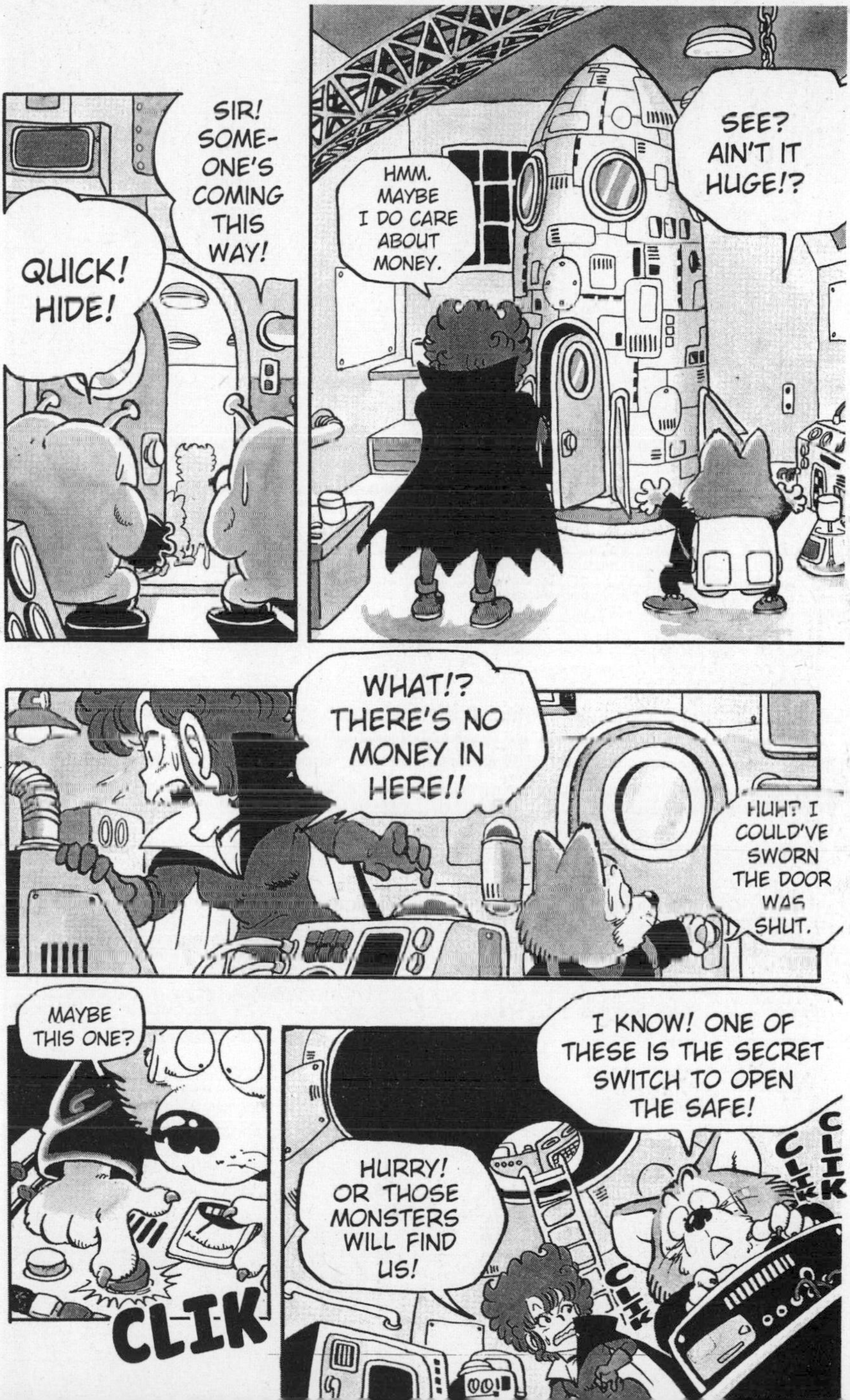
SEE? AIN'T IT HUGE!?
HMM. MAYBE I DO CARE ABOUT MONEY.
SIR! SOME-ONE'S COMING THIS WAY!
QUICK! HIDE!
WHAT!? THERE'S NO MONEY IN HERE!!
HUH? I COULD'VE SWORN THE DOOR WAS SHUT.
I KNOW! ONE OF THESE IS THE SECRET SWITCH TO OPEN THE SAFE!
CLIK CLIK
HURRY! OR THOSE MONSTERS WILL FIND US!
CLIK
MAYBE THIS ONE?
CLIK

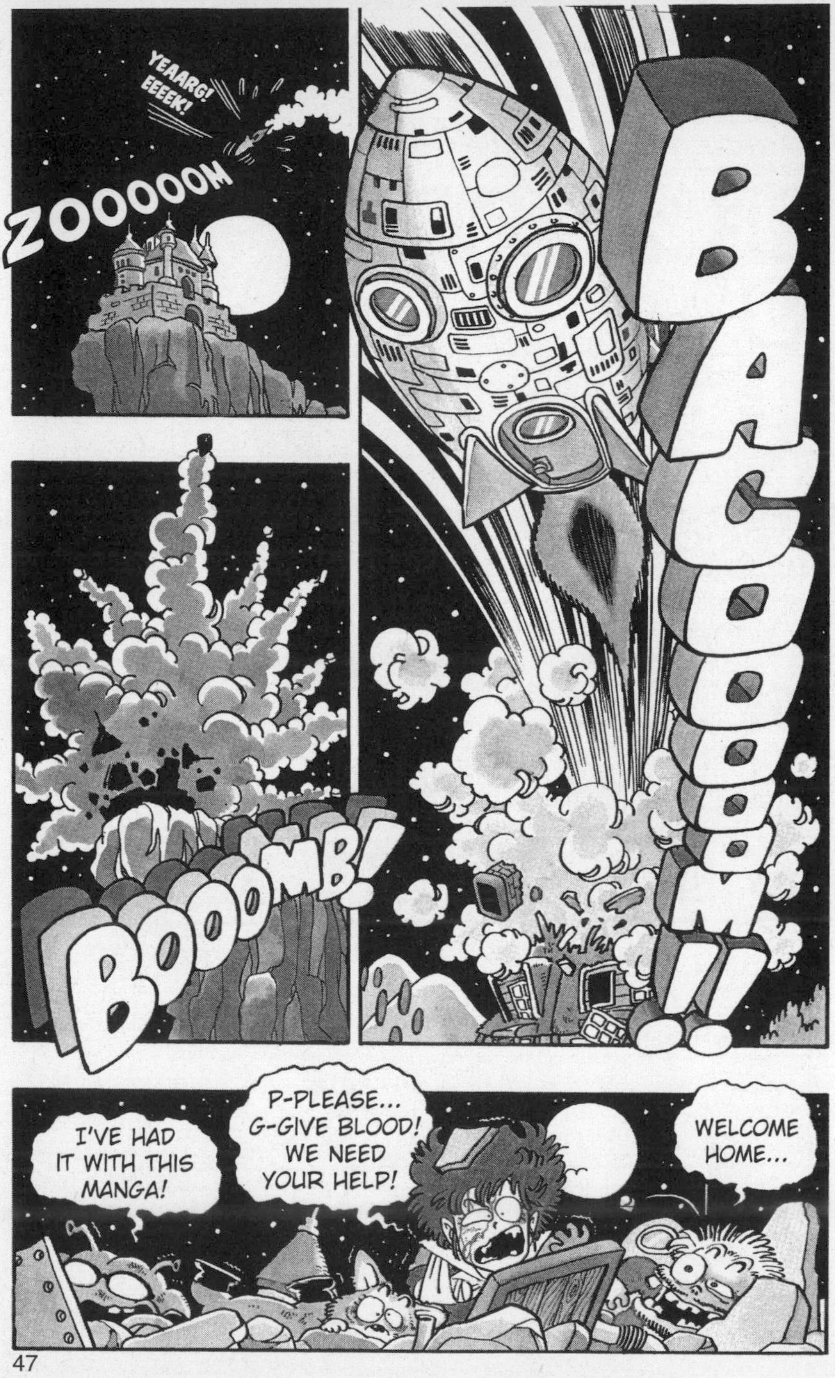
BACOOOOOM!!
YEAARG! EEEEK!
ZOOOOOM
BOOOOMB!
WELCOME HOME...
P-PLEASE... G-GIVE BLOOD! WE NEED YOUR HELP!
I'VE HAD IT WITH THIS MANGA!

The Doodle Manga Version of

The Non-Fiction Theater's

ME BACK THEN

3 Who Needs Hiswashi?

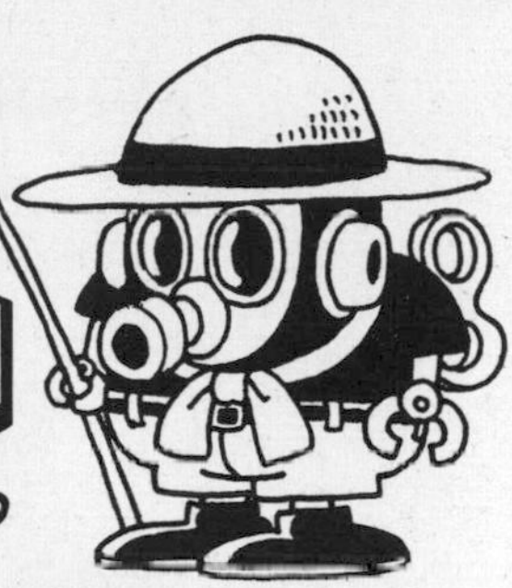

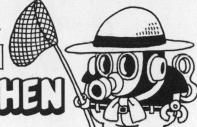

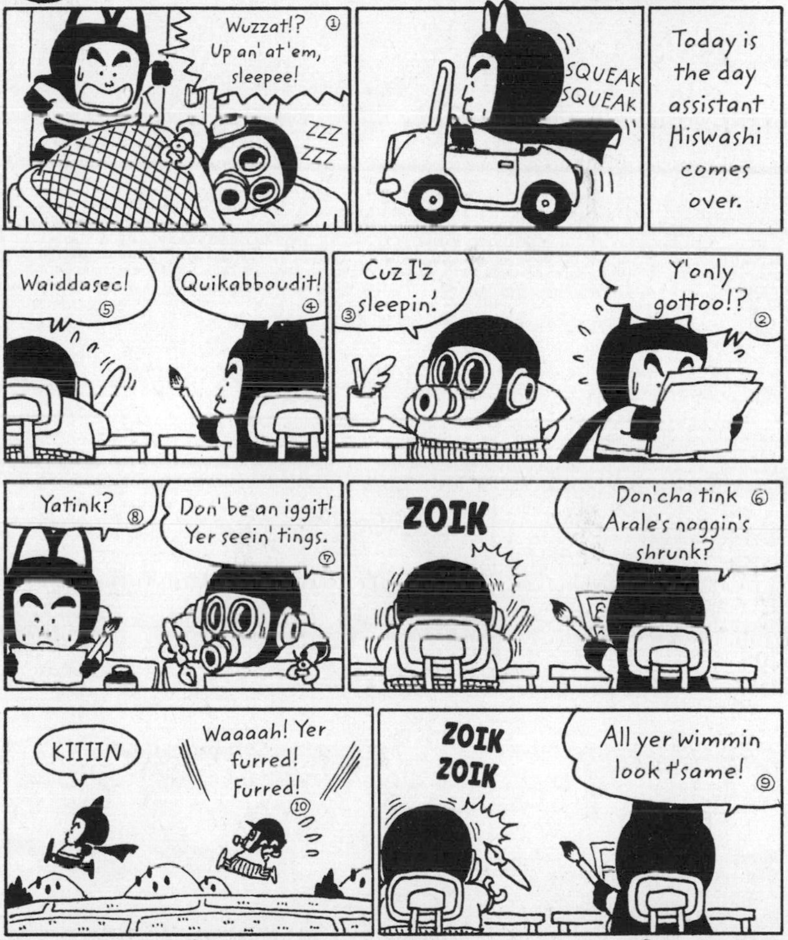
Today is the day assistant Hiswashi comes over.
SQUEAK SQUEAK
Wuzzat!? Up an' at'em, sleepee! ①
ZZZ ZZZ
Y'only gottoo!? ②
Cuz I'z sleepin'. ③
Quikabboudit! ④
Waiddasec! ⑤
Don'cha tink Arale's noggin's shrunk? ⑥
ZOIK
Don' be an iggit! Yer seein' tings. ⑦
Yatink? ⑧
All yer wimmin look t'same! ⑨
ZOIK ZOIK
Waaaah! Yer furred! Furred! ⑩
KIIIIN

Trans-lation: ① What's this? Get up, sleepyhead! ② You've done only two pages? ③ Because I was asleep. ④ Do hurry up! ⑤ One moment, please! ⑥ Has Arale's face gotten smaller of late? ⑦ Don't be foolish. You're imagining it. ⑧ Am I now? ⑨ All the women you draw look identical! ⑩ Waaah! I'm releasing you from my employ!

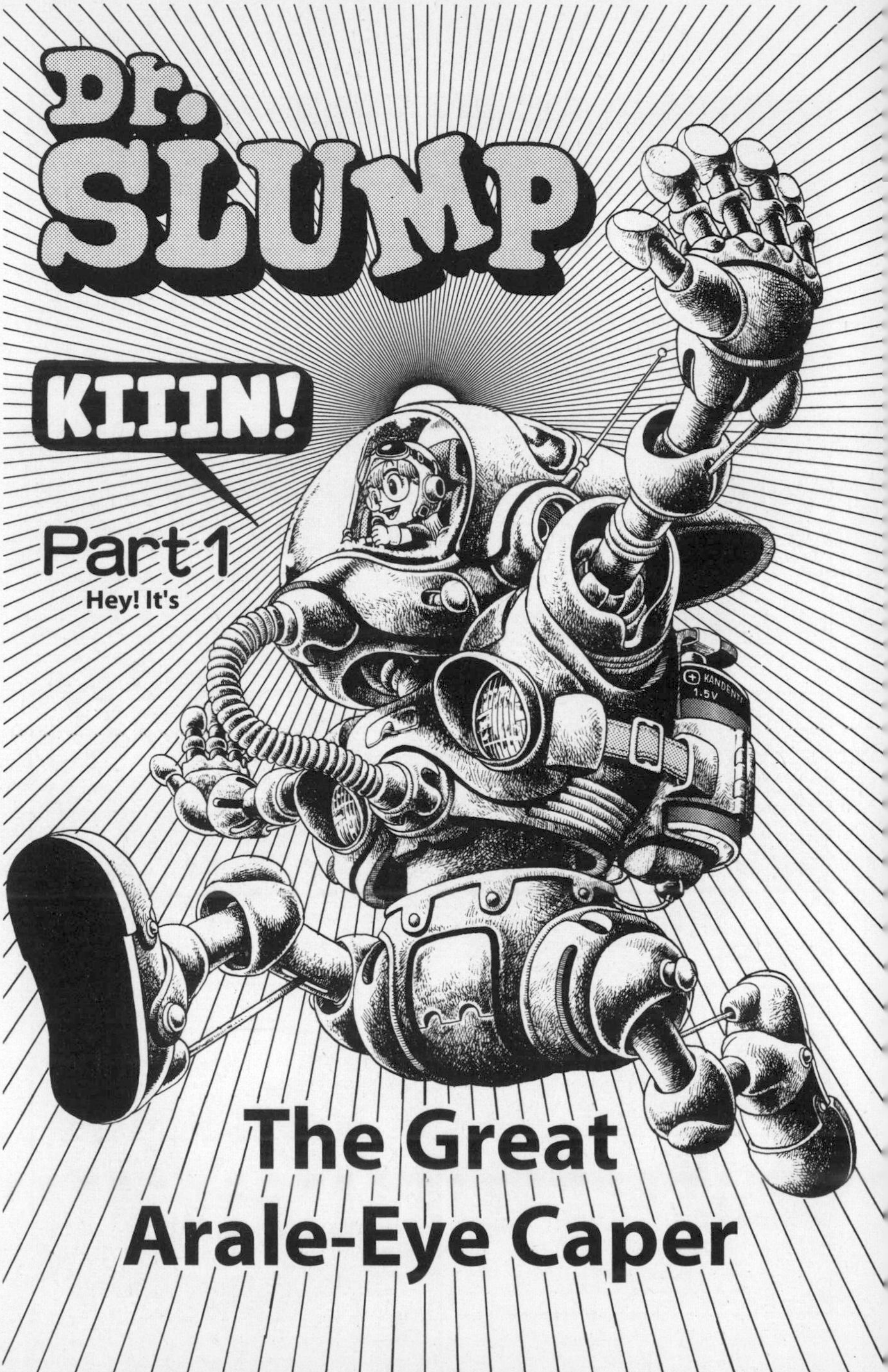
Dr. SLUMP
KIIIN!
Part 1
Hey! It's
KANDENT
1.5V
The Great
Arale-Eye Caper

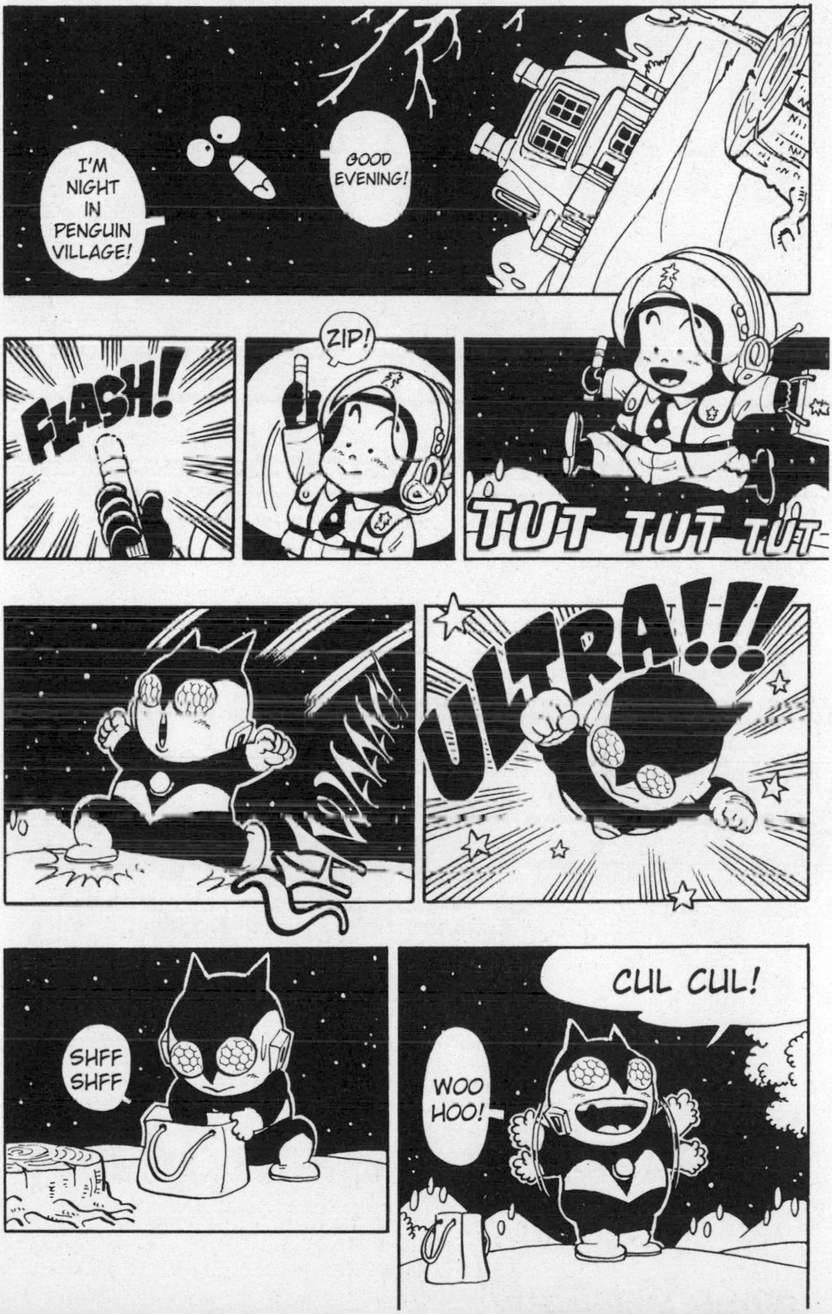
GOOD EVENING!
I'M NIGHT IN PENGUIN VILLAGE!
TUT TUT TUT
ZIP!
FLASH!
ULTRA!!!
CUL CUL!
WOO HOO!
SHFF SHFF

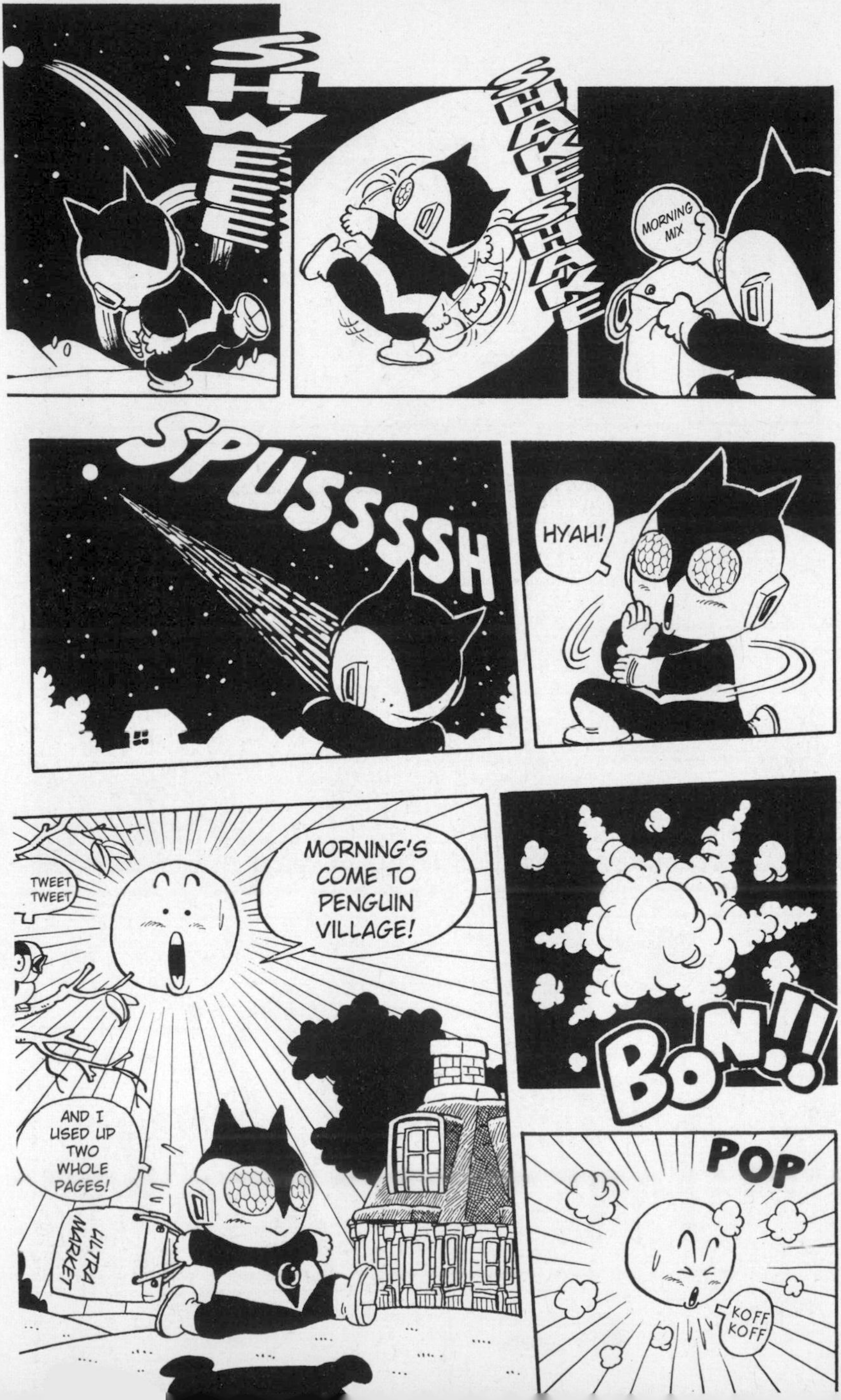
MORNING MIX
SHAKE SHAKE
SHWEEE
HYAH!
SPUSSSSH
BON!!
POP
KOFF KOFF
MORNING'S COME TO PENGUIN VILLAGE!
TWEET TWEET
AND I USED UP TWO WHOLE PAGES!
ULTRA MARKET

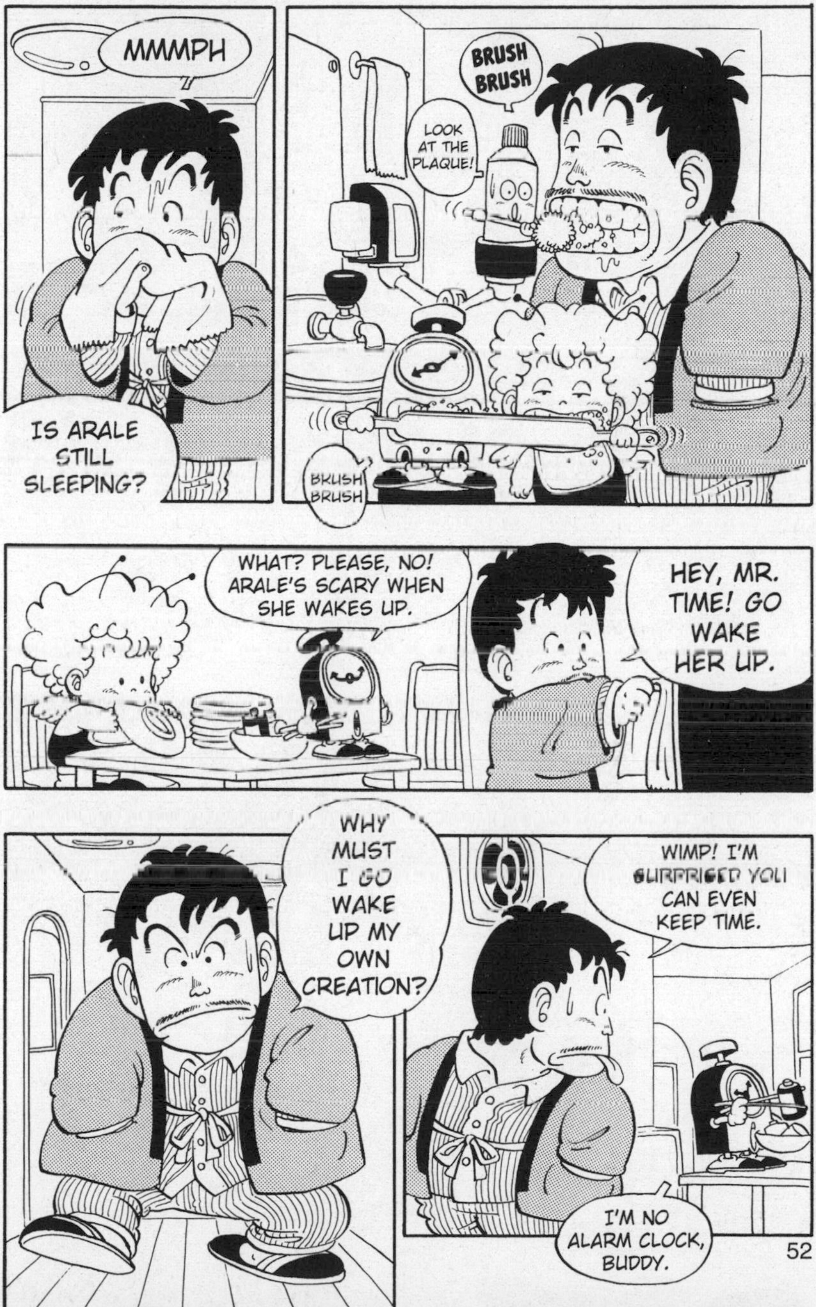
BRUSH BRUSH
LOOK AT THE PLAQUE!
BRUSH BRUSH
MMMPH
IS ARALE STILL SLEEPING?
HEY, MR. TIME! GO WAKE HER UP.
WHAT? PLEASE, NO! ARALE'S SCARY WHEN SHE WAKES UP.
WIMP! I'M SURPRISED YOU CAN EVEN KEEP TIME.
I'M NO ALARM CLOCK, BUDDY.
WHY MUST I GO WAKE UP MY OWN CREATION?

READ THIS WAY

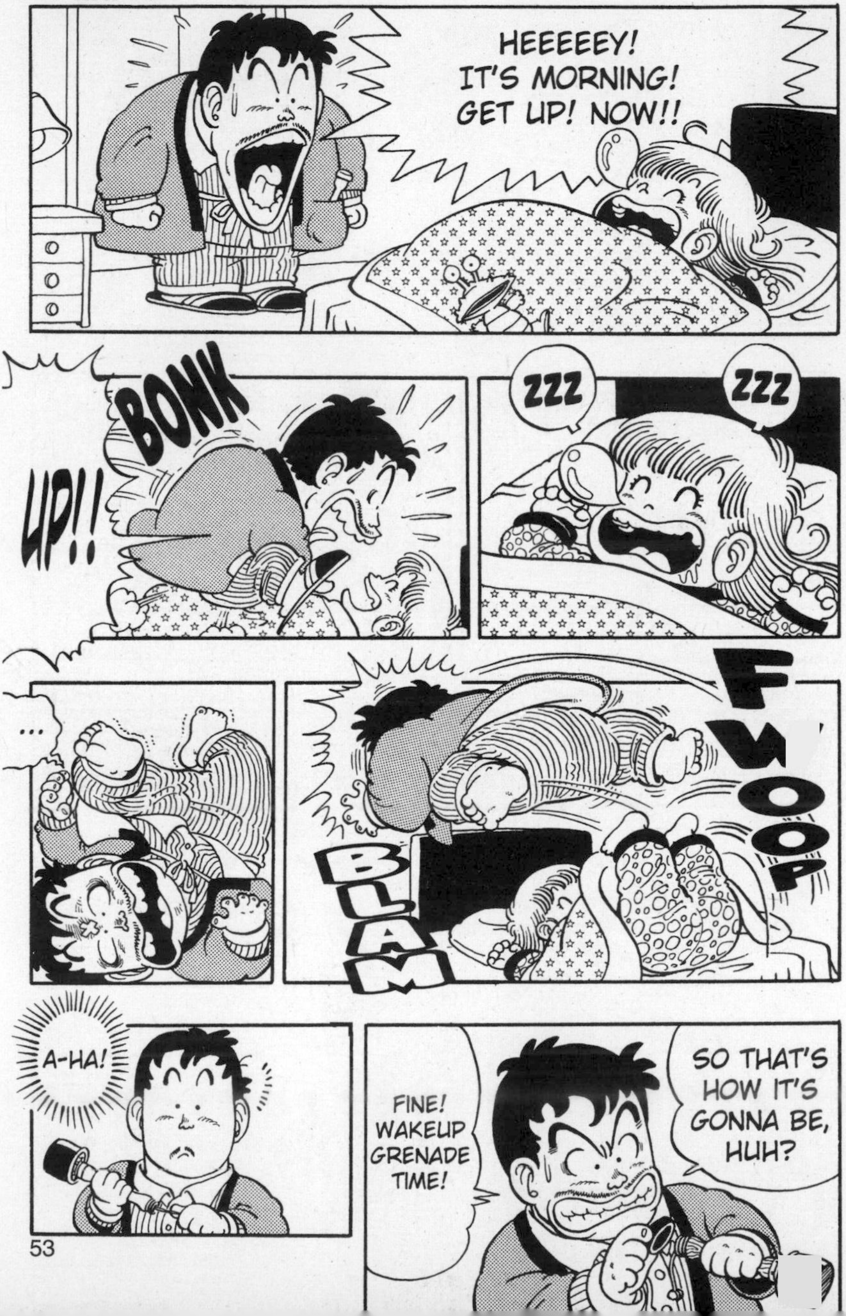

HEEEEEY! IT'S MORNING! GET UP! NOW!!
ZZZ
ZZZ
BONK
UP!!
FWOOP
BLAM
...
SO THAT'S HOW IT'S GONNA BE, HUH?
FINE! WAKEUP GRENADE TIME!
A-HA!

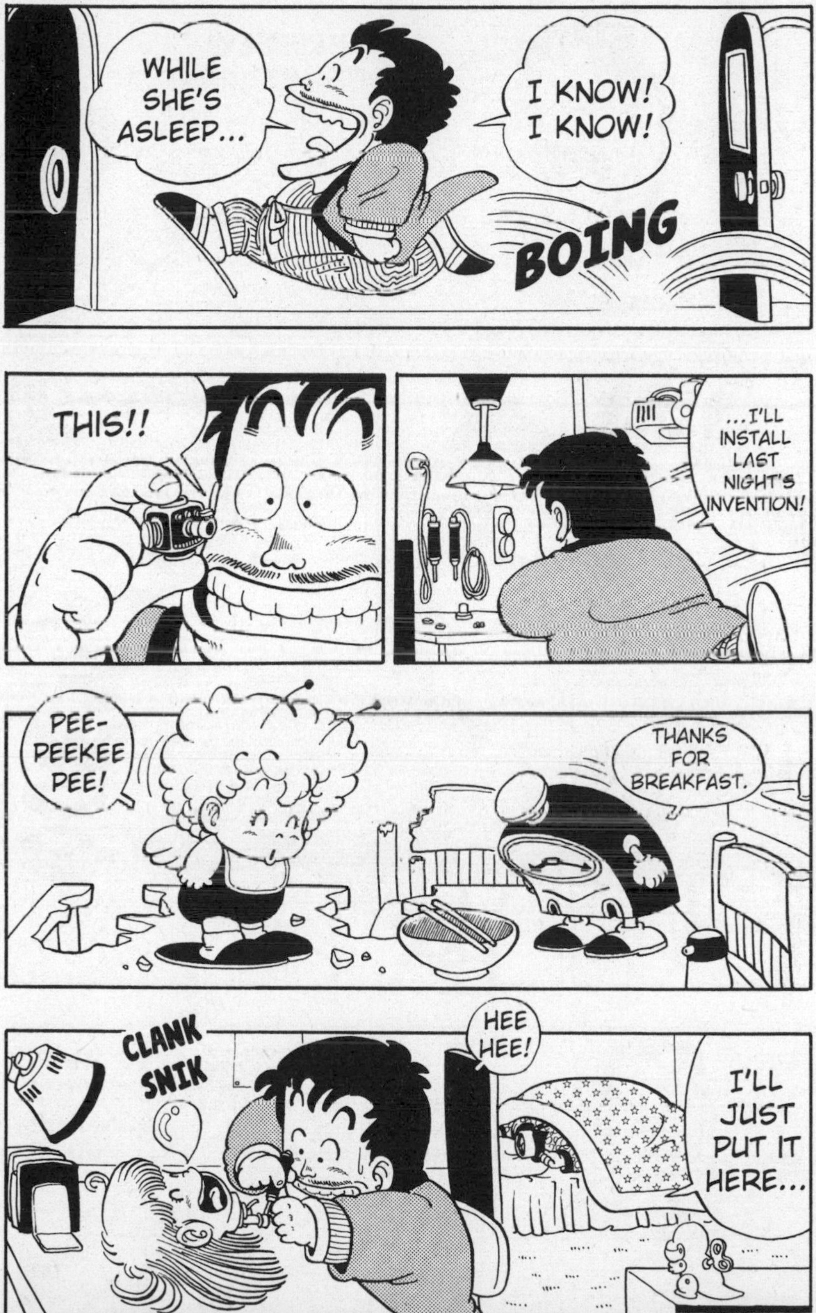
I KNOW! I KNOW!
WHILE SHE'S ASLEEP...
BOING
...I'LL INSTALL LAST NIGHT'S INVENTION!
THIS!!
THANKS FOR BREAKFAST.
PEE-PEEKEE PEE!
I'LL JUST PUT IT HERE...
HEE HEE!
CLANK SNIK

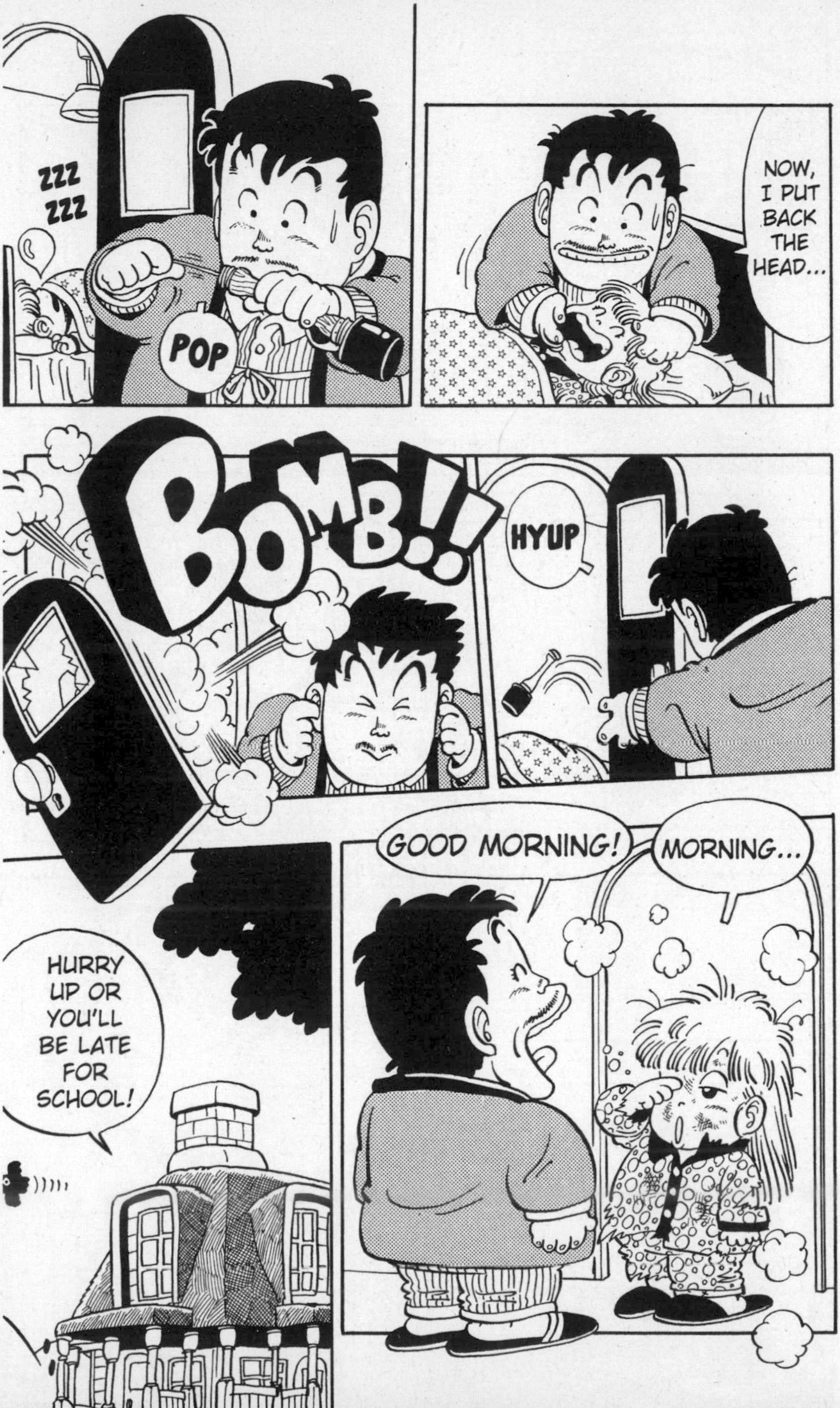
NOW, I PUT BACK THE HEAD...
ZZZ ZZZ
POP
HYUP
BOMB!!
MORNING...
GOOD MORNING!
HURRY UP OR YOU'LL BE LATE FOR SCHOOL!

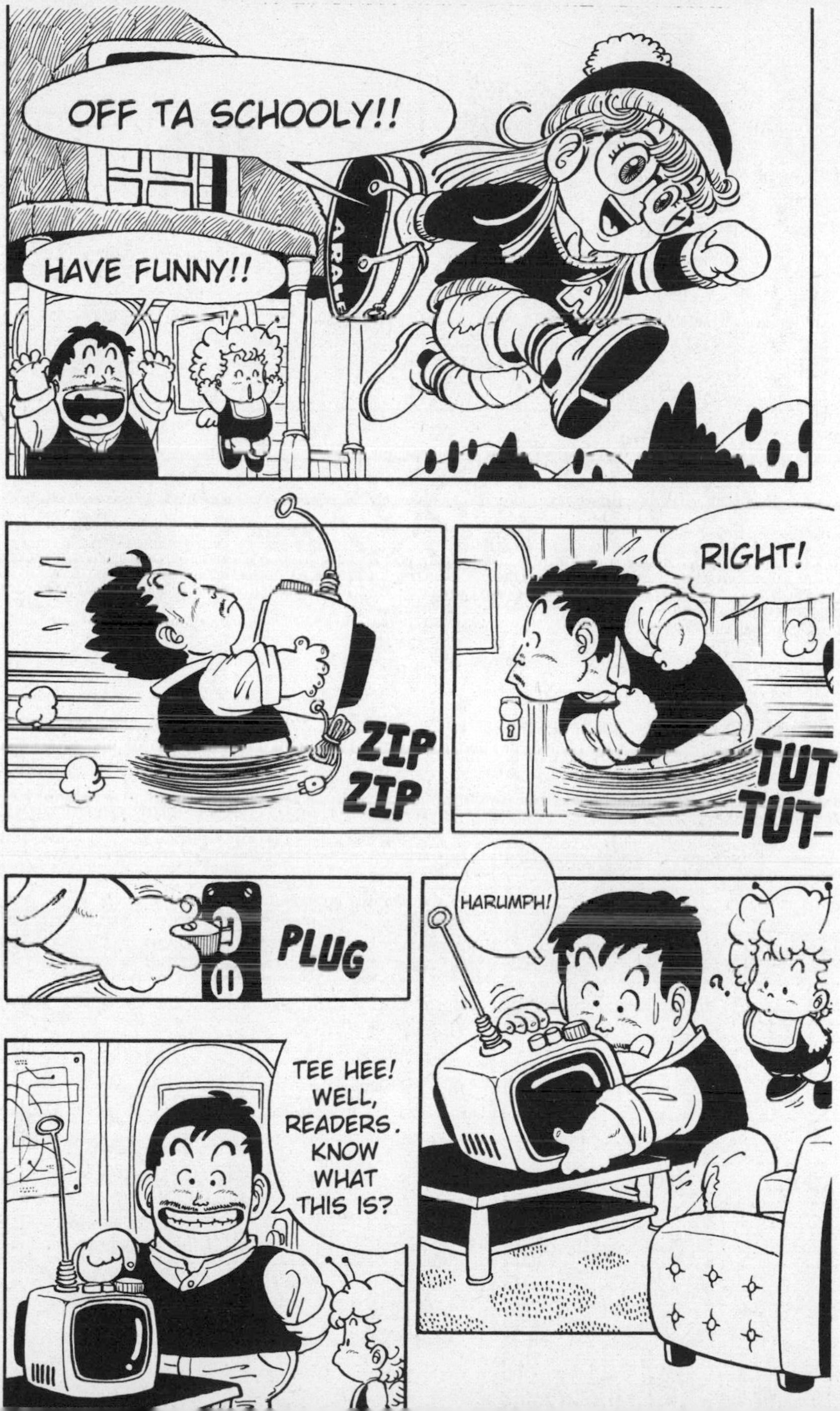
OFF TA SCHOOLY!!
HAVE FUNNY!!
RIGHT!
TUT TUT
ZIP ZIP
HARUMPH!
?
PLUG
TEE HEE! WELL, READERS. KNOW WHAT THIS IS?

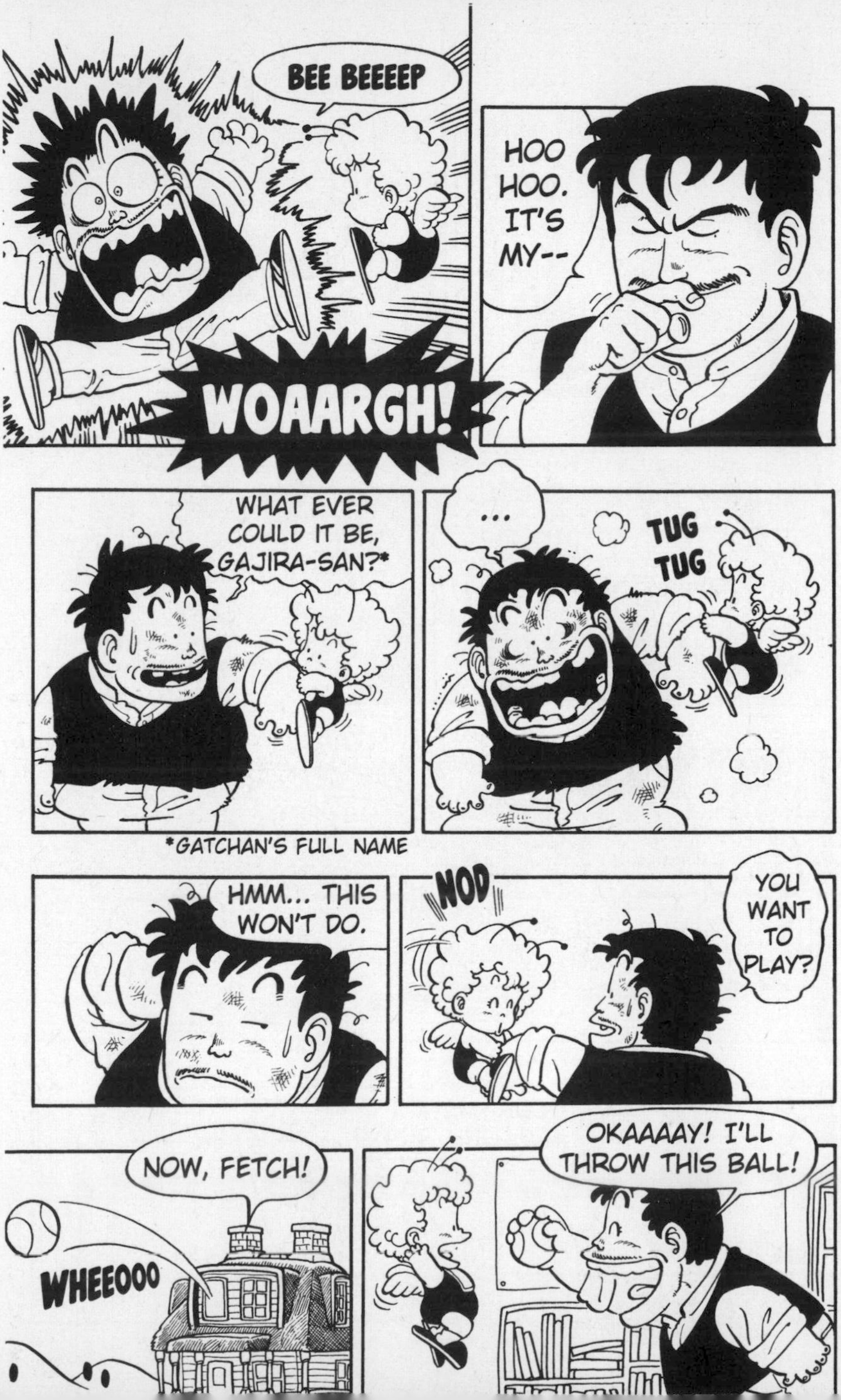
HOO HOO. IT'S MY--
BEE BEEEEP
WOAARGH!
...
TUG TUG
WHAT EVER COULD IT BE, GAJIRA-SAN?*
*GATCHAN'S FULL NAME
NOD
YOU WANT TO PLAY?
HMM... THIS WON'T DO.
OKAAAAY! I'LL THROW THIS BALL!
NOW, FETCH!
WHEEOOO

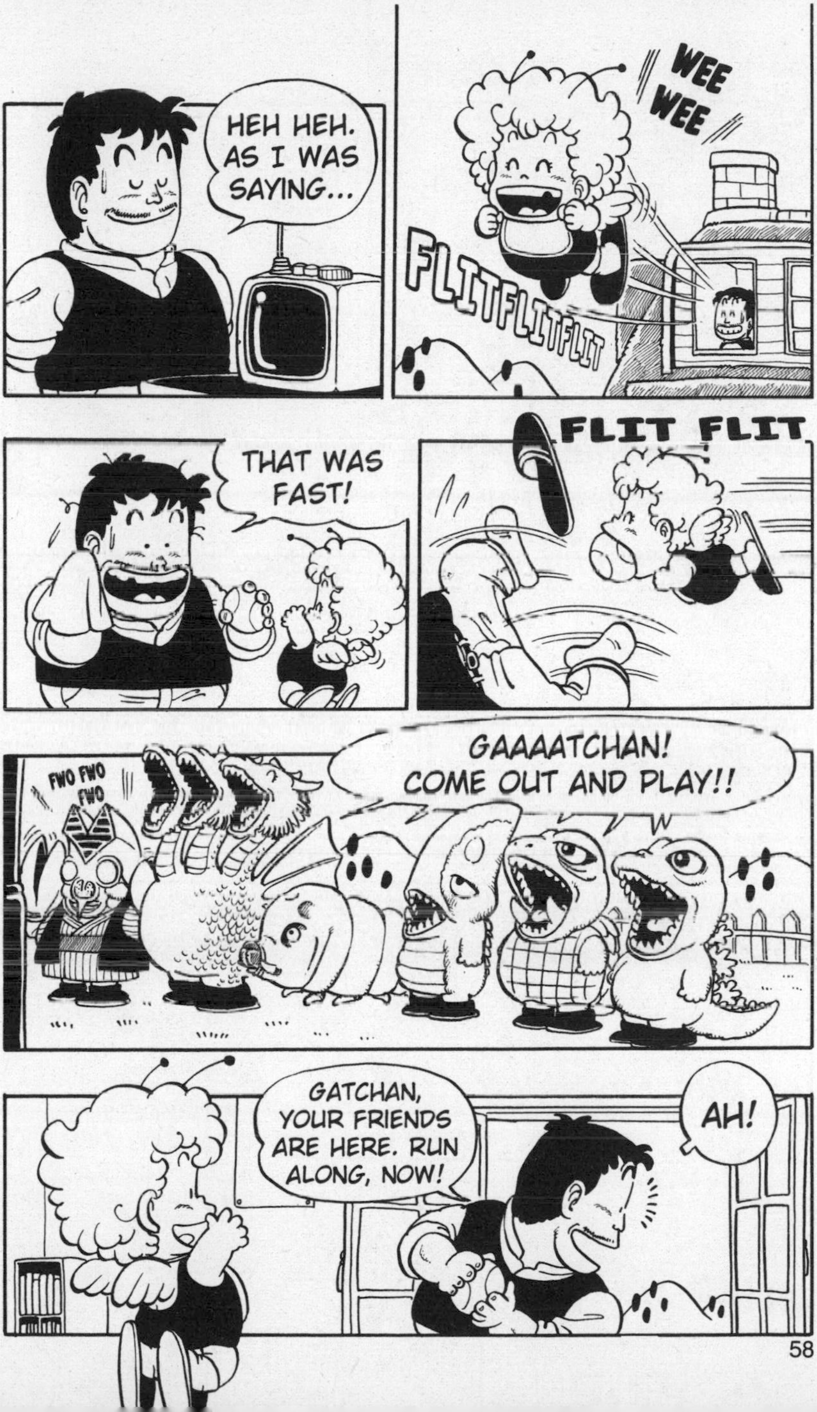
WEE WEE
FLITFLITFLIT
HEH HEH. AS I WAS SAYING...
FLIT FLIT
THAT WAS FAST!
GAAAATCHAN! COME OUT AND PLAY!!
FWO FWO FWO
AH!
GATCHAN, YOUR FRIENDS ARE HERE. RUN ALONG, NOW!

READ THIS WAY

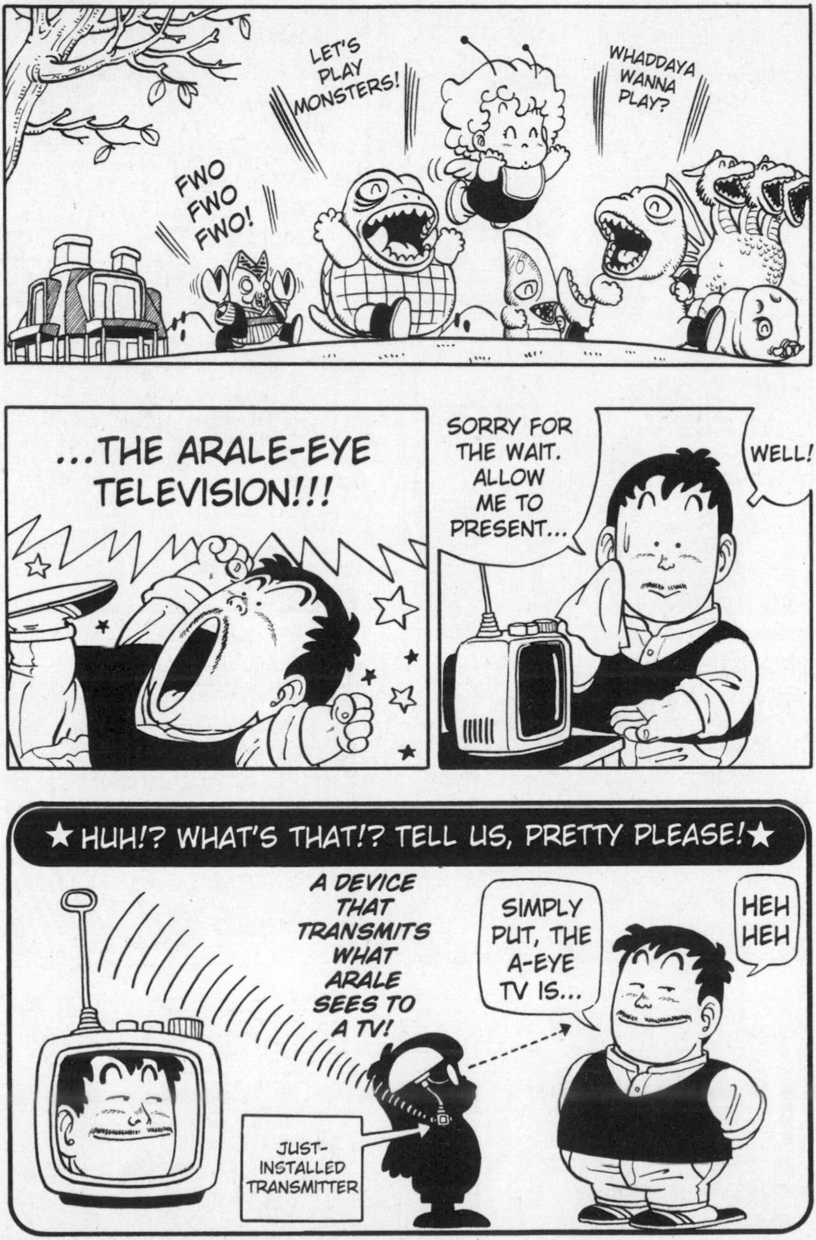
WHADDAYA WANNA PLAY?
LET'S PLAY MONSTERS!
FWO FWO FWO!
WELL!
SORRY FOR THE WAIT. ALLOW ME TO PRESENT...
...THE ARALE-EYE TELEVISION!!!
★HUH!? WHAT'S THAT!? TELL US, PRETTY PLEASE!★
HEH HEH
SIMPLY PUT, THE A-EYE TV IS...
A DEVICE THAT TRANSMITS WHAT ARALE SEES TO A TV!
JUST-INSTALLED TRANSMITTER

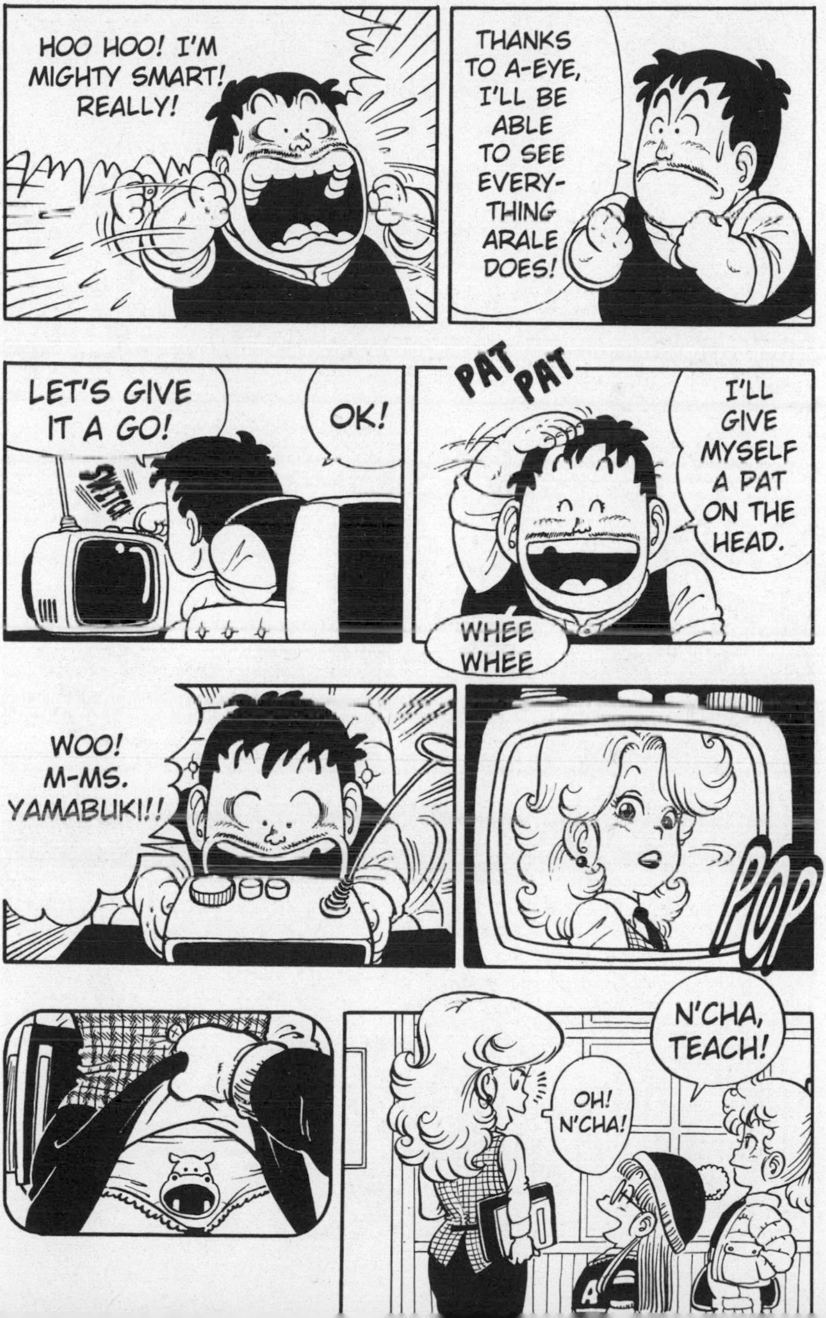
THANKS TO A-EYE, I'LL BE ABLE TO SEE EVERY-THING ARALE DOES!
HOO HOO! I'M MIGHTY SMART! REALLY!
PAT PAT
I'LL GIVE MYSELF A PAT ON THE HEAD.
WHEE WHEE
OK!
LET'S GIVE IT A GO!
SWITCH
POP
WOO! M-MS. YAMABUKI!!
N'CHA, TEACH!
OH! N'CHA!

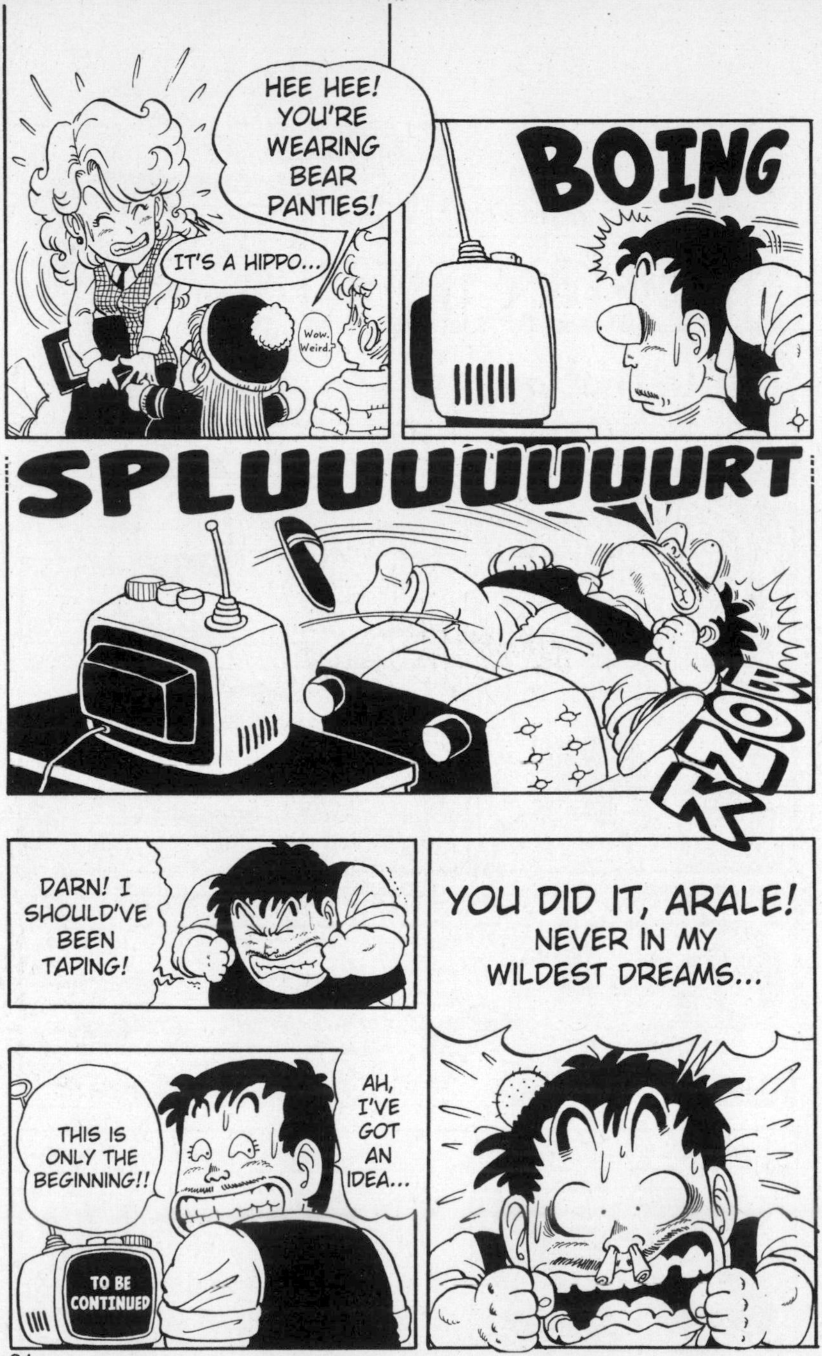
BOING
HEE HEE! YOU'RE WEARING BEAR PANTIES!
IT'S A HIPPO...
Wow. Weird.
SPLUUUUUUURT
KONK
YOU DID IT, ARALE! NEVER IN MY WILDEST DREAMS...
DARN! I SHOULD'VE BEEN TAPING!
AH, I'VE GOT AN IDEA...
THIS IS ONLY THE BEGINNING!!
TO BE CONTINUED

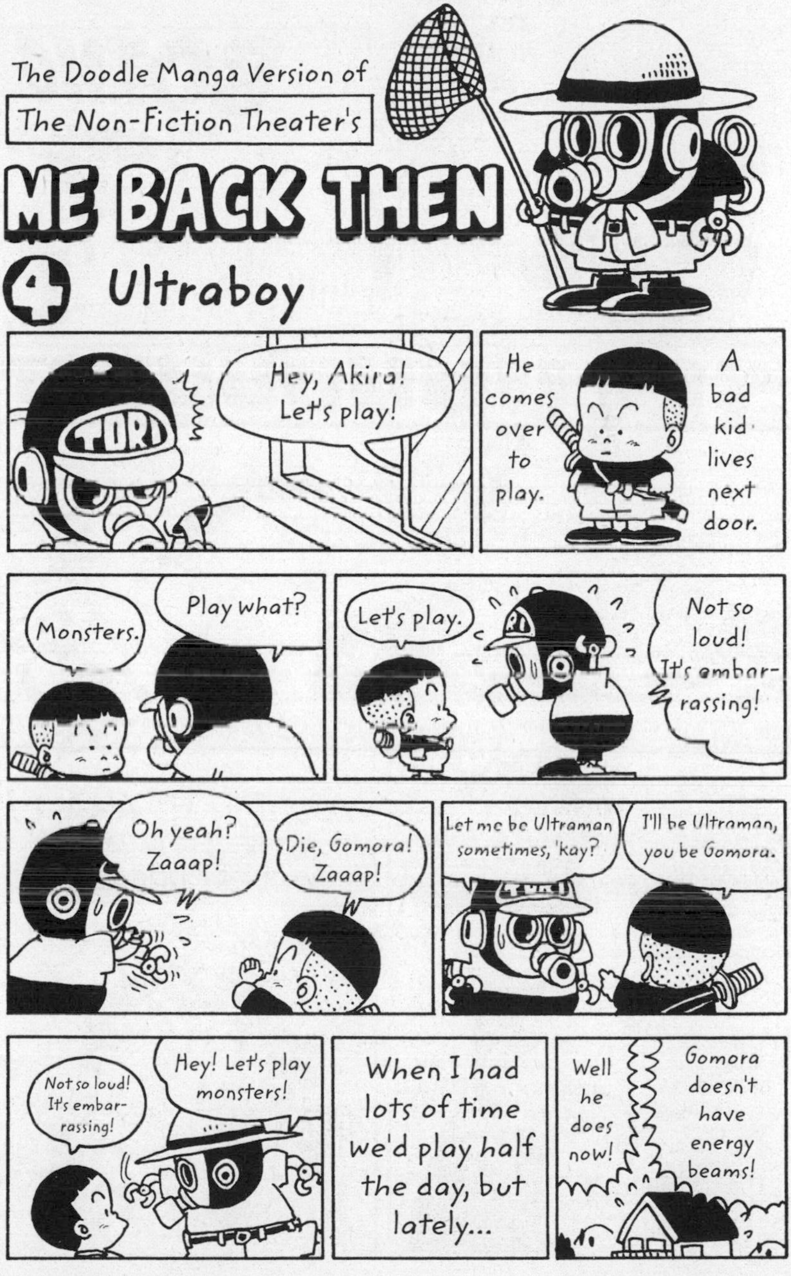
The Doodle Manga Version of
The Non-Fiction Theater's
ME BACK THEN
4 Ultraboy
A bad kid lives next door.
He comes over to play.
Hey, Akira! Let's play!
Not so loud! It's embarrassing!
Let's play.
Play what?
Monsters.
I'll be Ultraman, you be Gomora.
Let me be Ultraman sometimes, 'kay?
Die, Gomora! Zaaap!
Oh yeah? Zaaap!
Gomora doesn't have energy beams!
Well he does now!
When I had lots of time we'd play half the day, but lately...
Hey! Let's play monsters!
Not so loud! It's embarrassing!

The Great Arale-Eye Caper Part 2

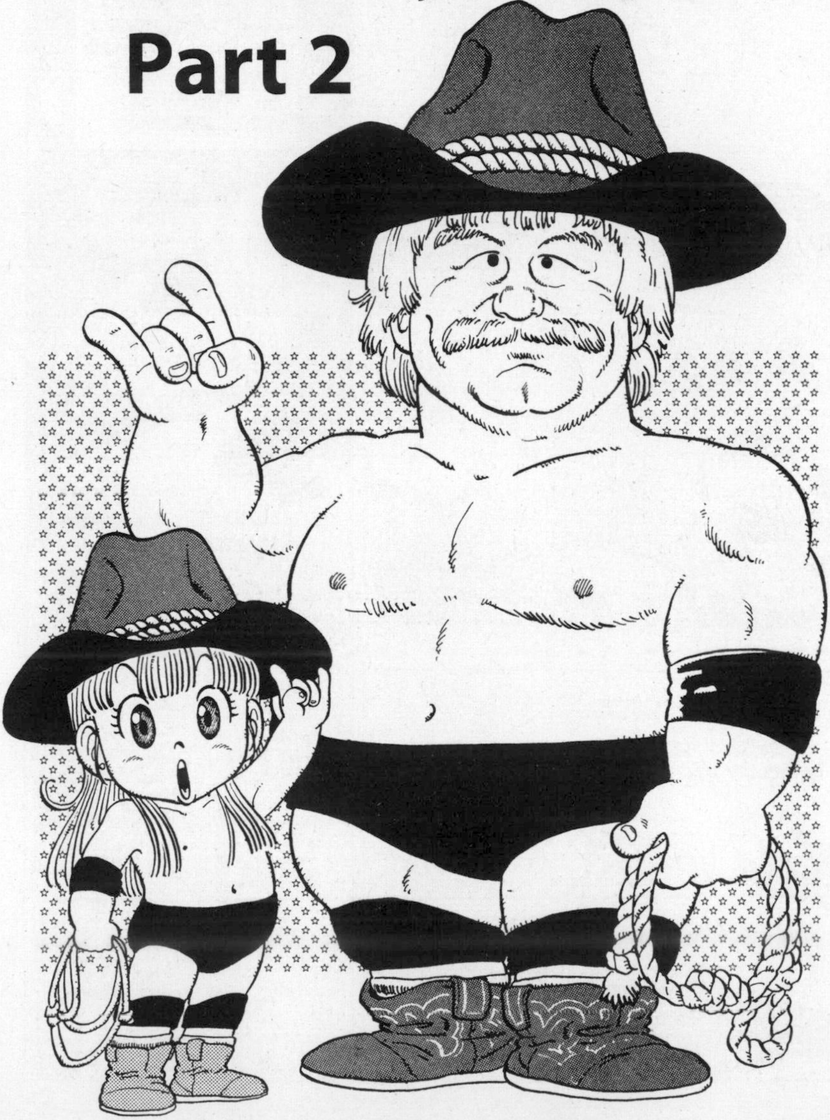

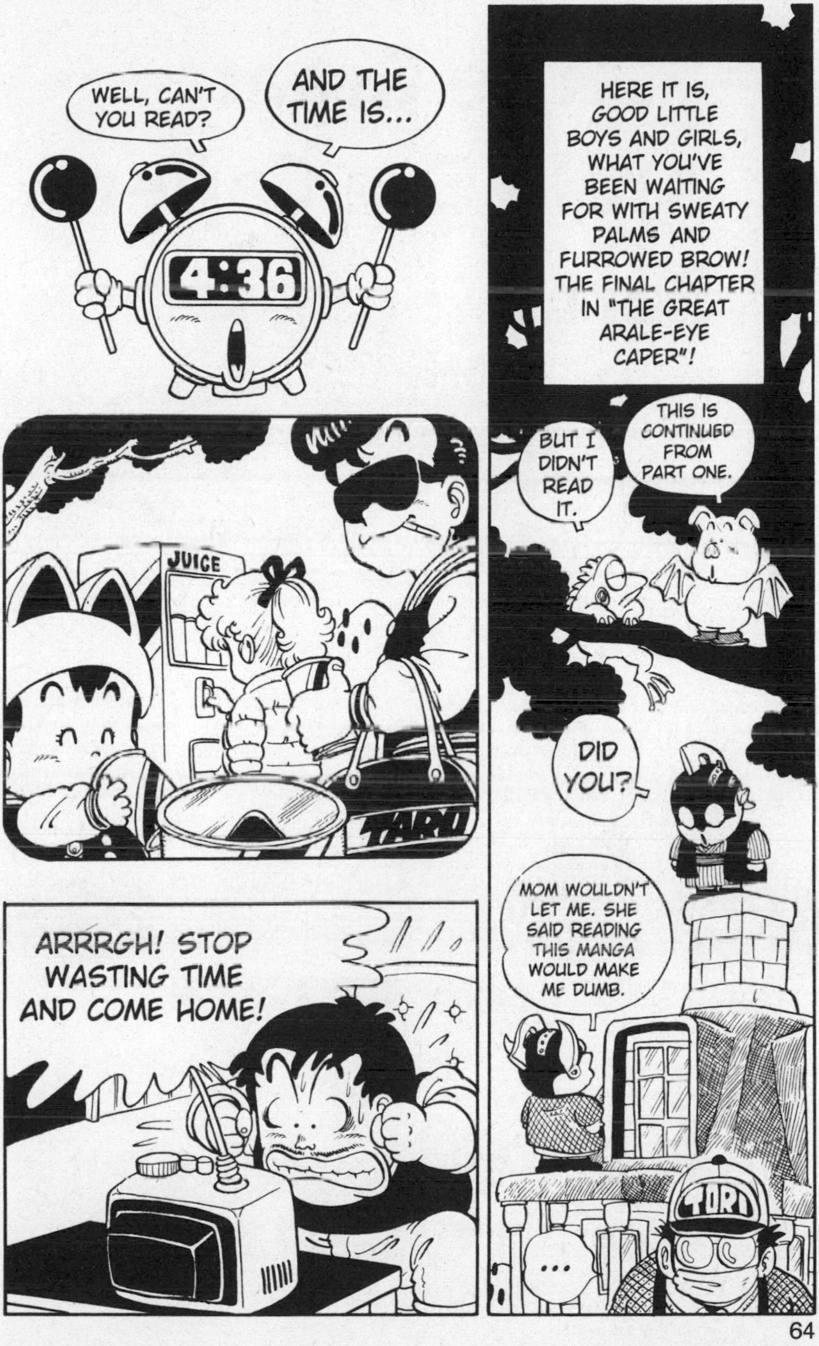
HERE IT IS, GOOD LITTLE BOYS AND GIRLS, WHAT YOU'VE BEEN WAITING FOR WITH SWEATY PALMS AND FURROWED BROW! THE FINAL CHAPTER IN "THE GREAT ARALE-EYE CAPER"!
THIS IS CONTINUED FROM PART ONE.
BUT I DIDN'T READ IT.
DID YOU?
MOM WOULDN'T LET ME. SHE SAID READING THIS MANGA WOULD MAKE ME DUMB.
...
TORI
AND THE TIME IS...
WELL, CAN'T YOU READ?
4:36
JUICE
TARO
ARRRGH! STOP WASTING TIME AND COME HOME!

READ THIS WAY

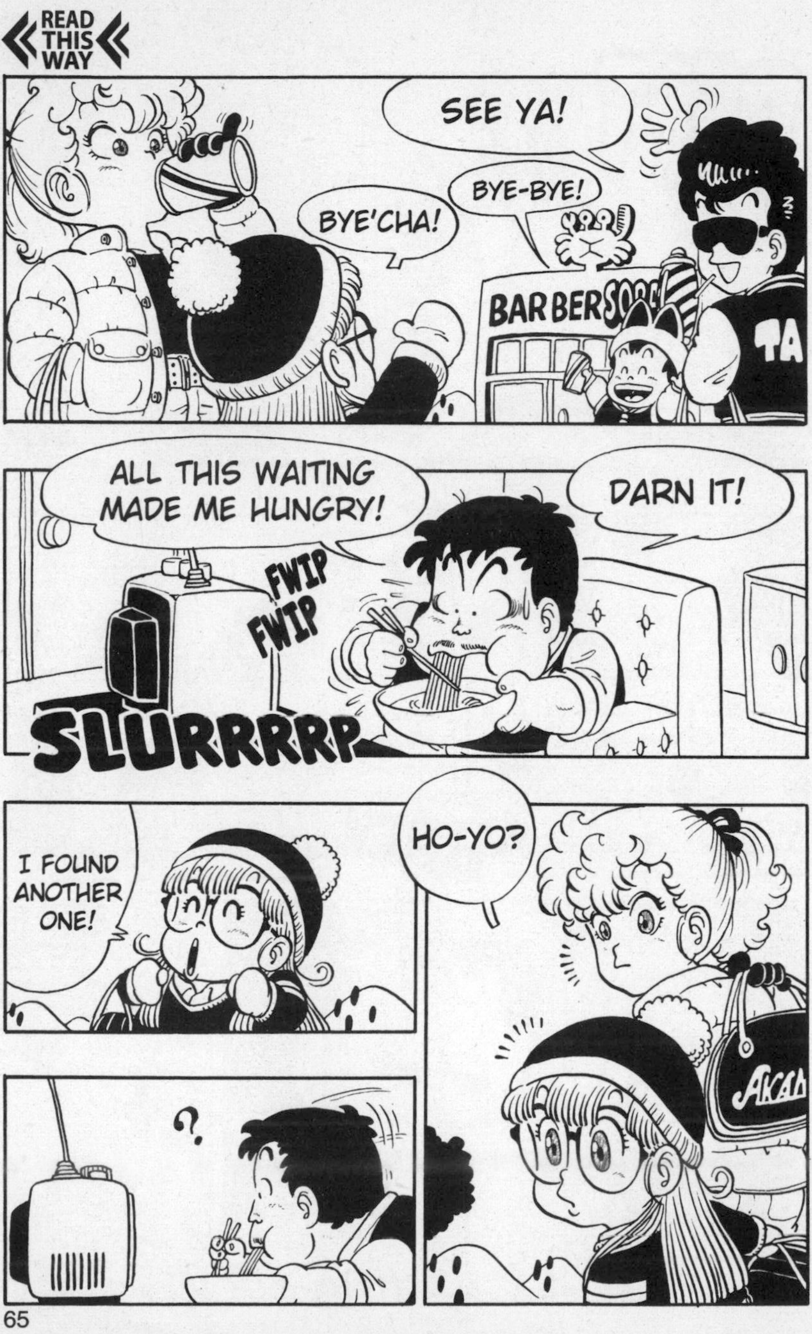
SEE YA!
BYE-BYE!
BYE'CHA!
BARBER
DARN IT!
ALL THIS WAITING MADE ME HUNGRY!
FWIP FWIP
SLURRRRP
HO-YO?
I FOUND ANOTHER ONE!
?

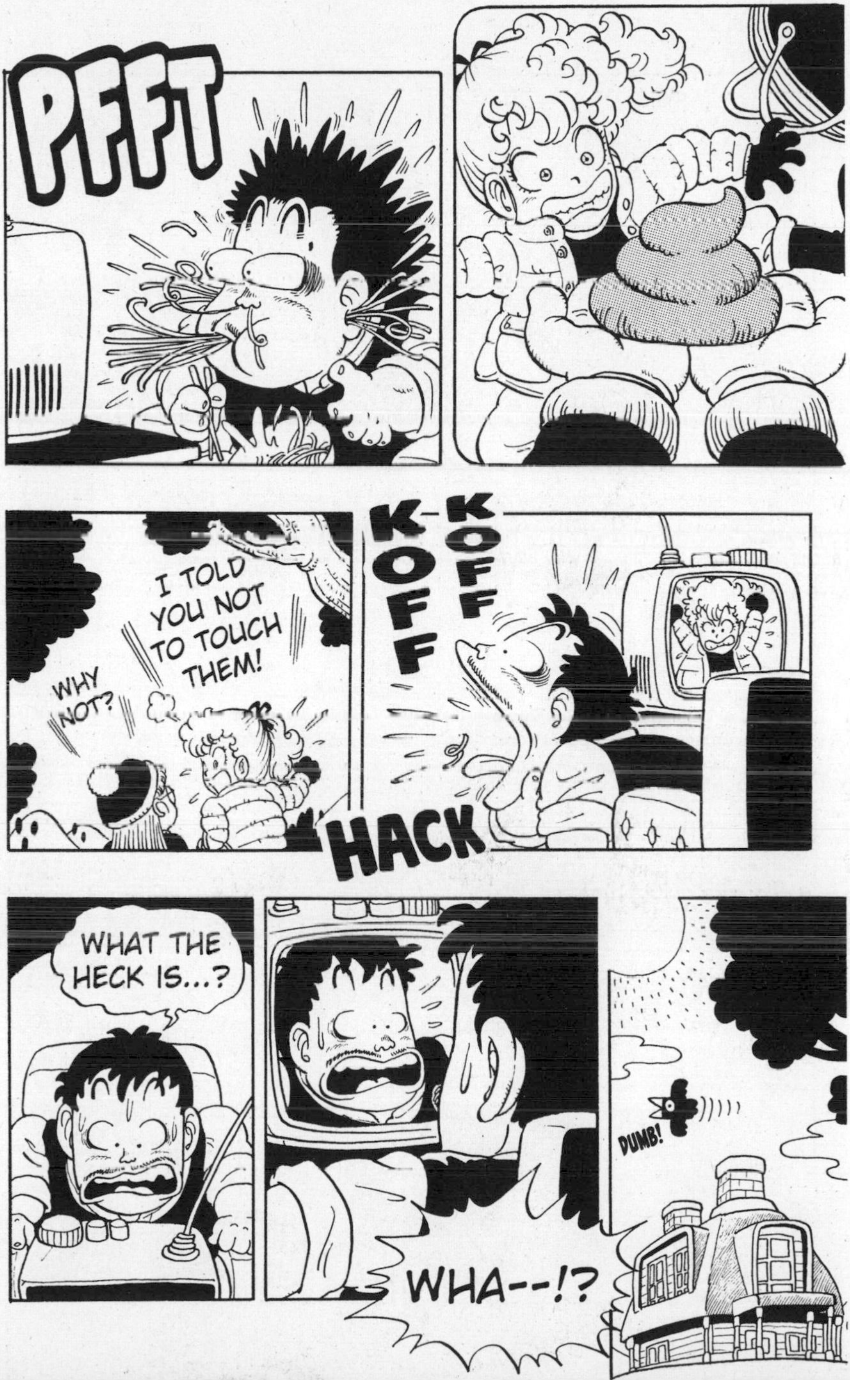
PFFT
KOFF
K-KOFF
HACK
I TOLD YOU NOT TO TOUCH THEM!
WHY NOT?
DUMB!
WHA--!?
WHAT THE HECK IS...?

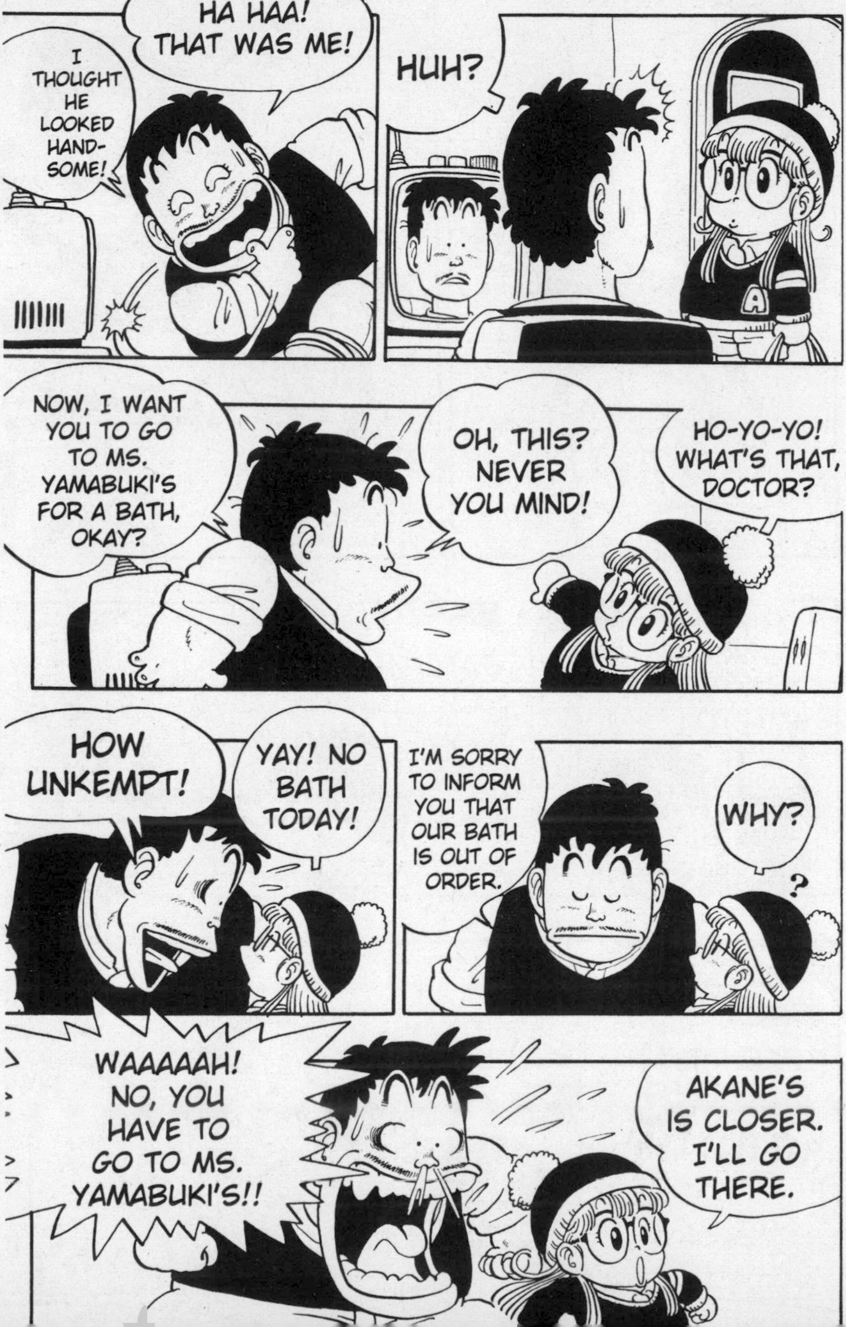
HUH?
HA HAA! THAT WAS ME!
I THOUGHT HE LOOKED HAND-SOME!
HO-YO-YO! WHAT'S THAT, DOCTOR?
OH, THIS? NEVER YOU MIND!
NOW, I WANT YOU TO GO TO MS. YAMABUKI'S FOR A BATH, OKAY?
I'M SORRY TO INFORM YOU THAT OUR BATH IS OUT OF ORDER.
WHY?
?
YAY! NO BATH TODAY!
HOW UNKEMPT!
AKANE'S IS CLOSER. I'LL GO THERE.
WAAAAAH! NO, YOU HAVE TO GO TO MS. YAMABUKI'S!!

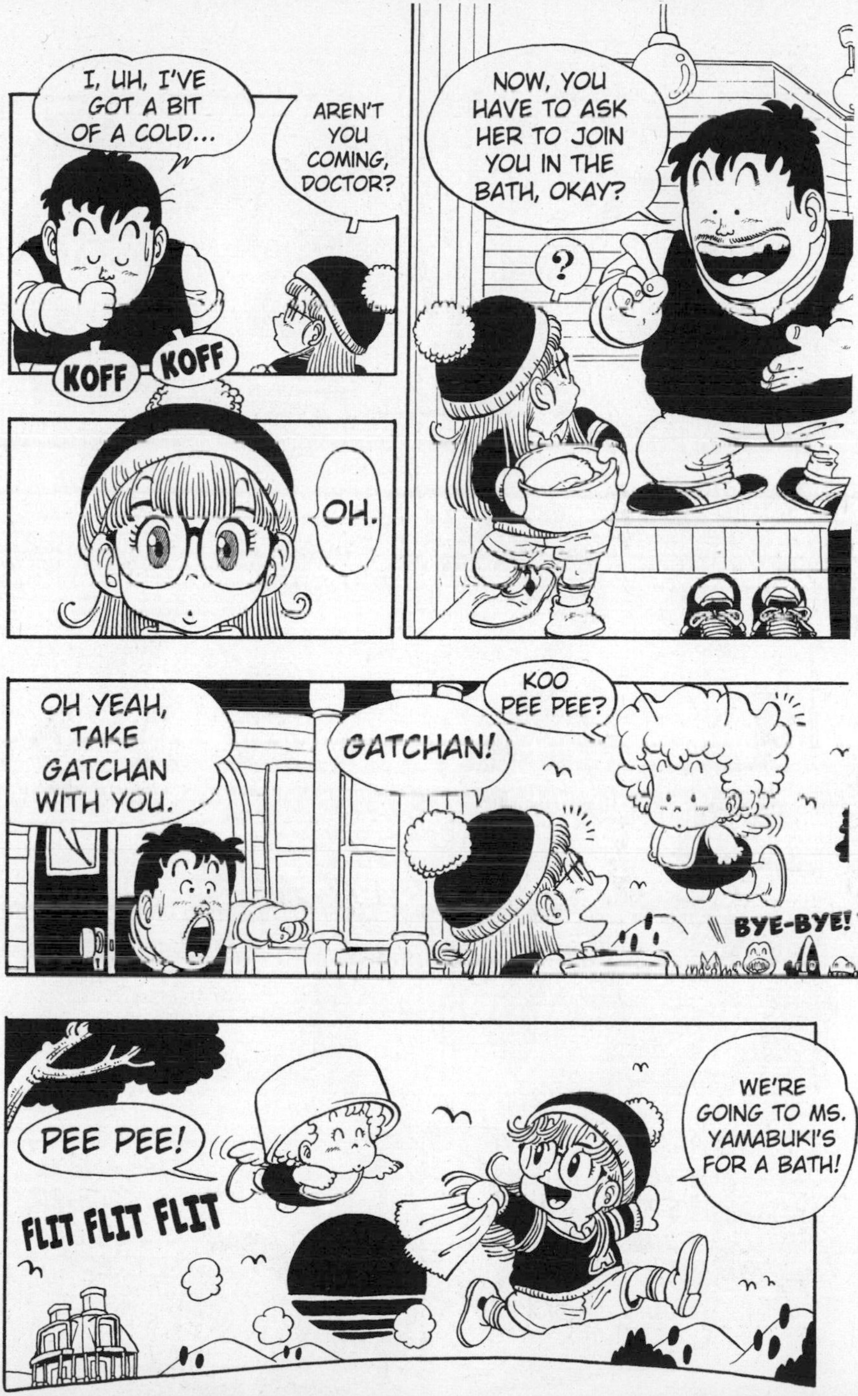
NOW, YOU HAVE TO ASK HER TO JOIN YOU IN THE BATH, OKAY?
?
AREN'T YOU COMING, DOCTOR?
I, UH, I'VE GOT A BIT OF A COLD...
KOFF
KOFF
OH.
OH YEAH, TAKE GATCHAN WITH YOU.
GATCHAN!
KOO PEE PEE?
BYE-BYE!
WE'RE GOING TO MS. YAMABUKI'S FOR A BATH!
PEE PEE!
FLIT FLIT FLIT

READ THIS WAY

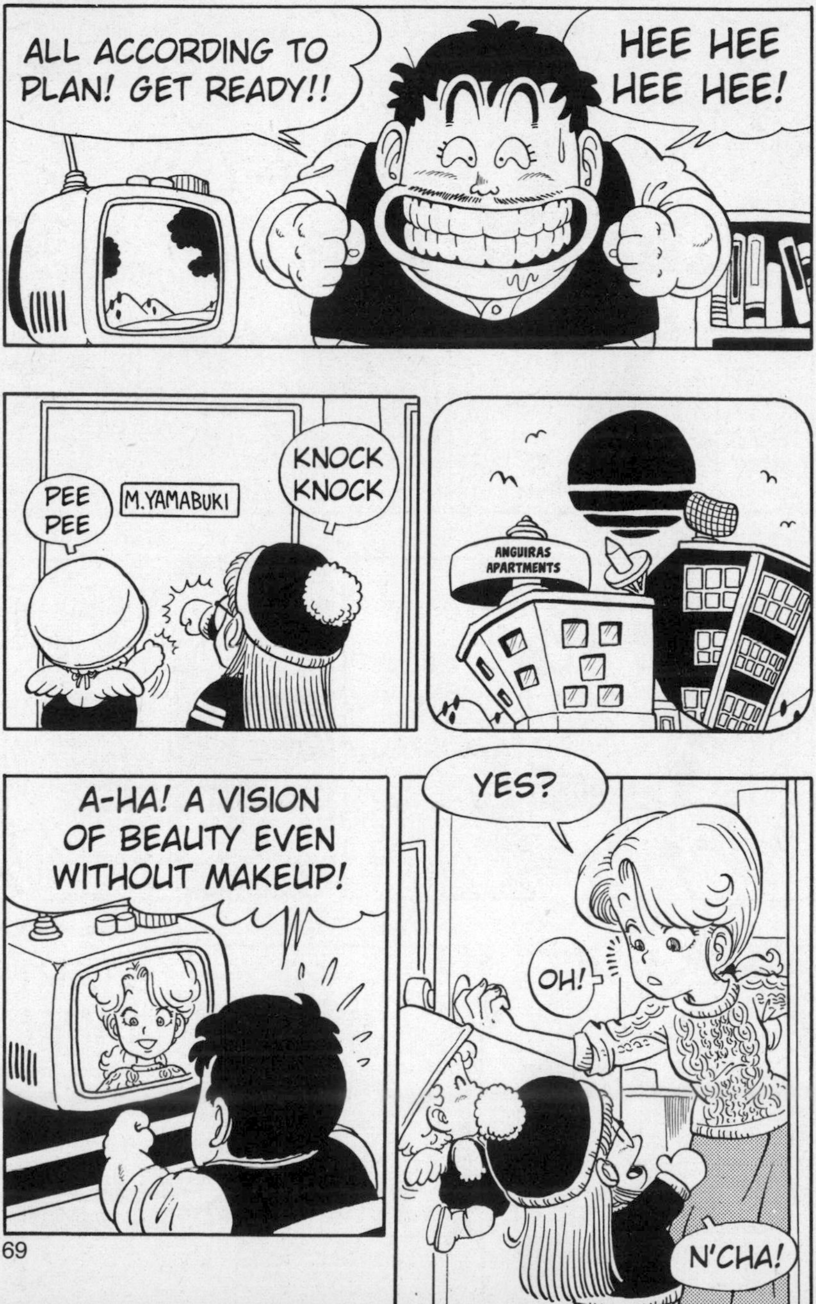

HEE HEE HEE HEE!
ALL ACCORDING TO PLAN! GET READY!!
ANGUIRAS APARTMENTS
KNOCK KNOCK
M.YAMABUKI
PEE PEE
YES?
OH!
N'CHA!
A-HA! A VISION OF BEAUTY EVEN WITHOUT MAKEUP!

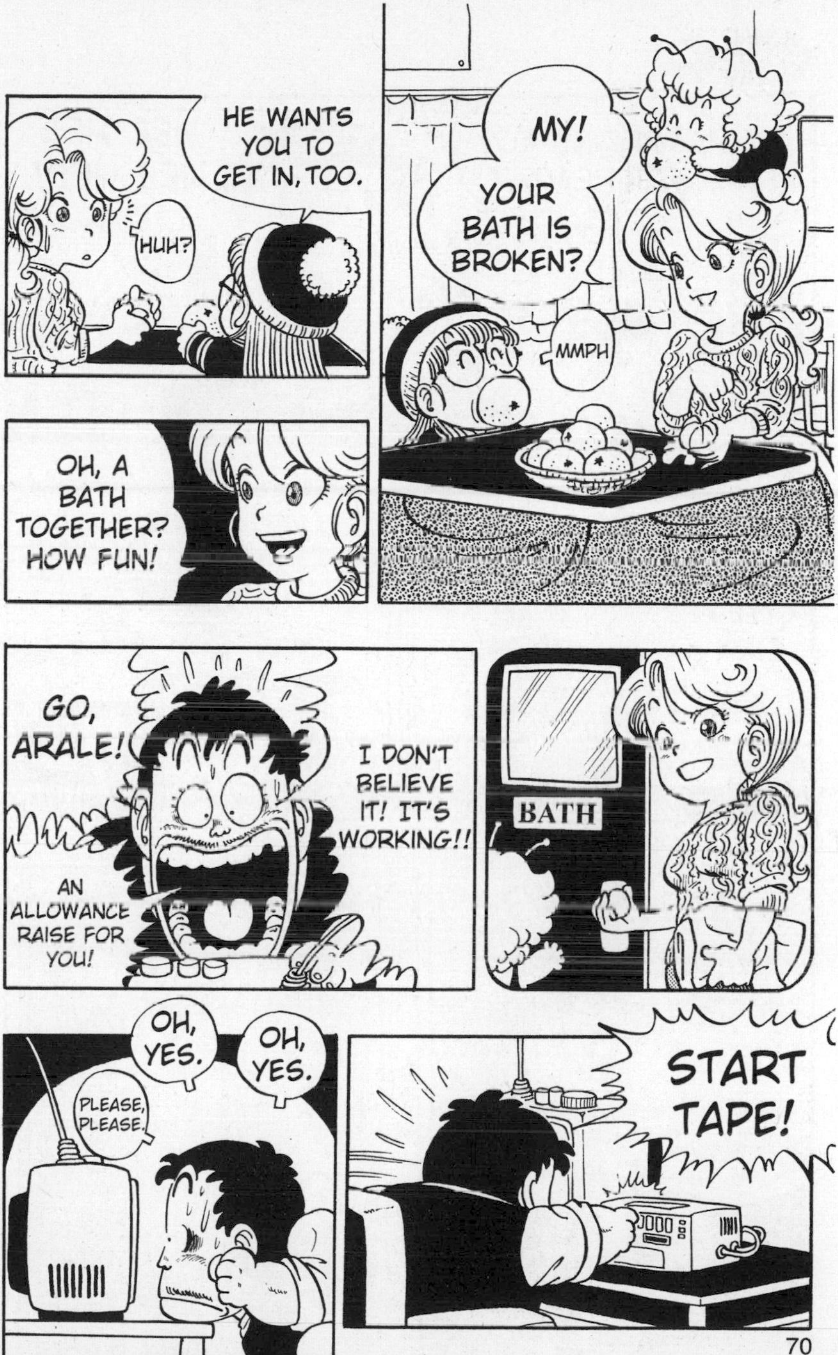
MY!
YOUR BATH IS BROKEN?
MMPH
HE WANTS YOU TO GET IN, TOO.
HUH?
OH, A BATH TOGETHER? HOW FUN!
BATH
GO, ARALE!
I DON'T BELIEVE IT! IT'S WORKING!!
AN ALLOWANCE RAISE FOR YOU!
START TAPE!
OH, YES.
OH, YES.
PLEASE, PLEASE.

READ THIS WAY

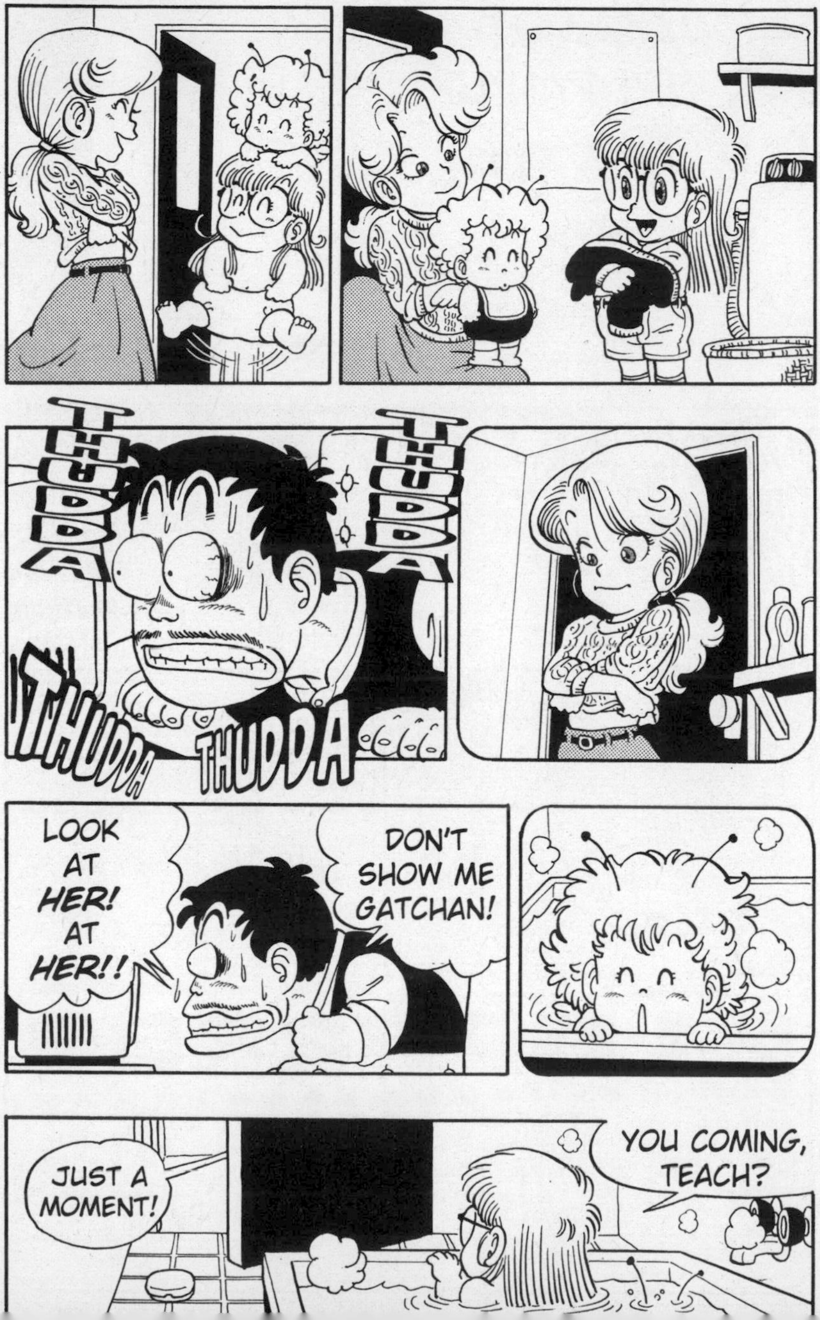
THUDDA
THUDDA
THUDDA
THUDDA
DON'T SHOW ME GATCHAN!
LOOK AT *HER!* AT *HER!!*
YOU COMING, TEACH?
JUST A MOMENT!

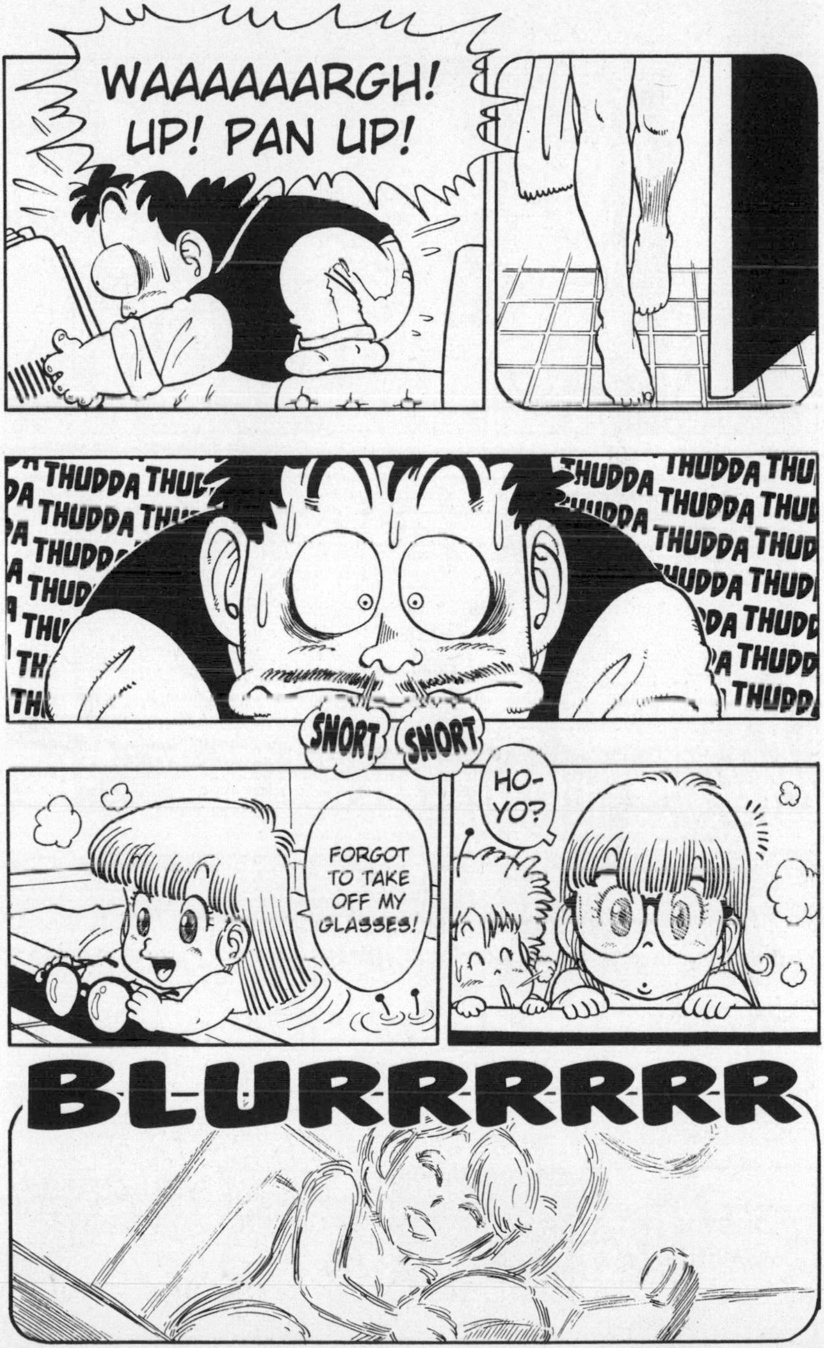
WAAAAAARGH! UP! PAN UP!
THUDDA THUDDA THUDDA THUDDA THUDDA THUDDA THUDDA THUDDA
SNORT
SNORT
HO-YO?
FORGOT TO TAKE OFF MY GLASSES!
BLURRRRRR

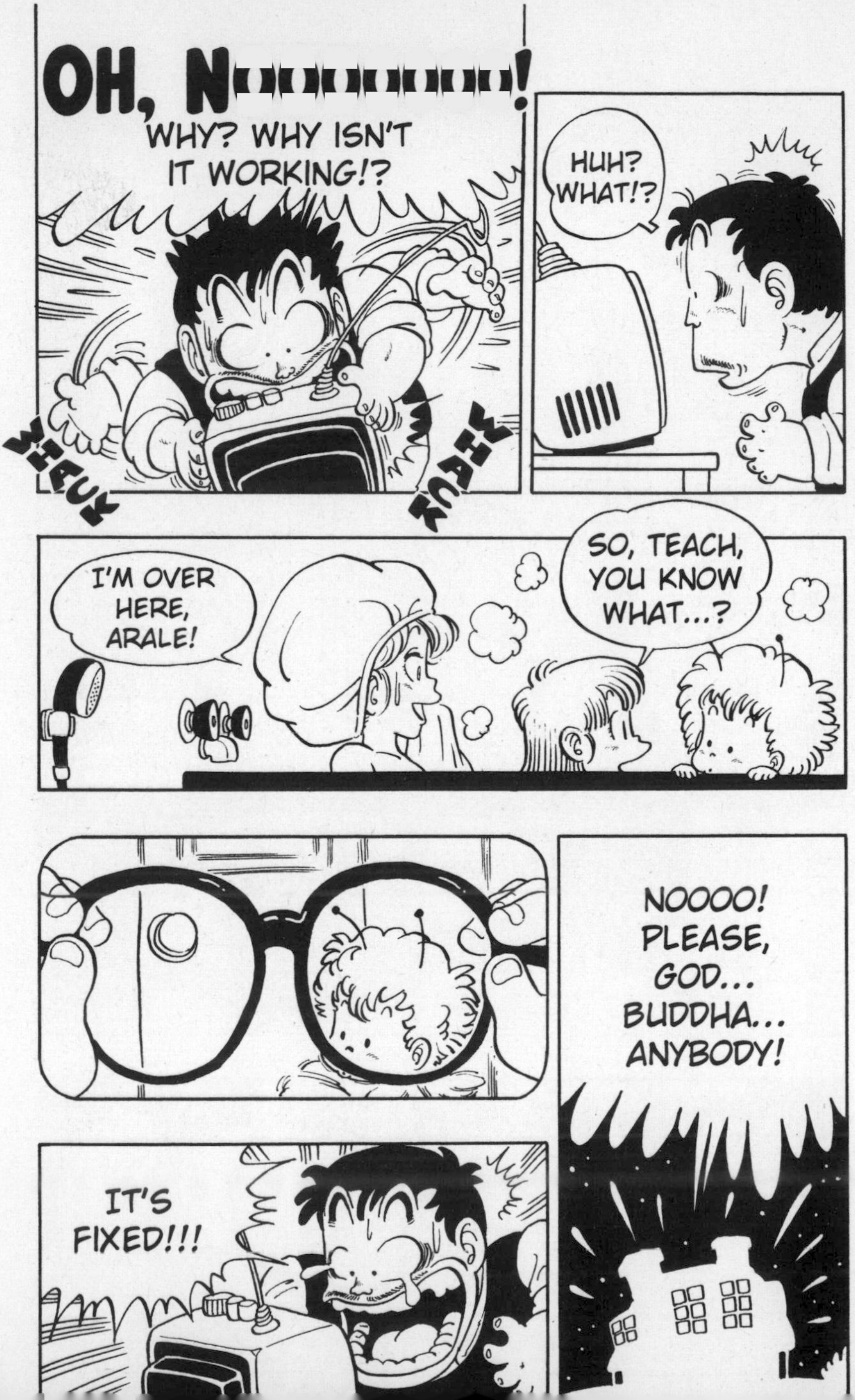
HUH? WHAT!?
OH, NOOOOOOOOOOOO!
WHY? WHY ISN'T IT WORKING!?
WHACK
WHACK
SO, TEACH, YOU KNOW WHAT...?
I'M OVER HERE, ARALE!
NOOOO! PLEASE, GOD... BUDDHA... ANYBODY!
IT'S FIXED!!!

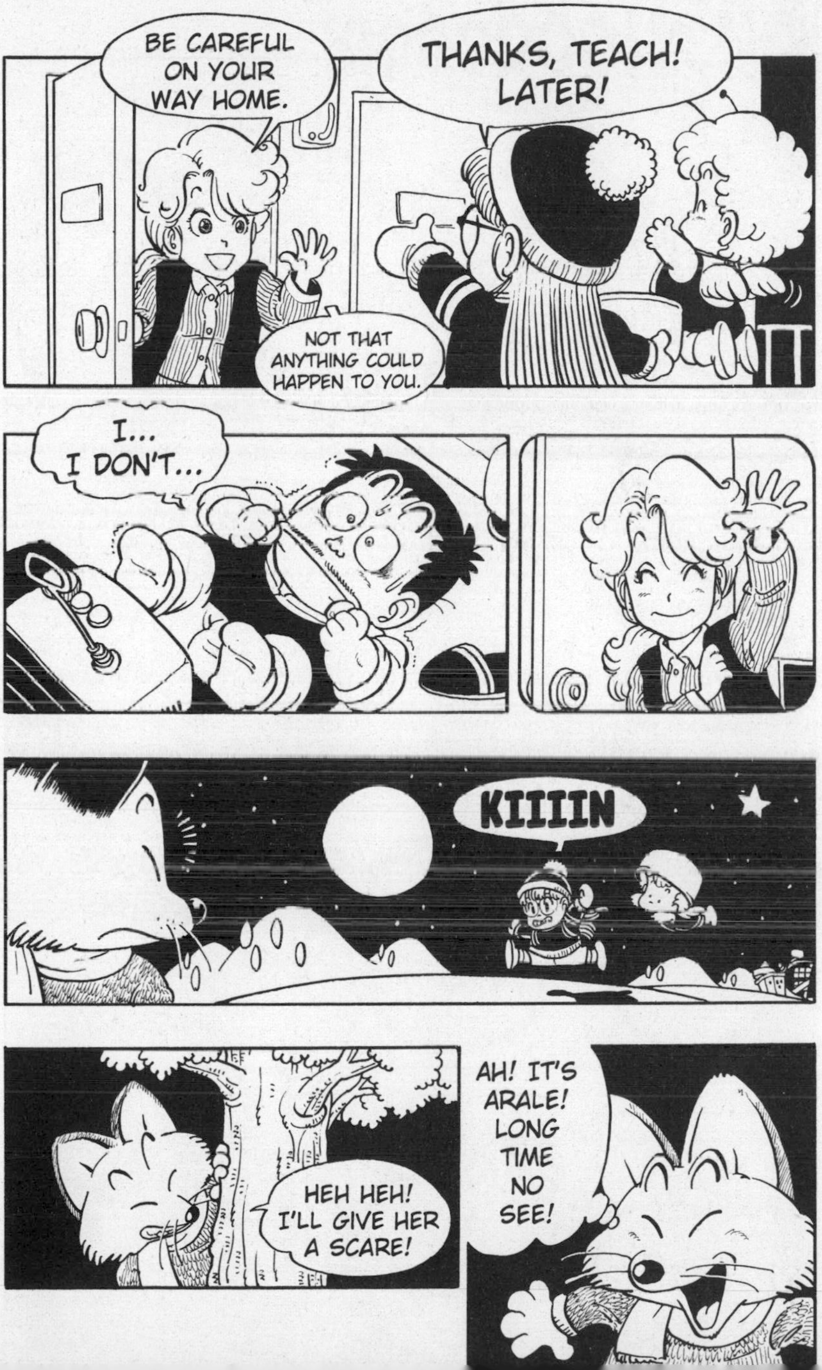
THANKS, TEACH! LATER!
BE CAREFUL ON YOUR WAY HOME.
NOT THAT ANYTHING COULD HAPPEN TO YOU.
I... I DON'T...
KIIIN
AH! IT'S ARALE! LONG TIME NO SEE!
HEH HEH! I'LL GIVE HER A SCARE!

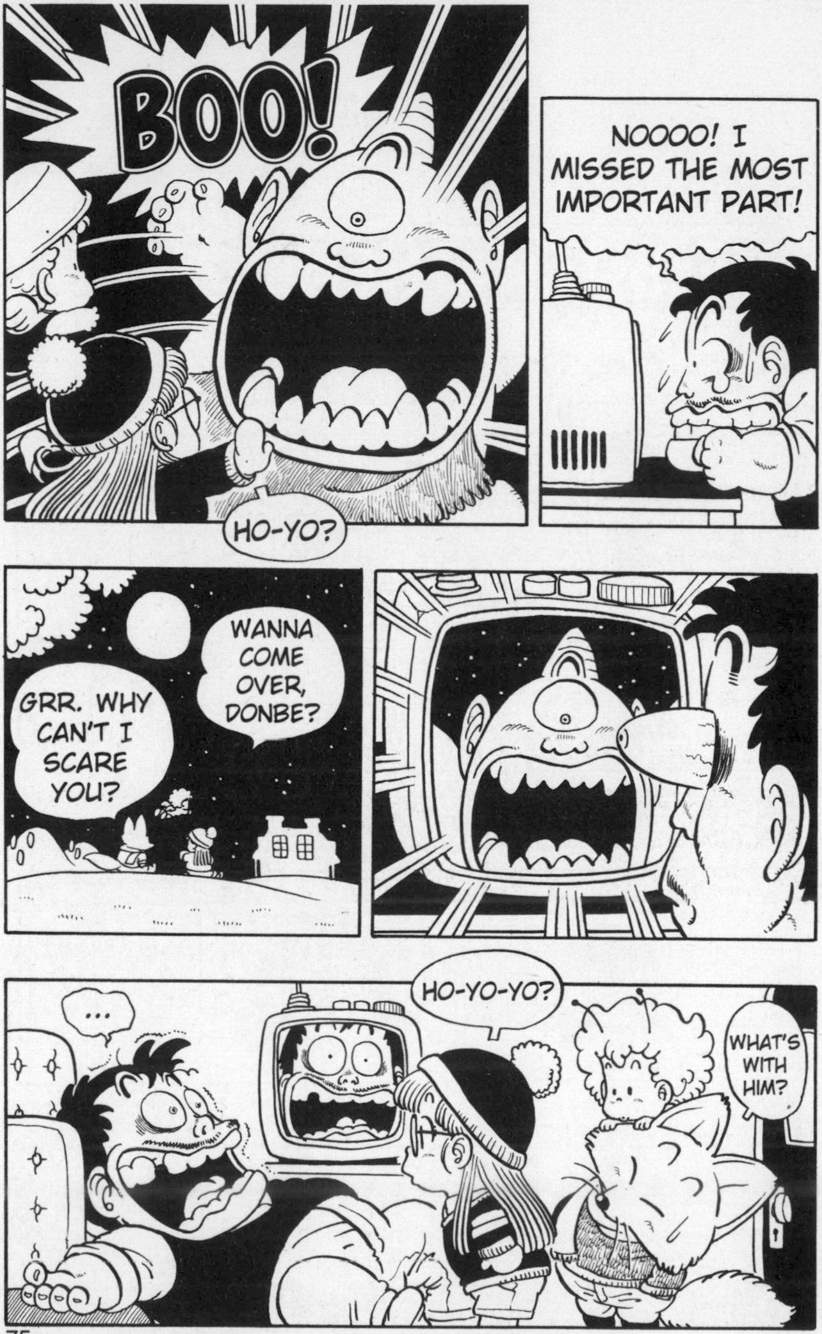
NOOOO! I MISSED THE MOST IMPORTANT PART!
BOO!
HO-YO?
WANNA COME OVER, DONBE?
GRR. WHY CAN'T I SCARE YOU?
WHAT'S WITH HIM?
HO-YO-YO?
...

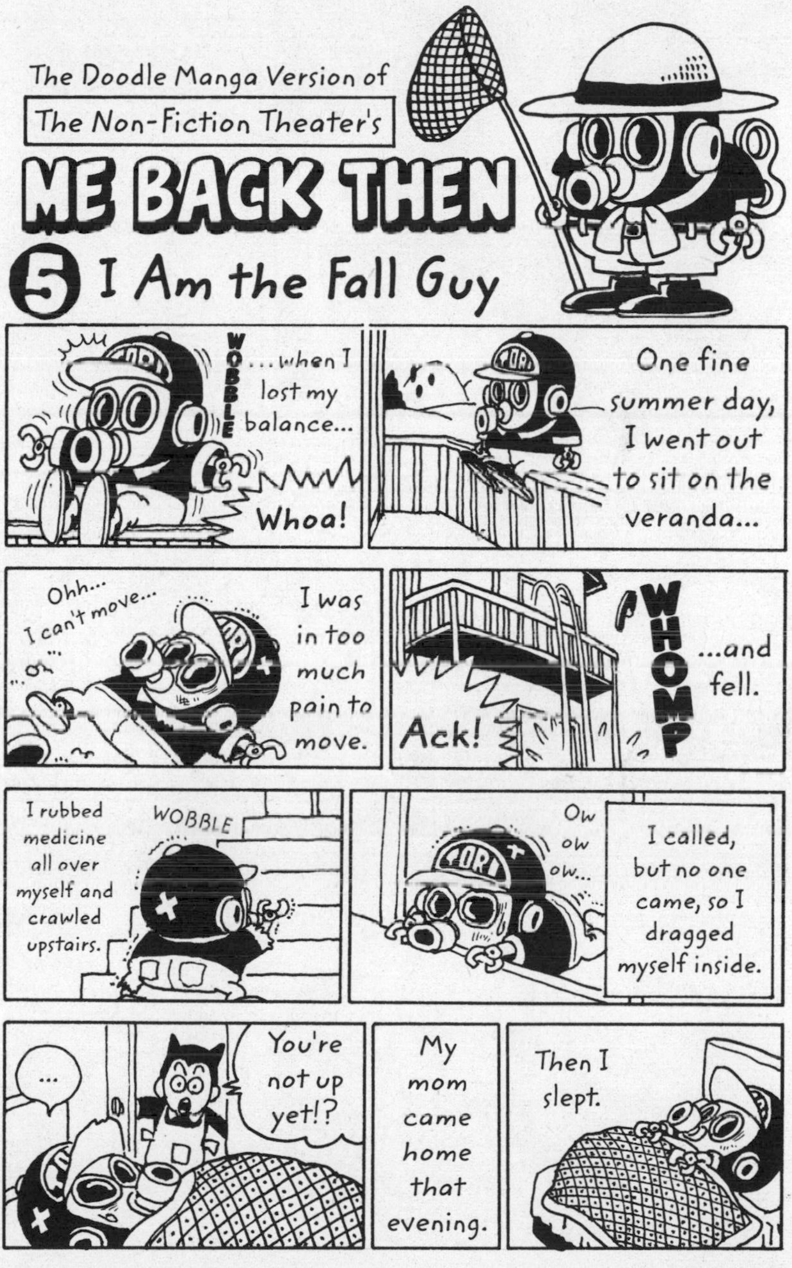
The Doodle Manga Version of
The Non-Fiction Theater's
ME BACK THEN
5 I Am the Fall Guy
One fine summer day, I went out to sit on the veranda...
WOBBLE
...when I lost my balance...
Whoa!
WHOMP
...and fell.
Ack!
Ohh... I can't move...
I was in too much pain to move.
Ow ow ow...
I called, but no one came, so I dragged myself inside.
I rubbed medicine all over myself and crawled upstairs.
WOBBLE
Then I slept.
My mom came home that evening.
You're not up yet!?
...

Kinoko on the Loose

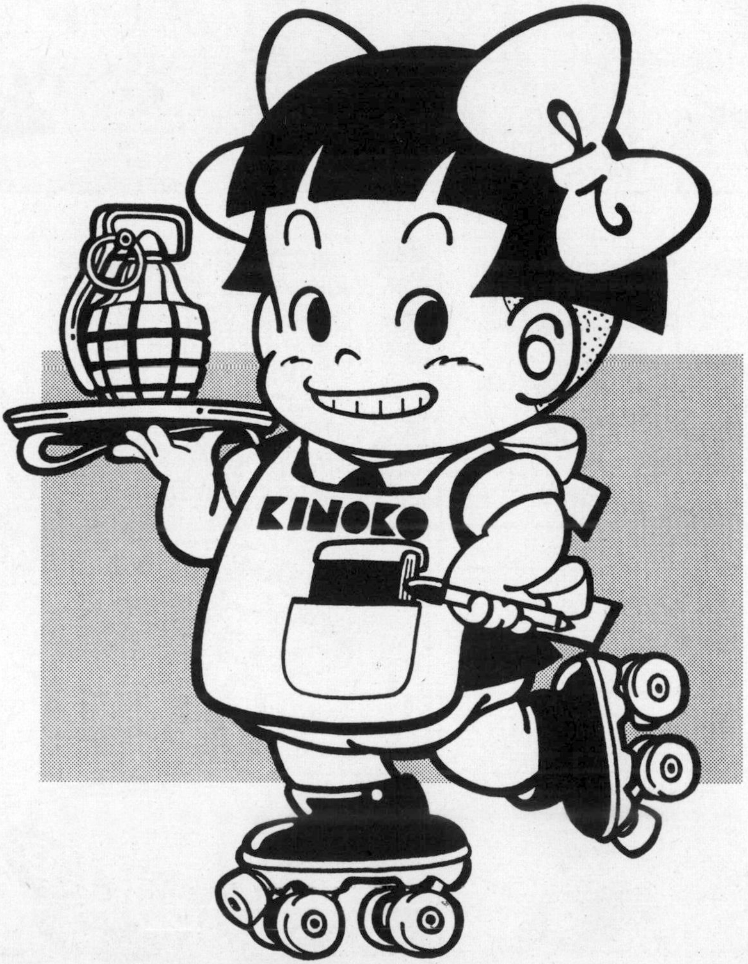
KINOKO

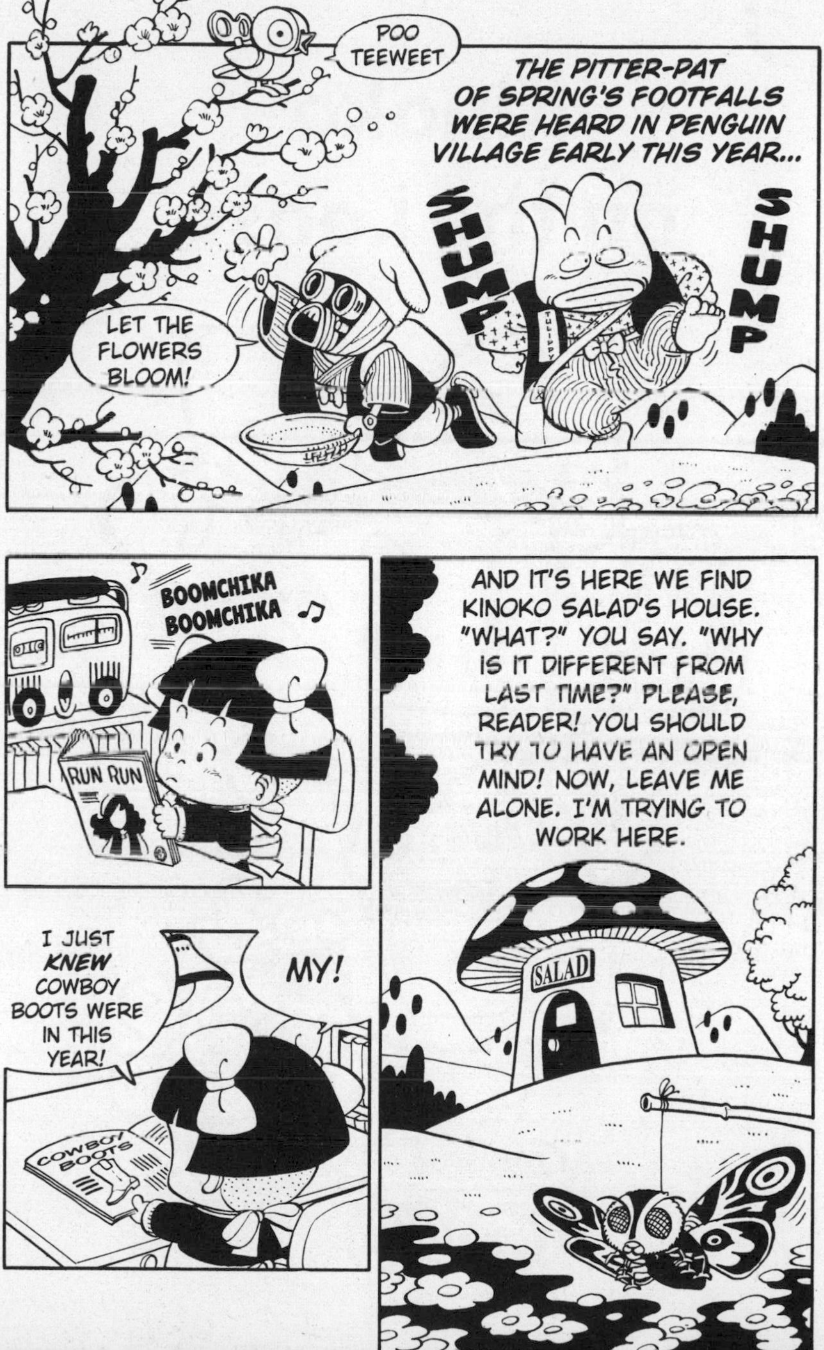
THE PITTER-PAT OF SPRING'S FOOTFALLS WERE HEARD IN PENGUIN VILLAGE EARLY THIS YEAR...
POO TEEWEET
SHUMP
SHUMP
LET THE FLOWERS BLOOM!
AND IT'S HERE WE FIND KINOKO SALAD'S HOUSE. "WHAT?" YOU SAY. "WHY IS IT DIFFERENT FROM LAST TIME?" PLEASE, READER! YOU SHOULD TRY TO HAVE AN OPEN MIND! NOW, LEAVE ME ALONE. I'M TRYING TO WORK HERE.
SALAD
BOOMCHIKA BOOMCHIKA
RUN RUN
MY!
I JUST *KNEW* COWBOY BOOTS WERE IN THIS YEAR!
COWBOY BOOTS

READ THIS WAY

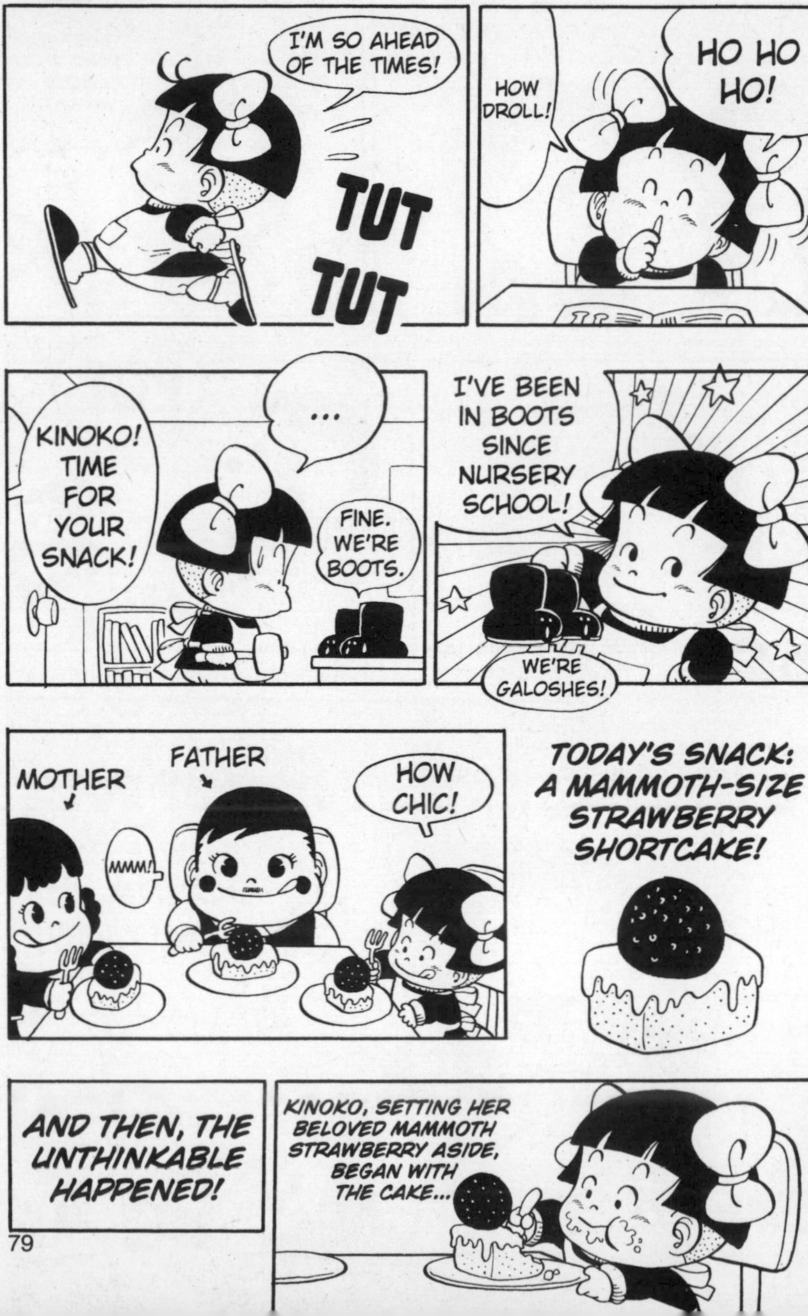

HO HO HO!
HOW DROLL!
I'M SO AHEAD OF THE TIMES!
TUT TUT
I'VE BEEN IN BOOTS SINCE NURSERY SCHOOL!
WE'RE GALOSHES!
...
KINOKO! TIME FOR YOUR SNACK!
FINE. WE'RE BOOTS.
TODAY'S SNACK: A MAMMOTH-SIZE STRAWBERRY SHORTCAKE!
HOW CHIC!
FATHER
MOTHER
MMM!
KINOKO, SETTING HER BELOVED MAMMOTH STRAWBERRY ASIDE, BEGAN WITH THE CAKE...
AND THEN, THE UNTHINKABLE HAPPENED!

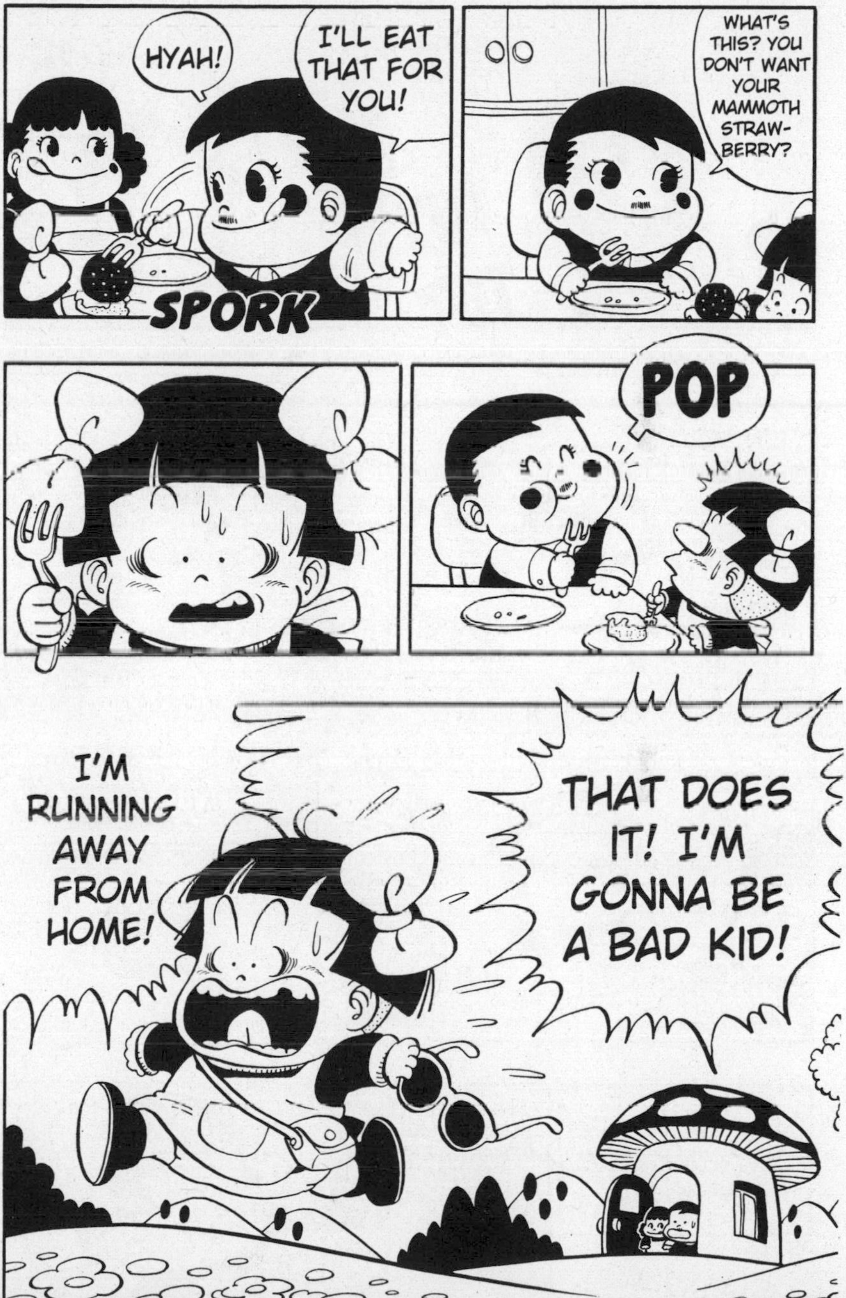
WHAT'S THIS? YOU DON'T WANT YOUR MAMMOTH STRAW-BERRY?
I'LL EAT THAT FOR YOU!
HYAH!
SPORK
POP
THAT DOES IT! I'M GONNA BE A BAD KID!
I'M RUNNING AWAY FROM HOME!

READ THIS WAY

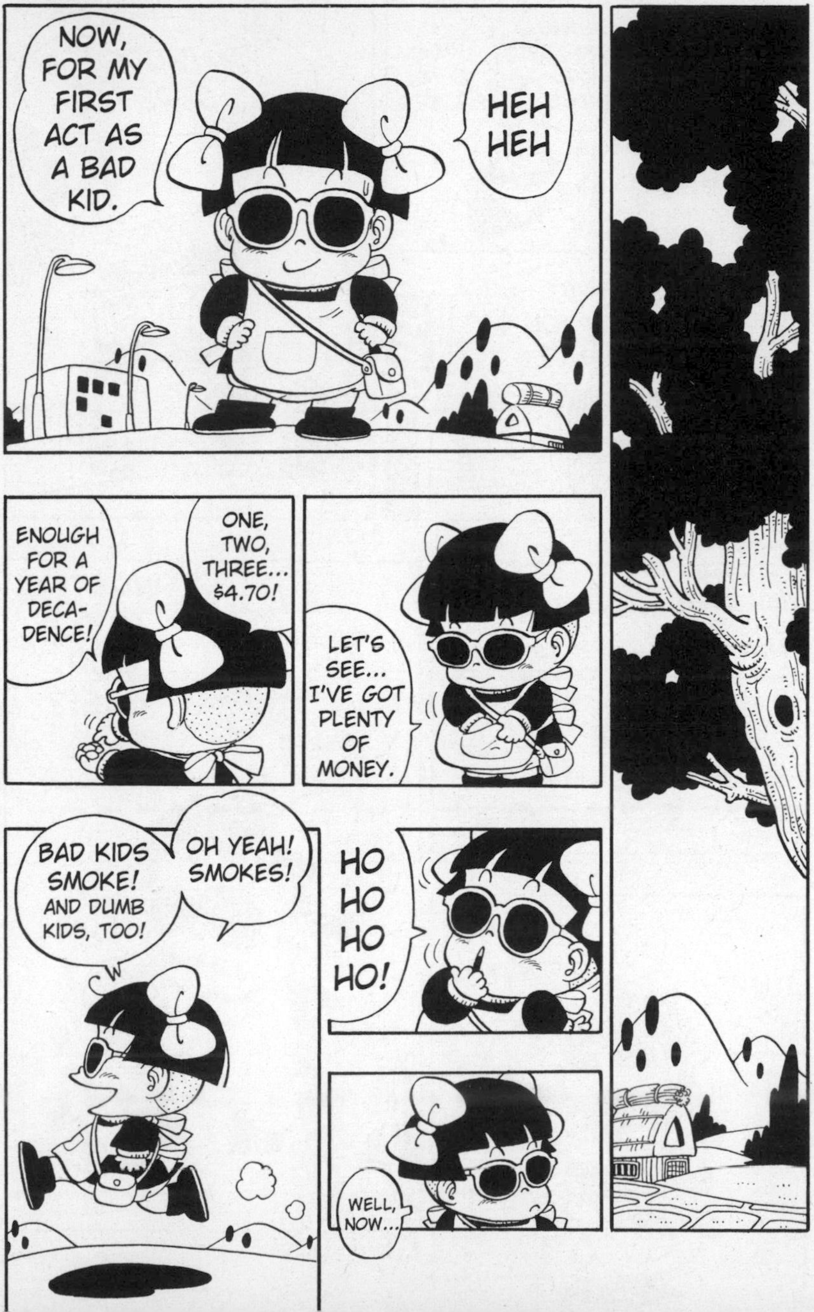
HEH HEH
NOW, FOR MY FIRST ACT AS A BAD KID.
LET'S SEE... I'VE GOT PLENTY OF MONEY.
ONE, TWO, THREE... $4.70!
ENOUGH FOR A YEAR OF DECADENCE!
HO HO HO HO!
WELL, NOW...
OH YEAH! SMOKES!
BAD KIDS SMOKE! AND DUMB KIDS, TOO!

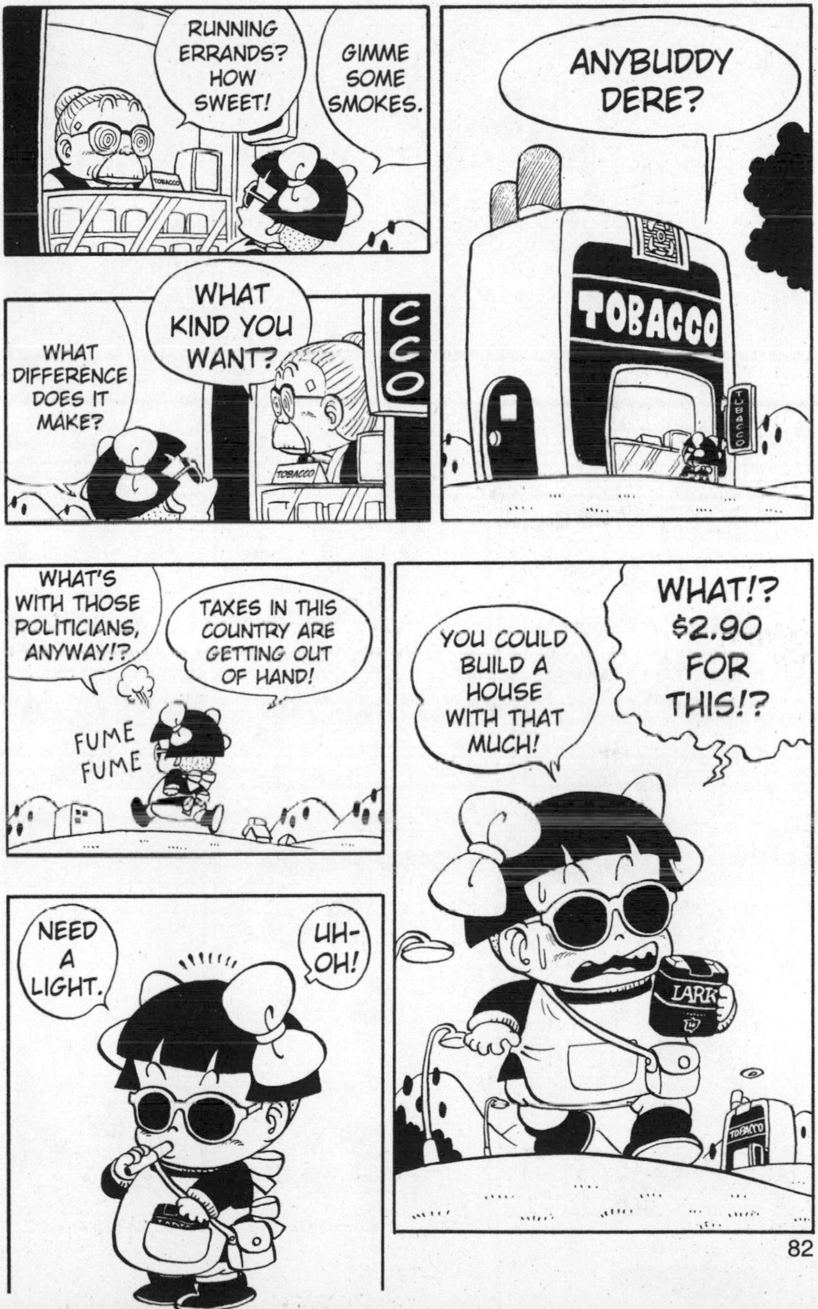
ANYBUDDY DERE?
GIMME SOME SMOKES.
RUNNING ERRANDS? HOW SWEET!
TOBACCO
WHAT KIND YOU WANT?
WHAT DIFFERENCE DOES IT MAKE?
WHAT!? $2.90 FOR THIS!?
YOU COULD BUILD A HOUSE WITH THAT MUCH!
LARK
TAXES IN THIS COUNTRY ARE GETTING OUT OF HAND!
WHAT'S WITH THOSE POLITICIANS, ANYWAY!?
FUME FUME
UH-OH!
NEED A LIGHT.

READ THIS WAY

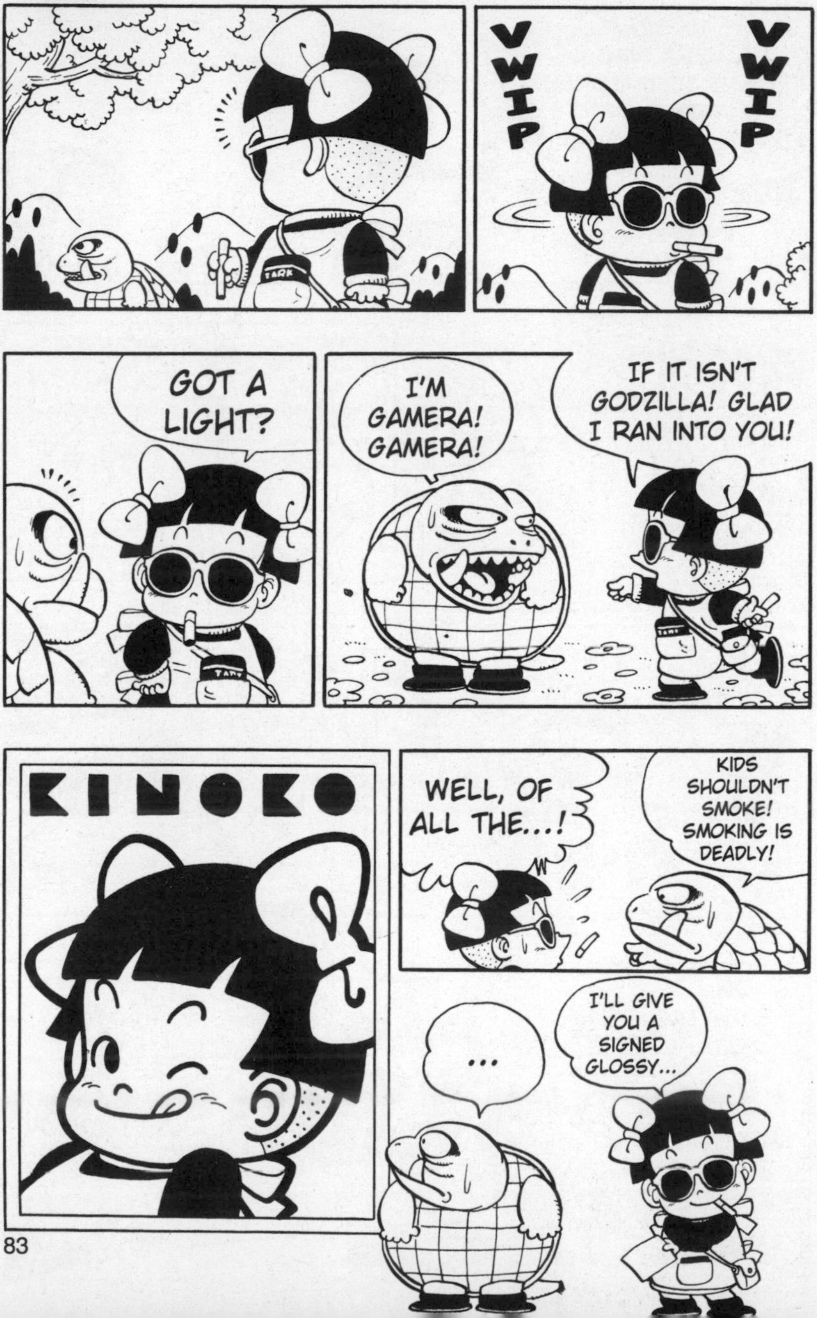
VWIP VWIP
IF IT ISN'T GODZILLA! GLAD I RAN INTO YOU!
I'M GAMERA! GAMERA!
GOT A LIGHT?
KIDS SHOULDN'T SMOKE! SMOKING IS DEADLY!
WELL, OF ALL THE...!
I'LL GIVE YOU A SIGNED GLOSSY...
...
KINOKO

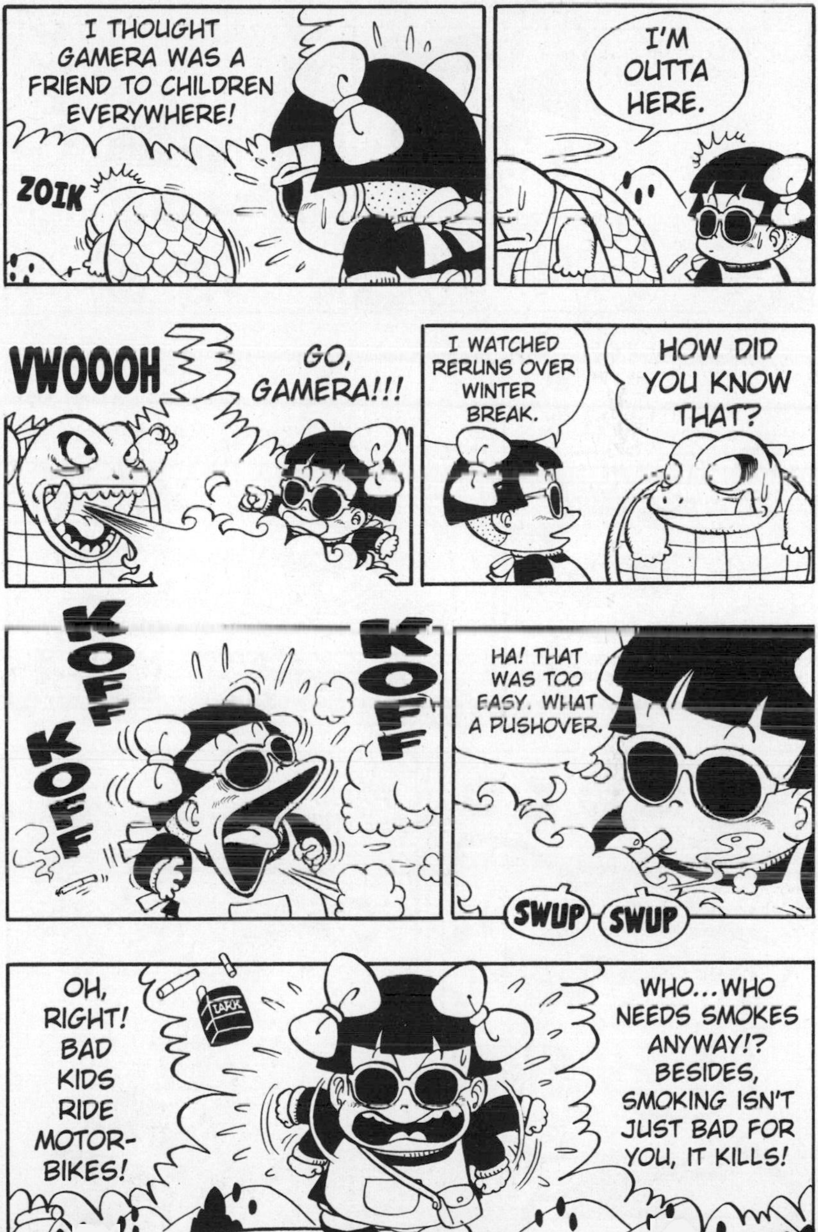
I'M OUTTA HERE.
I THOUGHT GAMERA WAS A FRIEND TO CHILDREN EVERYWHERE!
ZOIK
HOW DID YOU KNOW THAT?
I WATCHED RERUNS OVER WINTER BREAK.
GO, GAMERA!!!
VWOOOH
HA! THAT WAS TOO EASY. WHAT A PUSHOVER.
SWUP SWUP
KOFF KOFF
KOFF KOFF
WHO...WHO NEEDS SMOKES ANYWAY!? BESIDES, SMOKING ISN'T JUST BAD FOR YOU, IT KILLS!
OH, RIGHT! BAD KIDS RIDE MOTOR-BIKES!

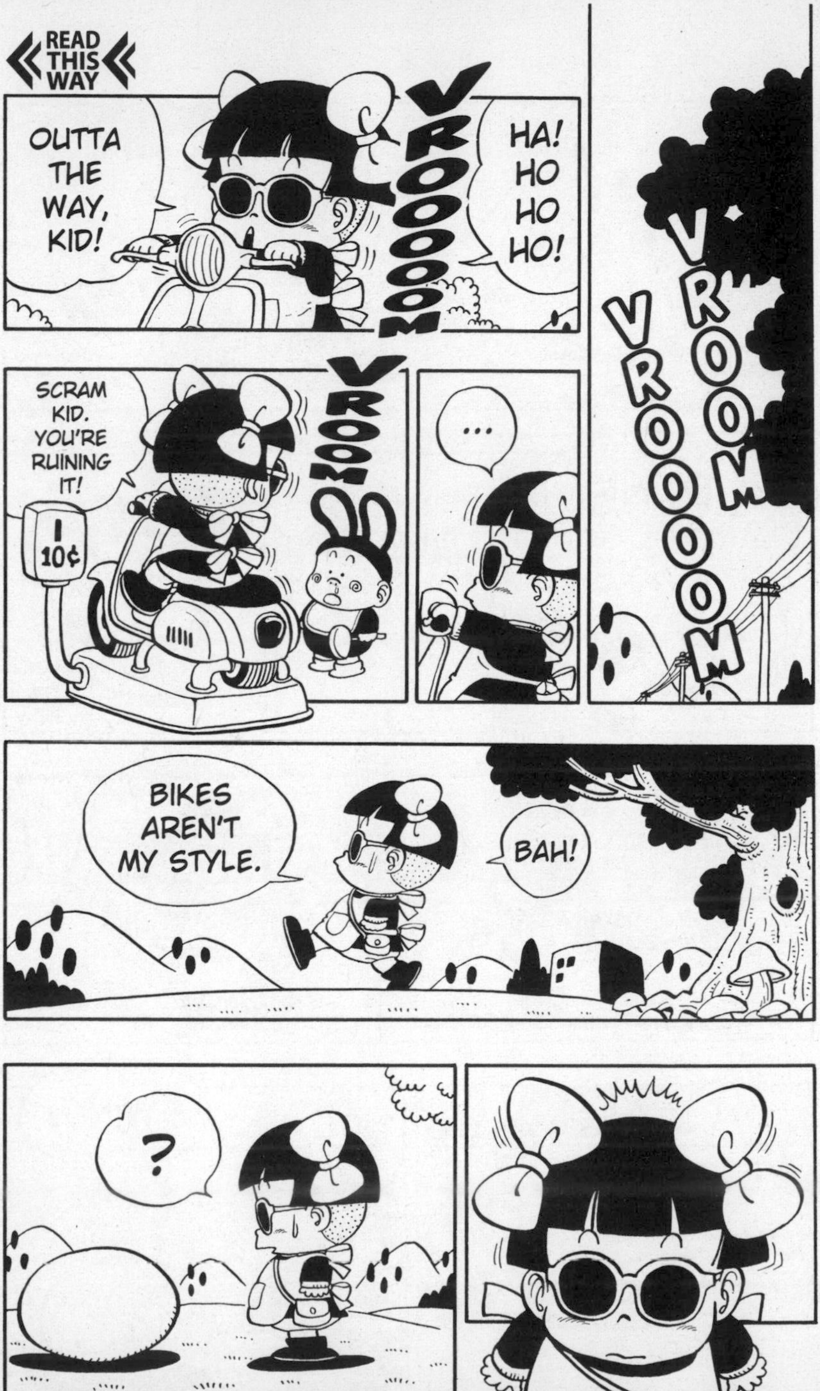
READ THIS WAY
VROOOOM
VROOOOOM
HA! HO HO HO!
VROOOOOOM
OUTTA THE WAY, KID!
...
VROOM
SCRAM KID. YOU'RE RUINING IT!
1 10¢
BAH!
BIKES AREN'T MY STYLE.
?

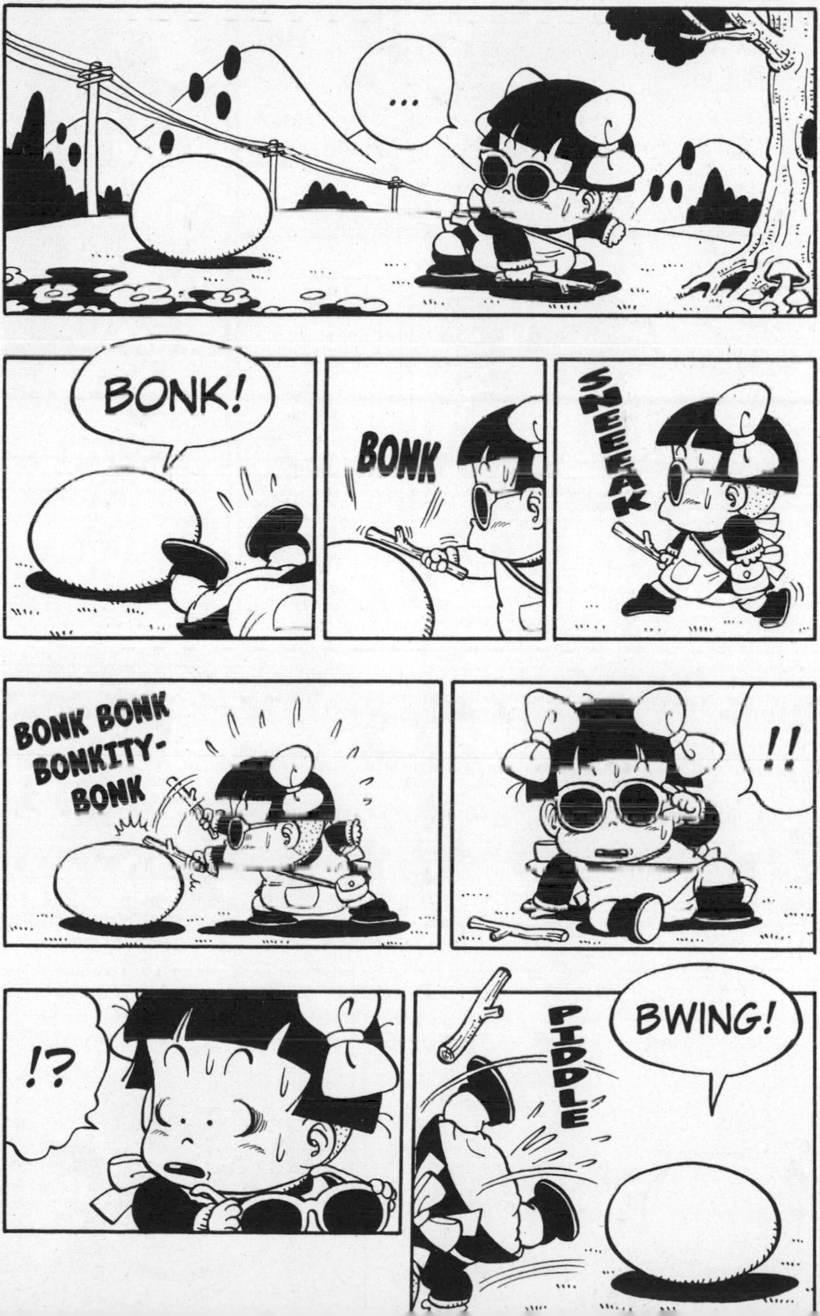
...
SNEEEAK
BONK
BONK!
!!
BONK BONK BONKITY-BONK
BWING!
PIDDLE
!?

READ THIS WAY

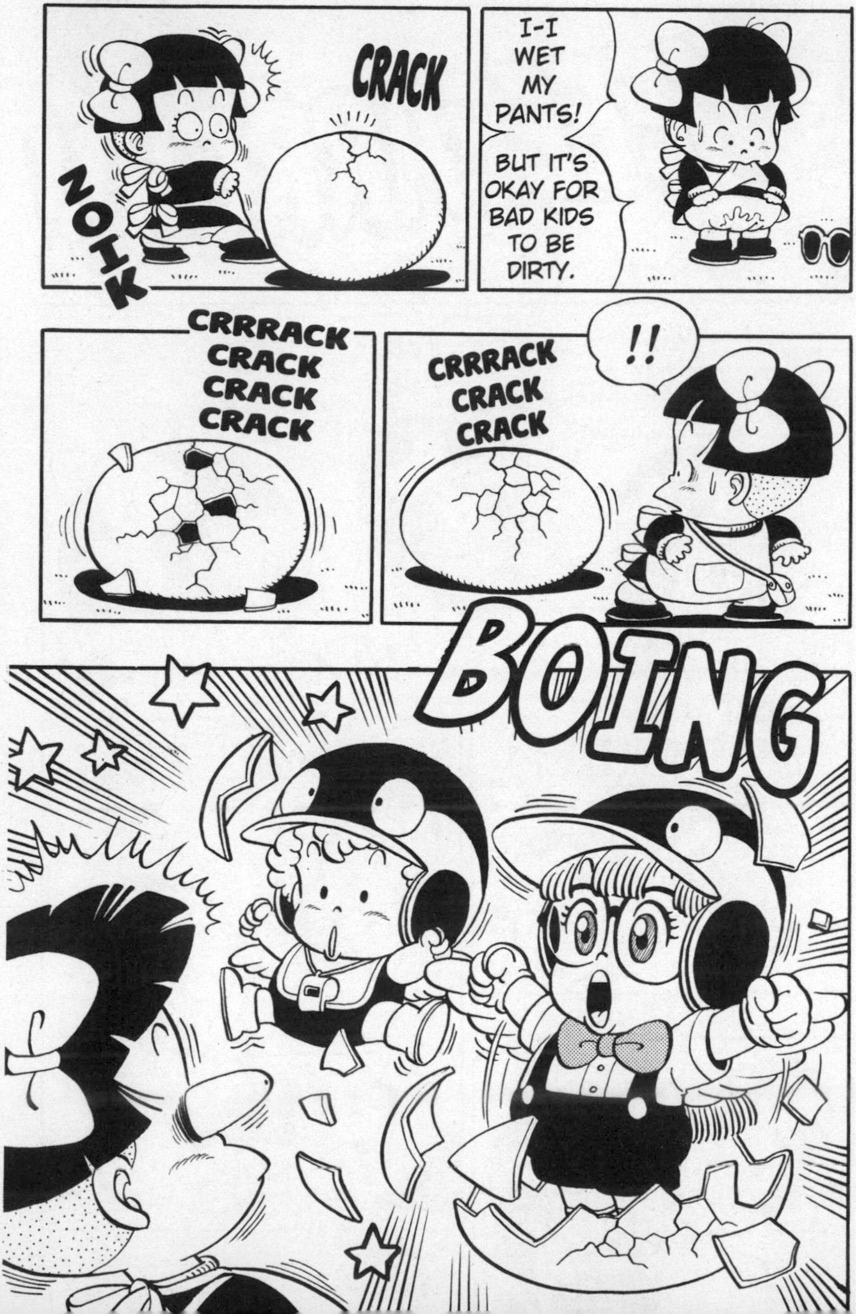

I-I WET MY PANTS!
BUT IT'S OKAY FOR BAD KIDS TO BE DIRTY.
CRACK
ZOIK
!!
CRRRACK CRACK CRACK
CRRRACK CRACK CRACK CRACK
BOING

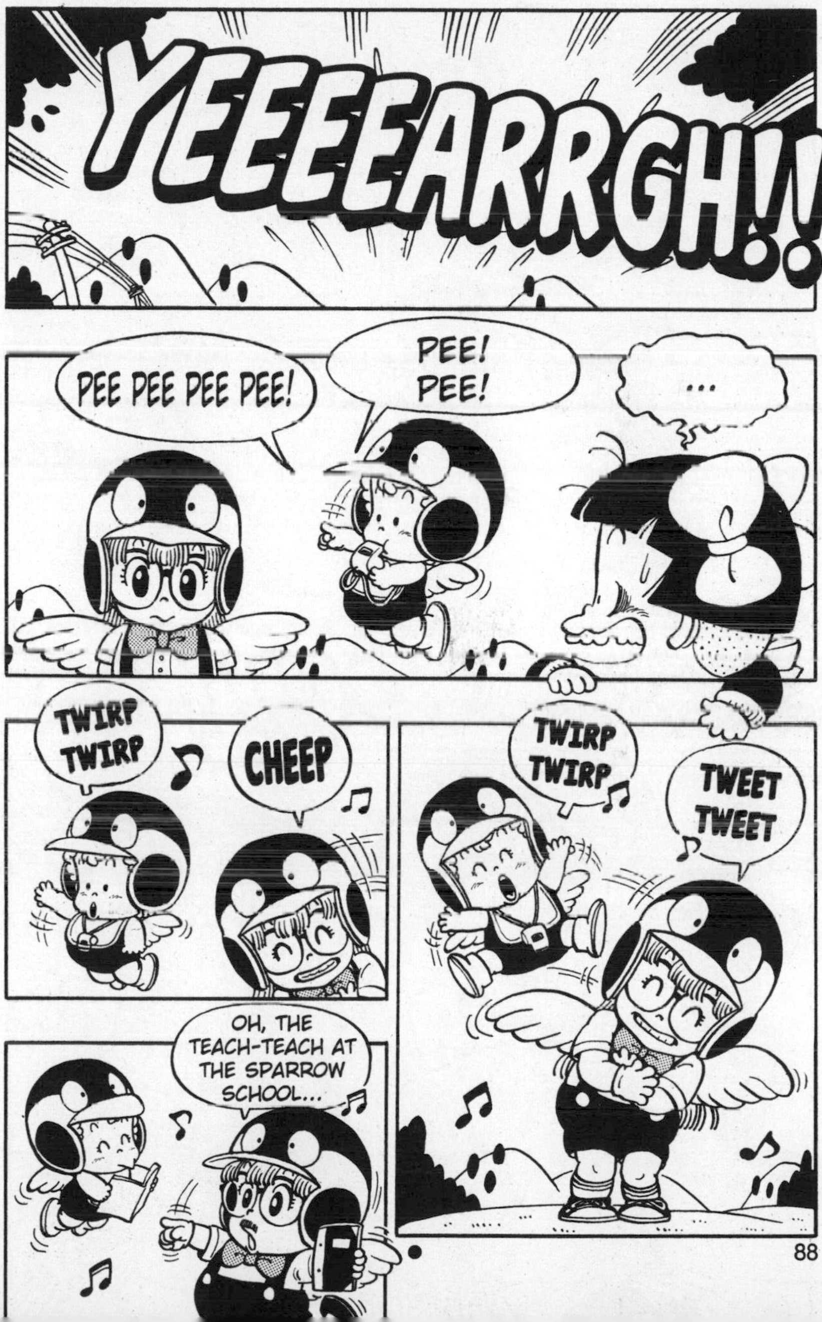
YEEEEARRGH!!
...
PEE! PEE!
PEE PEE PEE PEE!
TWEET TWEET
TWIRP TWIRP
CHEEP
TWIRP TWIRP
OH, THE TEACH-TEACH AT THE SPARROW SCHOOL...

READ THIS WAY

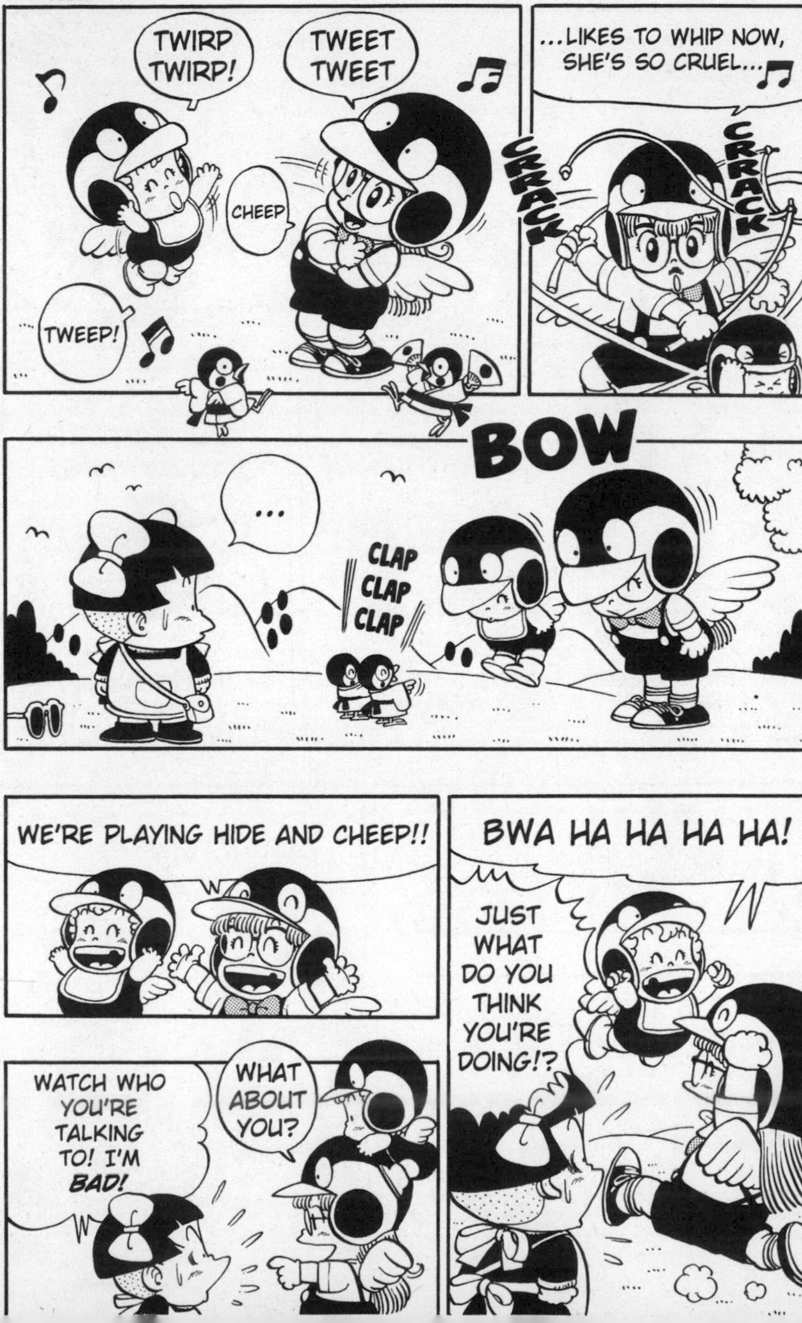
...LIKES TO WHIP NOW, SHE'S SO CRUEL...
CRRACK
CRRACK
TWEET TWEET
TWIRP TWIRP!
CHEEP
TWEEP!
BOW
CLAP CLAP CLAP
...
BWA HA HA HA HA!
JUST WHAT DO YOU THINK YOU'RE DOING!?
WE'RE PLAYING HIDE AND CHEEP!!
WHAT ABOUT YOU?
WATCH WHO YOU'RE TALKING TO! I'M *BAD*!

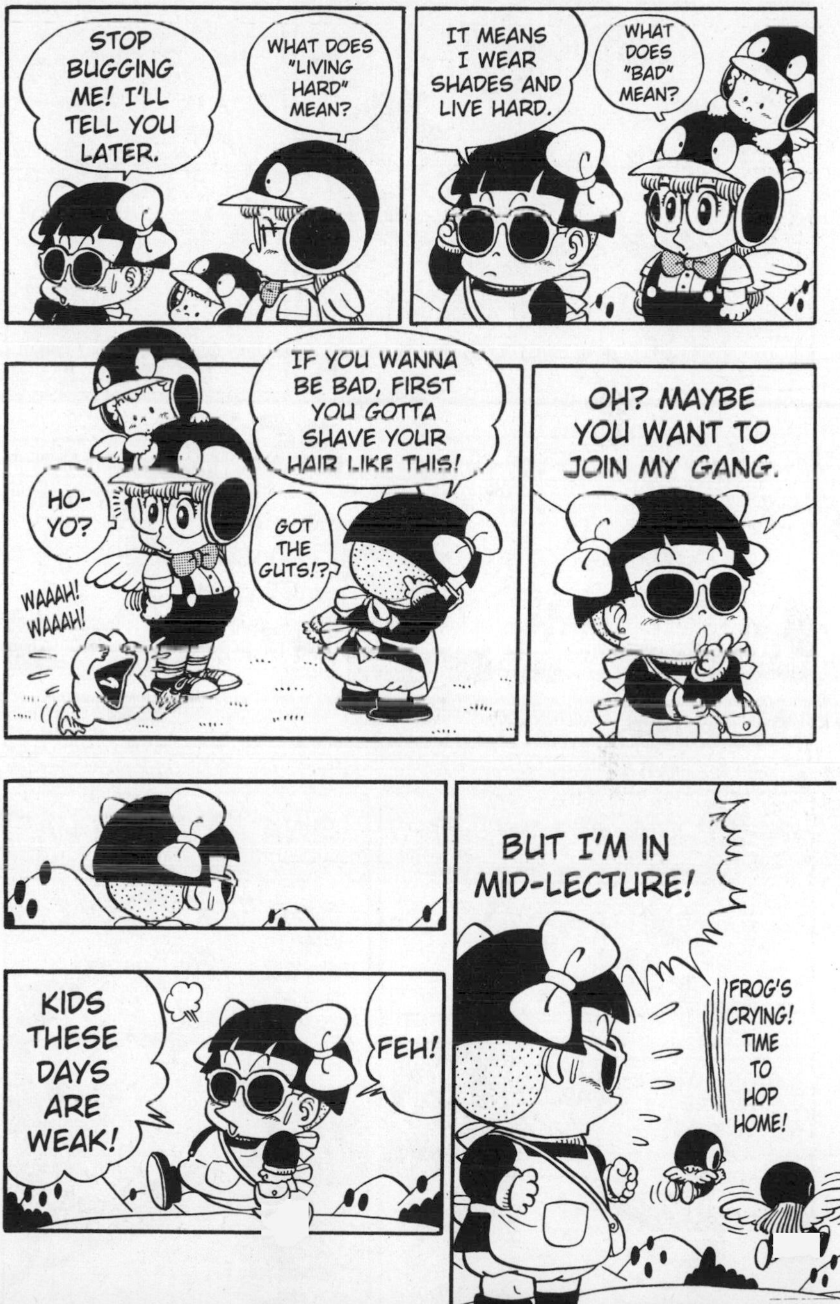
WHAT DOES "BAD" MEAN?
IT MEANS I WEAR SHADES AND LIVE HARD.
WHAT DOES "LIVING HARD" MEAN?
STOP BUGGING ME! I'LL TELL YOU LATER.
OH? MAYBE YOU WANT TO JOIN MY GANG.
IF YOU WANNA BE BAD, FIRST YOU GOTTA SHAVE YOUR HAIR LIKE THIS!
GOT THE GUTS!?
HO-YO?
WAAAH! WAAAH!
BUT I'M IN MID-LECTURE!
FROG'S CRYING! TIME TO HOP HOME!
FEH!
KIDS THESE DAYS ARE WEAK!

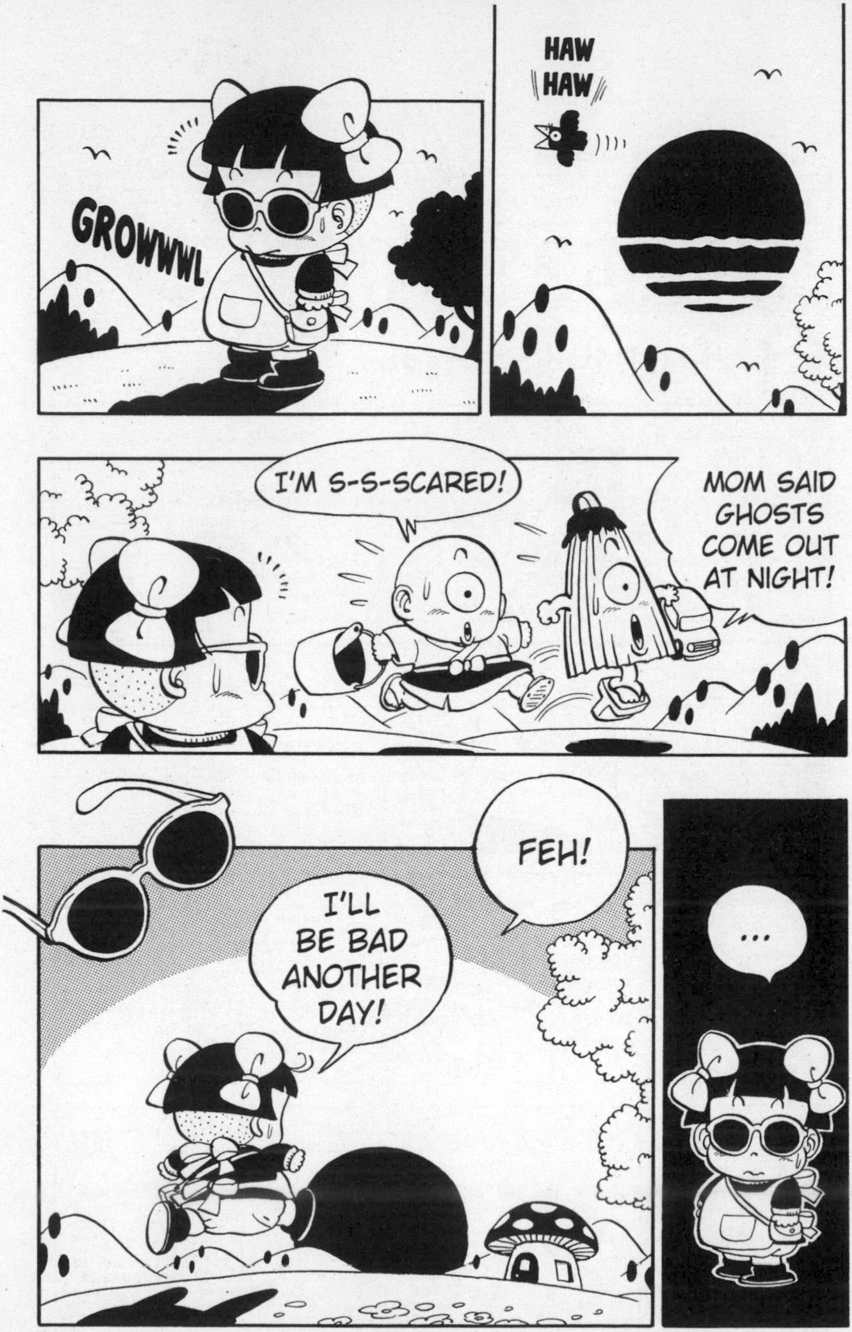
HAW HAW
GROWWWL
MOM SAID GHOSTS COME OUT AT NIGHT!
I'M S-S-SCARED!
...
FEH!
I'LL BE BAD ANOTHER DAY!

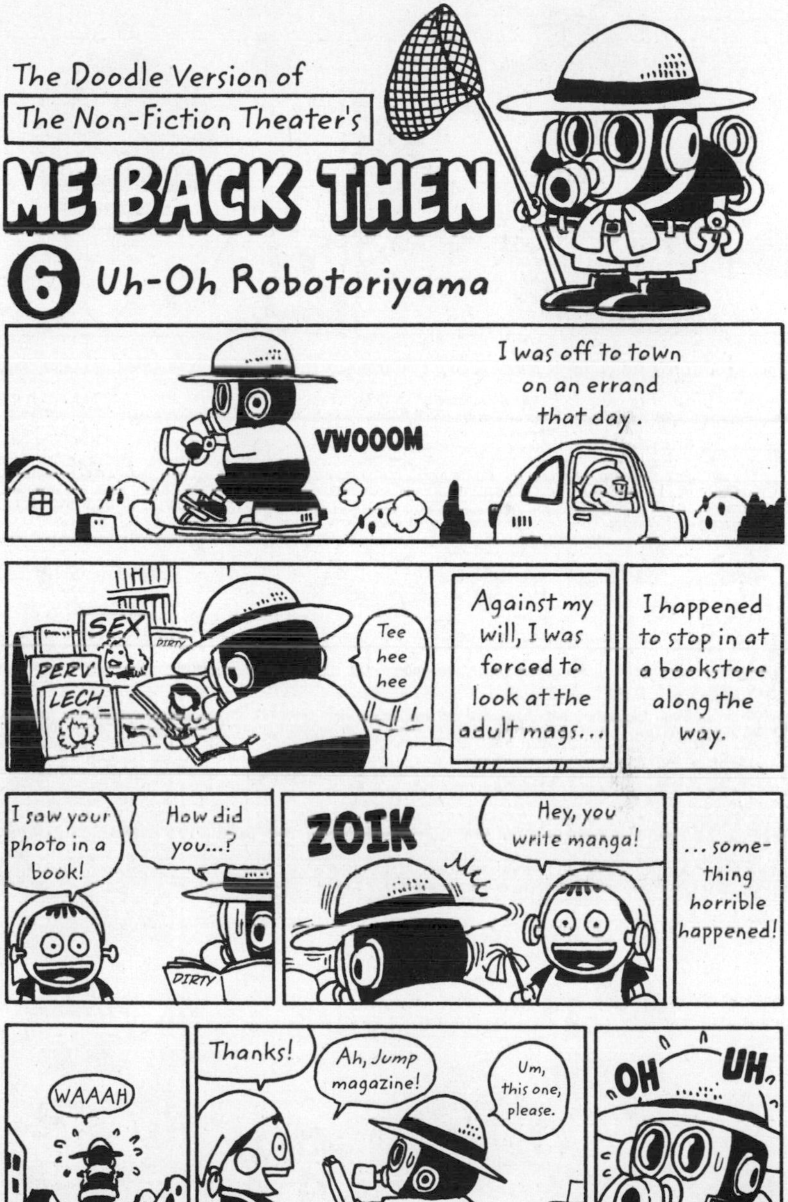

The Doodle Version of
The Non-Fiction Theater's
ME BACK THEN
6 Uh-Oh Robotoriyama
I was off to town on an errand that day.
VWOOOM
I happened to stop in at a bookstore along the way.
Against my will, I was forced to look at the adult mags...
Tee hee hee
SEX
DIRTY
PERV
LECH
... some-thing horrible happened!
Hey, you write manga!
ZOIK
How did you...?
I saw your photo in a book!
DIRTY
OH UH
Um, this one, please.
Ah, Jump magazine!
Thanks!
WAAAH

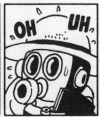

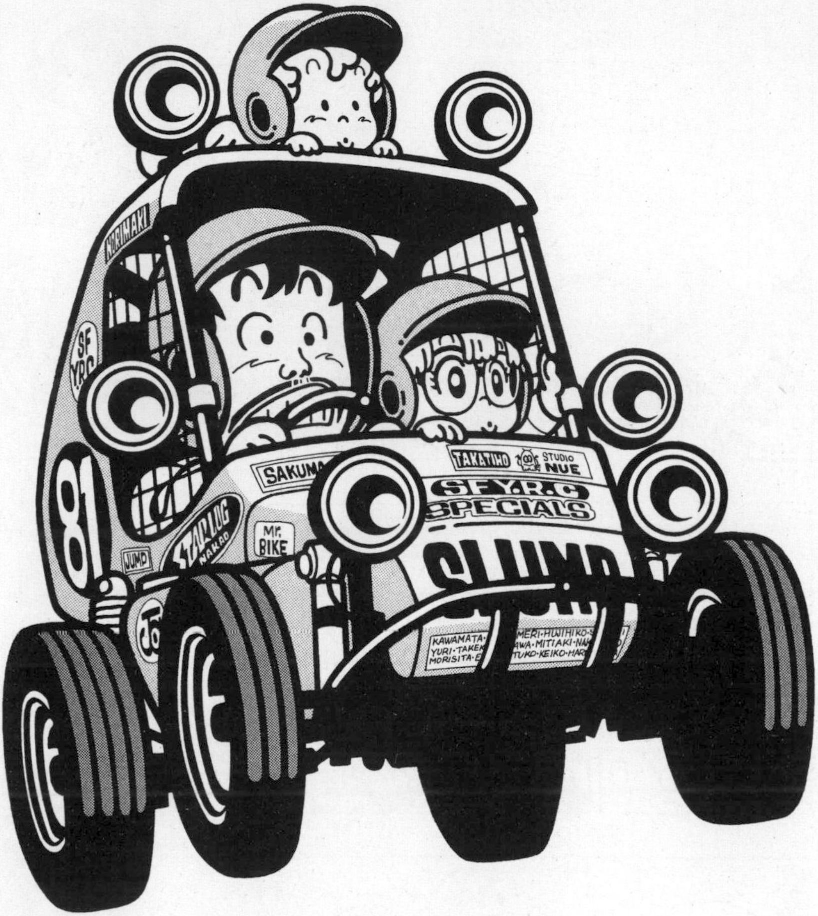
NORIMAKI
SF
YRC
81
SAKUMA
TAKATIHO
STUDIO
NUE
SF.Y.R.C
SPECIALS
Mr.
BIKE
JUMP

Heel, Achilles!

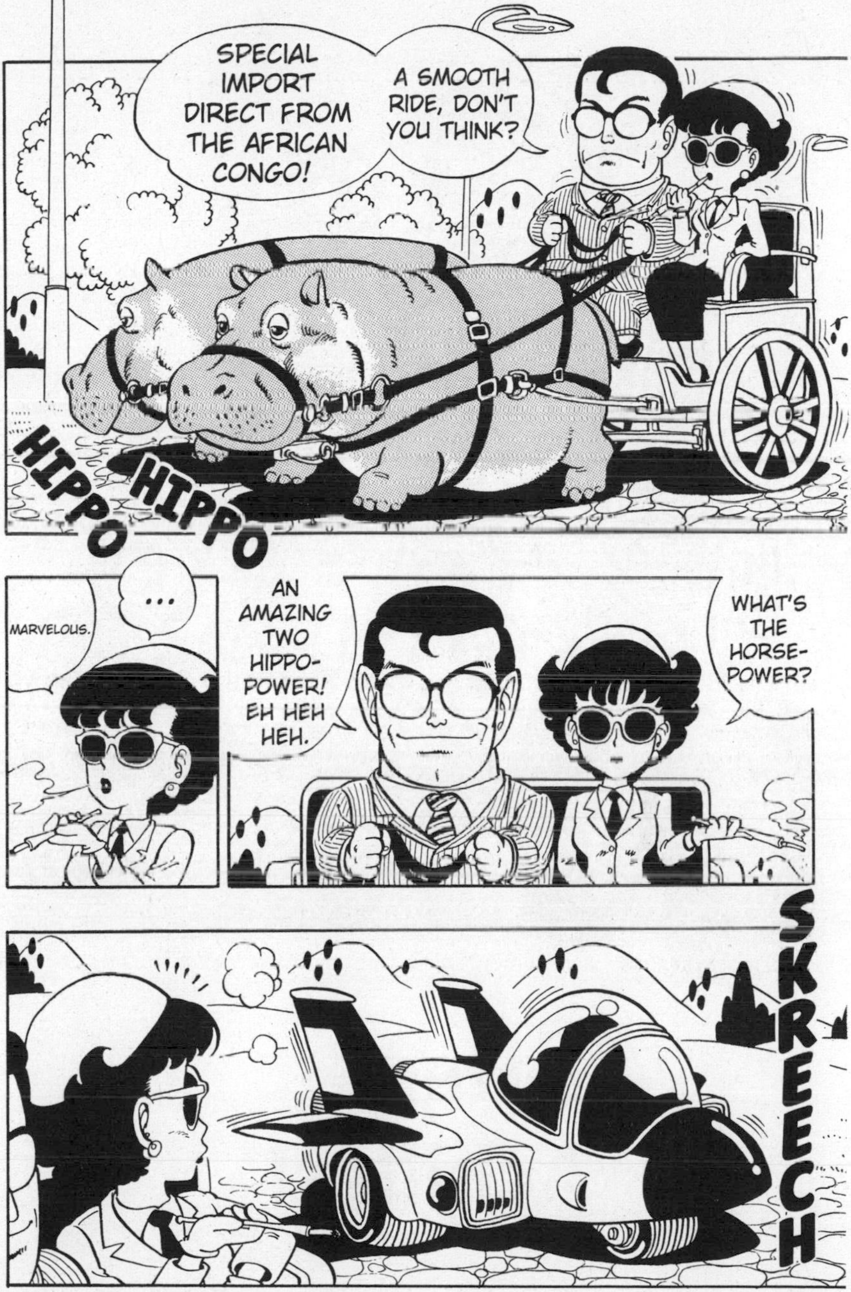
A SMOOTH RIDE, DON'T YOU THINK?
SPECIAL IMPORT DIRECT FROM THE AFRICAN CONGO!
HIPPO HIPPO
WHAT'S THE HORSE-POWER?
AN AMAZING TWO HIPPO-POWER! EH HEH HEH.
...
MARVELOUS.
SKREECH

READ THIS WAY

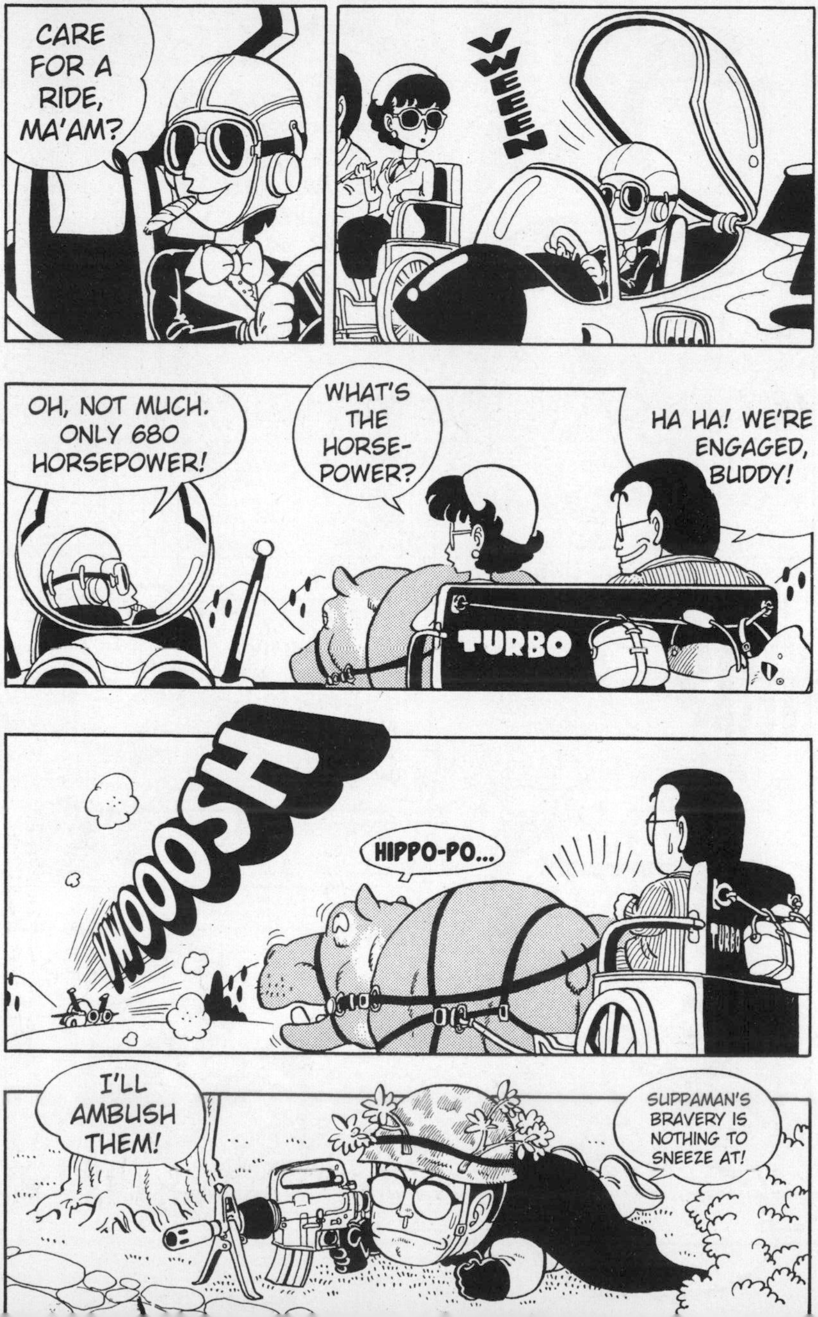
VWEEN
CARE FOR A RIDE, MA'AM?
HA HA! WE'RE ENGAGED, BUDDY!
WHAT'S THE HORSE-POWER?
OH, NOT MUCH. ONLY 680 HORSEPOWER!
TURBO
HIPPO-PO...
WHOOOSH
TURBO
SUPPAMAN'S BRAVERY IS NOTHING TO SNEEZE AT!
I'LL AMBUSH THEM!

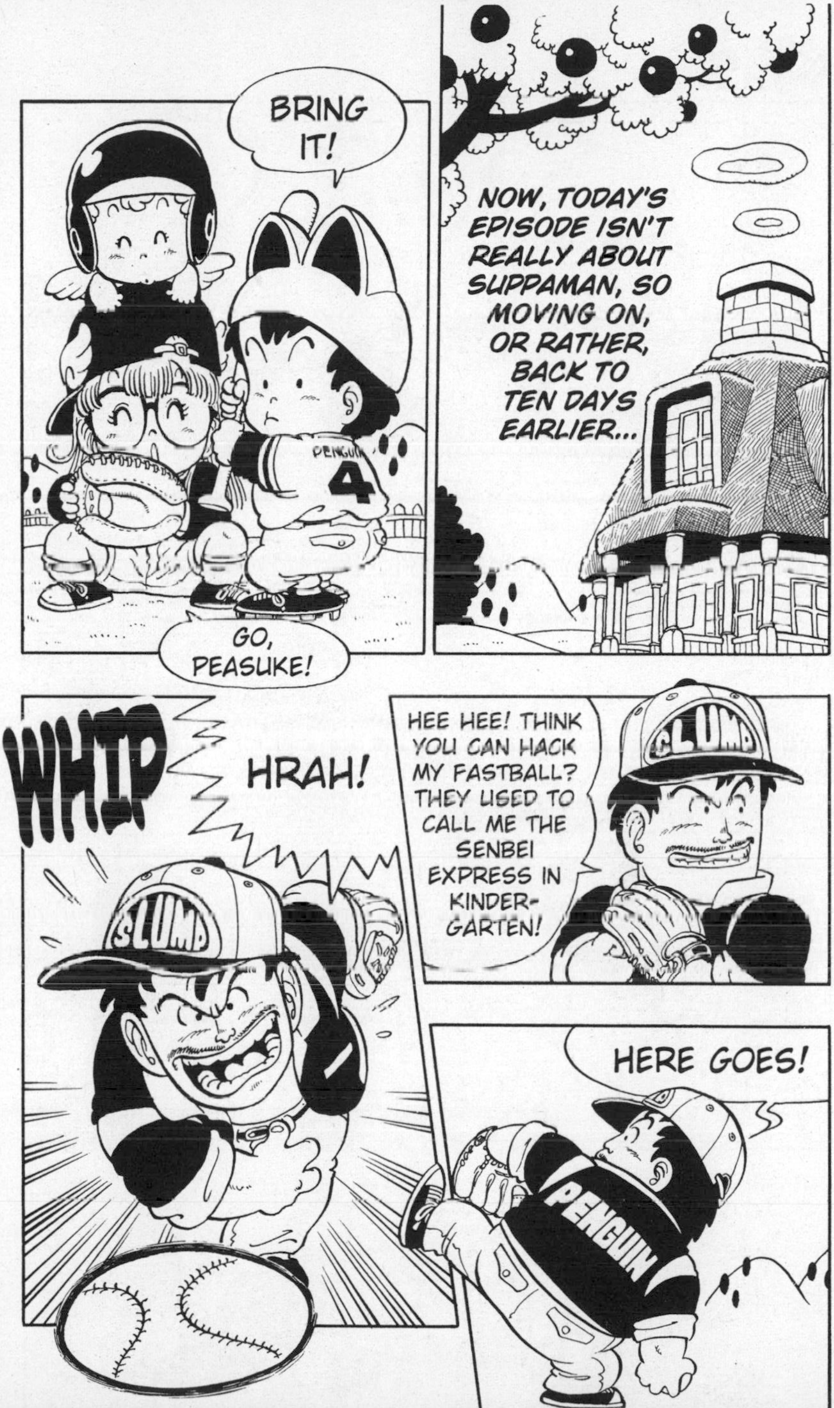
NOW, TODAY'S EPISODE ISN'T REALLY ABOUT SUPPAMAN, SO MOVING ON, OR RATHER, BACK TO TEN DAYS EARLIER...
BRING IT!
PENGUIN 4
GO, PEASUKE!
HEE HEE! THINK YOU CAN HACK MY FASTBALL? THEY USED TO CALL ME THE SENBEI EXPRESS IN KINDER-GARTEN!
SLUMP
HERE GOES!
PENGUIN
WHIP
HRAH!
SLUMP

READ THIS WAY

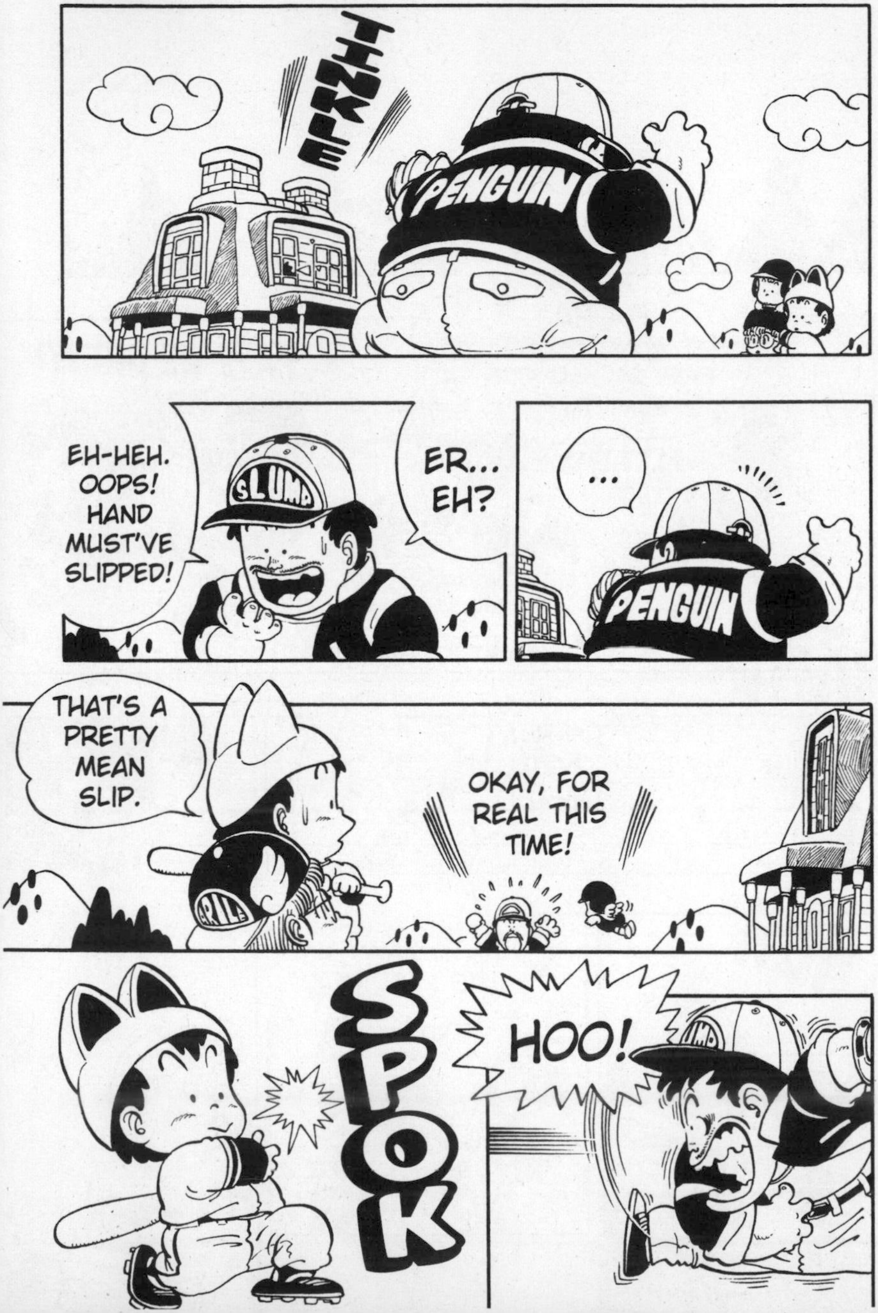
TINKLE
PENGUIN
...
PENGUIN
ER... EH?
EH-HEH. OOPS! HAND MUST'VE SLIPPED!
SLUMP
OKAY, FOR REAL THIS TIME!
THAT'S A PRETTY MEAN SLIP.
HOO!
SPOK

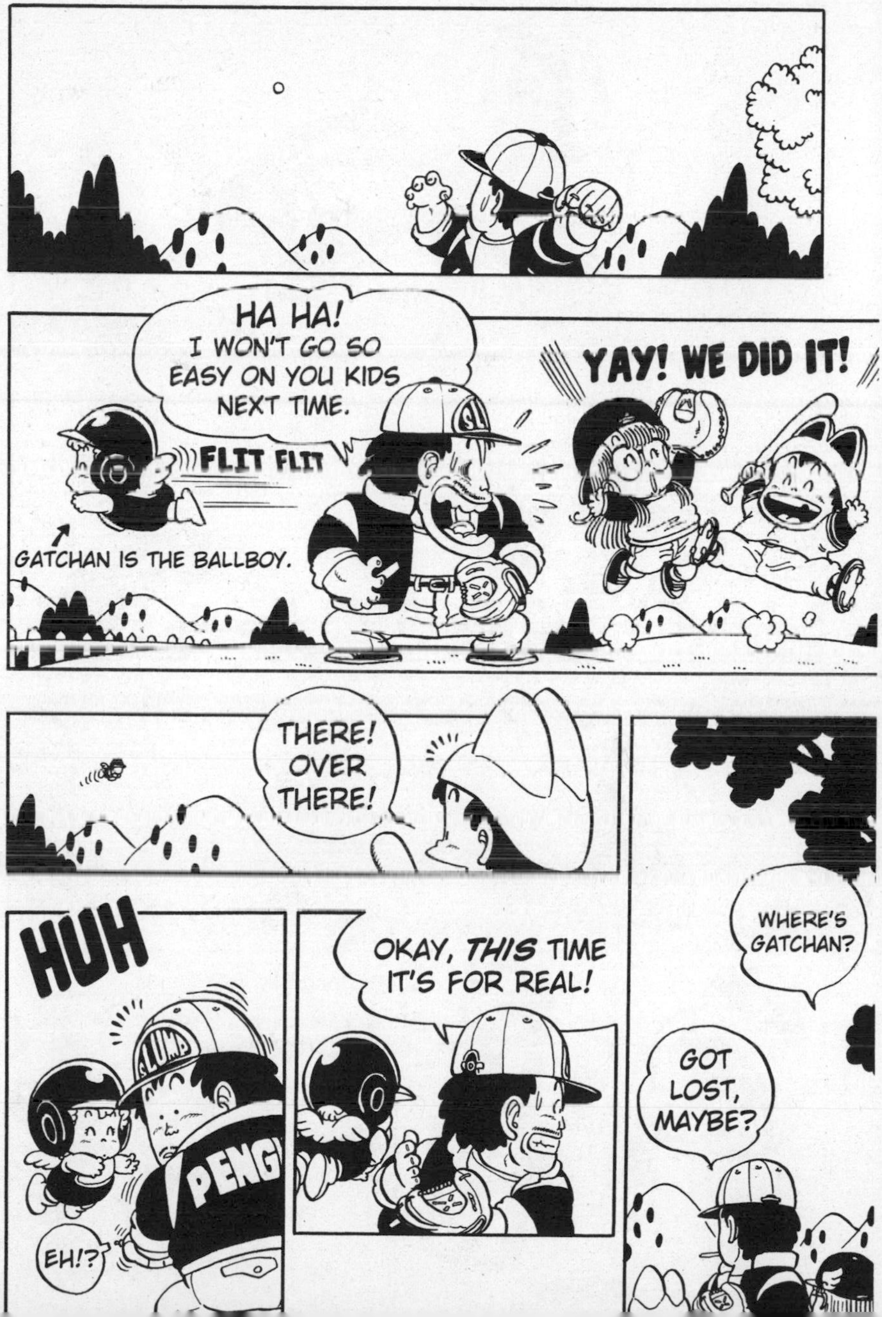
YAY! WE DID IT!
HA HA! I WON'T GO SO EASY ON YOU KIDS NEXT TIME.
FLIT FLIT
GATCHAN IS THE BALLBOY.
WHERE'S GATCHAN?
GOT LOST, MAYBE?
THERE! OVER THERE!
OKAY, *THIS* TIME IT'S FOR REAL!
HUH
SLUMP
PENG
EH!?

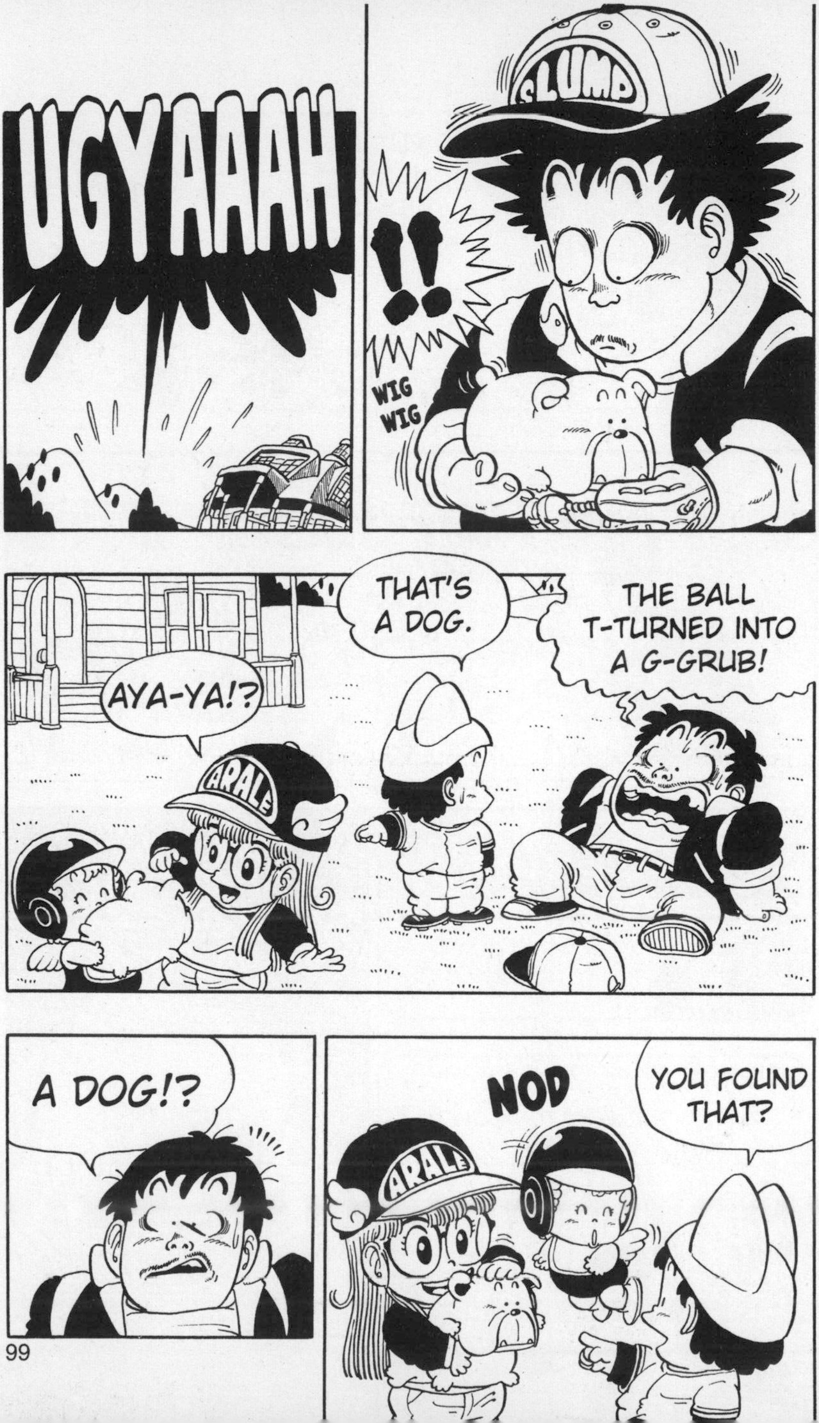
SLUMP
!!
WIG WIG
UGYAAAH
THE BALL T-TURNED INTO A G-GRUB!
THAT'S A DOG.
AYA-YA!?
ARALE
YOU FOUND THAT?
NOD
ARALE
A DOG!?

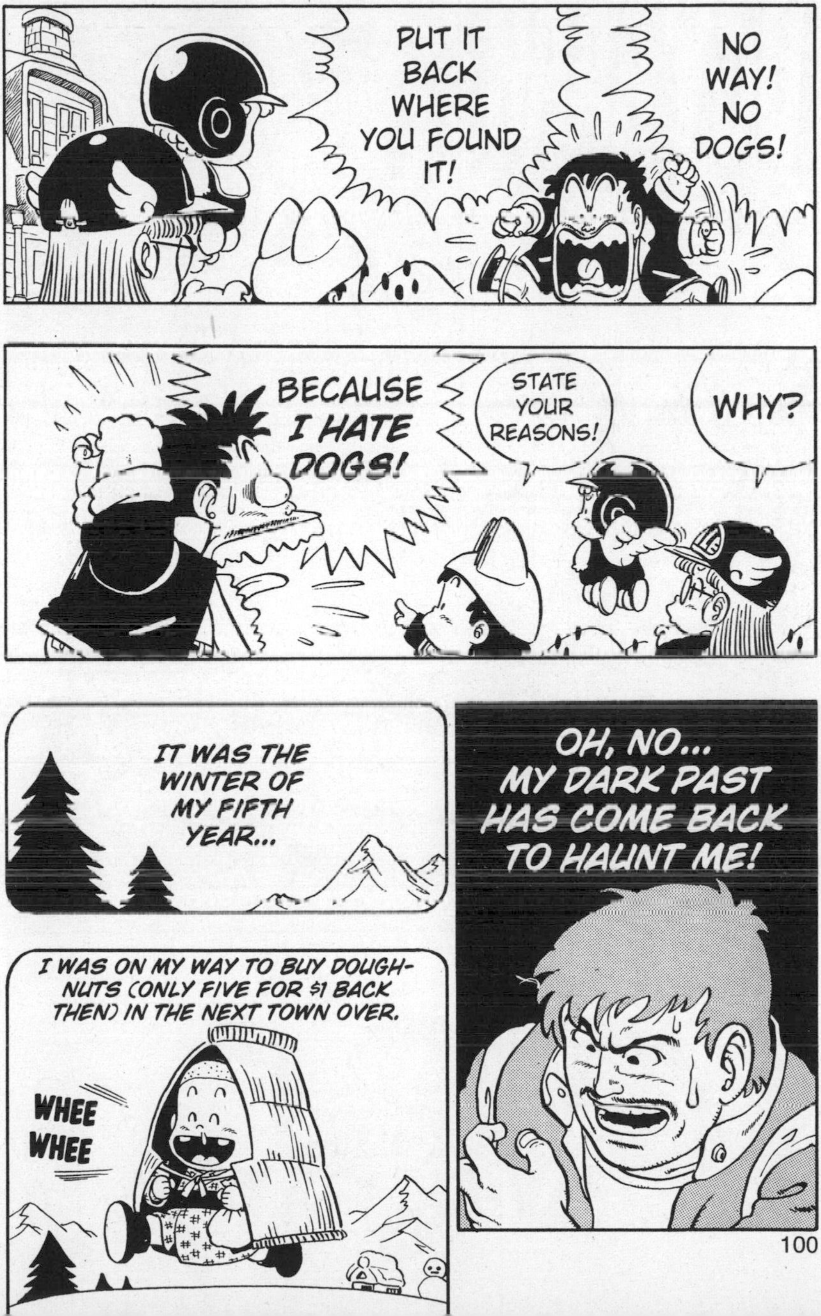
NO WAY! NO DOGS!
PUT IT BACK WHERE YOU FOUND IT!
WHY?
STATE YOUR REASONS!
BECAUSE I HATE DOGS!
OH, NO... MY DARK PAST HAS COME BACK TO HAUNT ME!
IT WAS THE WINTER OF MY FIFTH YEAR...
I WAS ON MY WAY TO BUY DOUGH-NUTS (ONLY FIVE FOR $1 BACK THEN) IN THE NEXT TOWN OVER.
WHEE WHEE

READ THIS WAY

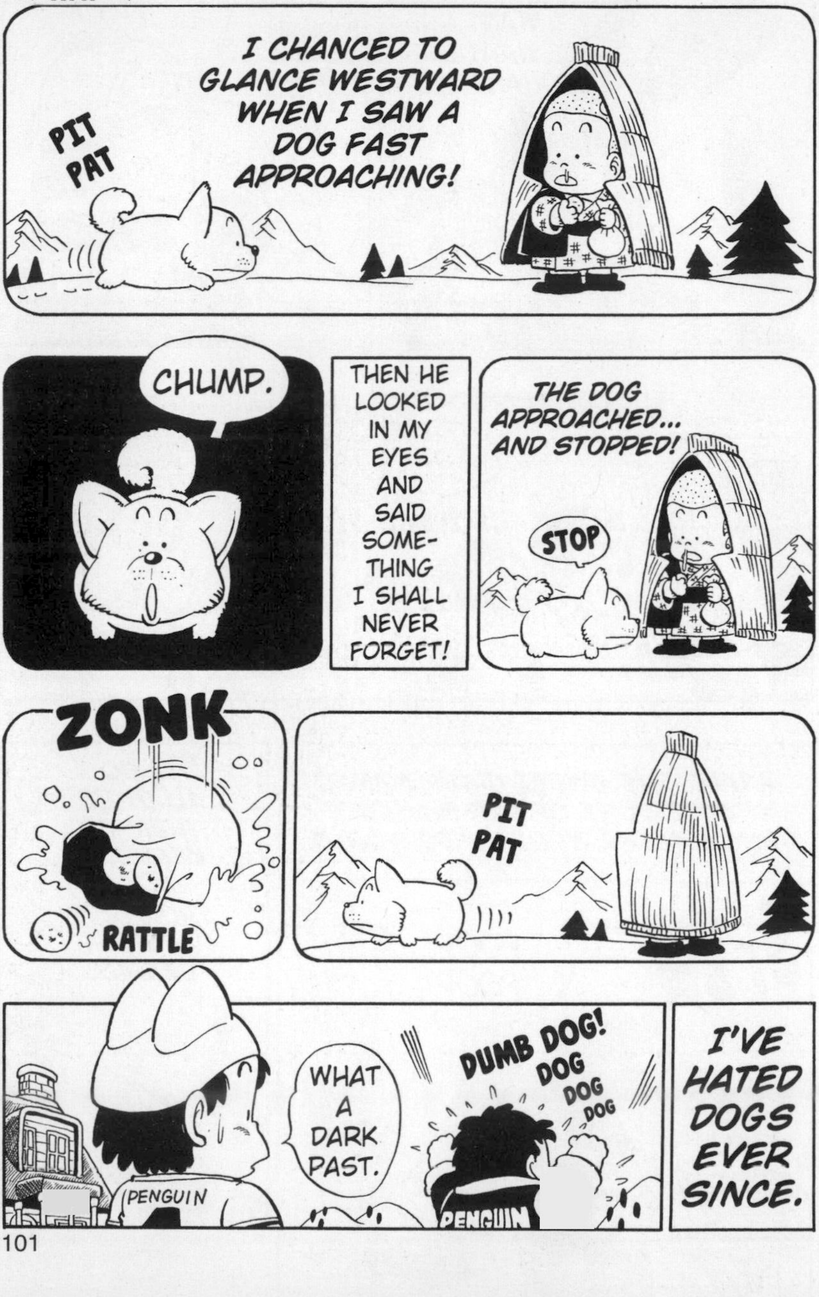
I CHANCED TO GLANCE WESTWARD WHEN I SAW A DOG FAST APPROACHING!
PIT PAT
THE DOG APPROACHED... AND STOPPED!
STOP
THEN HE LOOKED IN MY EYES AND SAID SOME-THING I SHALL NEVER FORGET!
CHUMP.
PIT PAT
ZONK
RATTLE
I'VE HATED DOGS EVER SINCE.
DUMB DOG! DOG DOG DOG
PENGUIN
WHAT A DARK PAST.
PENGUIN

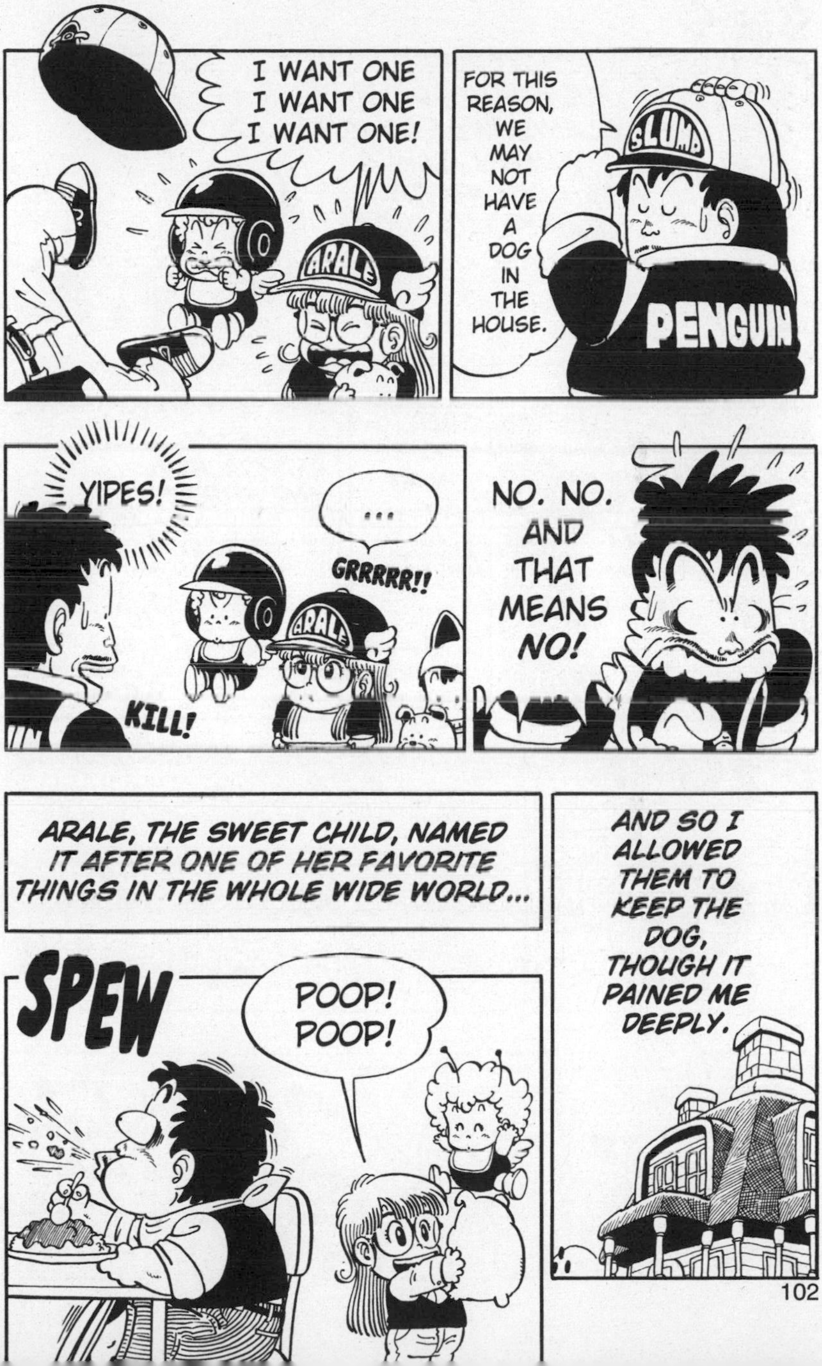
FOR THIS REASON, WE MAY NOT HAVE A DOG IN THE HOUSE.
PENGUIN
SLUMP
I WANT ONE I WANT ONE I WANT ONE!
ARALE
NO. NO. AND THAT MEANS NO!
YIPES!
...
GRRRRR!!
ARALE
KILL!
AND SO I ALLOWED THEM TO KEEP THE DOG, THOUGH IT PAINED ME DEEPLY.
ARALE, THE SWEET CHILD, NAMED IT AFTER ONE OF HER FAVORITE THINGS IN THE WHOLE WIDE WORLD...
SPEW
POOP! POOP!

READ THIS WAY

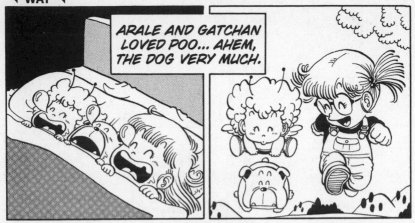

ARALE AND GATCHAN LOVED POO... AHEM, THE DOG VERY MUCH.
GATCHAN, IN PARTICULAR, WAS ENTHUSED TO FINALLY HAVE A PLAYMATE WHILE ARALE WAS AT SCHOOL.
FETCH
IN A WEEK, THE DOG HAD MASTERED A FEW WORDS.
ARACHA!
GATCHA!
GORILLA. GORILLA.
...
I STILL HATED DOGS.

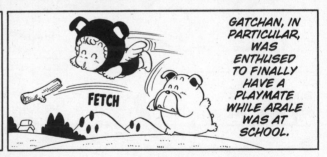

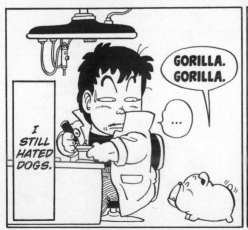

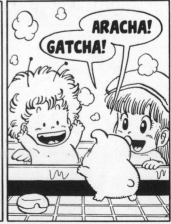

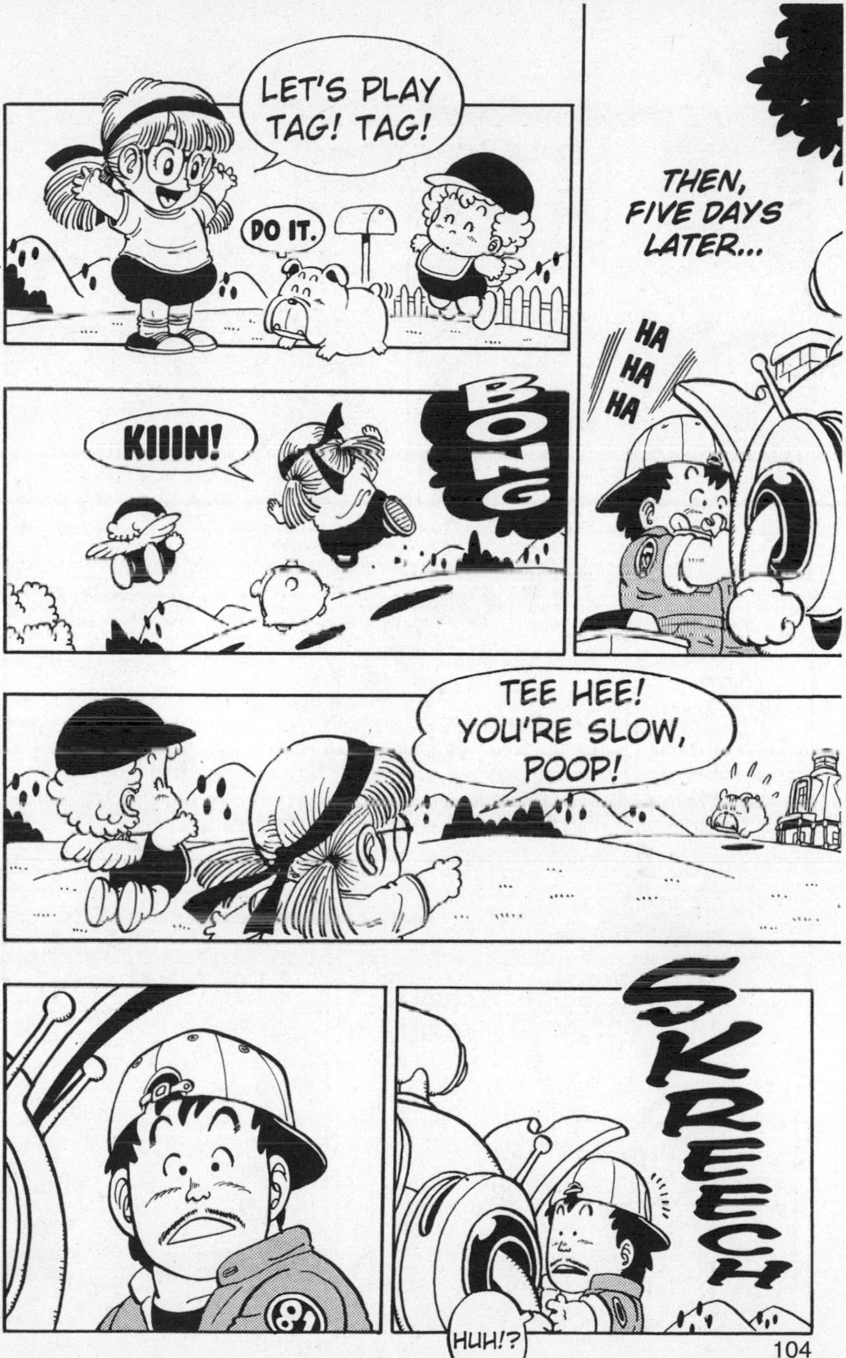
THEN, FIVE DAYS LATER...
HA HA HA
LET'S PLAY TAG! TAG!
DO IT.
KIIIN!
BONG
TEE HEE! YOU'RE SLOW, POOP!
SKREECH
HUH!?

READ THIS WAY

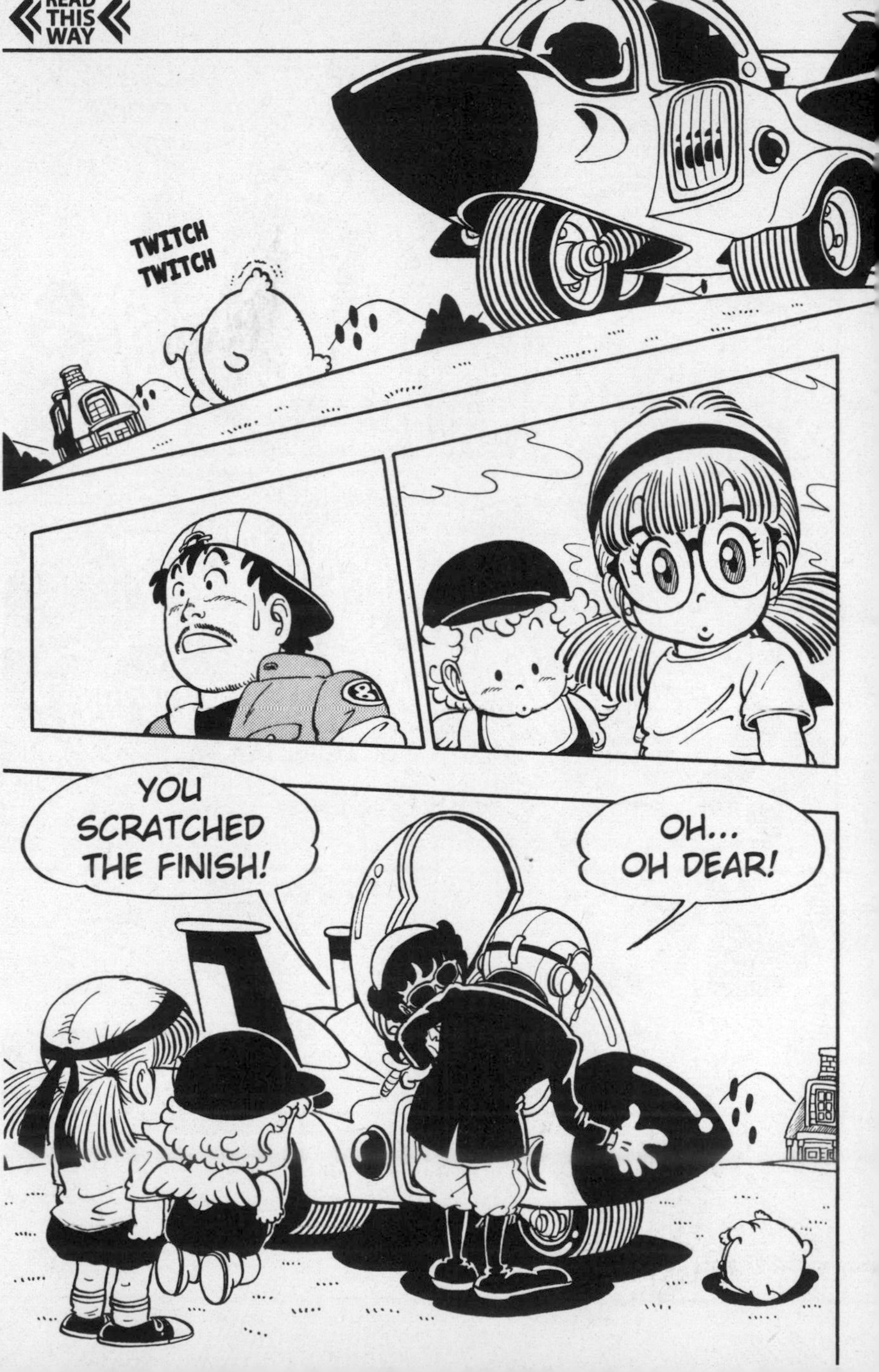
TWITCH TWITCH
OH... OH DEAR!
YOU SCRATCHED THE FINISH!

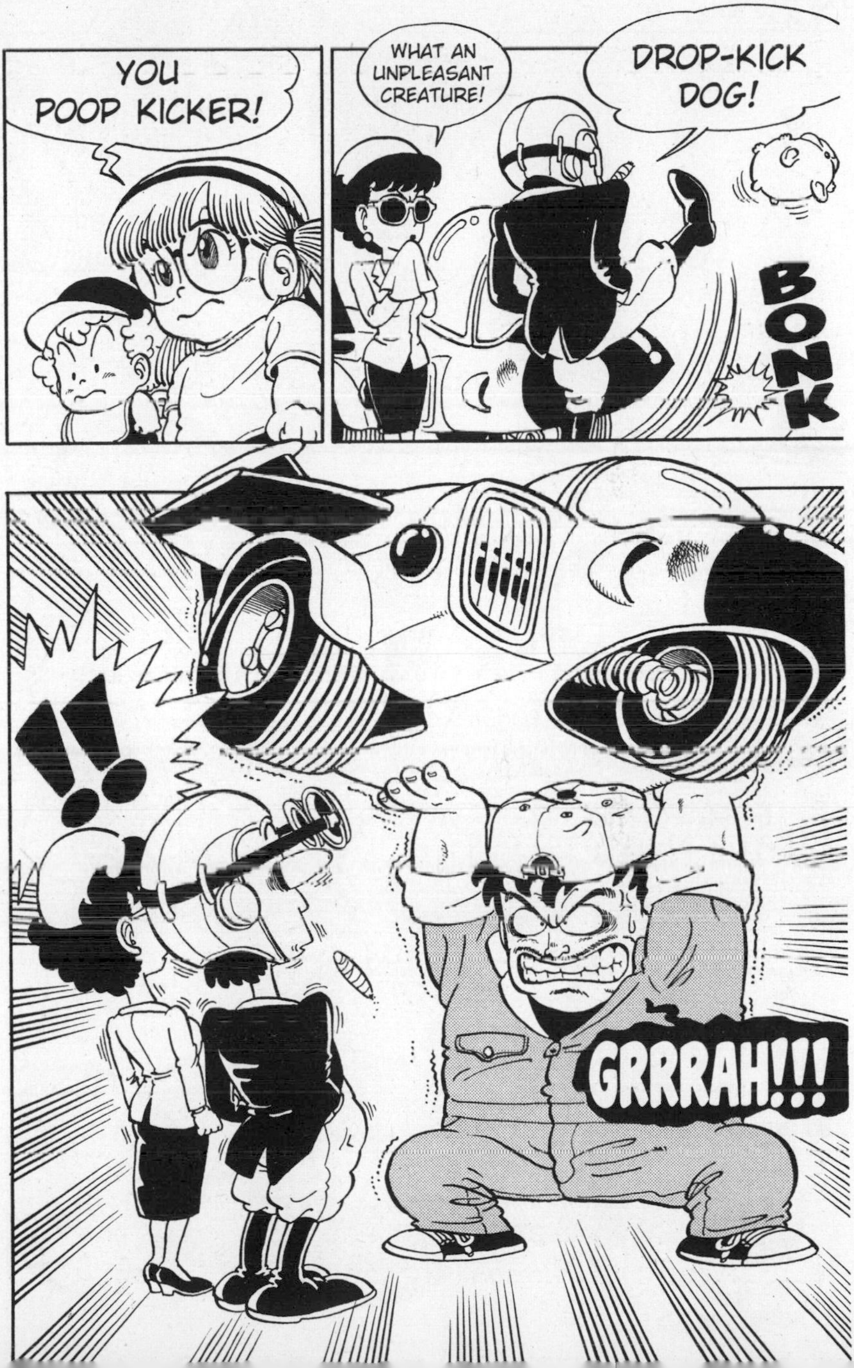
DROP-KICK DOG!
WHAT AN UNPLEASANT CREATURE!
BONK
YOU POOP KICKER!
GRRRAH!!!

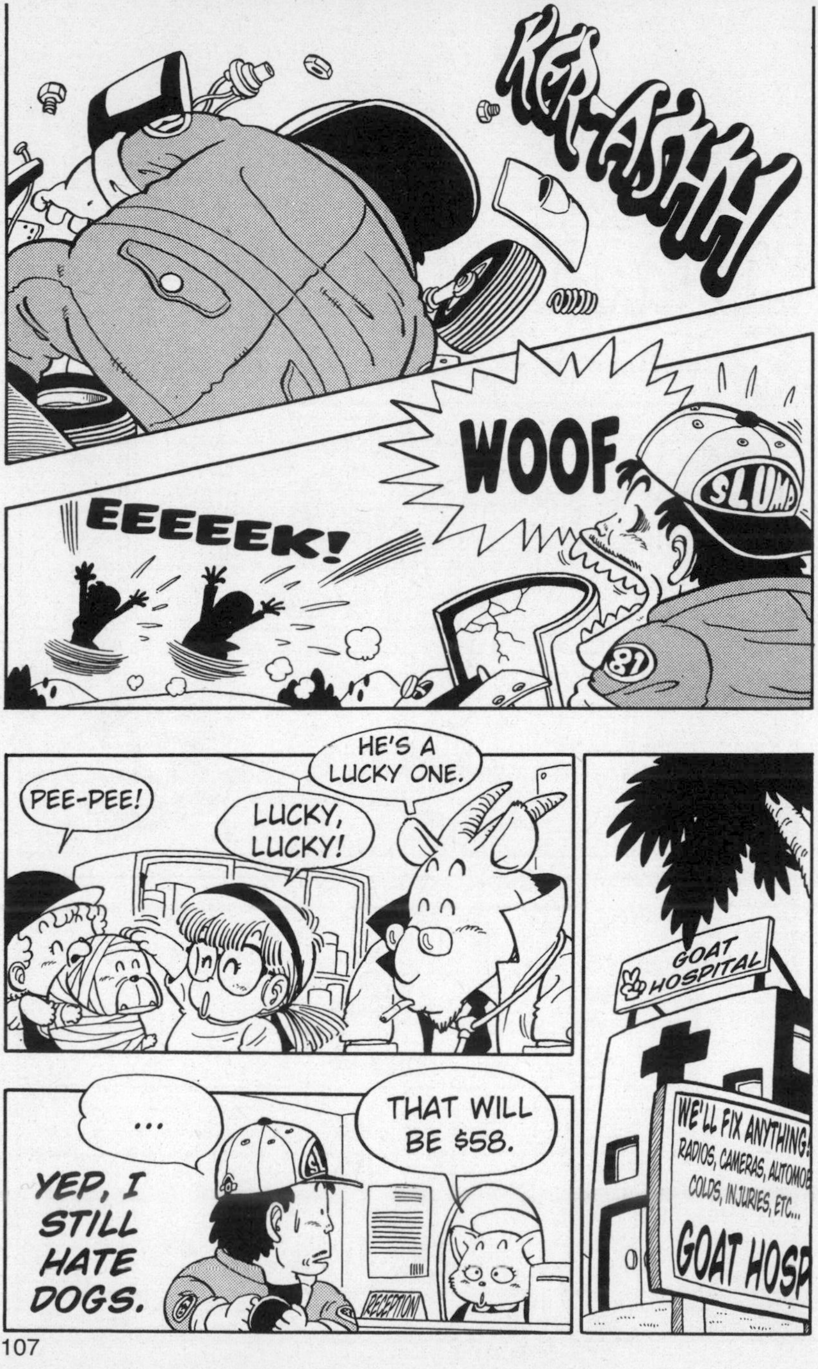
KER-ASHHH
WOOF
EEEEEK!
GOAT HOSPITAL
WE'LL FIX ANYTHING!
RADIOS, CAMERAS, AUTOMOB
COLDS, INJURIES, ETC...
GOAT HOSP
HE'S A LUCKY ONE.
LUCKY, LUCKY!
PEE-PEE!
THAT WILL BE $58.
...
RECEPTION
YEP, I STILL HATE DOGS.

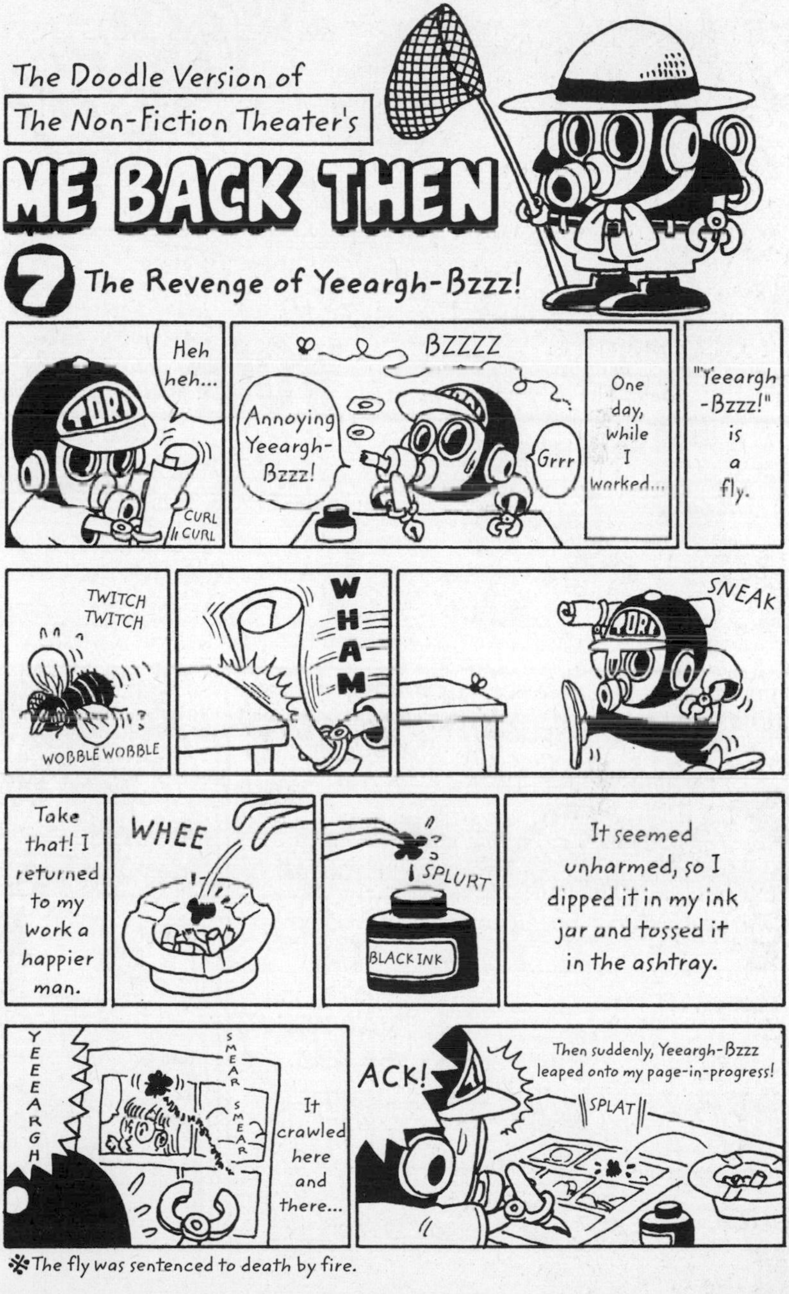

The Doodle Version of
The Non-Fiction Theater's
ME BACK THEN
7 The Revenge of Yeeargh-Bzzz!
"Yeeargh-Bzzz!" is a fly.
One day, while I worked...
BZZZZ
Grrr
Annoying Yeeargh-Bzzz!
Heh heh...
CURL CURL
SNEAK
WHAM
TWITCH TWITCH
WOBBLE WOBBLE
It seemed unharmed, so I dipped it in my ink jar and tossed it in the ashtray.
SPLURT
BLACK INK
WHEE
Take that! I returned to my work a happier man.
Then suddenly, Yeeargh-Bzzz leaped onto my page-in-progress!
SPLAT
ACK!
It crawled here and there...
SMEAR SMEAR
YEEEEARGH

※The fly was sentenced to death by fire.

Good-bye, Gatchan!

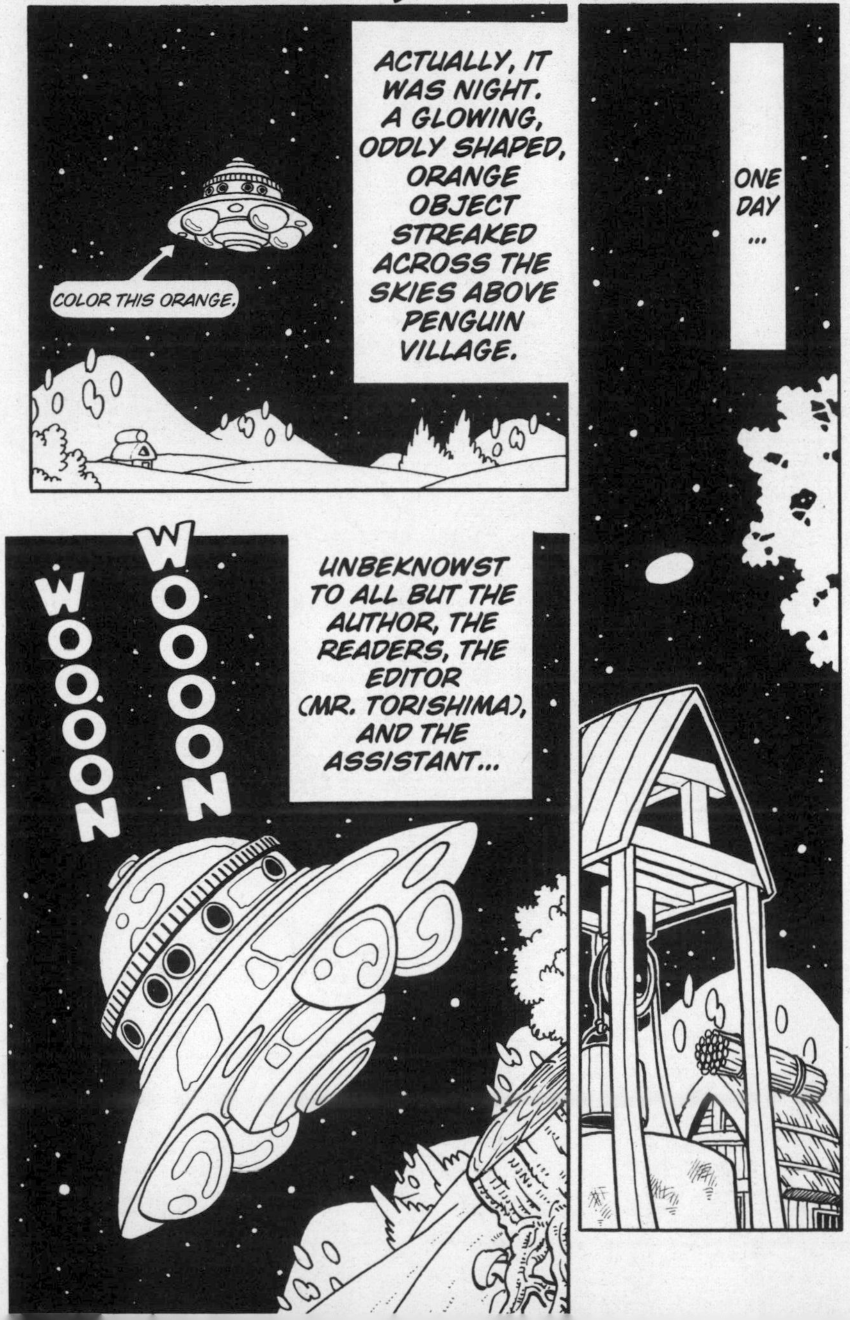

ONE DAY ...
ACTUALLY, IT WAS NIGHT. A GLOWING, ODDLY SHAPED, ORANGE OBJECT STREAKED ACROSS THE SKIES ABOVE PENGUIN VILLAGE.
COLOR THIS ORANGE.
UNBEKNOWST TO ALL BUT THE AUTHOR, THE READERS, THE EDITOR (MR. TORISHIMA), AND THE ASSISTANT...
WOOOON
WOOOON

Good-bye, Gatchan!

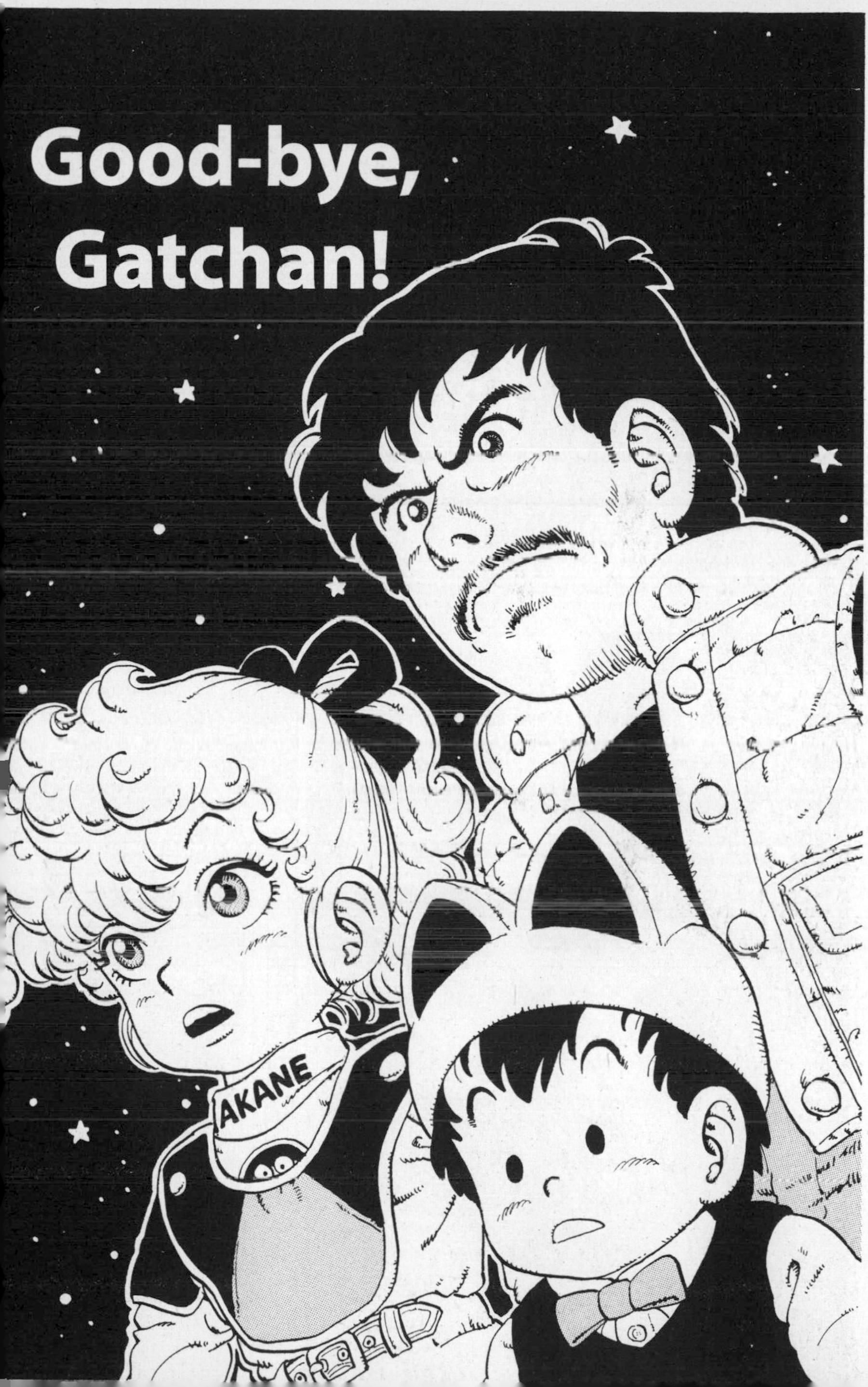
AKANE

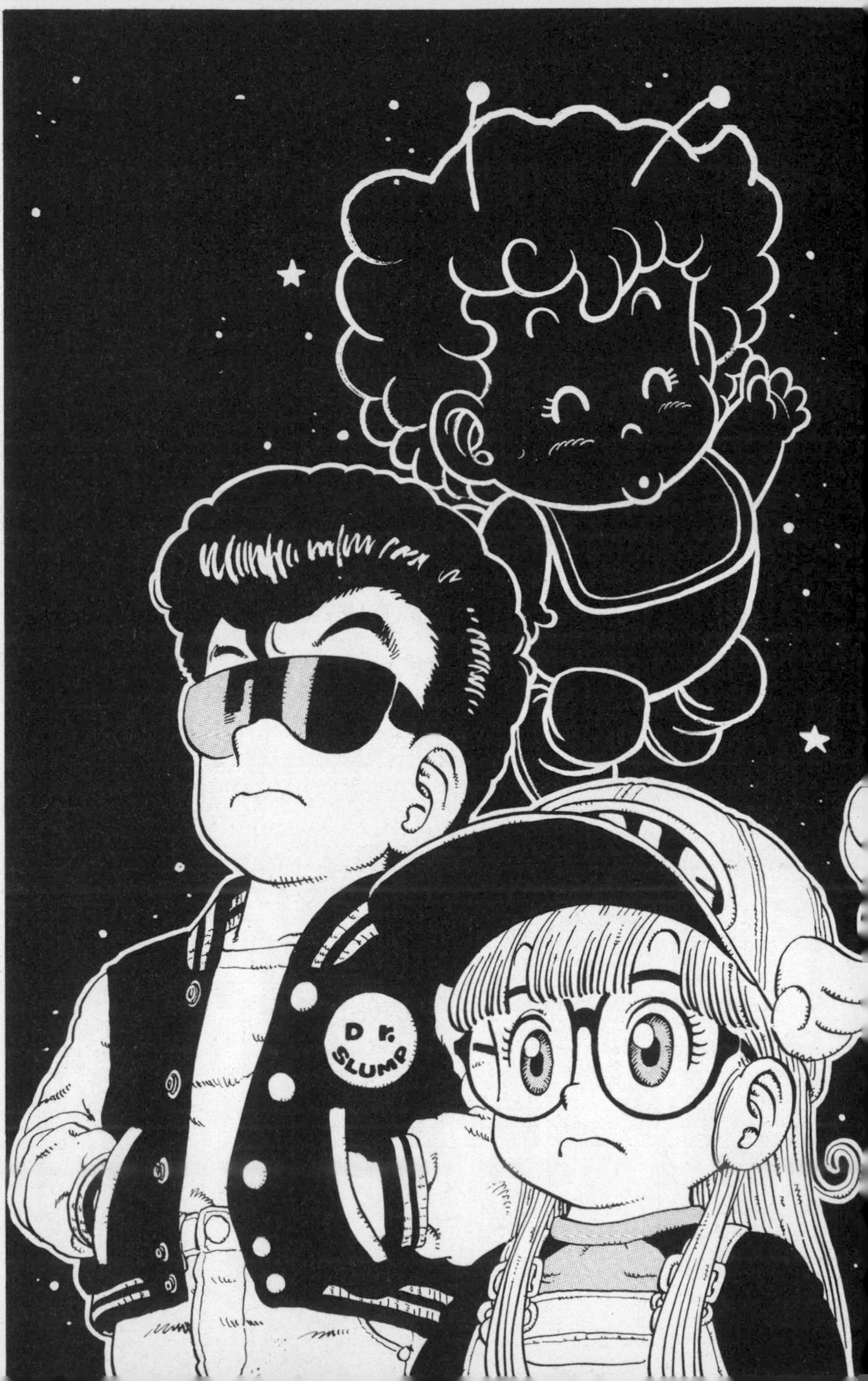
Dr.
SLUMP

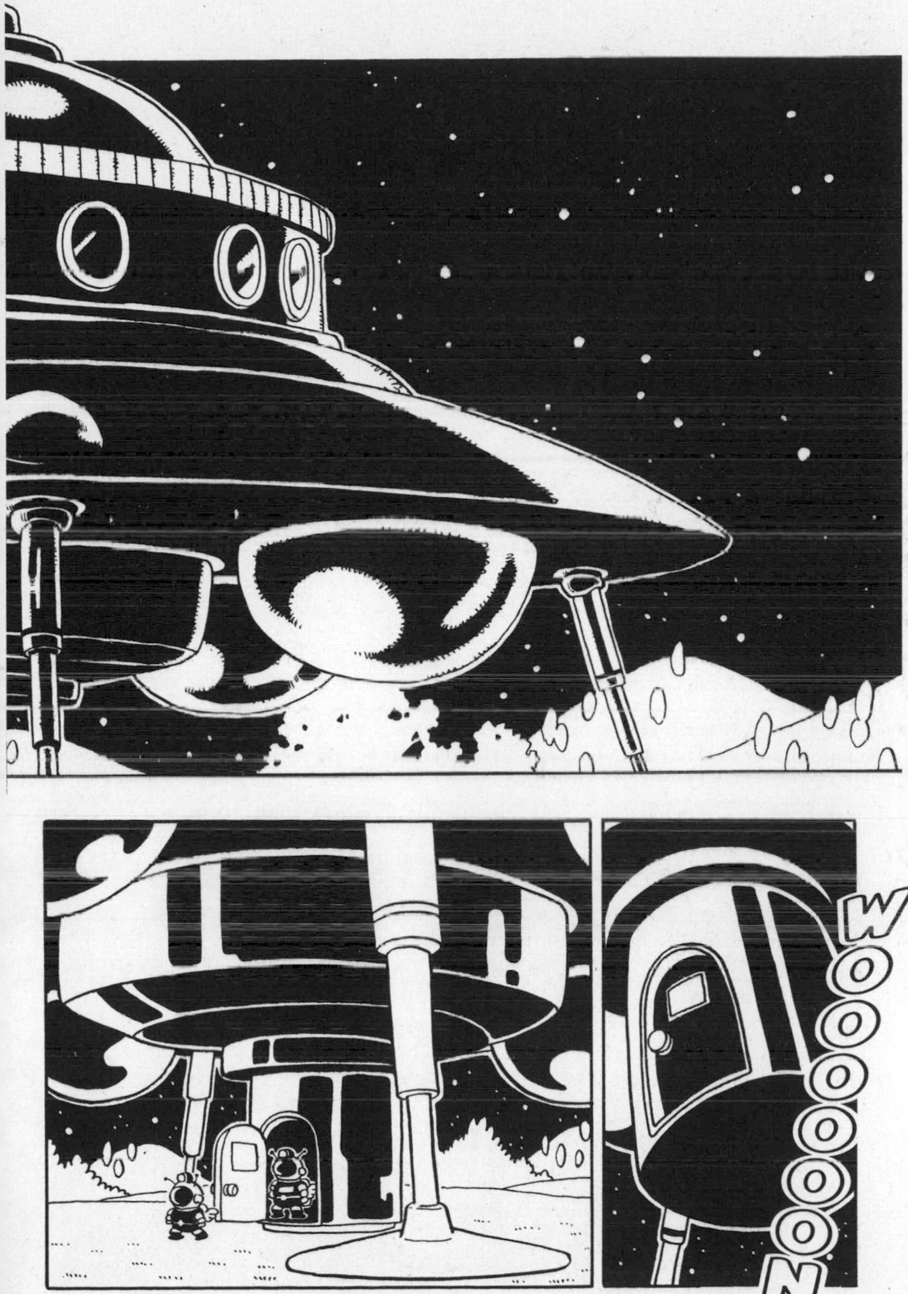
WOOOOOOOON

READ THIS WAY

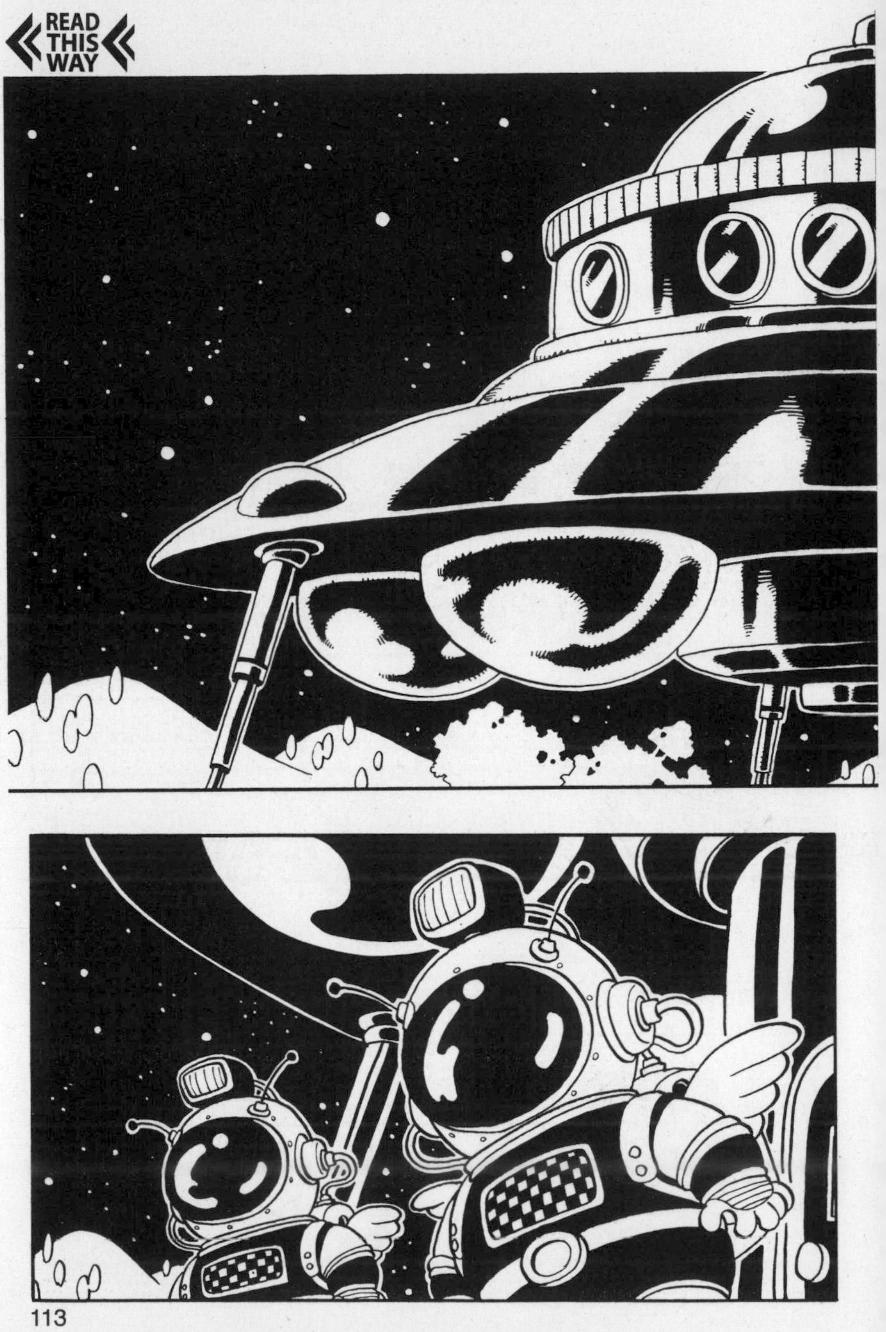

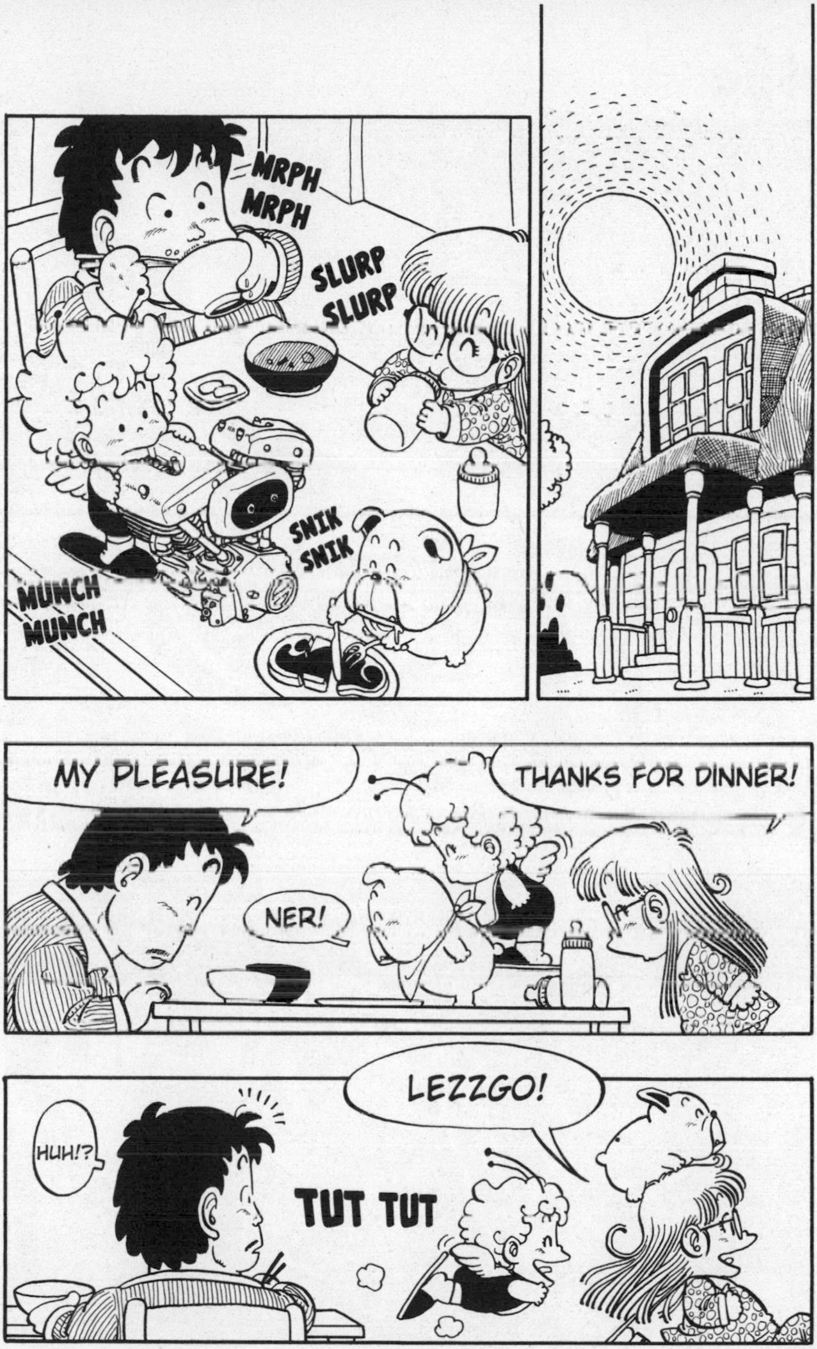
MRPH MRPH
SLURP SLURP
SNIK SNIK
MUNCH MUNCH
THANKS FOR DINNER!
MY PLEASURE!
NER!
LEZZGO!
TUT TUT
HUH!?

READ THIS WAY

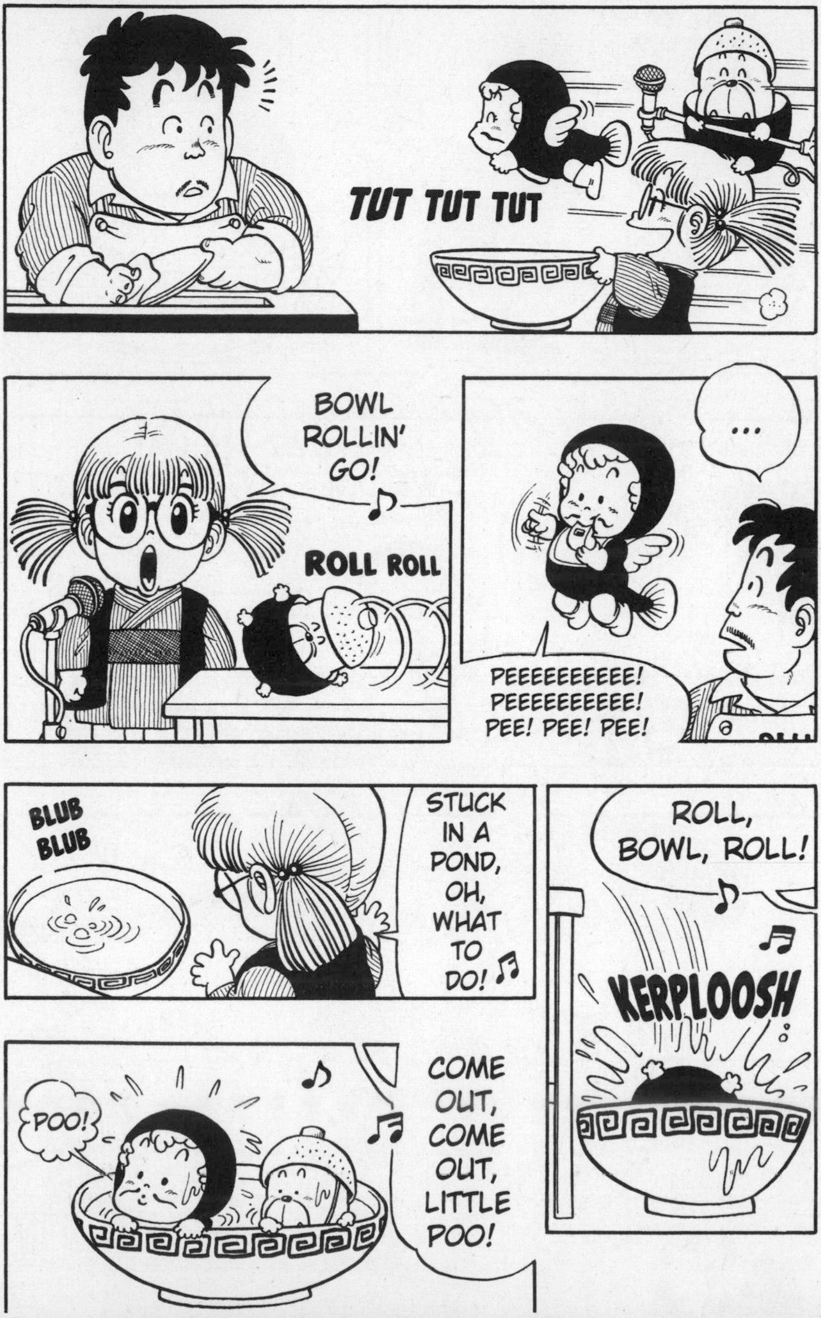
TUT TUT TUT
...
PEEEEEEEEEE! PEEEEEEEEEE! PEE! PEE! PEE!
BOWL ROLLIN' GO!
ROLL ROLL
ROLL, BOWL, ROLL!
KERPLOOSH
STUCK IN A POND, OH, WHAT TO DO!
BLUB BLUB
COME OUT, COME OUT, LITTLE POO!
POO!

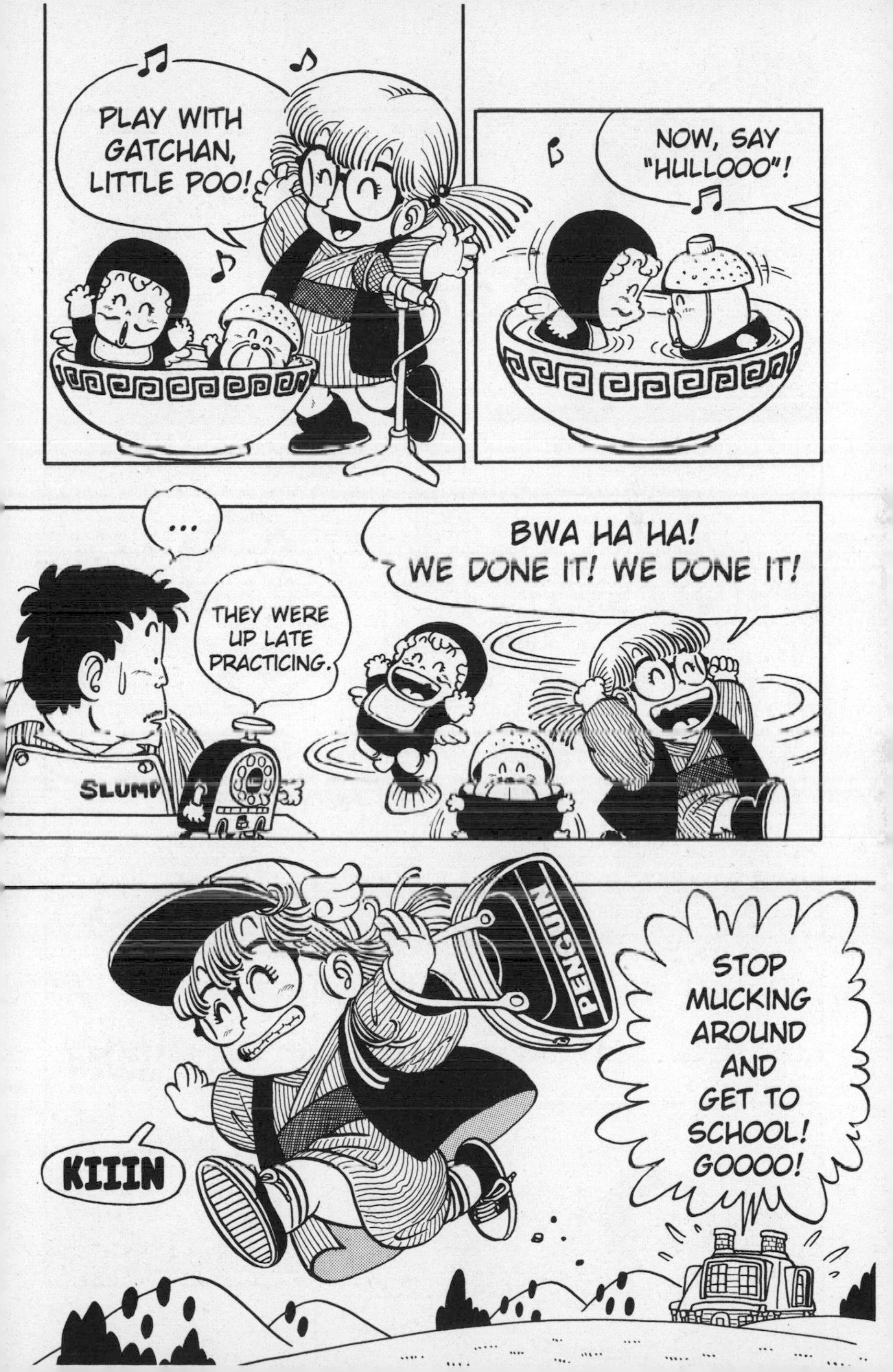
NOW, SAY "HULLOOO"!
PLAY WITH GATCHAN, LITTLE POO!
BWA HA HA! WE DONE IT! WE DONE IT!
THEY WERE UP LATE PRACTICING.
...
SLUMP
PENGUIN
STOP MUCKING AROUND AND GET TO SCHOOL! GOOOO!
KIIN

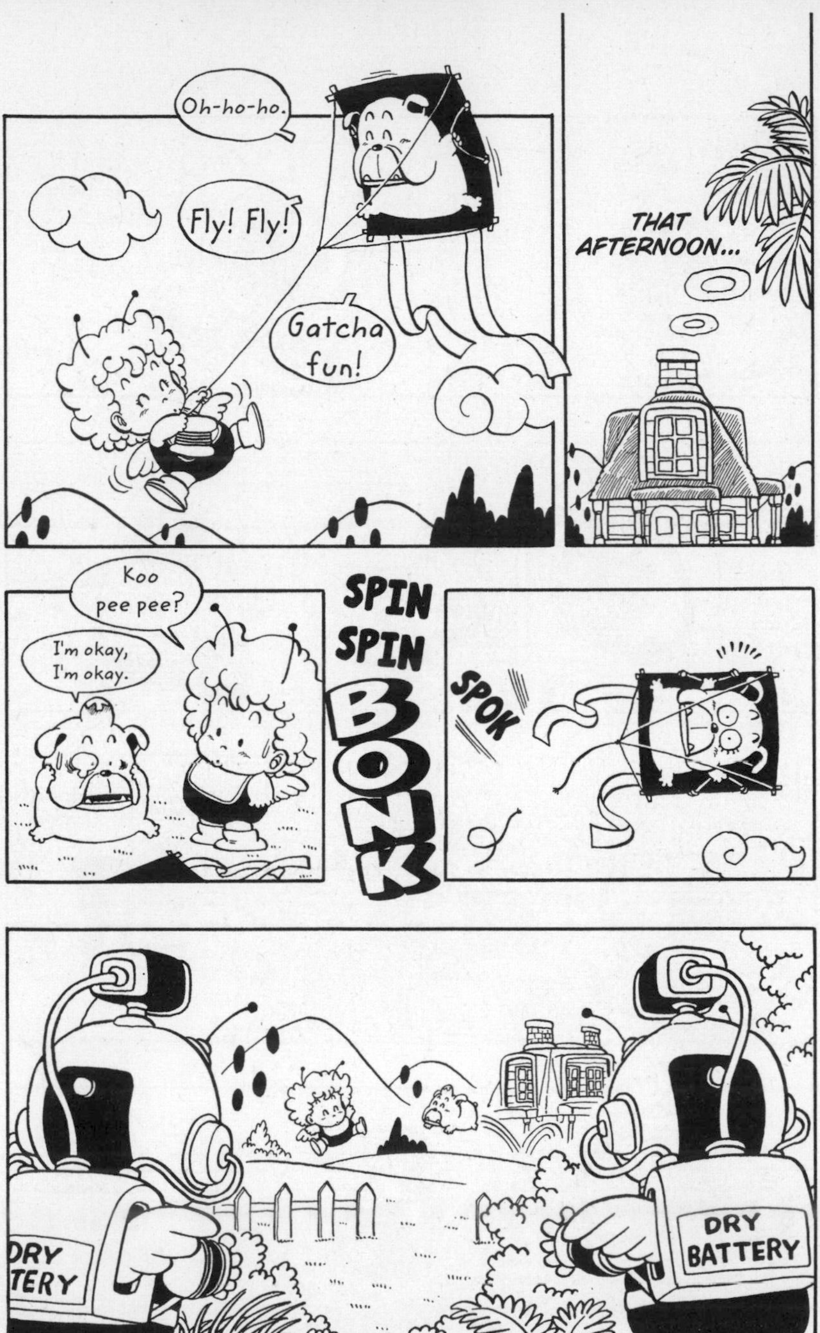
THAT AFTERNOON...
Oh-ho-ho.
Fly! Fly!
Gatcha fun!
SPOK
SPIN SPIN BONK
Koo pee pee?
I'm okay, I'm okay.
DRY BATTERY
DRY TERY

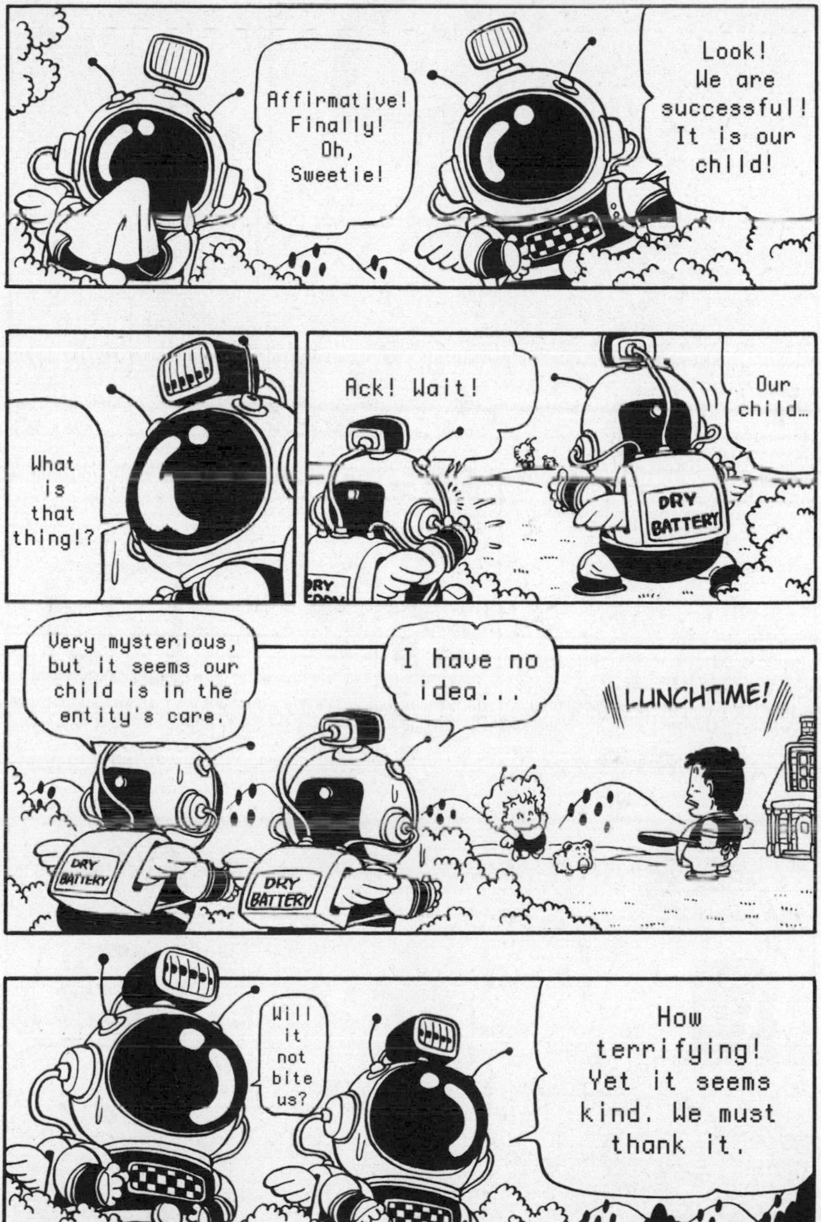
Look! We are successful! It is our child!
Affirmative! Finally! Oh, Sweetie!
Our child...
DRY BATTERY
Ack! Wait!
What is that thing!?
LUNCHTIME!
I have no idea...
Very mysterious, but it seems our child is in the entity's care.
DRY BATTERY
DRY BATTERY
How terrifying! Yet it seems kind. We must thank it.
Will it not bite us?

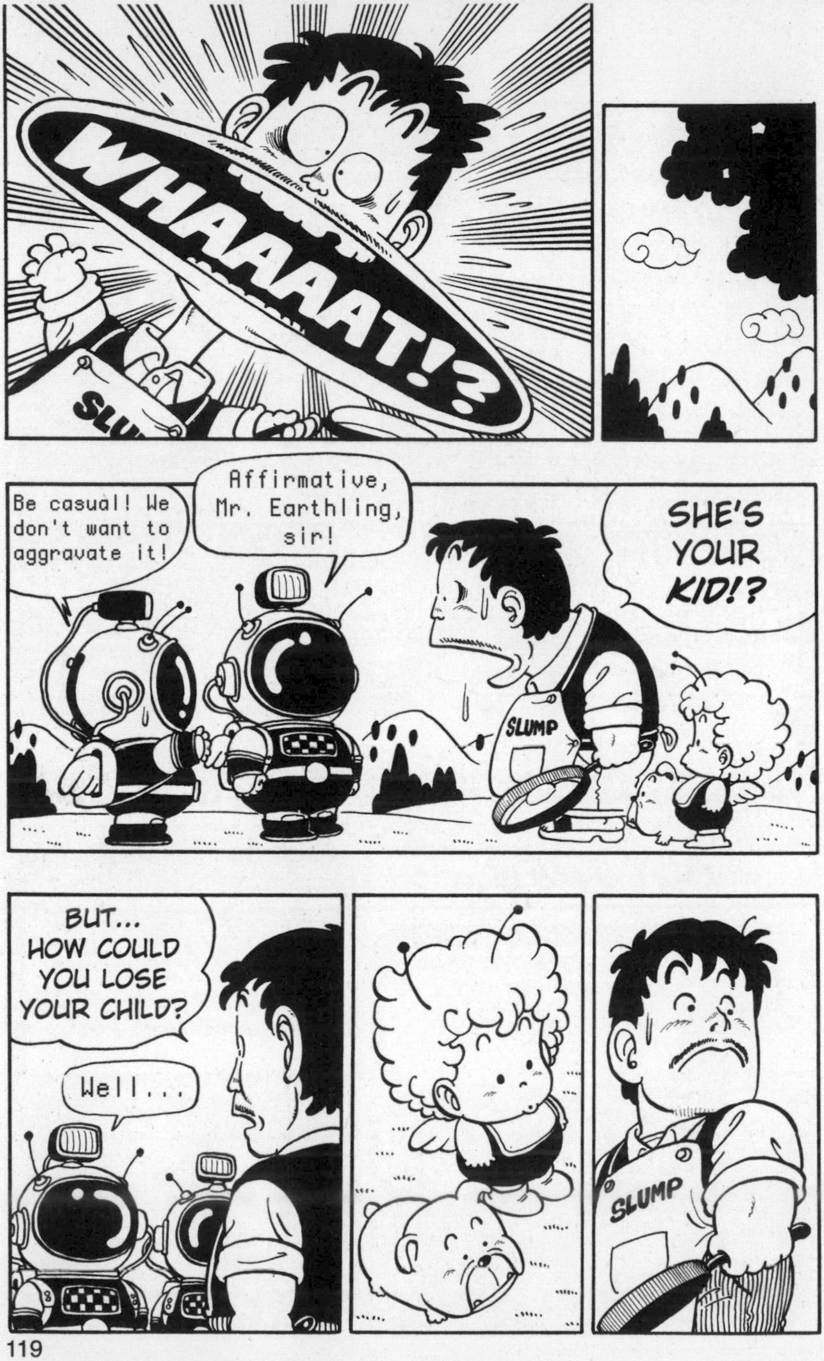
WHAAAT!?
SHE'S YOUR KID!?
SLUMP
Affirmative, Mr. Earthling, sir!
Be casual! We don't want to aggravate it!
SLUMP
BUT... HOW COULD YOU LOSE YOUR CHILD?
Well...

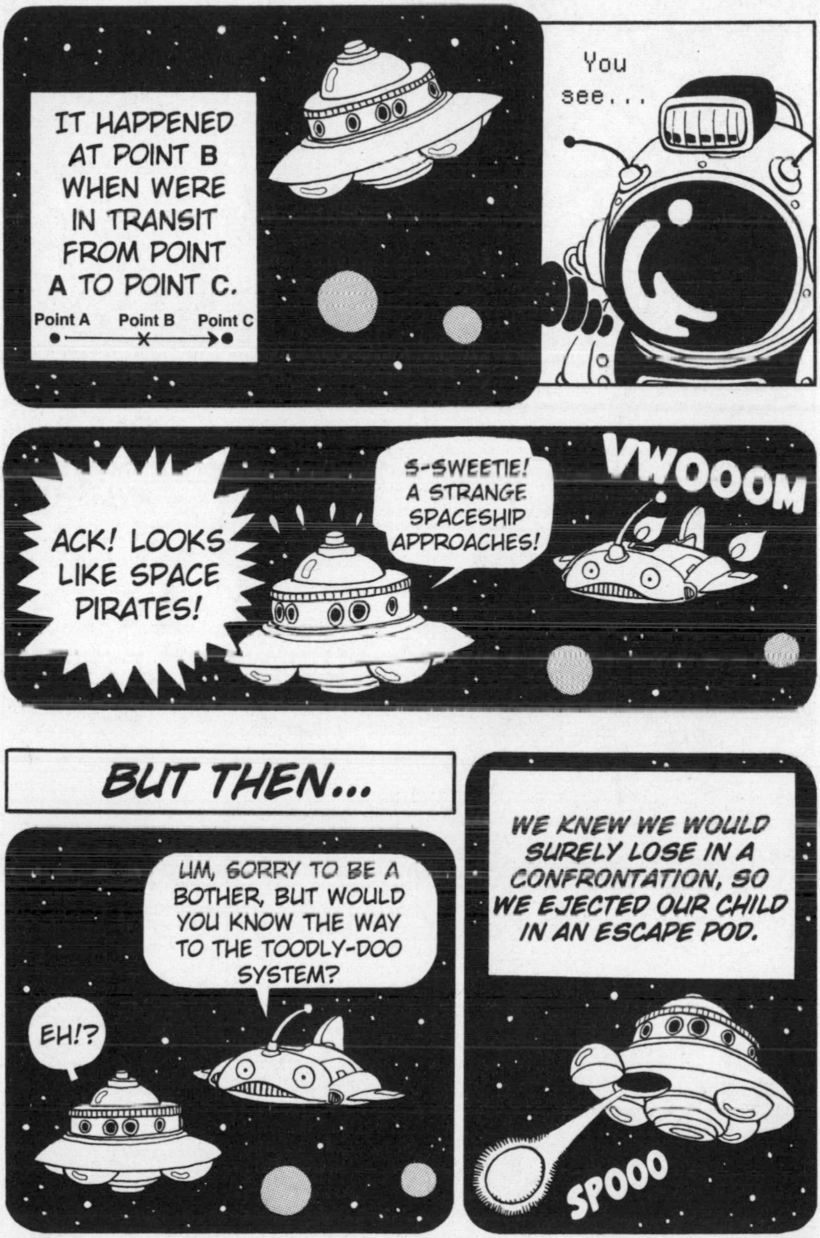
You see...
IT HAPPENED AT POINT B WHEN WERE IN TRANSIT FROM POINT A TO POINT C.
Point A
Point B
Point C
VWOOOM
S-SWEETIE! A STRANGE SPACESHIP APPROACHES!
ACK! LOOKS LIKE SPACE PIRATES!
WE KNEW WE WOULD SURELY LOSE IN A CONFRONTATION, SO WE EJECTED OUR CHILD IN AN ESCAPE POD.
SPOOO
BUT THEN...
UM, SORRY TO BE A BOTHER, BUT WOULD YOU KNOW THE WAY TO THE TOODLY-DOO SYSTEM?
EH!?

READ THIS WAY

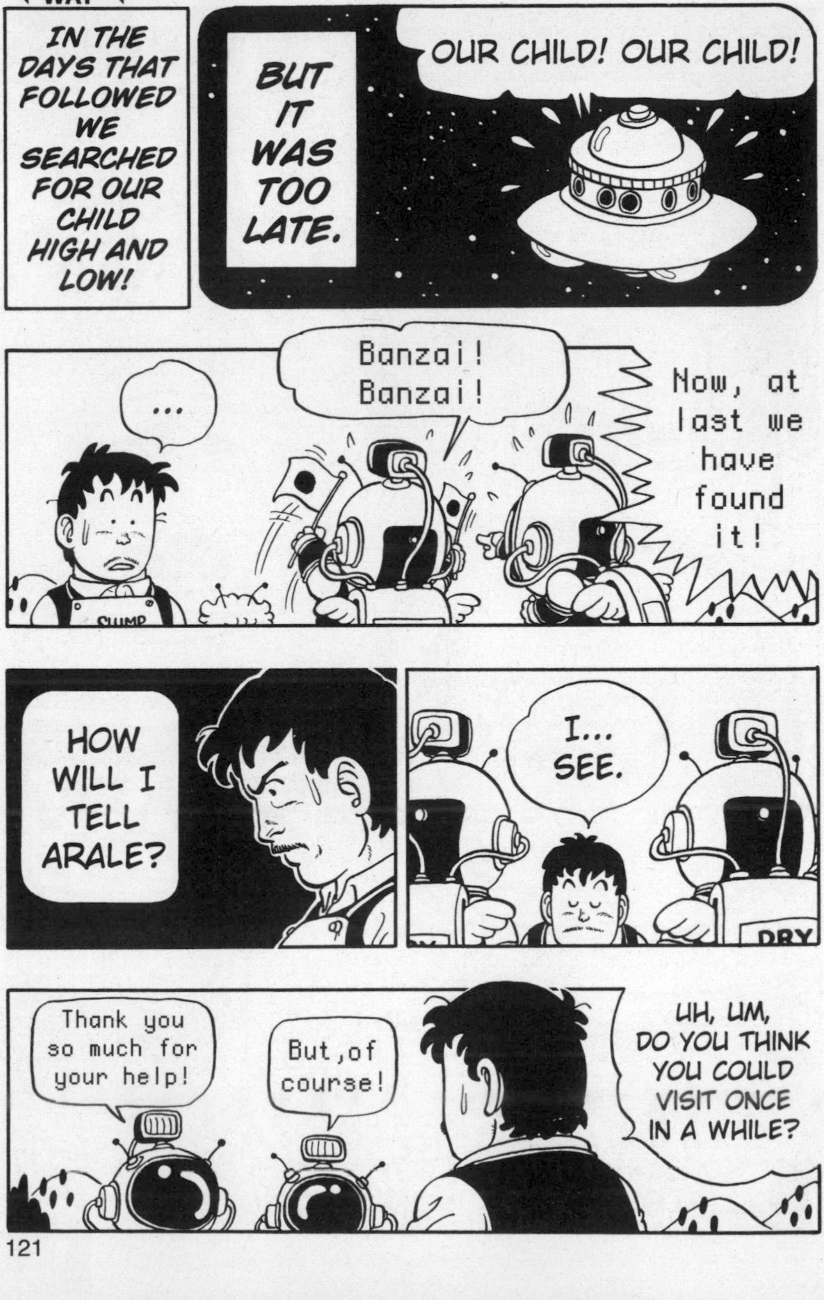
OUR CHILD! OUR CHILD!
BUT IT WAS TOO LATE.
IN THE DAYS THAT FOLLOWED WE SEARCHED FOR OUR CHILD HIGH AND LOW!
Now, at last we have found it!
Banzai! Banzai!
...
I... SEE.
HOW WILL I TELL ARALE?
UH, UM, DO YOU THINK YOU COULD VISIT ONCE IN A WHILE?
But,of course!
Thank you so much for your help!

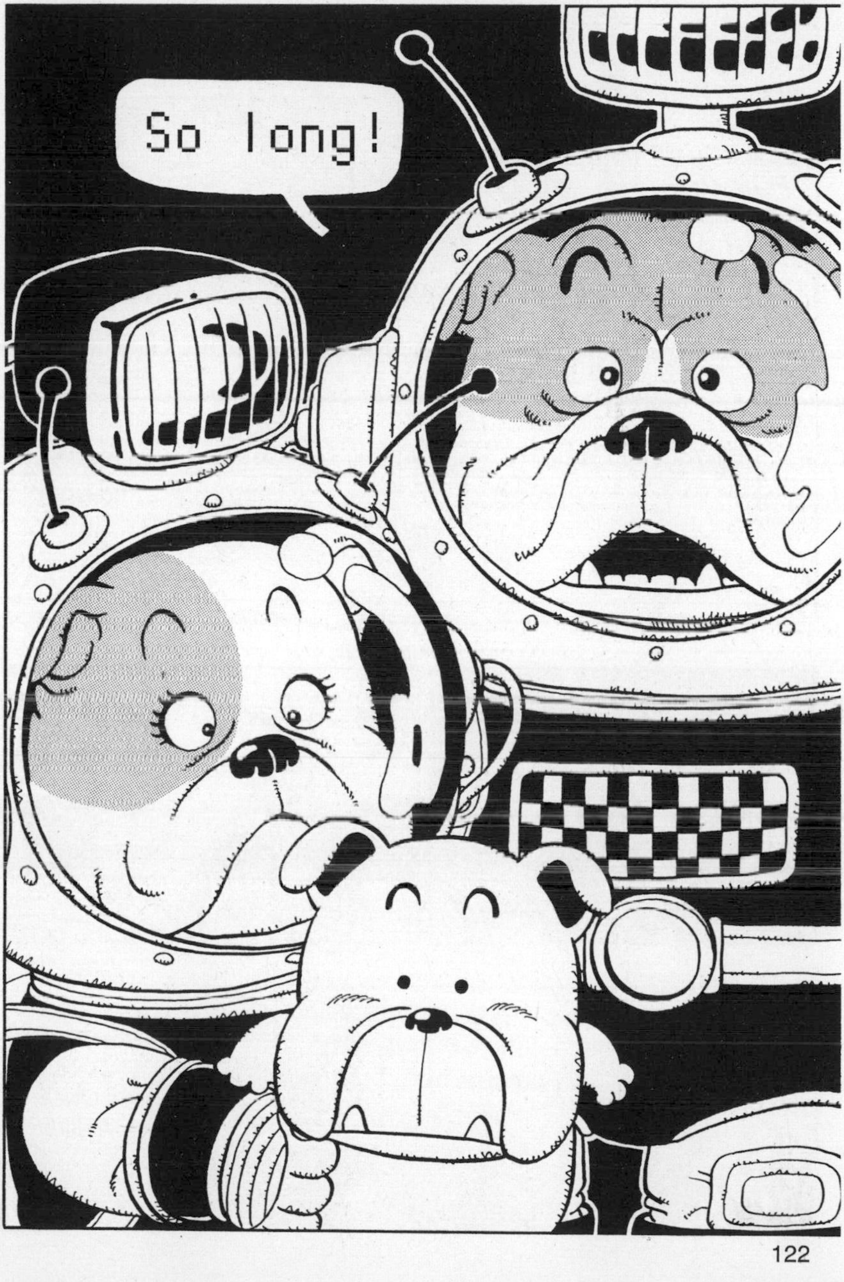
So long!

READ THIS WAY

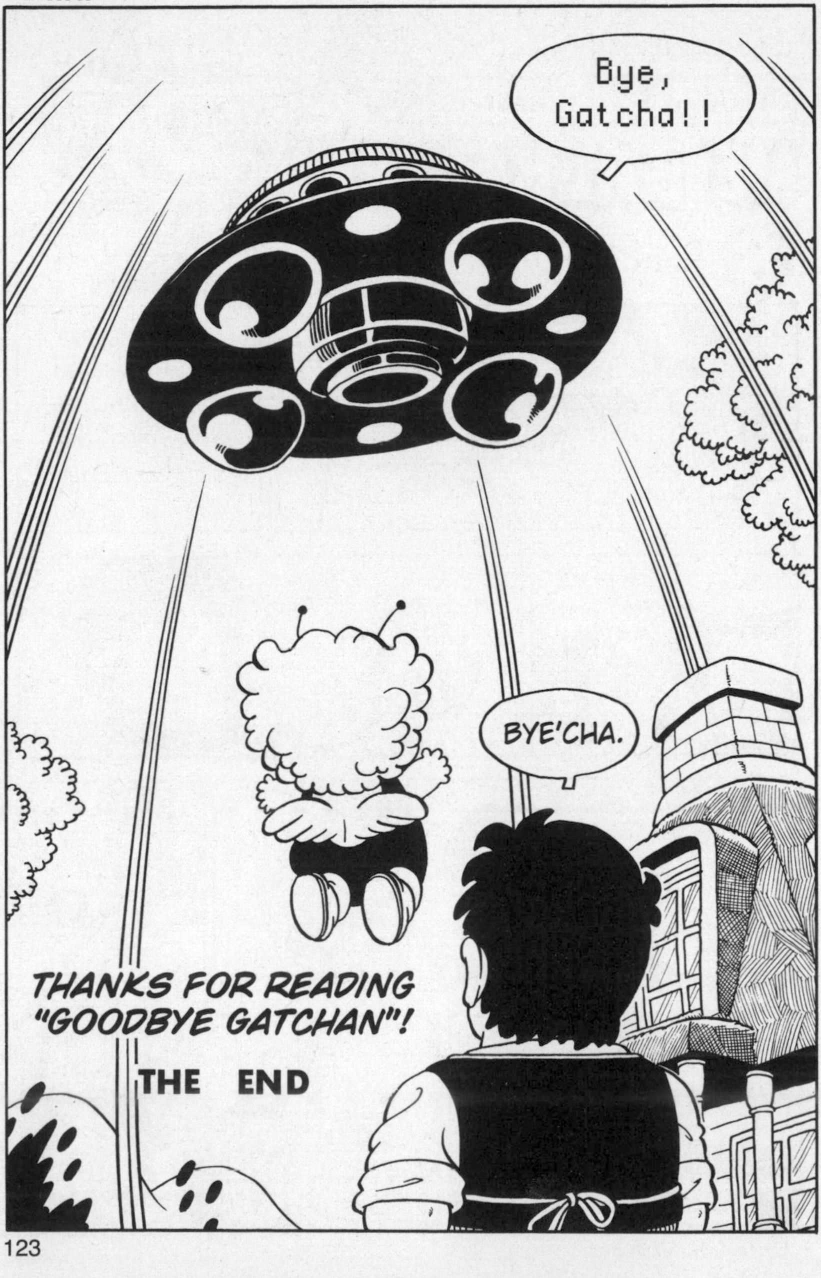
Bye, Gatcha!!
BYE'CHA.
THANKS FOR READING "GOODBYE GATCHAN"!
THE END

The Doodle Version of
The Non-Fiction Theater's
ME BACK THEN
8 Punch-Punch Mashirito

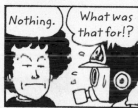

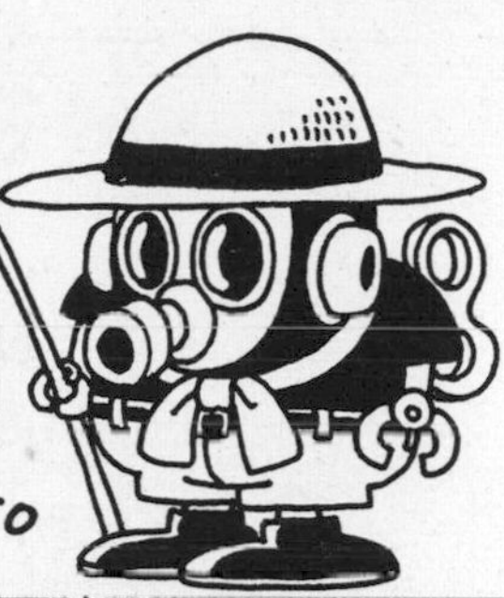

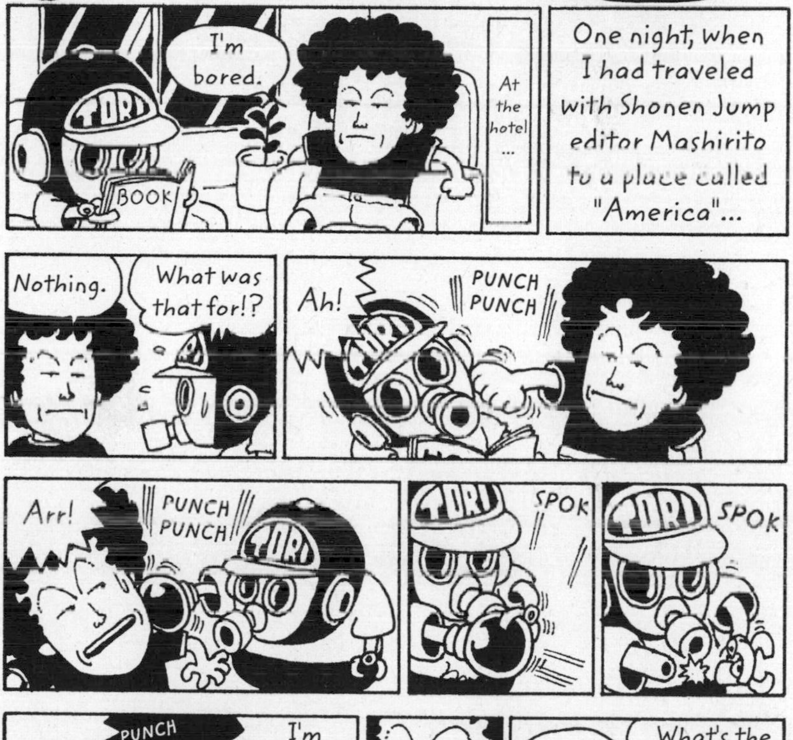

I'm bored.

BOOK

At the hotel...

One night, when I had traveled with Shonen Jump editor Mashirito to a place called "America"...

Nothing.

What was that for!?

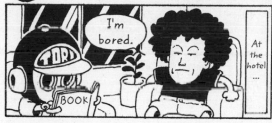

Ah!

PUNCH PUNCH

Arr!

PUNCH PUNCH

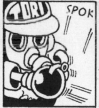

SPOK

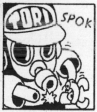

SPOK

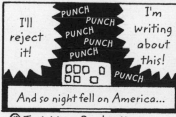

I'll reject it!

PUNCH PUNCH PUNCH PUNCH PUNCH PUNCH

I'm writing about this!

And so night fell on America...

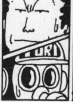

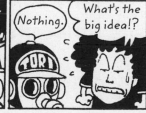

Nothing.

What's the big idea!?

© Torishima Productions

The Big-City Student

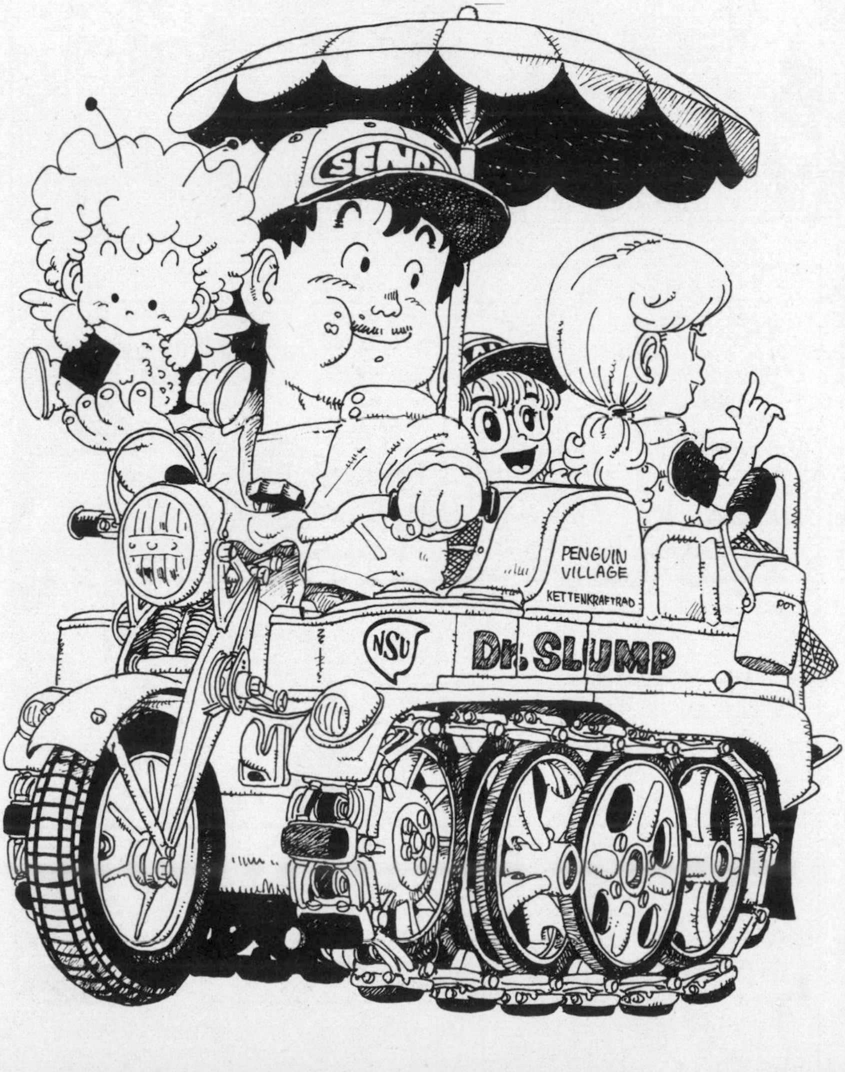
SENDI
PENGUIN
VILLAGE
KETTENKRAFTRAD
NSU
Dr. SLUMP

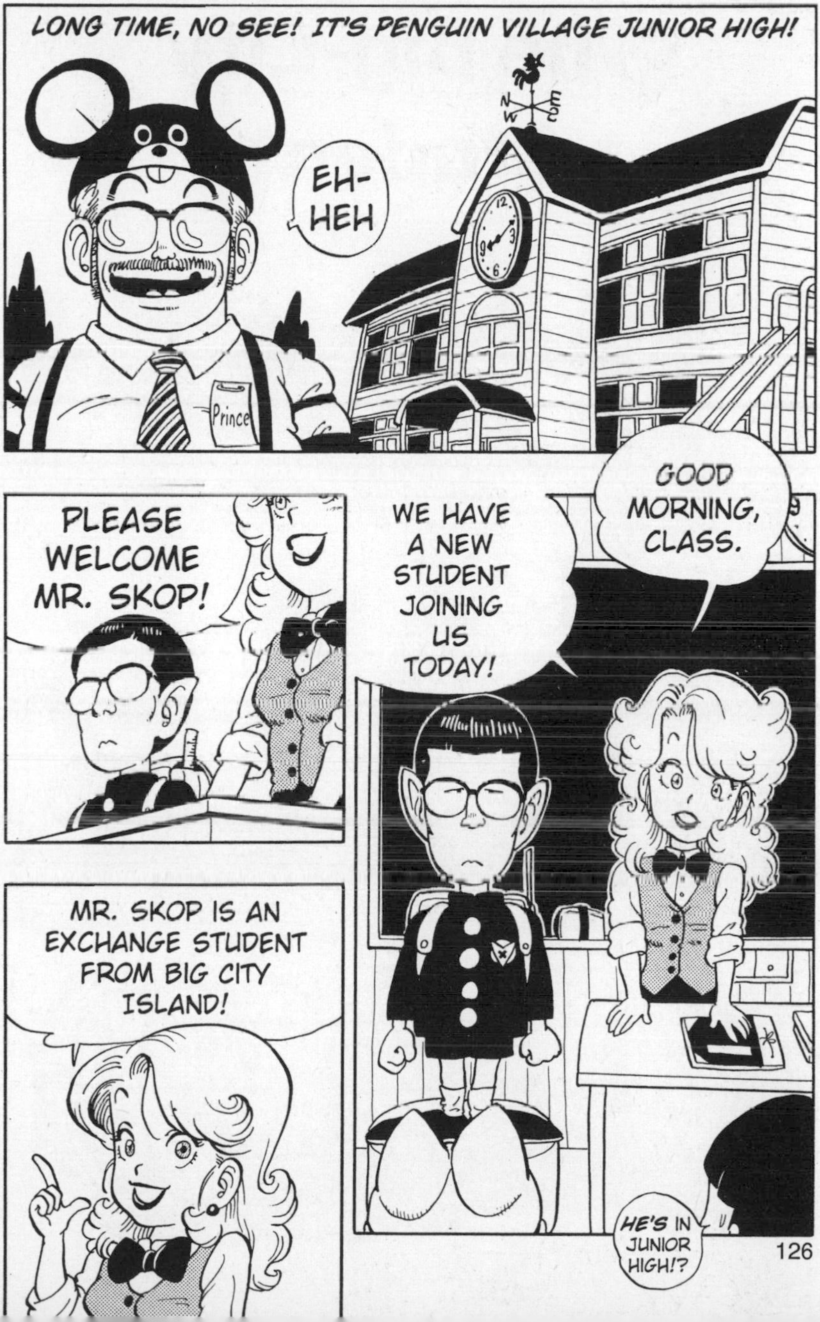
LONG TIME, NO SEE! IT'S PENGUIN VILLAGE JUNIOR HIGH!
EH-HEH
Prince
GOOD MORNING, CLASS.
WE HAVE A NEW STUDENT JOINING US TODAY!
HE'S IN JUNIOR HIGH!?
PLEASE WELCOME MR. SKOP!
MR. SKOP IS AN EXCHANGE STUDENT FROM BIG CITY ISLAND!

READ THIS WAY

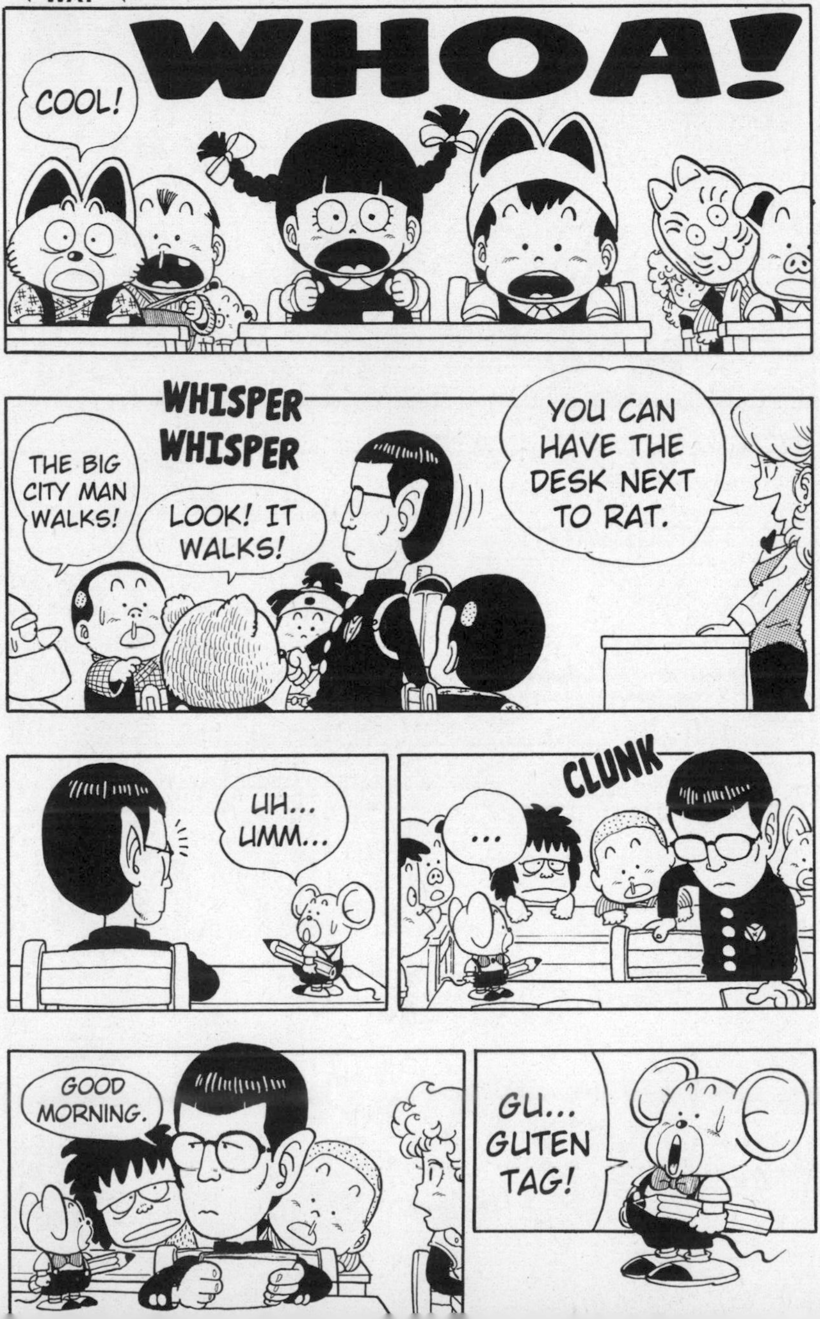
WHOA!
COOL!
YOU CAN HAVE THE DESK NEXT TO RAT.
WHISPER WHISPER
LOOK! IT WALKS!
THE BIG CITY MAN WALKS!
CLUNK
...
UH... UMM...
GU... GUTEN TAG!
GOOD MORNING.

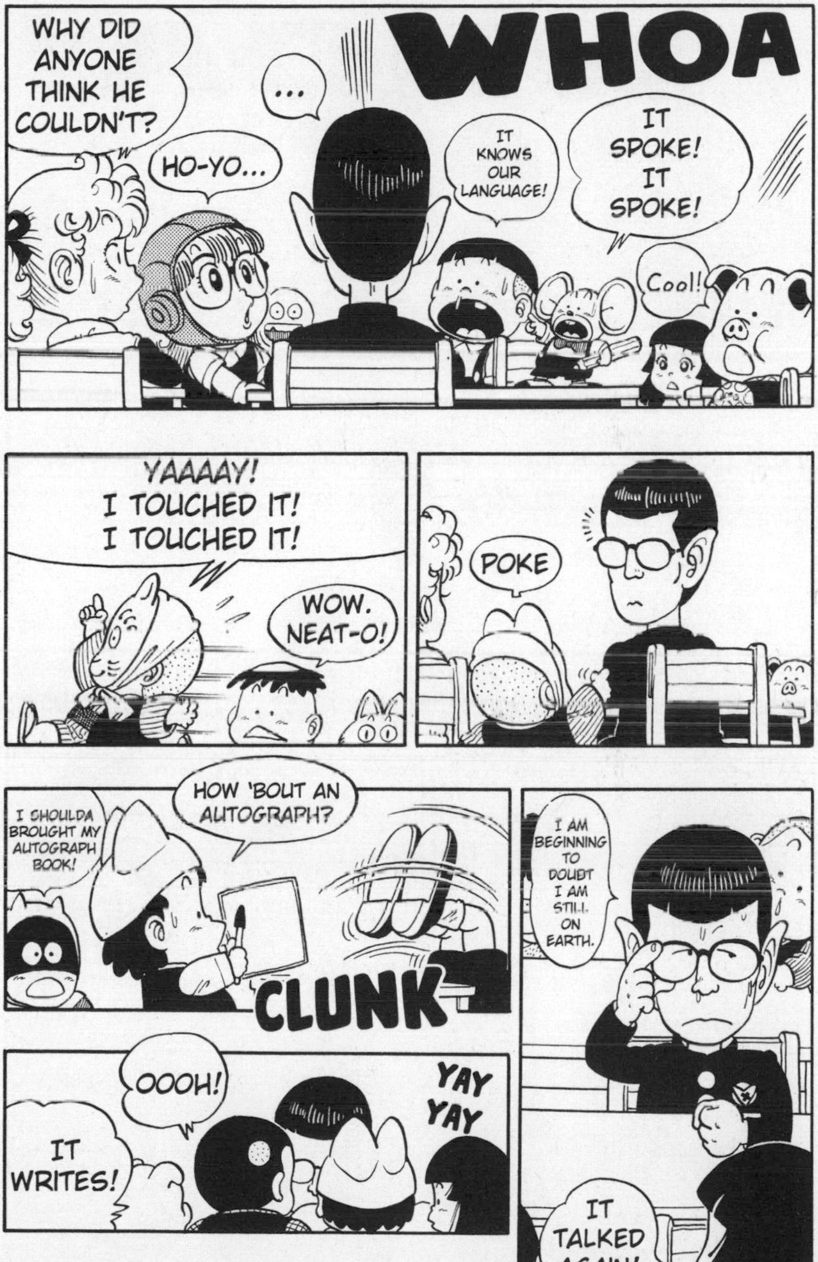
WHOA
IT SPOKE! IT SPOKE!
Cool!
IT KNOWS OUR LANGUAGE!
...
HO-YO...
WHY DID ANYONE THINK HE COULDN'T?
POKE
YAAAAY! I TOUCHED IT! I TOUCHED IT!
WOW. NEAT-O!
I AM BEGINNING TO DOUBT I AM STILL ON EARTH.
HOW 'BOUT AN AUTOGRAPH?
I SHOULDA BROUGHT MY AUTOGRAPH BOOK!
CLUNK
YAY YAY
OOOH!
IT WRITES!
IT TALKED AGAIN!

READ THIS WAY

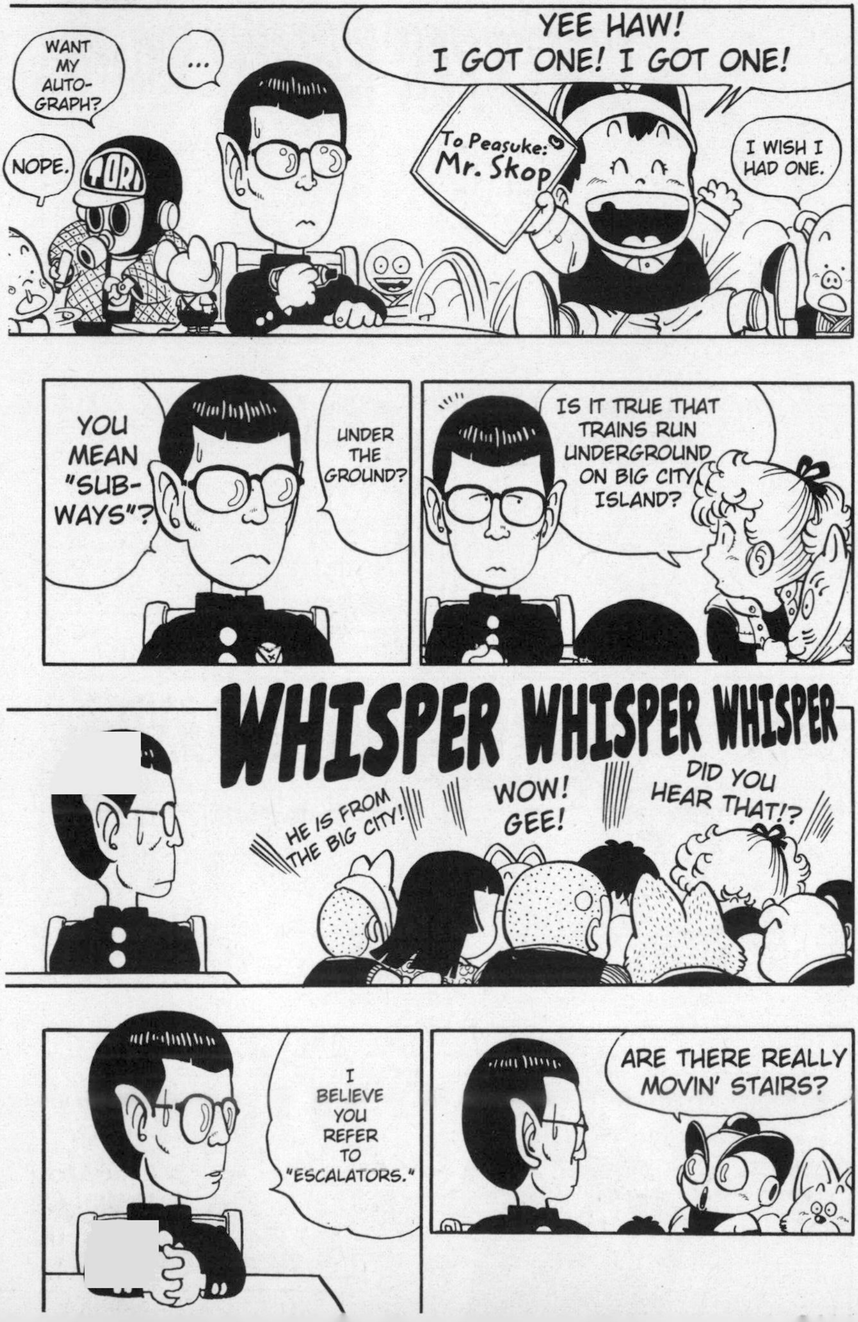
YEE HAW! I GOT ONE! I GOT ONE!
I WISH I HAD ONE.
To Peasuke: Mr. Skop
...
WANT MY AUTO-GRAPH?
NOPE.
IS IT TRUE THAT TRAINS RUN UNDERGROUND ON BIG CITY ISLAND?
UNDER THE GROUND?
YOU MEAN "SUB-WAYS"?
WHISPER WHISPER WHISPER
DID YOU HEAR THAT!?
WOW! GEE!
HE IS FROM THE BIG CITY!
ARE THERE REALLY MOVIN' STAIRS?
I BELIEVE YOU REFER TO "ESCALATORS."

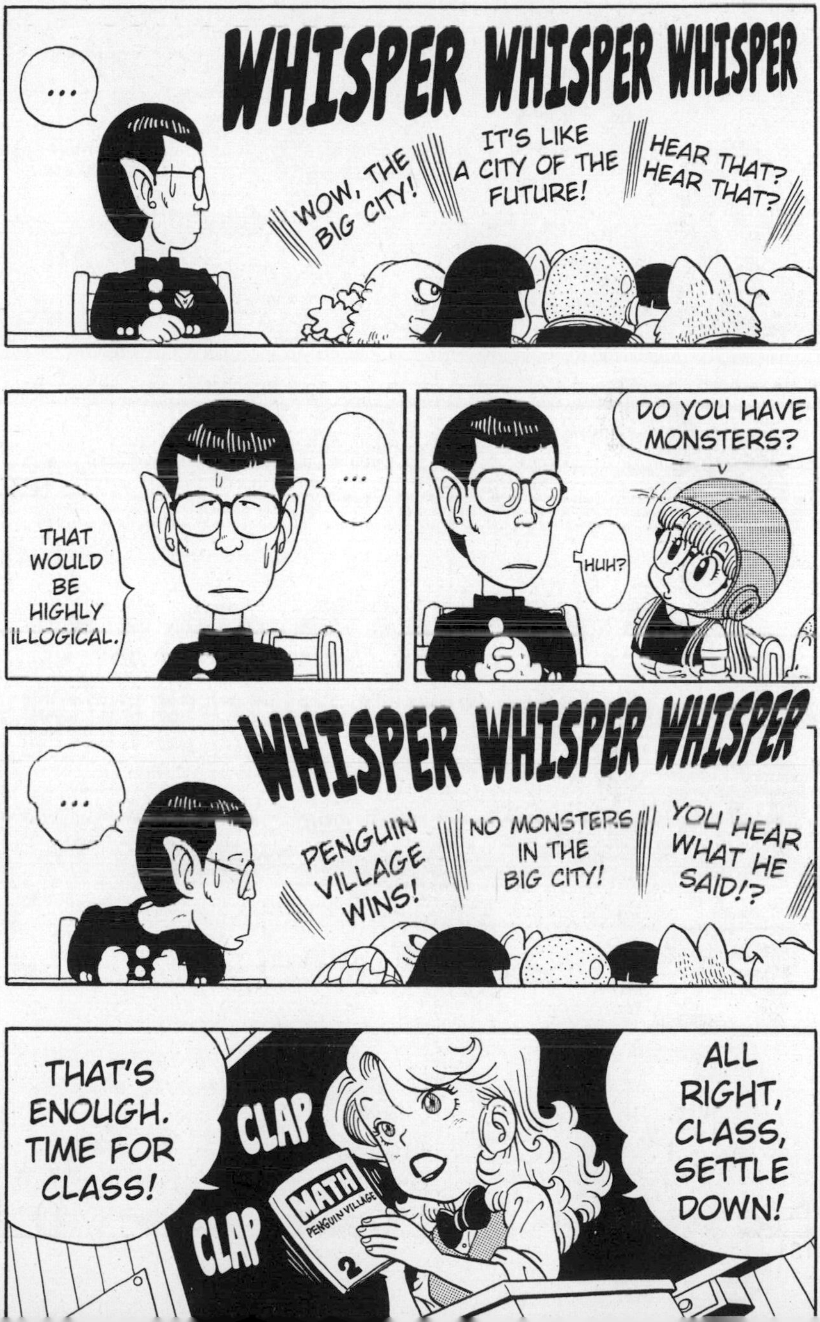
WHISPER WHISPER WHISPER
HEAR THAT? HEAR THAT?
IT'S LIKE A CITY OF THE FUTURE!
WOW, THE BIG CITY!
...
DO YOU HAVE MONSTERS?
HUH?
...
THAT WOULD BE HIGHLY ILLOGICAL.
WHISPER WHISPER WHISPER
YOU HEAR WHAT HE SAID!?
NO MONSTERS IN THE BIG CITY!
PENGUIN VILLAGE WINS!
...
ALL RIGHT, CLASS, SETTLE DOWN!
CLAP
CLAP
MATH
PENGUIN VILLAGE
2
THAT'S ENOUGH. TIME FOR CLASS!

READ THIS WAY

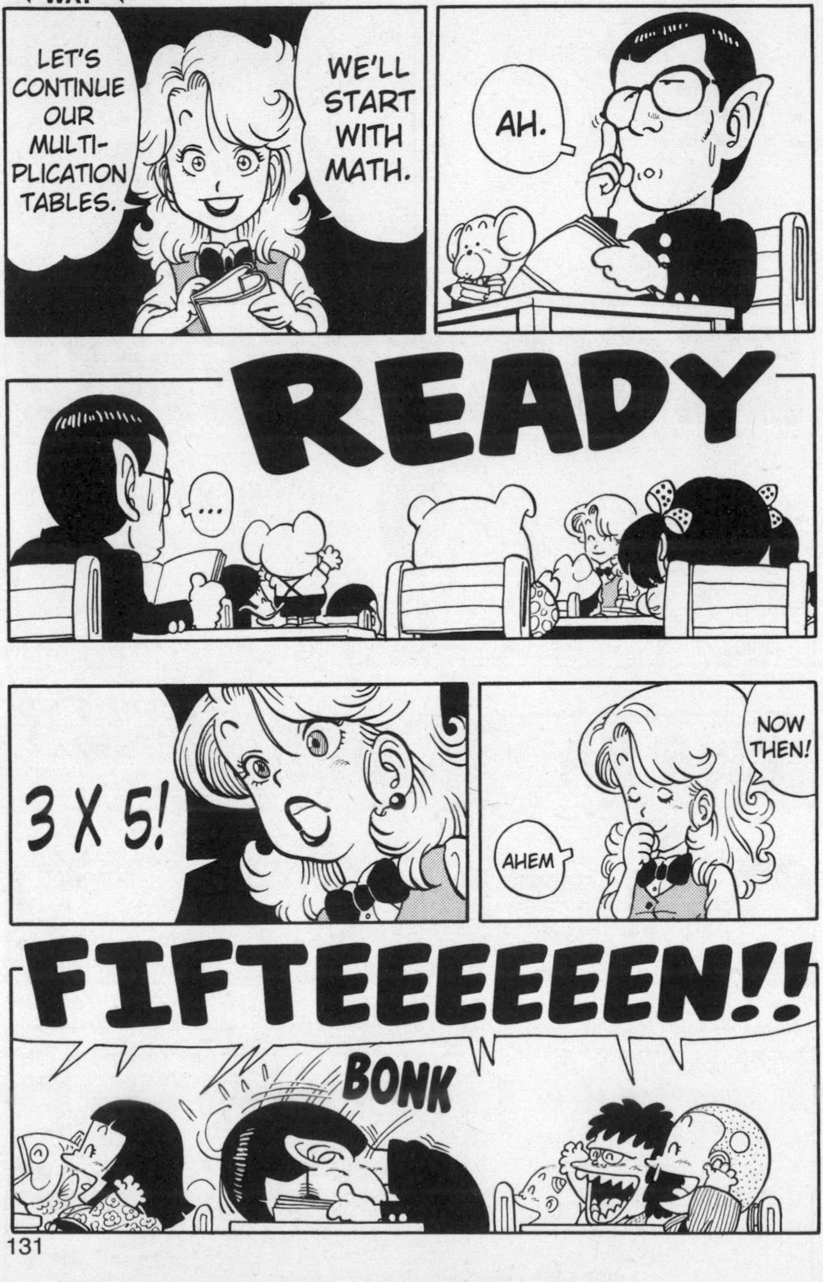
AH.
WE'LL START WITH MATH.
LET'S CONTINUE OUR MULTI-PLICATION TABLES.
READY
...
NOW THEN!
AHEM
3 X 5!
FIFTEEEEEEN!!
BONK

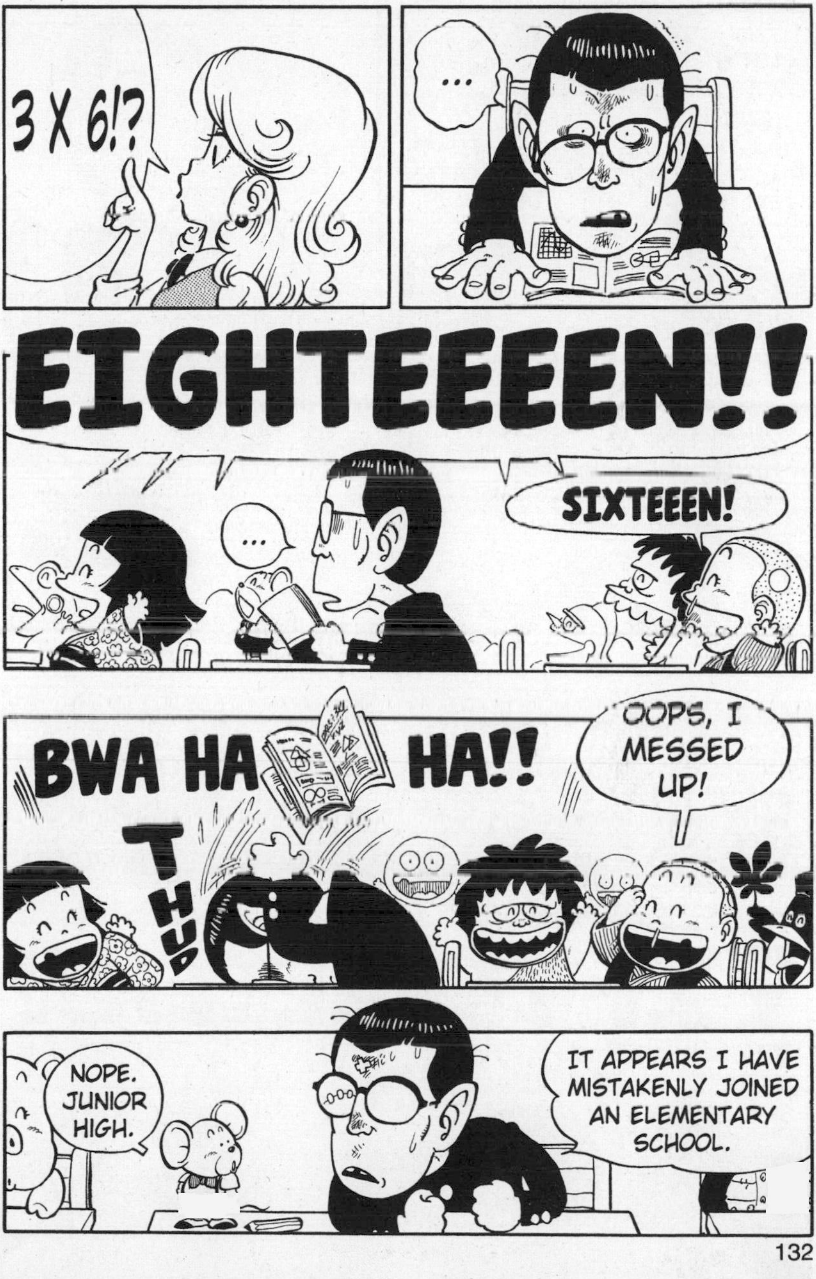
...
3 X 6!?
EIGHTEEEEN!!
SIXTEEEN!
...
OOPS, I MESSED UP!
BWA HA HA!!
THUD
IT APPEARS I HAVE MISTAKENLY JOINED AN ELEMENTARY SCHOOL.
NOPE. JUNIOR HIGH.

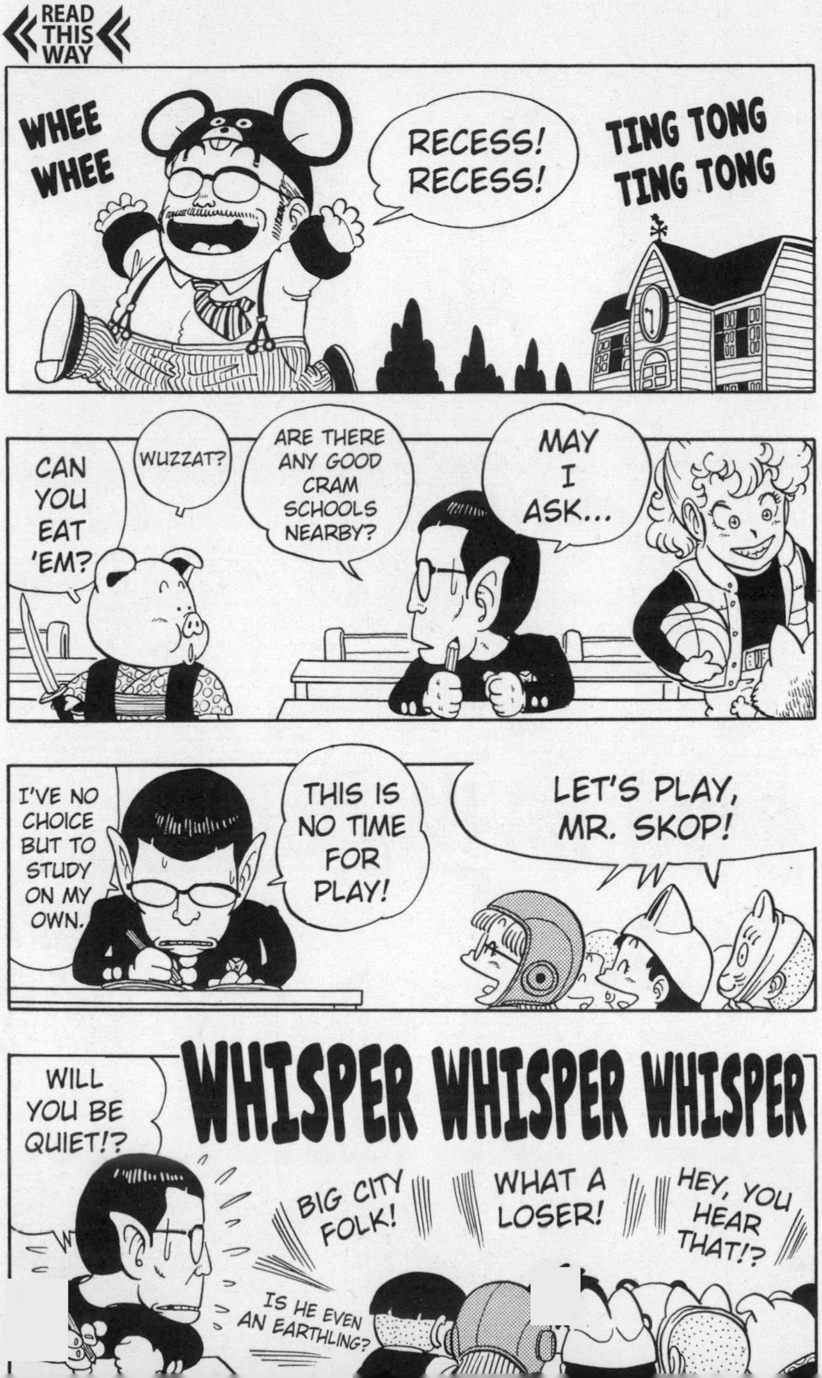
READ THIS WAY
TING TONG TING TONG
RECESS! RECESS!
WHEE WHEE
MAY I ASK...
ARE THERE ANY GOOD CRAM SCHOOLS NEARBY?
WUZZAT?
CAN YOU EAT 'EM?
LET'S PLAY, MR. SKOP!
THIS IS NO TIME FOR PLAY!
I'VE NO CHOICE BUT TO STUDY ON MY OWN.
WHISPER WHISPER WHISPER
HEY, YOU HEAR THAT!?
WHAT A LOSER!
BIG CITY FOLK!
IS HE EVEN AN EARTHLING?
WILL YOU BE QUIET!?

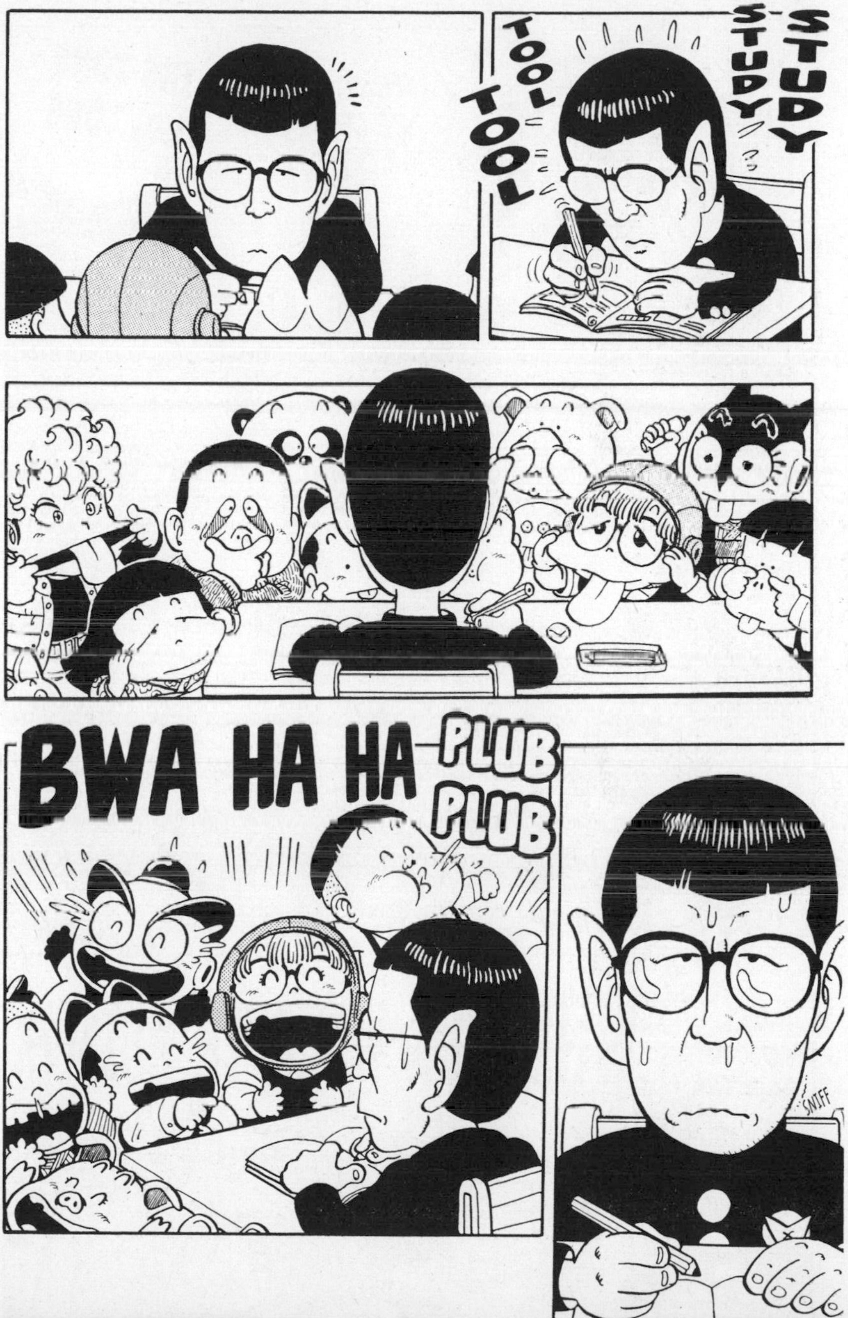
STUDY STUDY
STUDY
TOOL TOOL
TOOL TOOL
SNIFF
BWA HA HA
PLUB PLUB

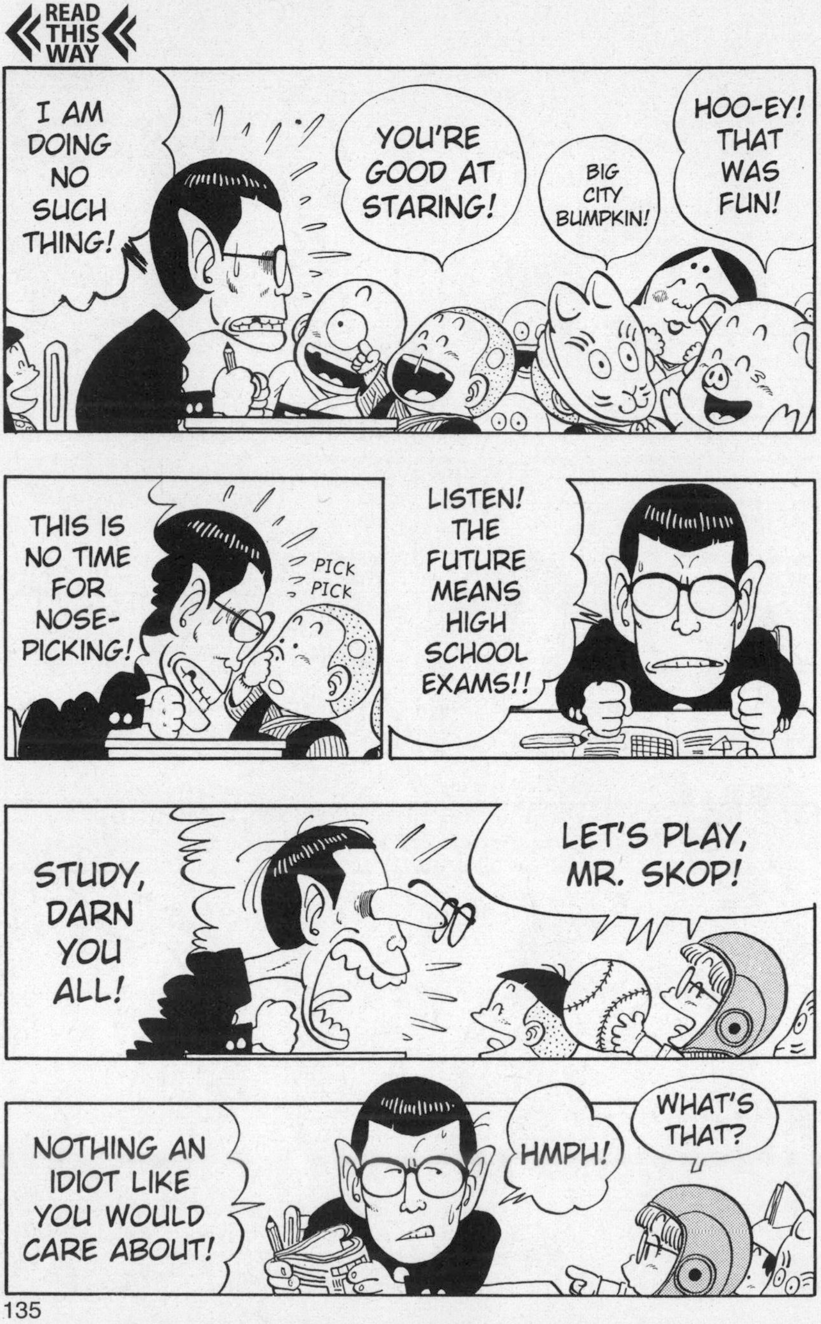
READ THIS WAY
HOO-EY! THAT WAS FUN!
BIG CITY BUMPKIN!
YOU'RE GOOD AT STARING!
I AM DOING NO SUCH THING!
LISTEN! THE FUTURE MEANS HIGH SCHOOL EXAMS!!
PICK PICK
THIS IS NO TIME FOR NOSE-PICKING!
LET'S PLAY, MR. SKOP!
STUDY, DARN YOU ALL!
WHAT'S THAT?
HMPH!
NOTHING AN IDIOT LIKE YOU WOULD CARE ABOUT!

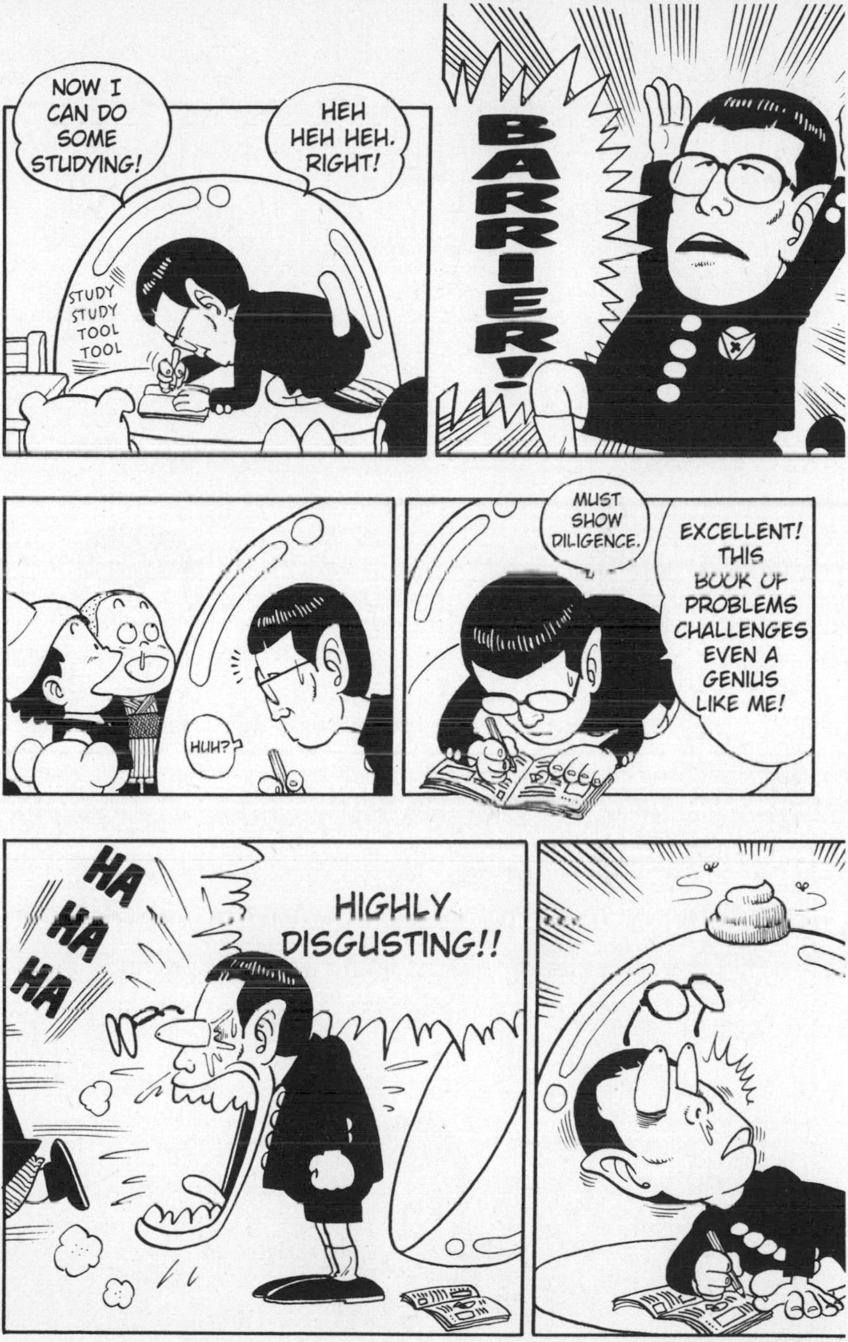
BARRIER!
HEH HEH HEH. RIGHT!
NOW I CAN DO SOME STUDYING!
STUDY STUDY TOOL TOOL
EXCELLENT! THIS BOOK OF PROBLEMS CHALLENGES EVEN A GENIUS LIKE ME!
MUST SHOW DILIGENCE.
HUH?
HIGHLY DISGUSTING!!
HA HA HA

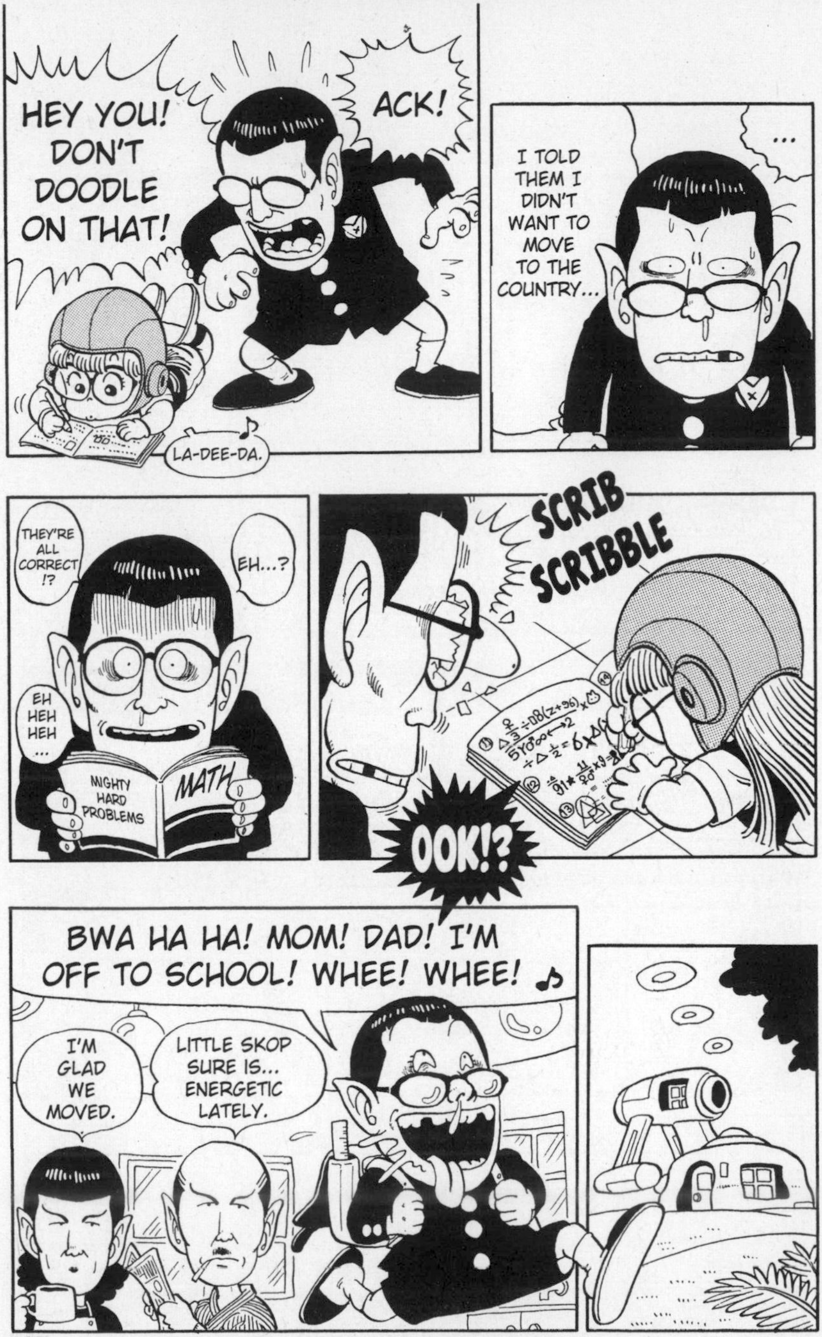
...
I TOLD THEM I DIDN'T WANT TO MOVE TO THE COUNTRY...
ACK!
HEY YOU! DON'T DOODLE ON THAT!
LA-DEE-DA.
SCRIB SCRIBBLE
OOK!?
EH...?
THEY'RE ALL CORRECT!?
EH HEH HEH ...
MATH
MIGHTY HARD PROBLEMS
BWA HA HA! MOM! DAD! I'M OFF TO SCHOOL! WHEE! WHEE!
LITTLE SKOP SURE IS... ENERGETIC LATELY.
I'M GLAD WE MOVED.

The Doodle Version of

The Non-Fiction Theater's

ME BACK THEN

9 Dumb Even in My Dreams?

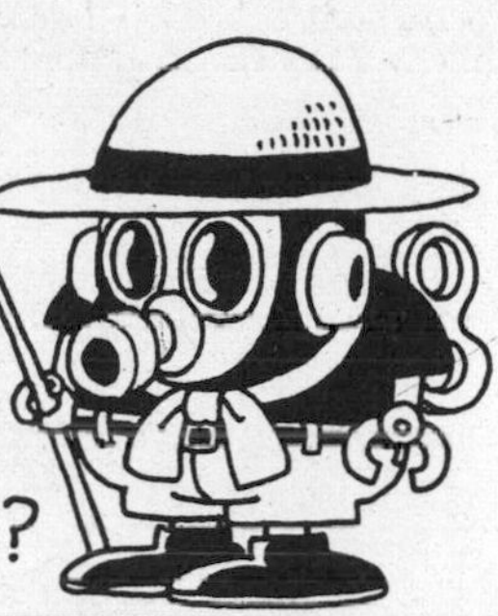

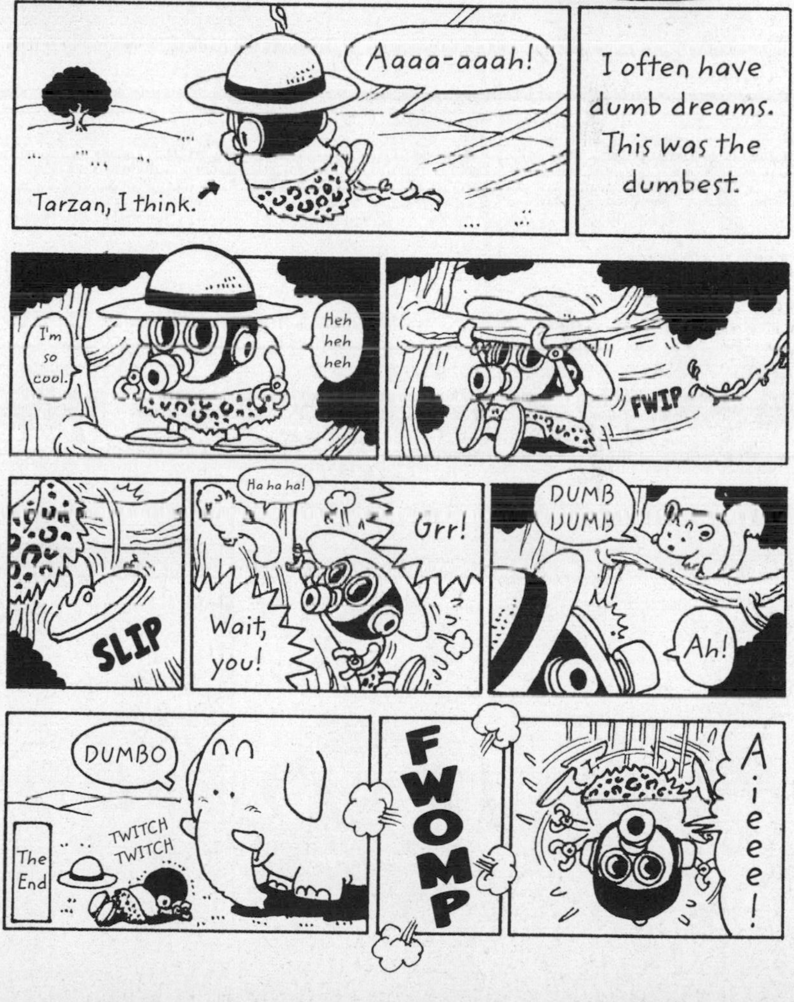
I often have dumb dreams. This was the dumbest.
Aaaa-aaah!
Tarzan, I think.
FWIP
Heh heh heh
I'm so cool.
DUMB DUMB
Ah!
Ha ha ha!
Grr!
Wait, you!
SLIP
Aieee!
FWOMP
DUMBO
TWITCH TWITCH
The End

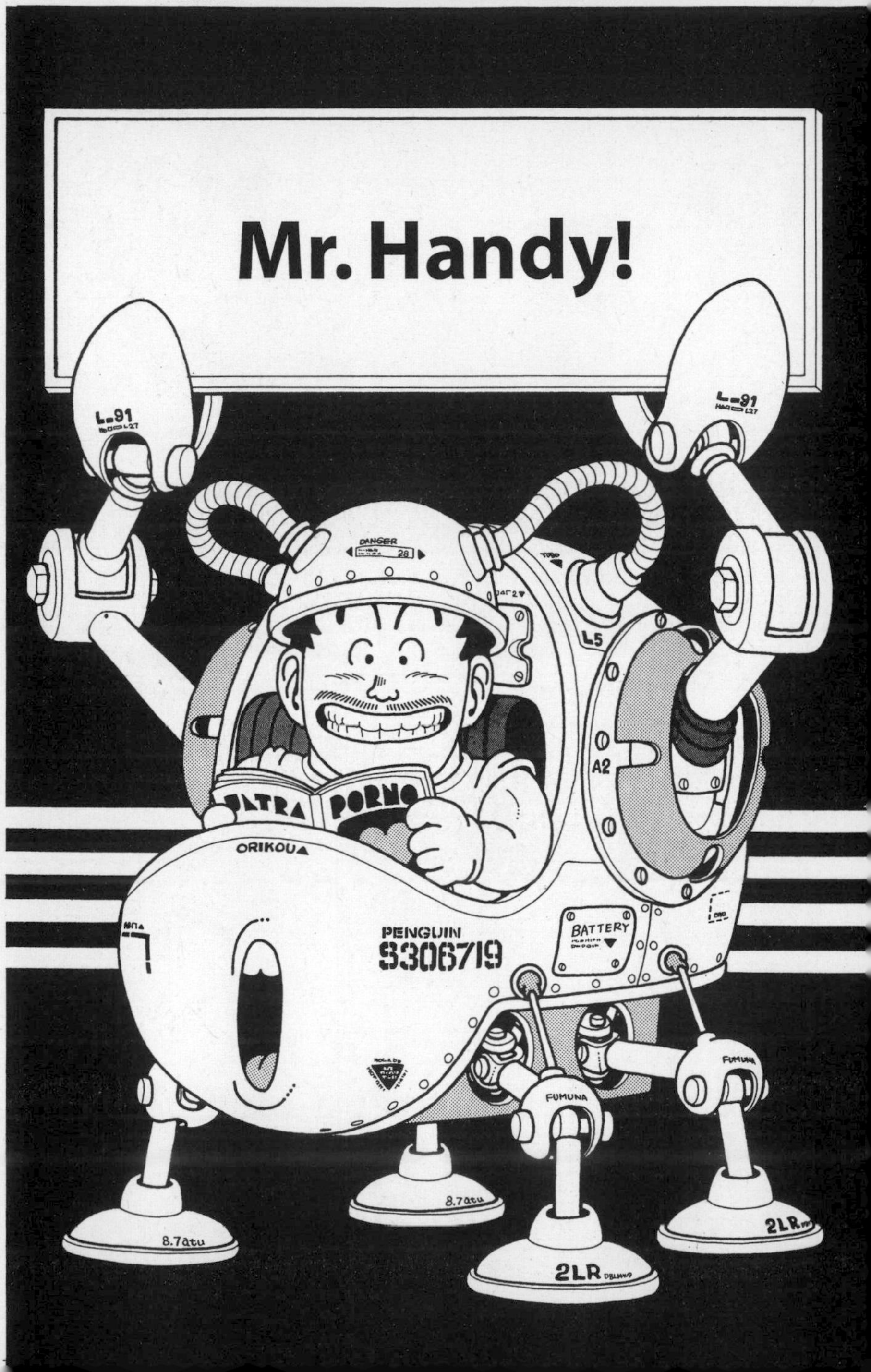
Mr. Handy!
L-91
L-91
DANGER
28
L5
A2
PORNO
ORIKOU
PENGUIN
S306719
BATTERY
FUMUNA
FUMUNA
8.7atu
8.7atu
2LR
2LR

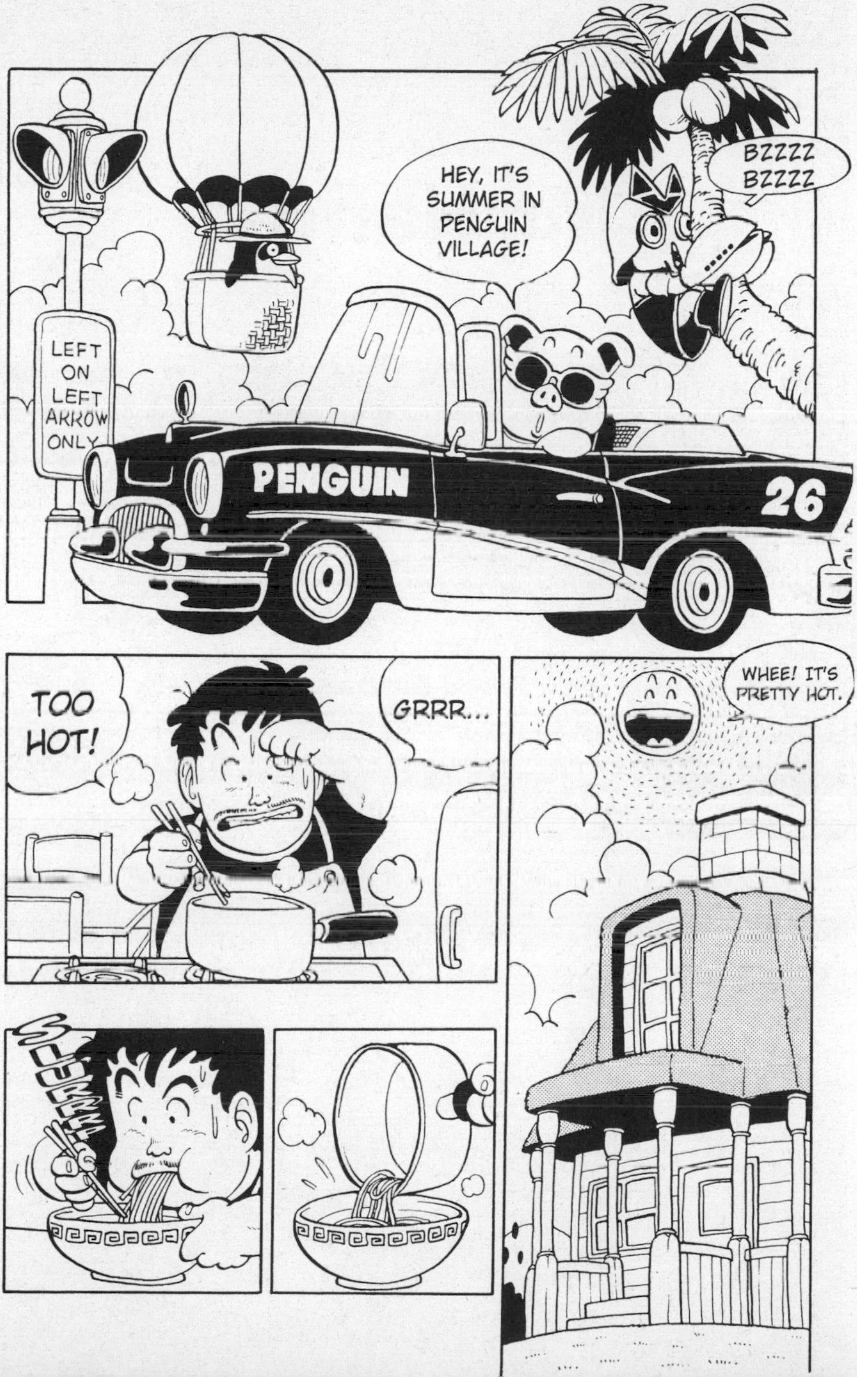
BZZZZ BZZZZ
HEY, IT'S SUMMER IN PENGUIN VILLAGE!
PENGUIN
26
LEFT ON LEFT ARROW ONLY
WHEE! IT'S PRETTY HOT.
GRRR...
TOO HOT!

READ THIS WAY

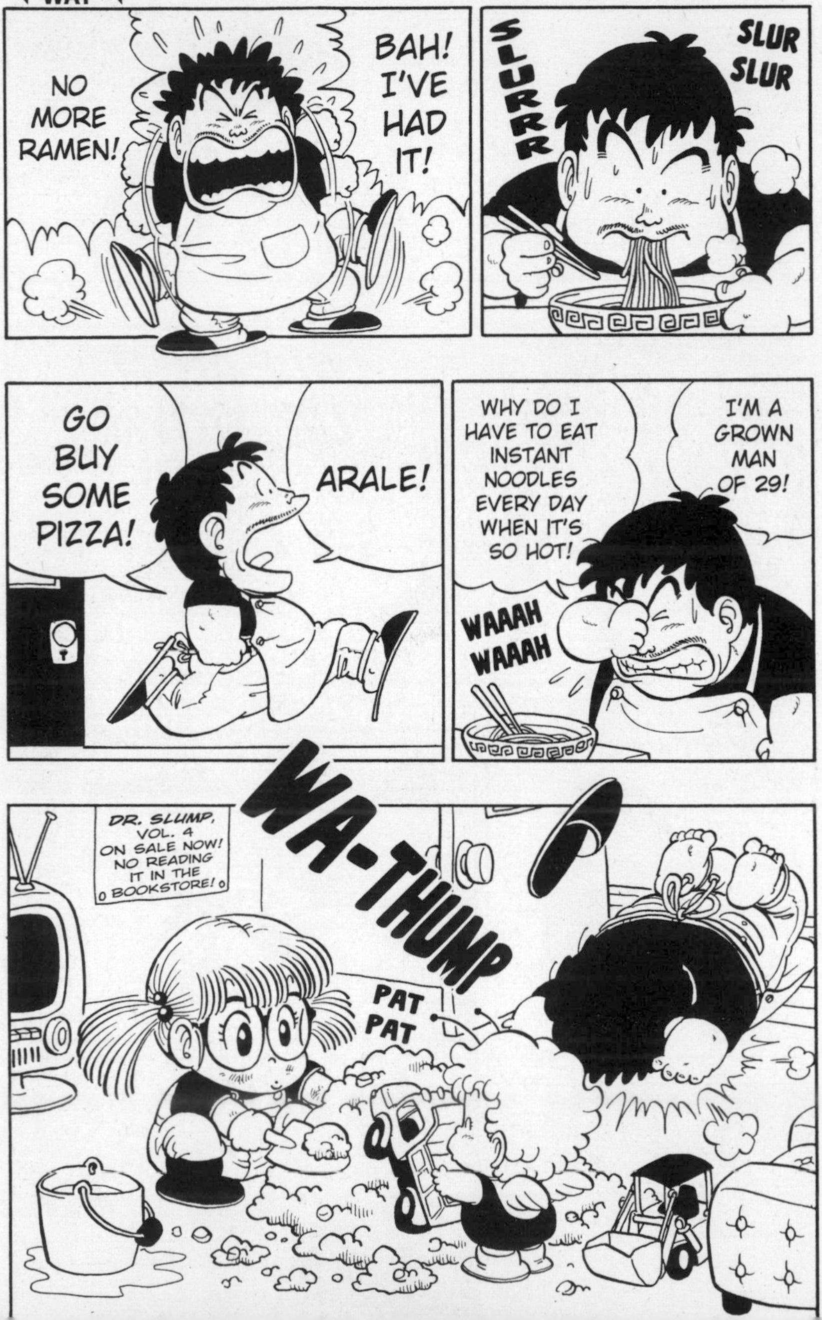

SLURRR
SLUR SLUR
BAH! I'VE HAD IT!
NO MORE RAMEN!
I'M A GROWN MAN OF 29!
WHY DO I HAVE TO EAT INSTANT NOODLES EVERY DAY WHEN IT'S SO HOT!
WAAAH WAAAH
ARALE!
GO BUY SOME PIZZA!
WA-THUMP
DR. SLUMP, VOL. 4 ON SALE NOW! NO READING IT IN THE BOOKSTORE!
PAT PAT

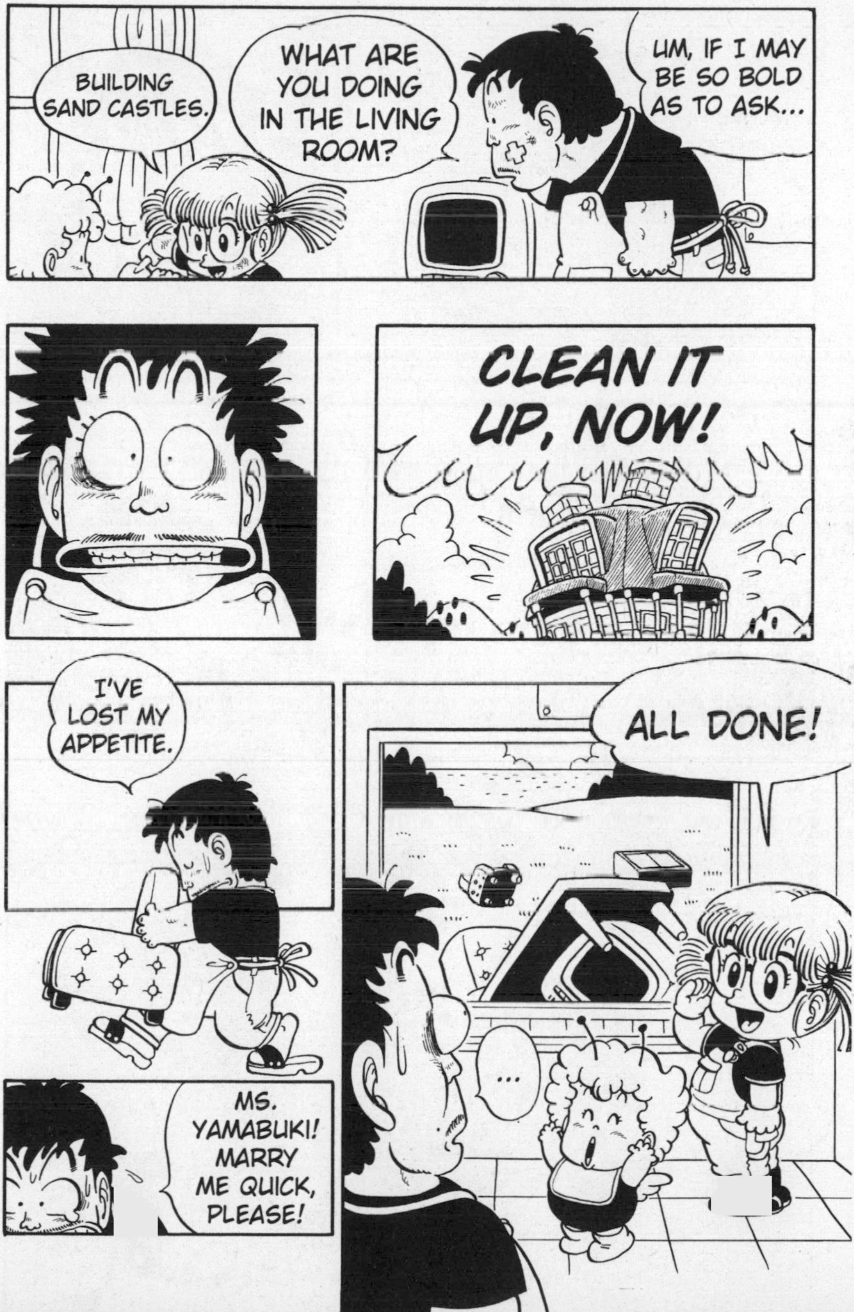
UM, IF I MAY BE SO BOLD AS TO ASK...
WHAT ARE YOU DOING IN THE LIVING ROOM?
BUILDING SAND CASTLES.
CLEAN IT UP, NOW!
ALL DONE!
...
I'VE LOST MY APPETITE.
MS. YAMABUKI! MARRY ME QUICK, PLEASE!

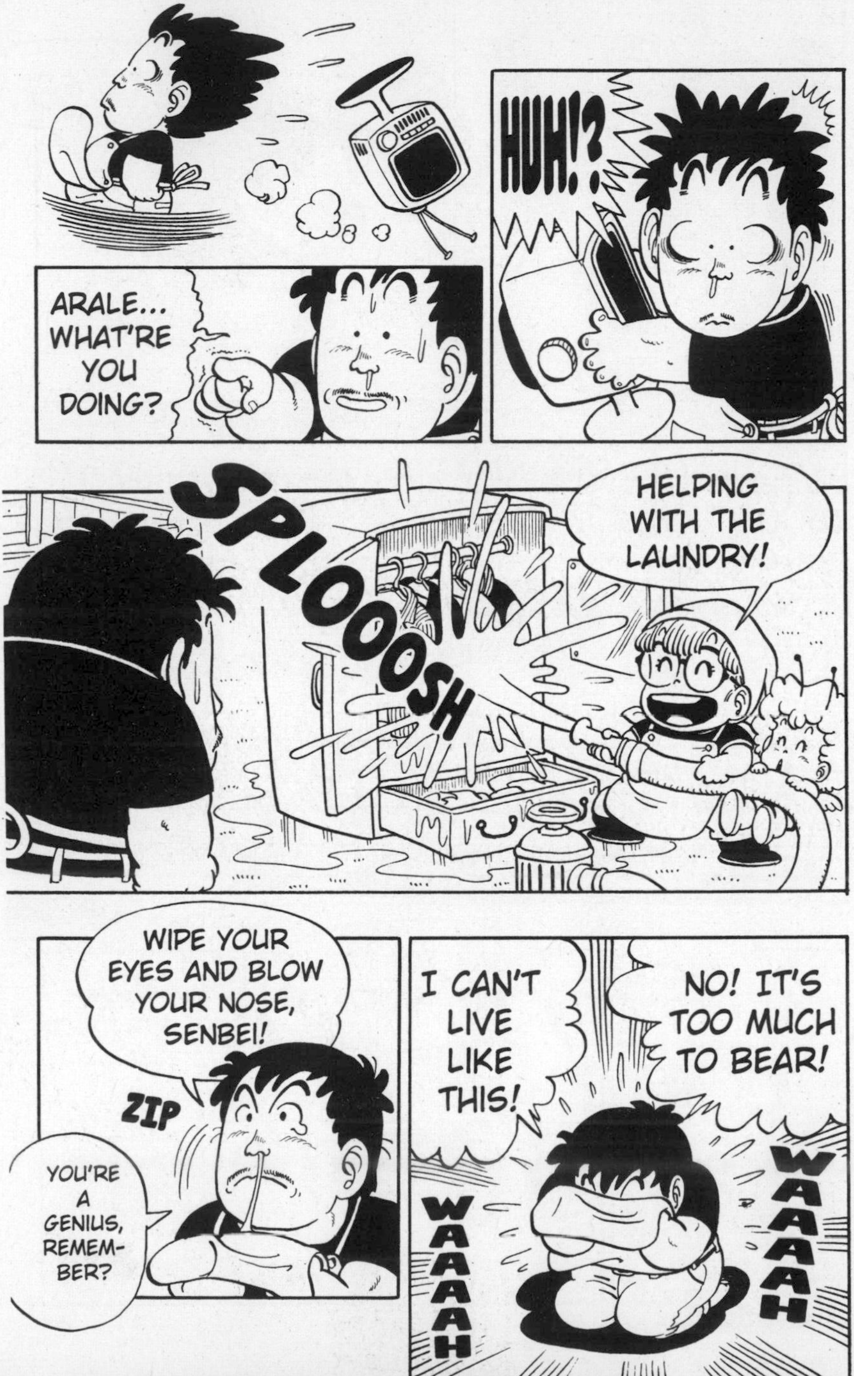
HUH!?
ARALE... WHAT'RE YOU DOING?
HELPING WITH THE LAUNDRY!
SPLOOOSH
NO! IT'S TOO MUCH TO BEAR!
I CAN'T LIVE LIKE THIS!
WAAAAAH
WAAAAAH
WIPE YOUR EYES AND BLOW YOUR NOSE, SENBEI!
ZIP
YOU'RE A GENIUS, REMEMBER-BER?

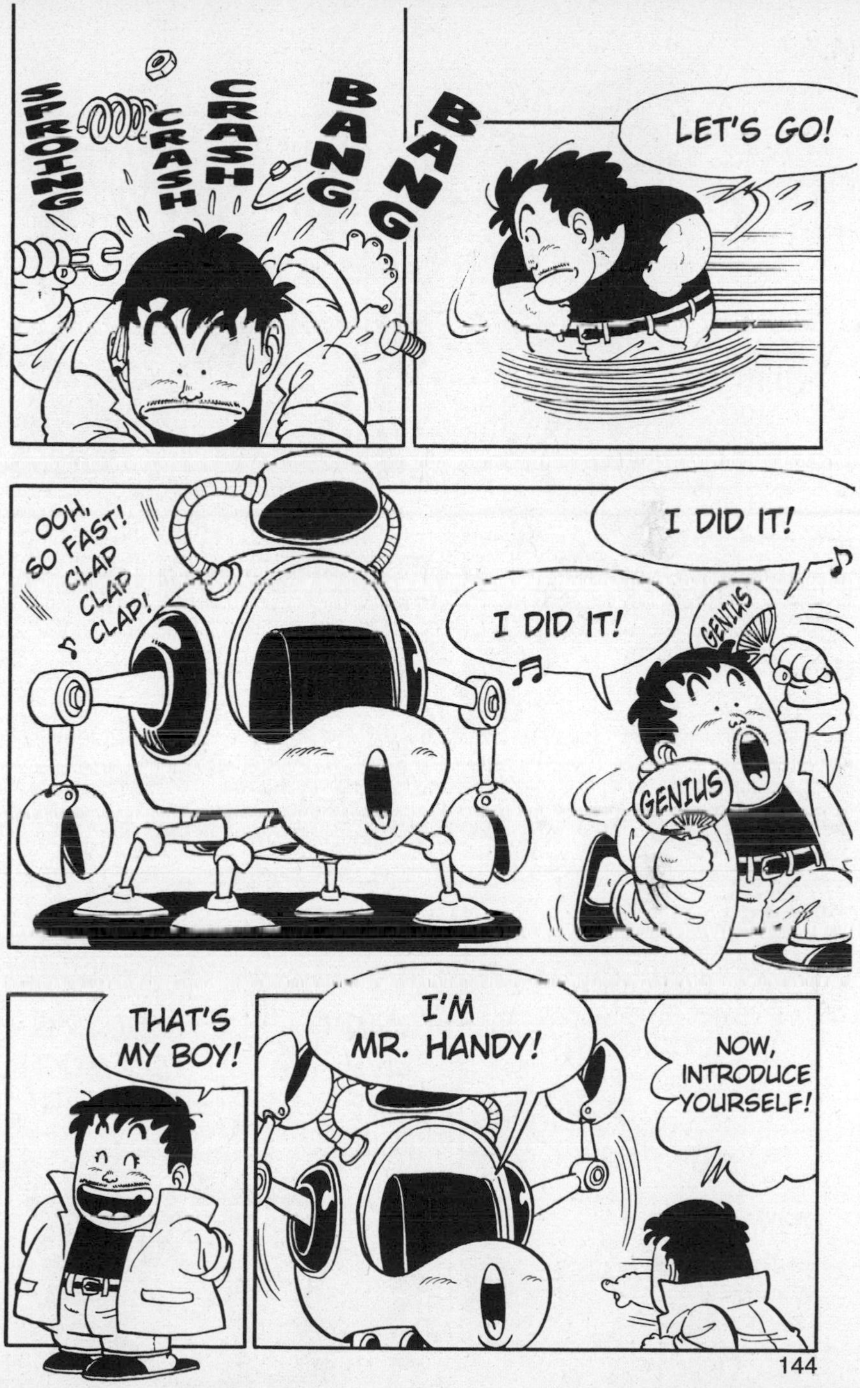
LET'S GO!
BANG
BANG
CRASH
CRASH
SPROING
I DID IT!
GENIUS
I DID IT!
GENIUS
OOH, SO FAST! CLAP CLAP CLAP!
NOW, INTRODUCE YOURSELF!
I'M MR. HANDY!
THAT'S MY BOY!

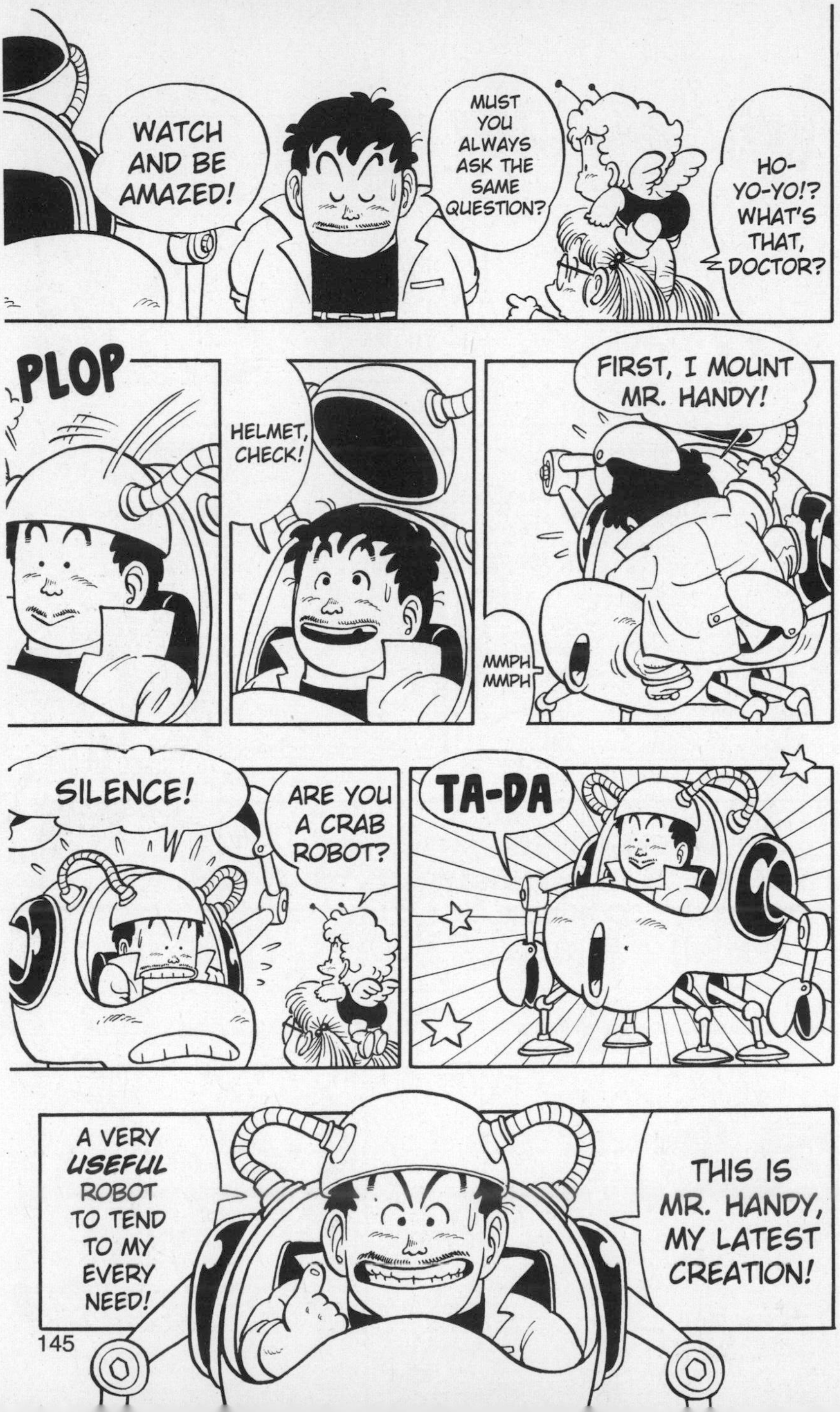
HO-YO-YO!? WHAT'S THAT, DOCTOR?
MUST YOU ALWAYS ASK THE SAME QUESTION?
WATCH AND BE AMAZED!
FIRST, I MOUNT MR. HANDY!
MMPH MMPH
HELMET, CHECK!
PLOP
TA-DA
ARE YOU A CRAB ROBOT?
SILENCE!
THIS IS MR. HANDY, MY LATEST CREATION!
A VERY *USEFUL* ROBOT TO TEND TO MY EVERY NEED!

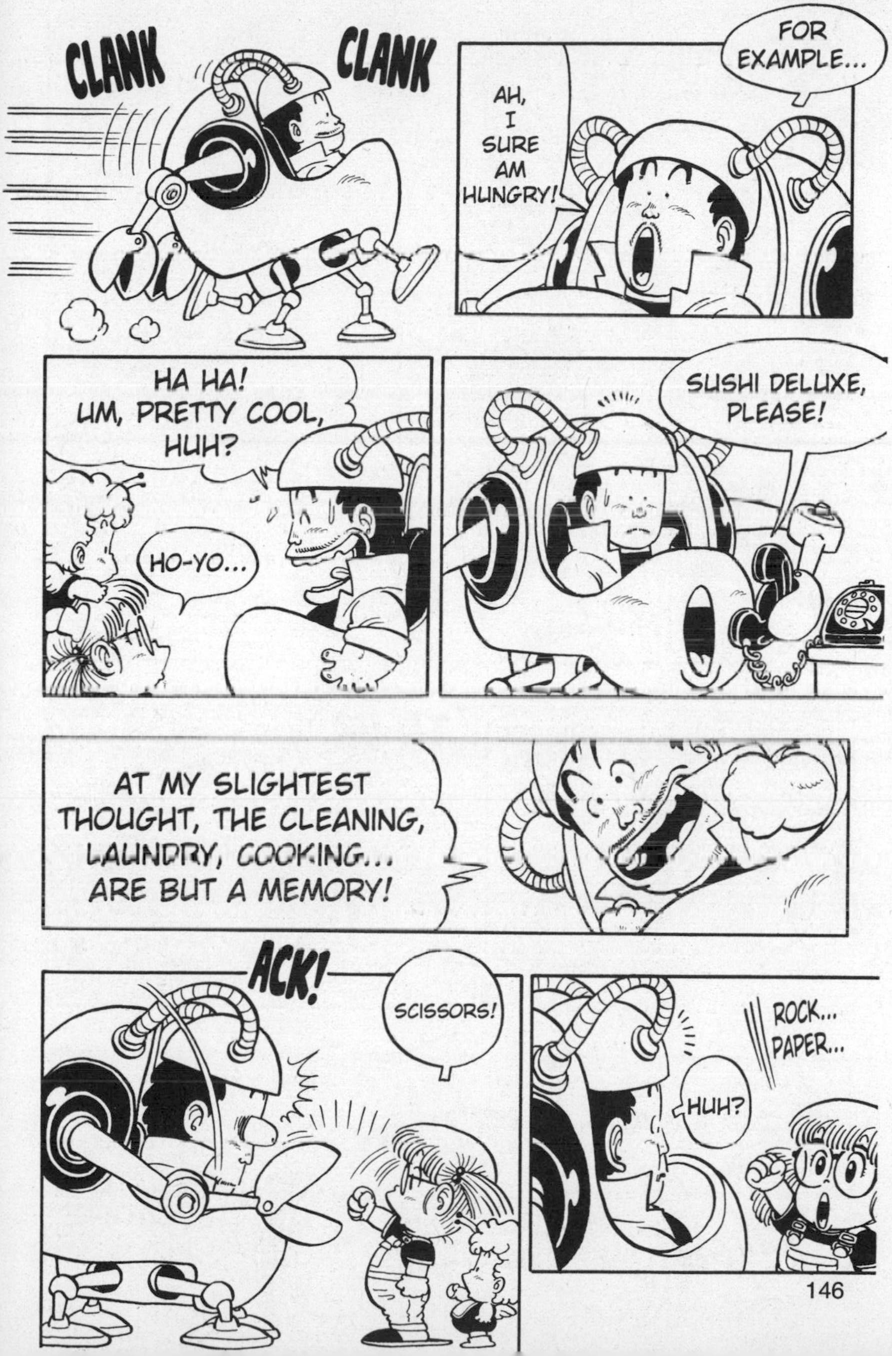
FOR EXAMPLE...
AH, I SURE AM HUNGRY!
CLANK
CLANK
SUSHI DELUXE, PLEASE!
HA HA! UM, PRETTY COOL, HUH?
HO-YO...
AT MY SLIGHTEST THOUGHT, THE CLEANING, LAUNDRY, COOKING... ARE BUT A MEMORY!
ROCK... PAPER...
HUH?
SCISSORS!
ACK!

READ THIS WAY

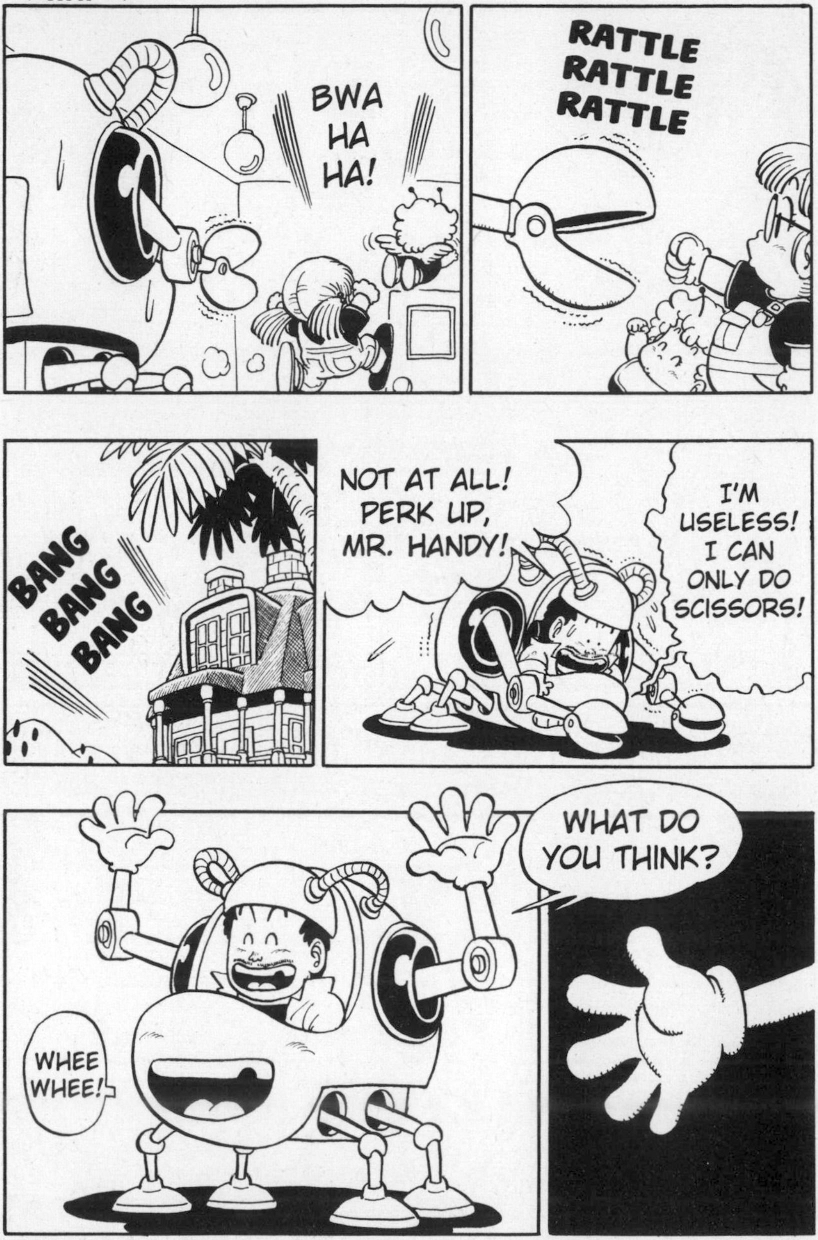

RATTLE RATTLE RATTLE
BWA HA HA!
I'M USELESS! I CAN ONLY DO SCISSORS!
NOT AT ALL! PERK UP, MR. HANDY!
BANG BANG BANG
WHAT DO YOU THINK?
WHEE WHEE!

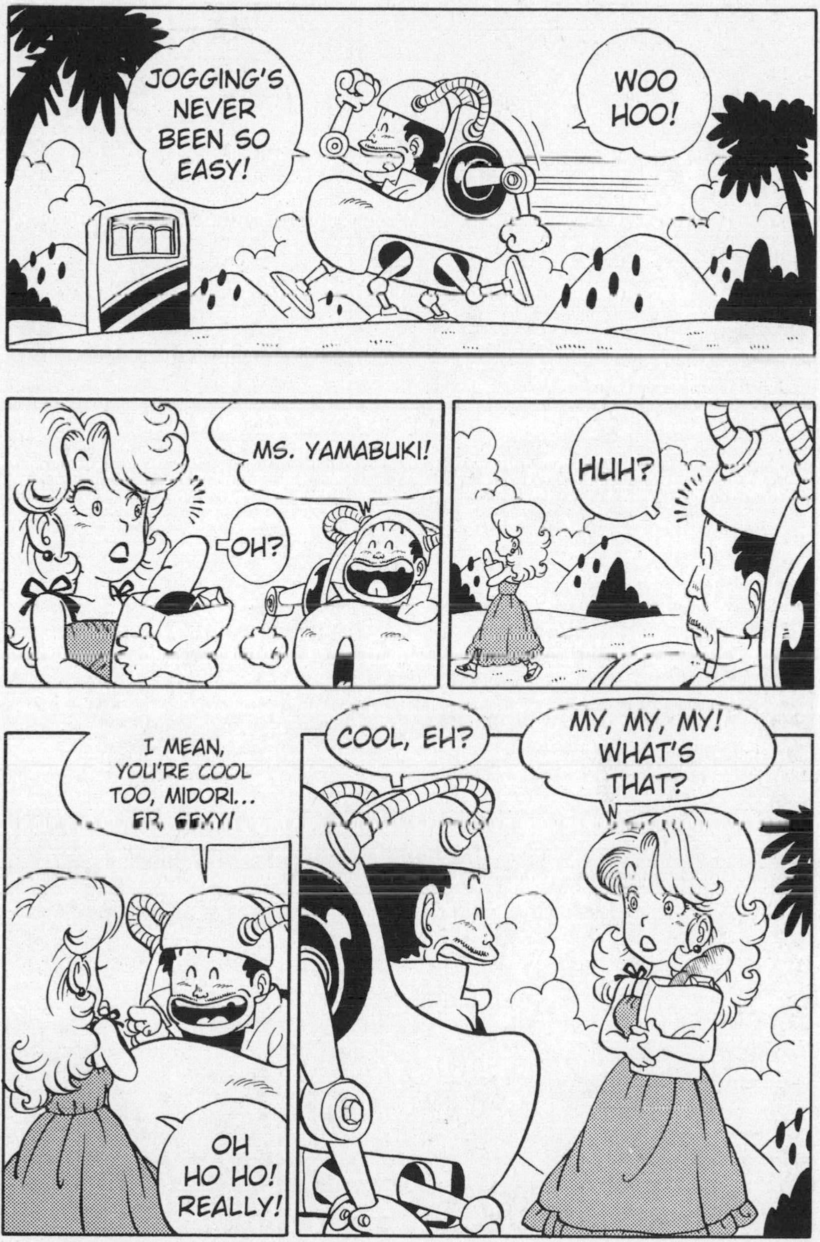

WOO HOO!
JOGGING'S NEVER BEEN SO EASY!
HUH?
MS. YAMABUKI!
OH?
MY, MY, MY! WHAT'S THAT?
COOL, EH?
I MEAN, YOU'RE COOL TOO, MIDORI... ER, SEXY!
OH HO HO! REALLY!

READ THIS WAY

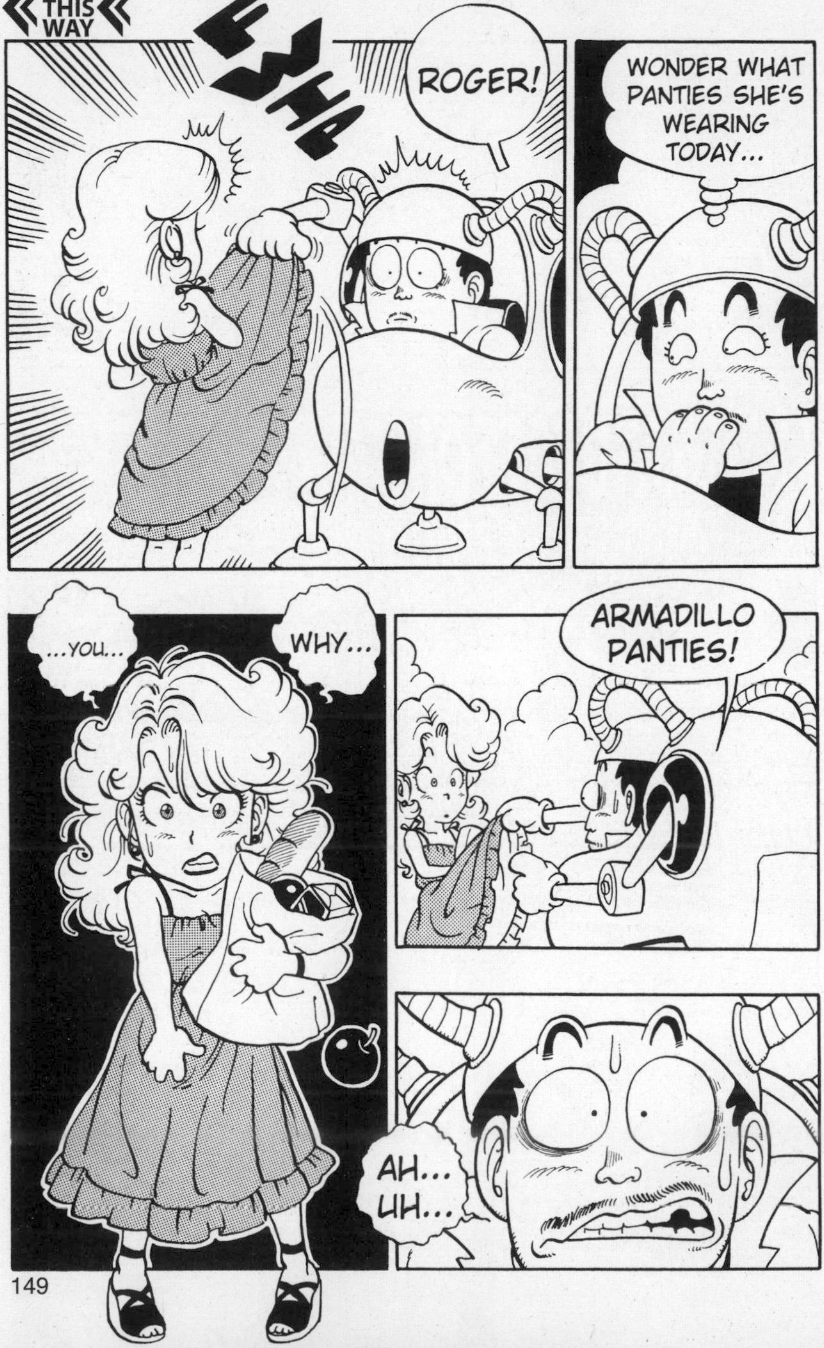

WONDER WHAT PANTIES SHE'S WEARING TODAY...
ROGER!
FWHA
ARMADILLO PANTIES!
AH... UH...
WHY...
...YOU...

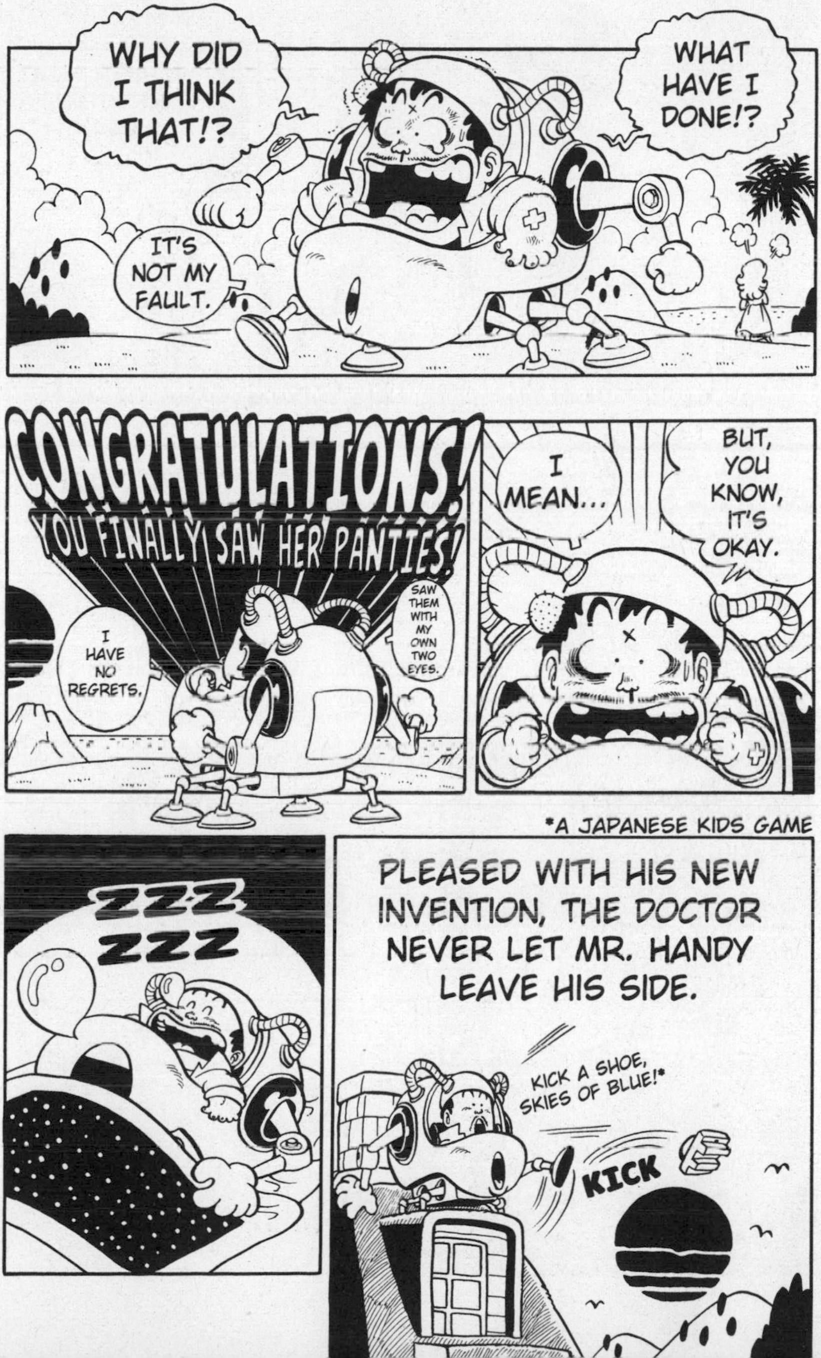
WHAT HAVE I DONE!?
WHY DID I THINK THAT!?
IT'S NOT MY FAULT.
BUT, YOU KNOW, IT'S OKAY.
I MEAN...
CONGRATULATIONS!
YOU FINALLY SAW HER PANTIES!
SAW THEM WITH MY OWN TWO EYES.
I HAVE NO REGRETS.
PLEASED WITH HIS NEW INVENTION, THE DOCTOR NEVER LET MR. HANDY LEAVE HIS SIDE.
KICK A SHOE, SKIES OF BLUE!*
KICK
ZZZ ZZZ
*A JAPANESE KIDS GAME

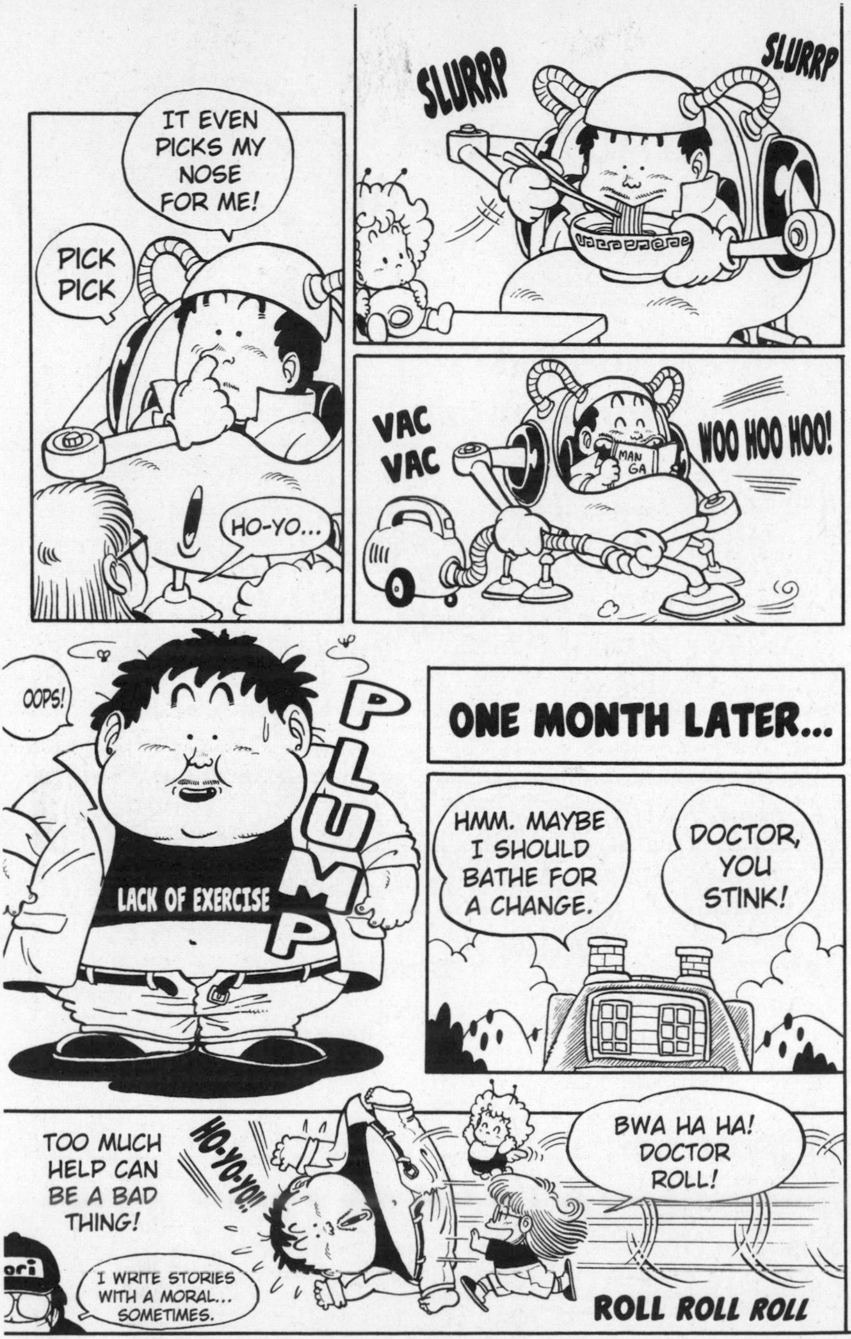
SLURRP
SLURRP
WOO HOO HOO!
VAC VAC
IT EVEN PICKS MY NOSE FOR ME!
PICK PICK
HO-YO...
ONE MONTH LATER...
DOCTOR, YOU STINK!
HMM. MAYBE I SHOULD BATHE FOR A CHANGE.
PLUMP
OOPS!
LACK OF EXERCISE
BWA HA HA! DOCTOR ROLL!
ROLL ROLL ROLL
HO-YO-YO!!
TOO MUCH HELP CAN BE A BAD THING!
I WRITE STORIES WITH A MORAL... SOMETIMES.

SPECIAL INSERT

FIRST TIME EVER!

Arale Norimaki's Very Short Manga!

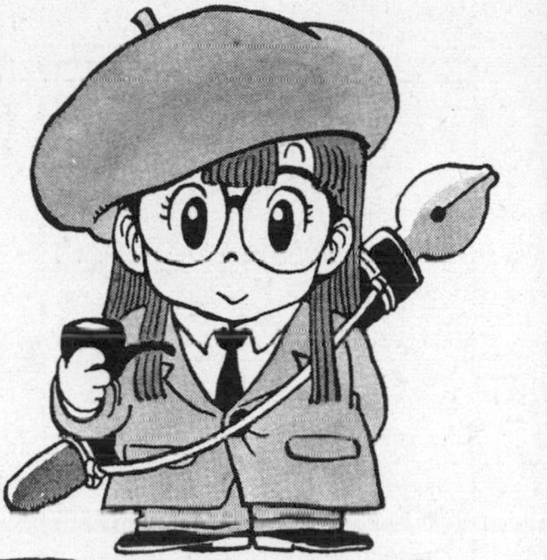

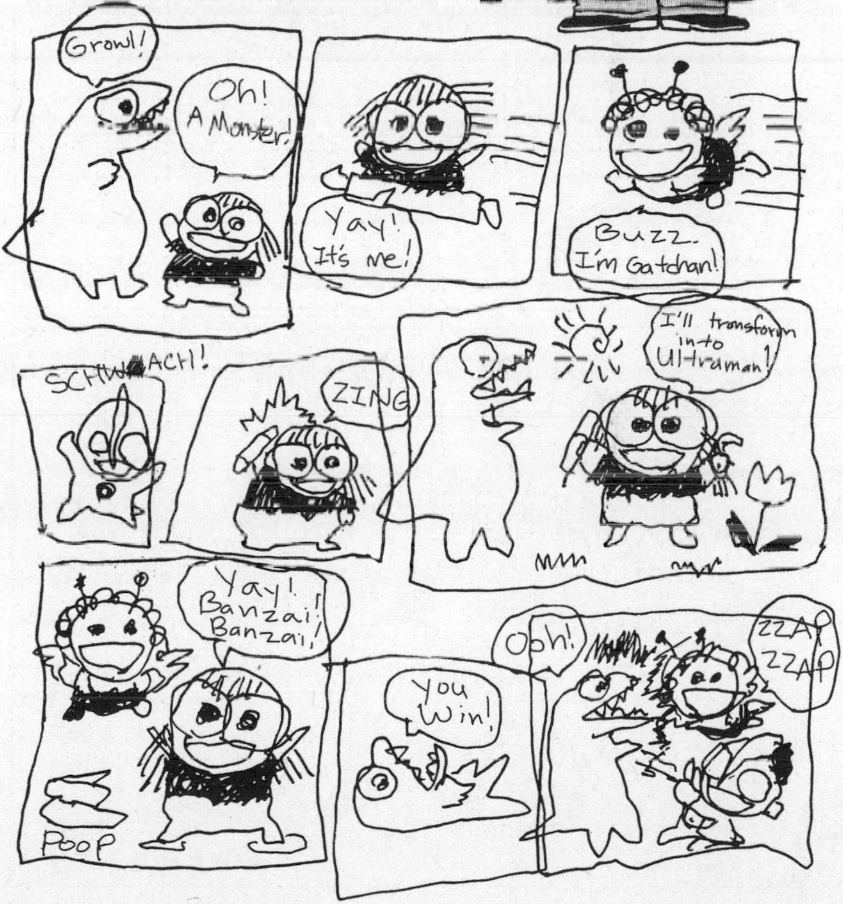
Buzz. I'm Gatchan!
Yay! It's me!
Growl!
Oh! A Monster!
I'll transform into Ultraman!
ZING
SCHWAACH!
ZZAP ZZAP
Ooh!
You Win!
Yay! Banzai! Banzai!
POOP

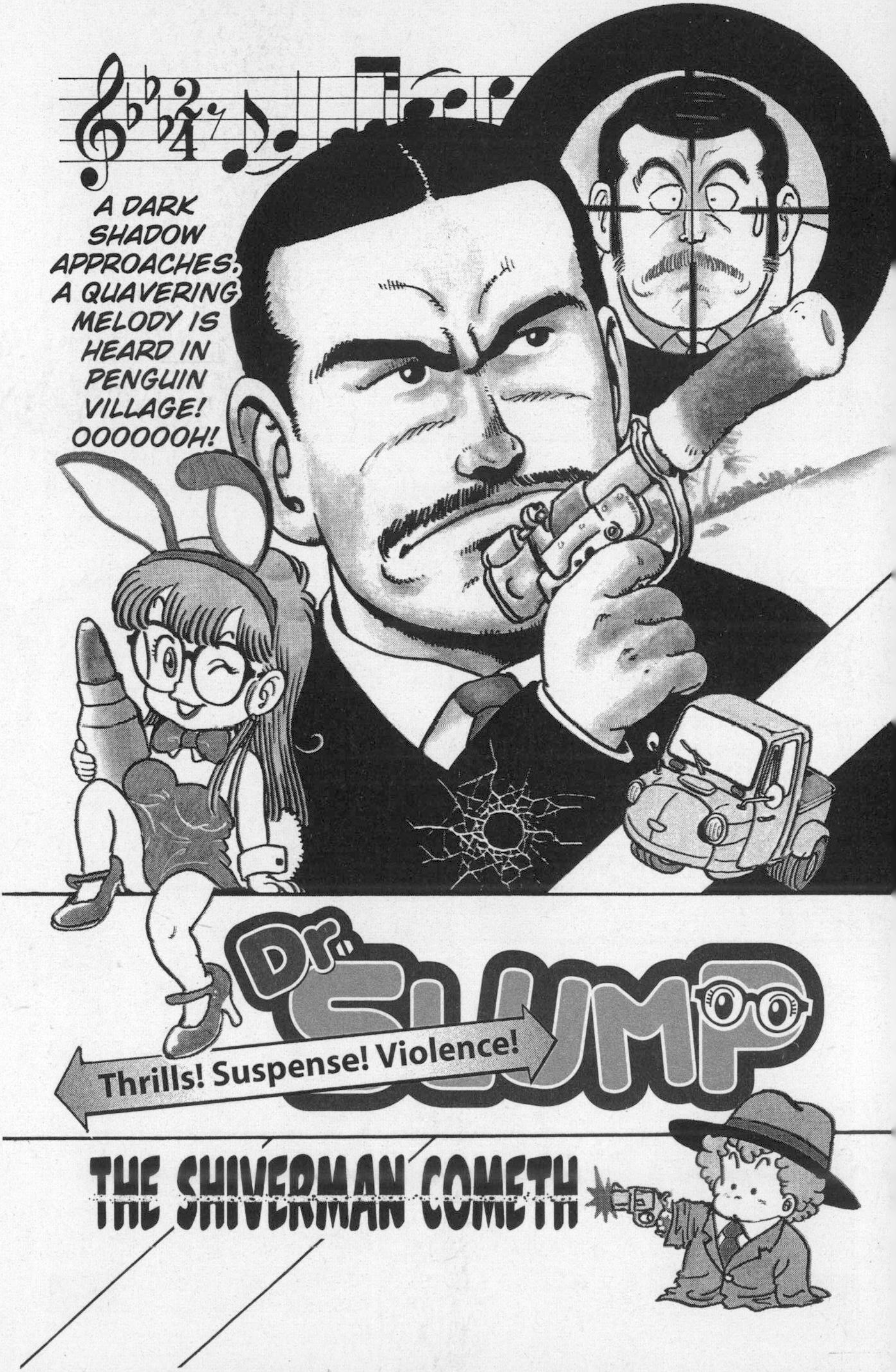
A DARK SHADOW APPROACHES. A QUAVERING MELODY IS HEARD IN PENGUIN VILLAGE! OOOOOOH!
Dr. SLUMP
Thrills! Suspense! Violence!
THE SHIVERMAN COMETH

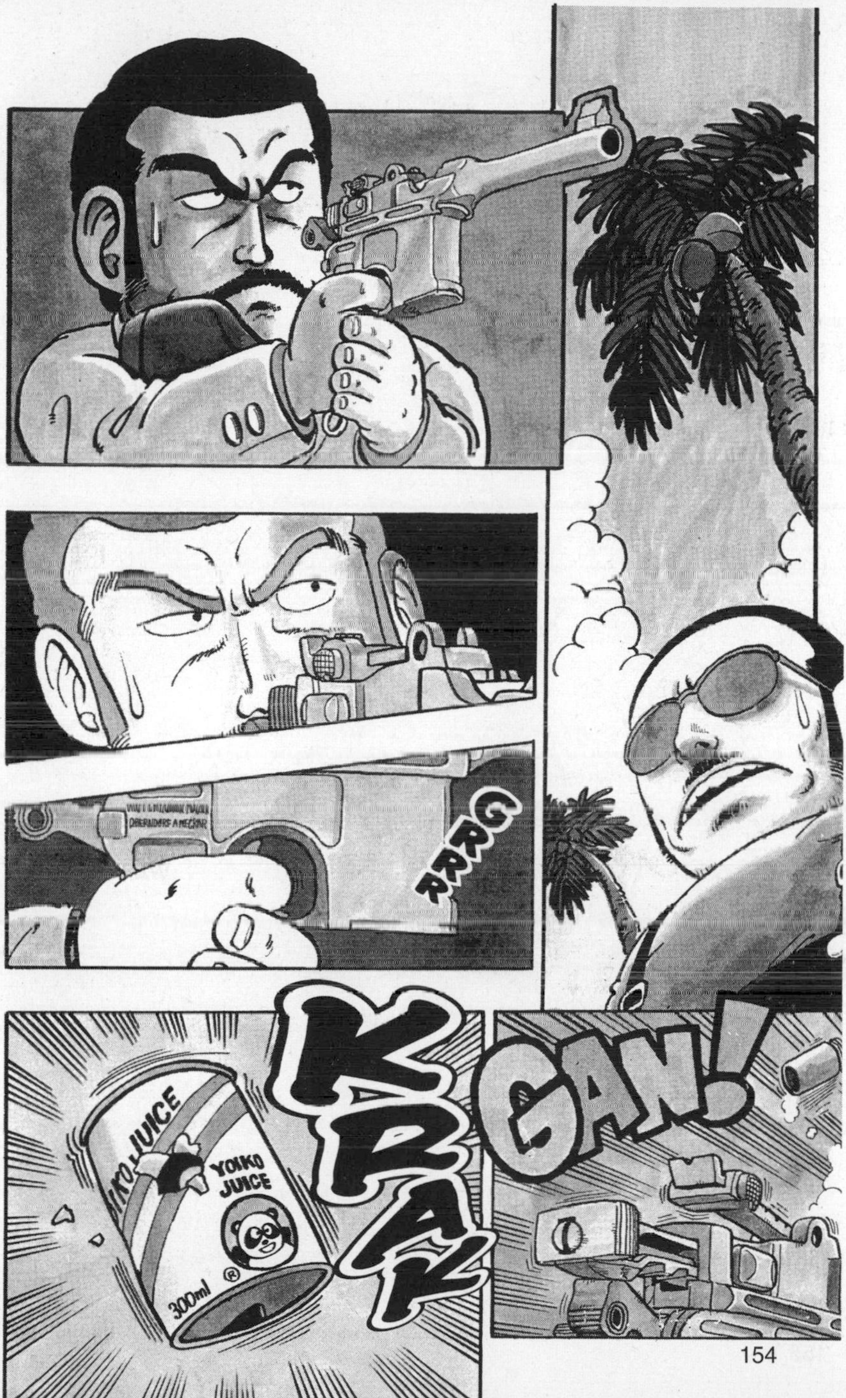
GRRR
GAN!
KRAK
YOIKO JUICE
300ml

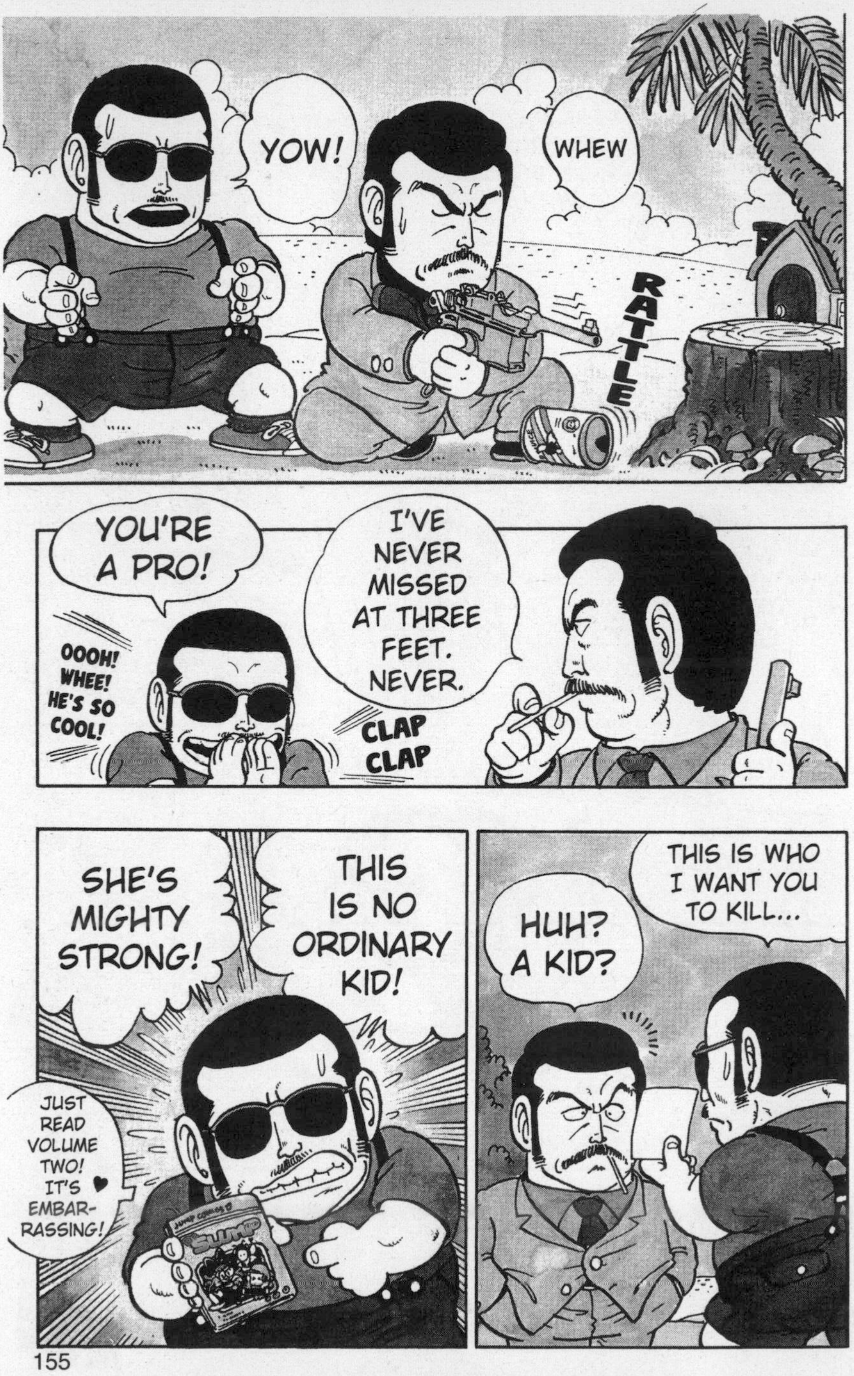
WHEW
YOW!
RATTLE
I'VE NEVER MISSED AT THREE FEET. NEVER.
YOU'RE A PRO!
OOOH! WHEE! HE'S SO COOL!
CLAP CLAP
THIS IS WHO I WANT YOU TO KILL...
HUH? A KID?
THIS IS NO ORDINARY KID!
SHE'S MIGHTY STRONG!
JUST READ VOLUME TWO! IT'S ♥ EMBARRASSING!

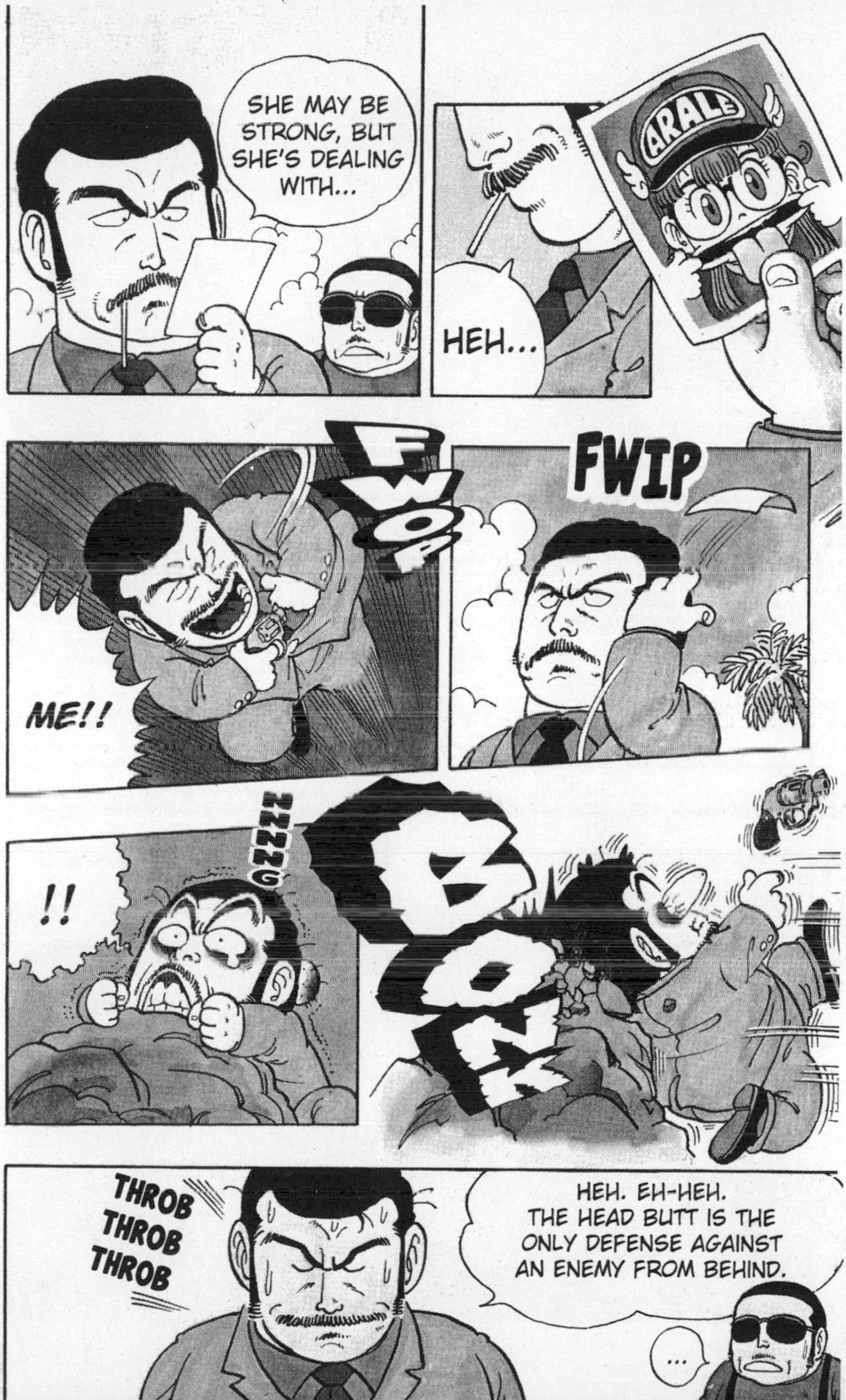
ARALE
HEH...
SHE MAY BE STRONG, BUT SHE'S DEALING WITH...
FWIP
FWOP
ME!!
BONK
HNNNG
!!
HEH. EH-HEH. THE HEAD BUTT IS THE ONLY DEFENSE AGAINST AN ENEMY FROM BEHIND.
THROB THROB THROB
...

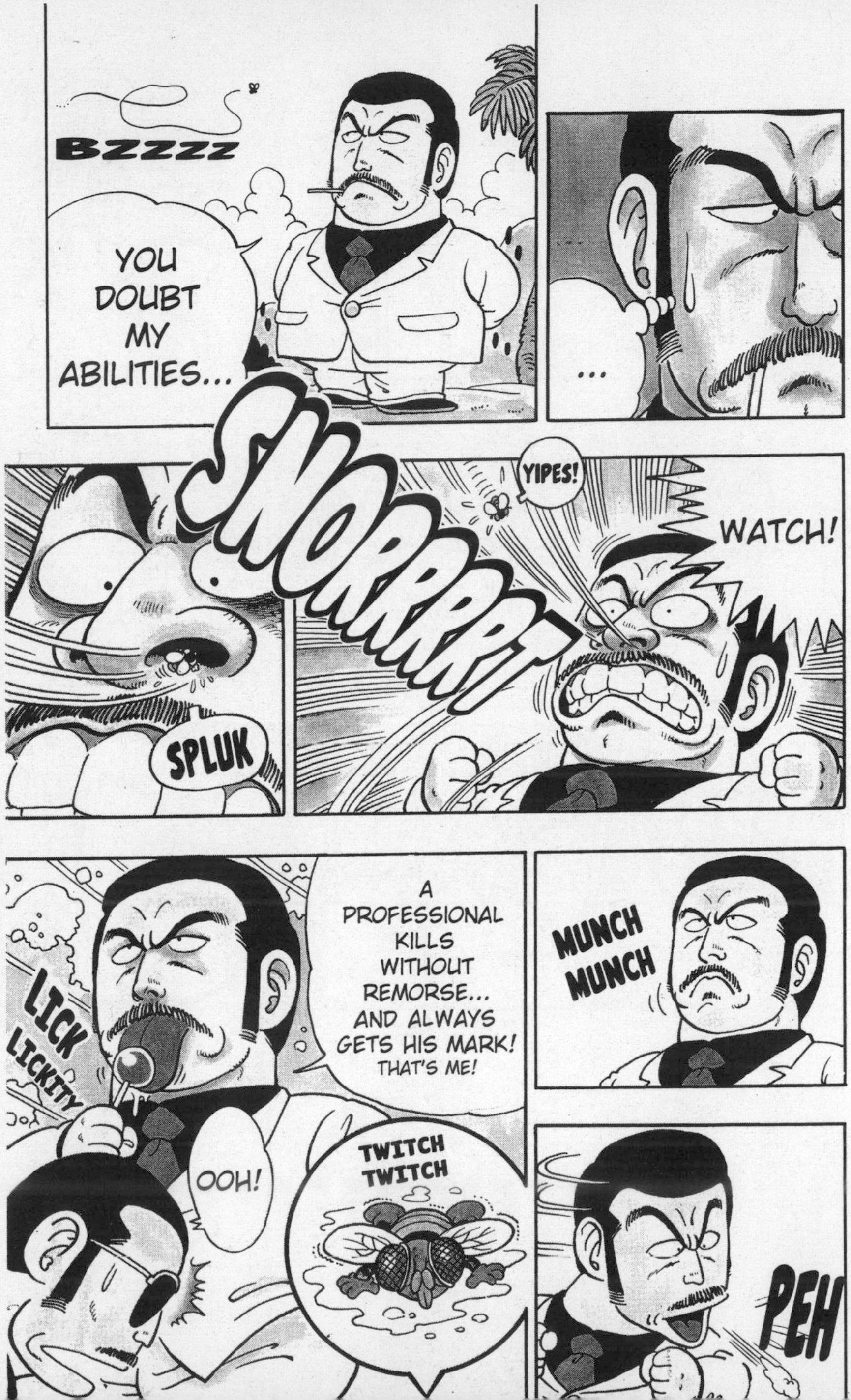
...
BZZZZ
YOU DOUBT MY ABILITIES...
SNORRRPT!
YIPES!
WATCH!
SPLUK
MUNCH MUNCH
PEH
A PROFESSIONAL KILLS WITHOUT REMORSE... AND ALWAYS GETS HIS MARK! THAT'S ME!
LICK LICKITY
TWITCH TWITCH
OOH!

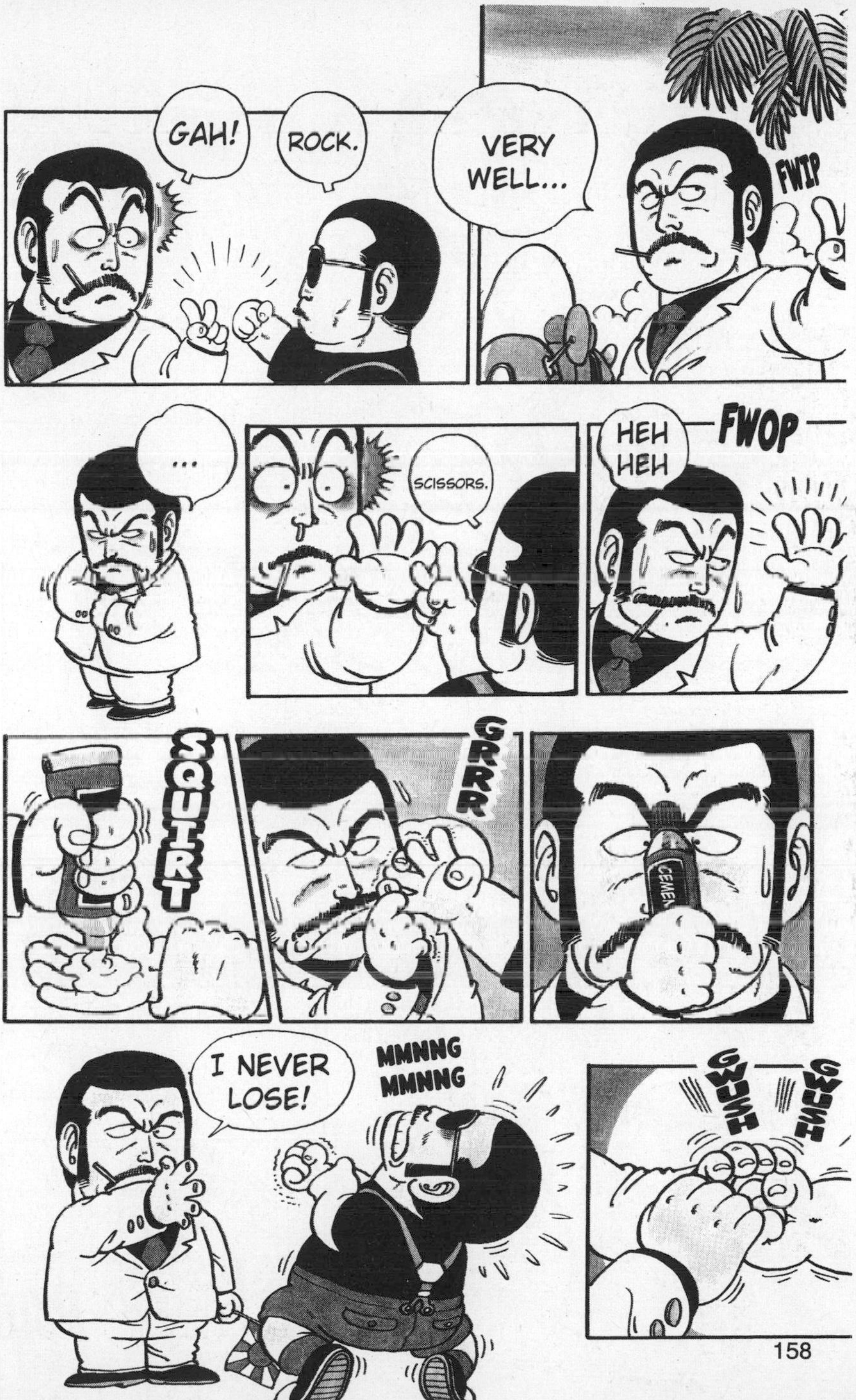
FWIP
VERY WELL...
ROCK.
GAH!
FWOP
HEH HEH
SCISSORS.
...
CEMEN
GRRR
SQUIRT
GWUSH
GWUSH
MMNNG MMNNG
I NEVER LOSE!

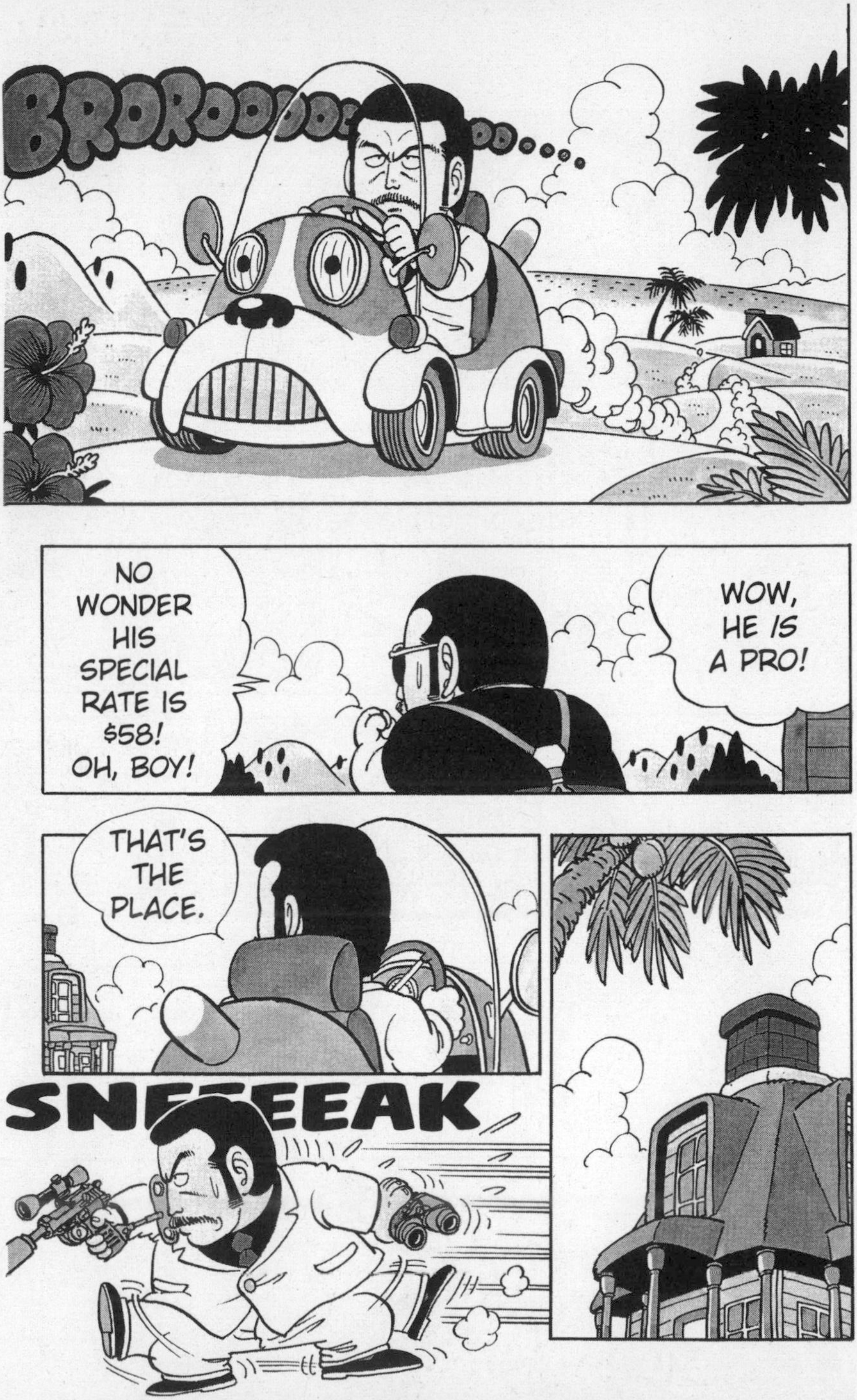
BROROOOO OOOO....
WOW, HE IS A PRO!
NO WONDER HIS SPECIAL RATE IS $58! OH, BOY!
THAT'S THE PLACE.
SNEEEAK

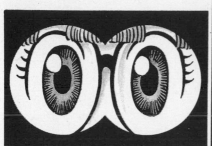

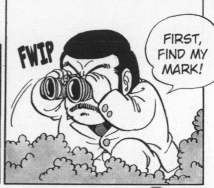
FWIP

FIRST, FIND MY MARK!

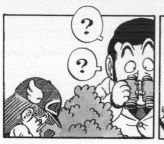
?
?

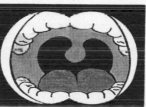
...

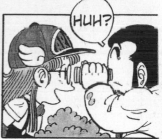
HUH?

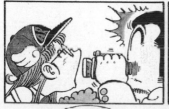

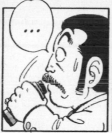

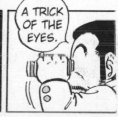
A TRICK OF THE EYES.

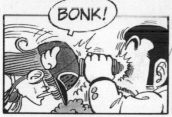
BONK!

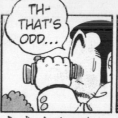
TH- THAT'S ODD...

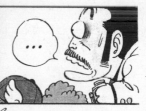
...

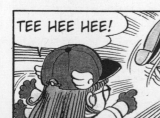
TEE HEE HEE!

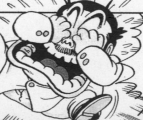
WAAAH! MY EYES!

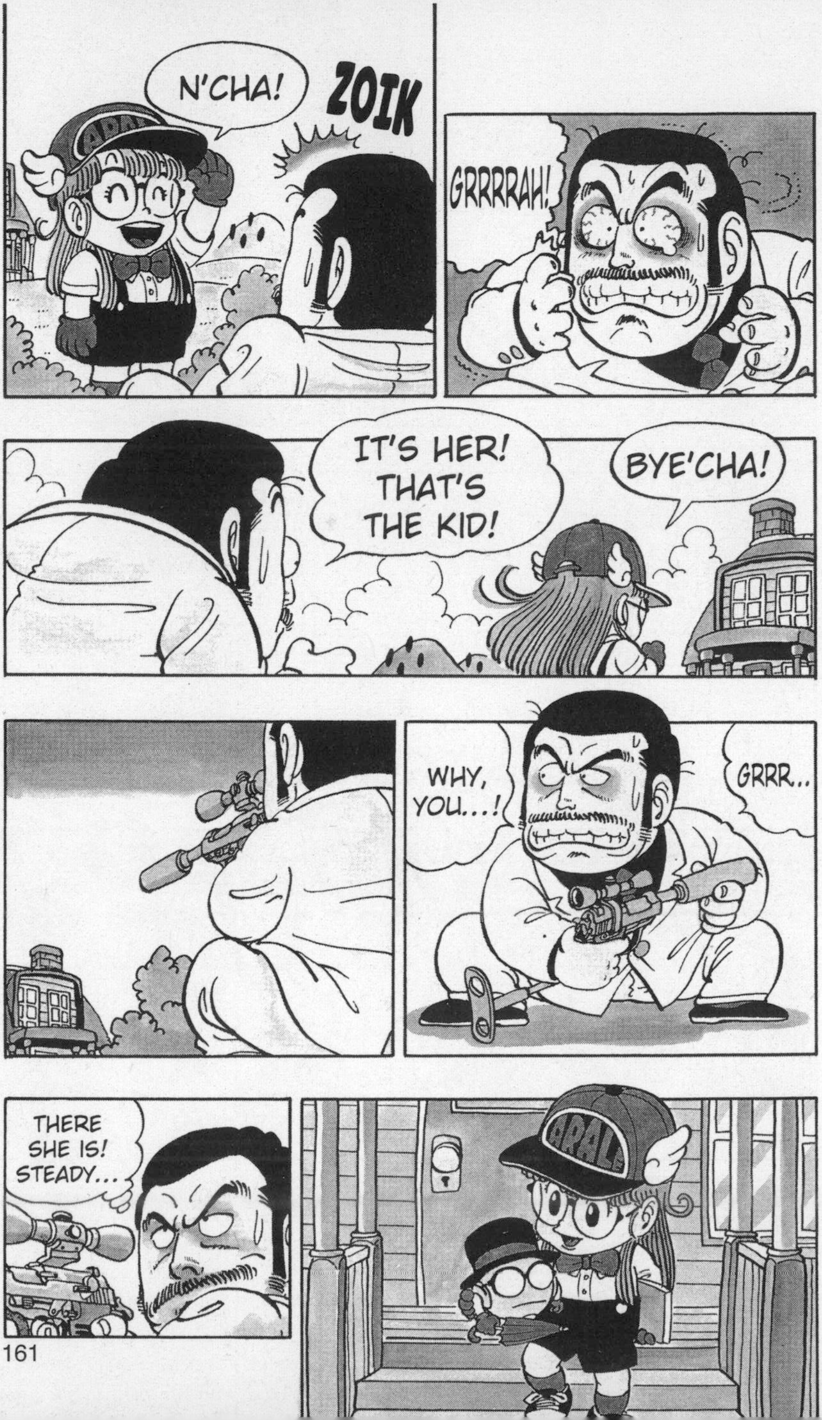
GRRRRAH!
N'CHA!
ZOIK
BYE'CHA!
IT'S HER! THAT'S THE KID!
GRRR...
WHY, YOU...!
THERE SHE IS! STEADY...

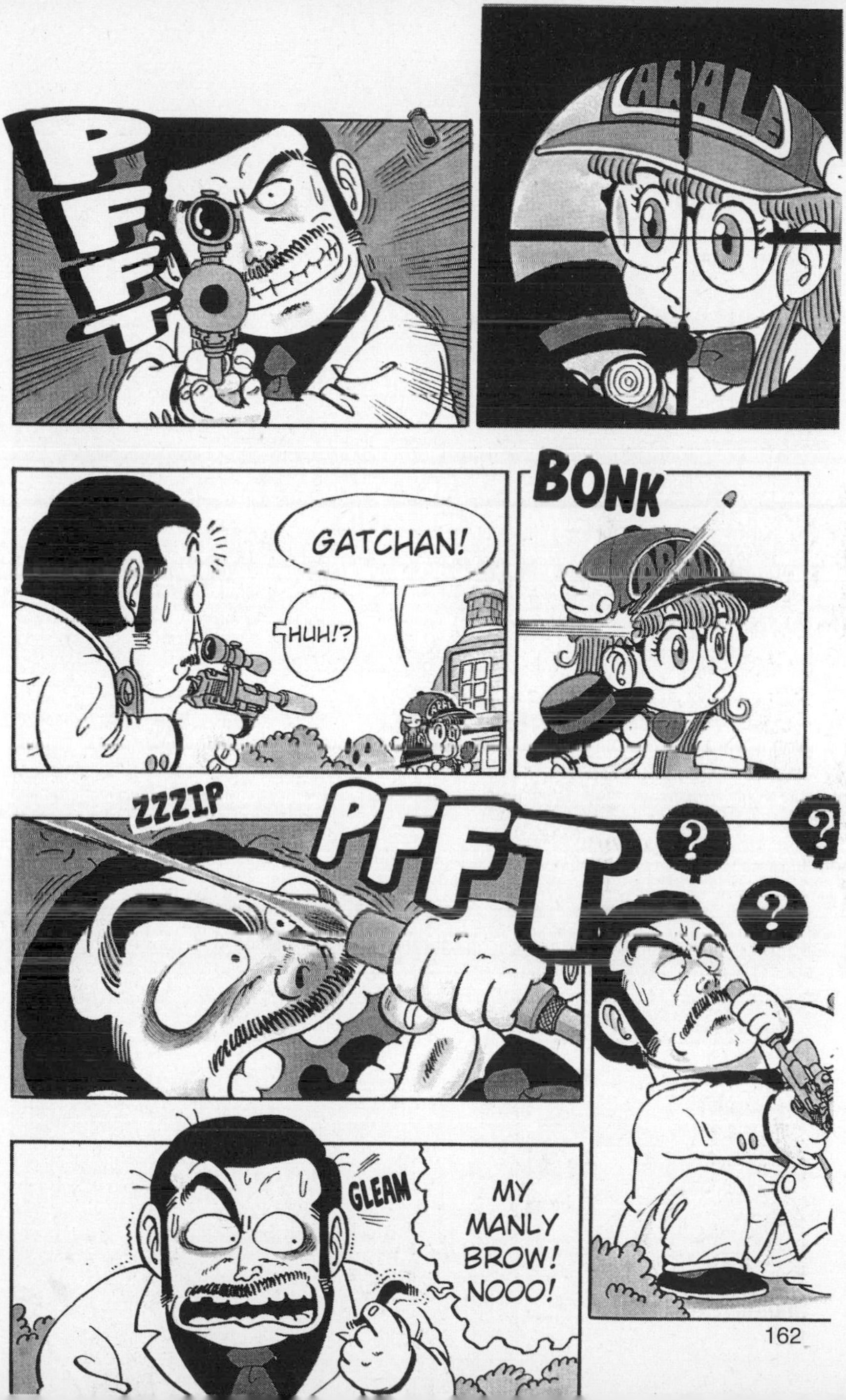
PFFT
BONK
GATCHAN!
HUH!?
? ? ?
ZZZIP
PFFT
GLEAM
MY MANLY BROW! NOOO!

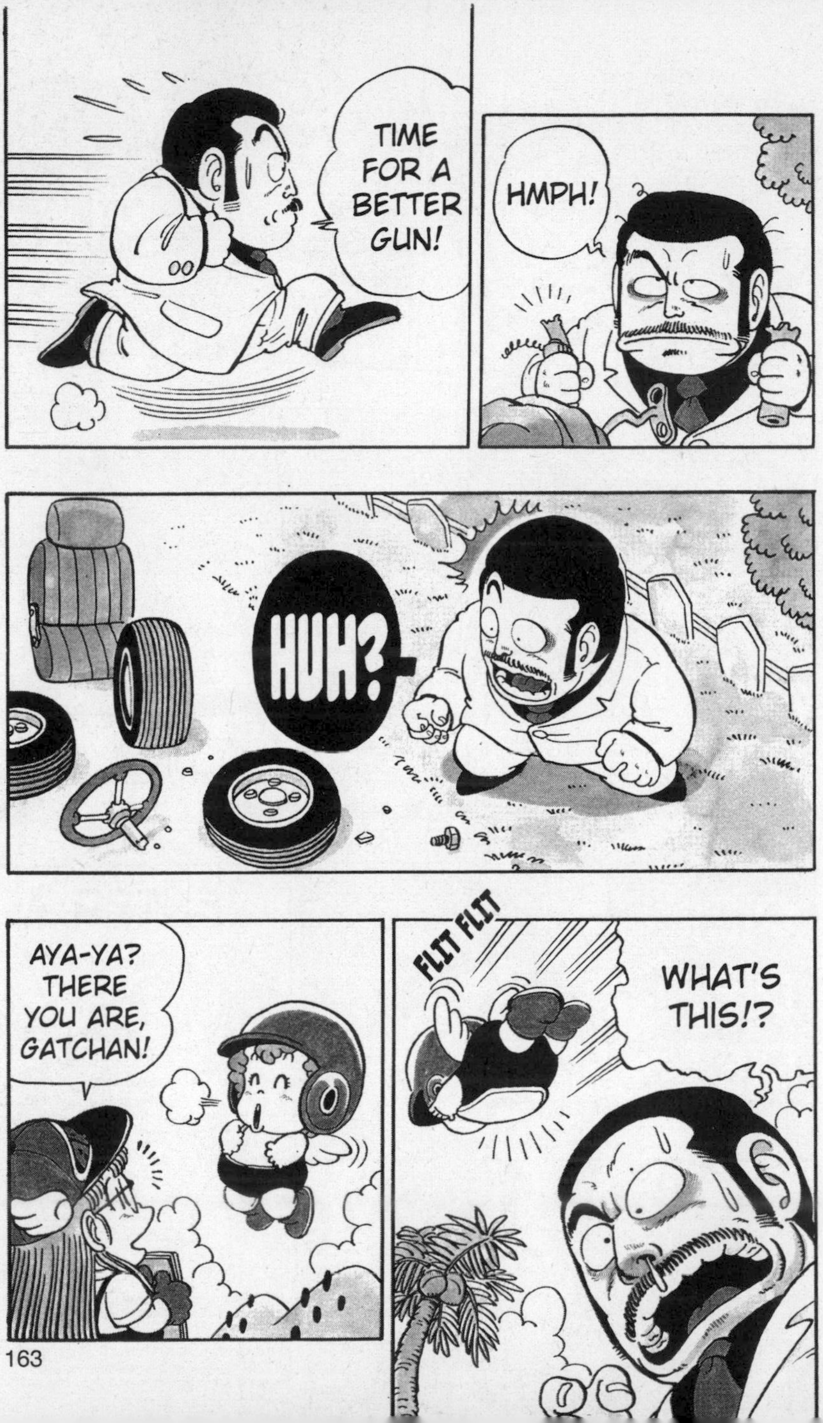
HMPH!
TIME FOR A BETTER GUN!
HUH?
FLIT FLIT
WHAT'S THIS!?
AYA-YA? THERE YOU ARE, GATCHAN!

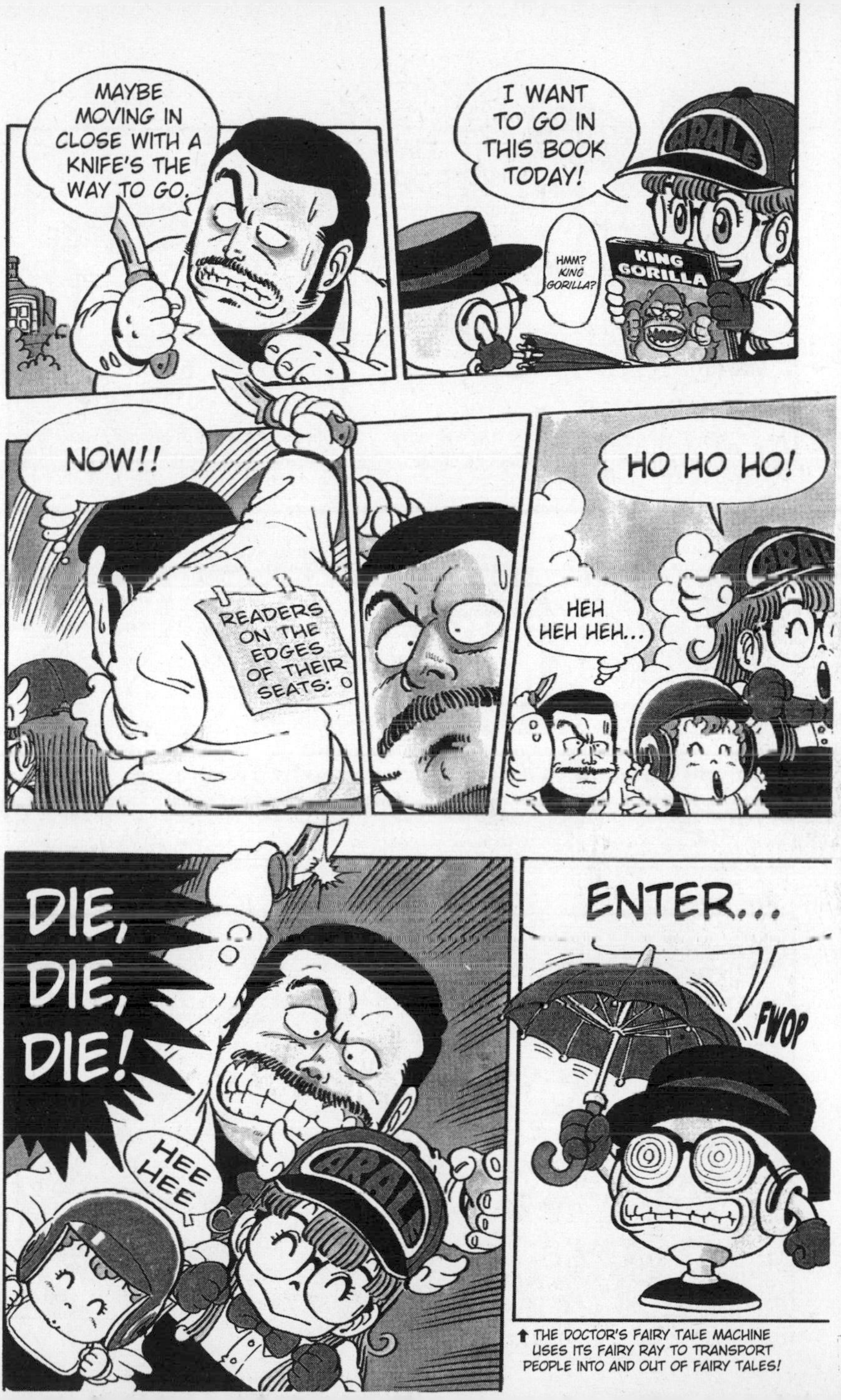
I WANT TO GO IN THIS BOOK TODAY!
HMM? KING GORILLA?
KING GORILLA
MAYBE MOVING IN CLOSE WITH A KNIFE'S THE WAY TO GO.
HO HO HO!
HEH HEH HEH...
NOW!!
READERS ON THE EDGES OF THEIR SEATS: 0
ENTER...
FWOP
DIE, DIE, DIE!
HEE HEE

↑ THE DOCTOR'S FAIRY TALE MACHINE USES ITS FAIRY RAY TO TRANSPORT PEOPLE INTO AND OUT OF FAIRY TALES!

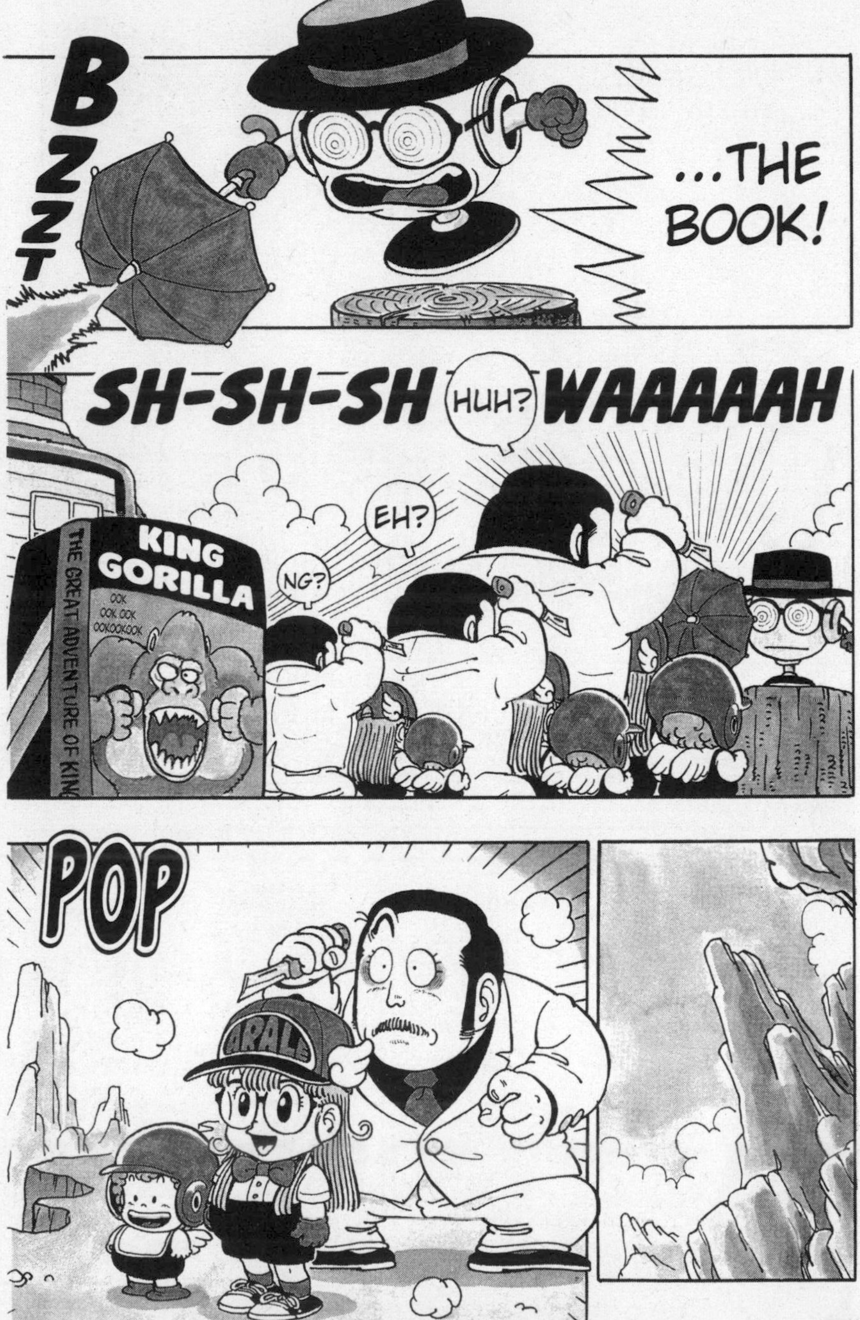
...THE BOOK!
BZZZT
WAAAAAH
HUH?
SH-SH-SH
EH?
NG?
KING GORILLA
OOK OOK OOK OOKOOKOOK
THE GREAT ADVENTURE OF KING
POP
ARALE

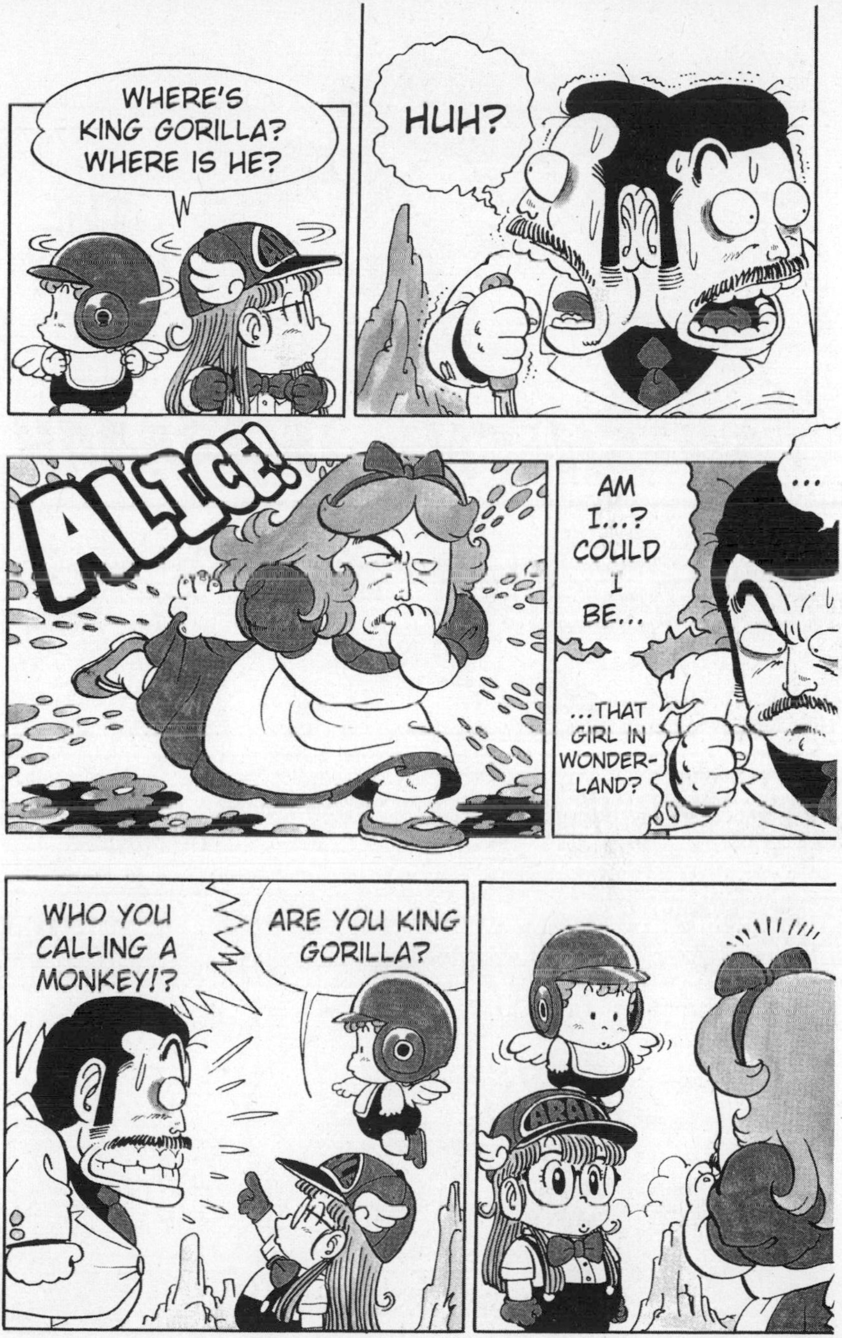
HUH?
WHERE'S KING GORILLA? WHERE IS HE?
...
AM I...? COULD I BE...
...THAT GIRL IN WONDERLAND?
ALICE!
ARE YOU KING GORILLA?
WHO YOU CALLING A MONKEY!?

READ THIS WAY

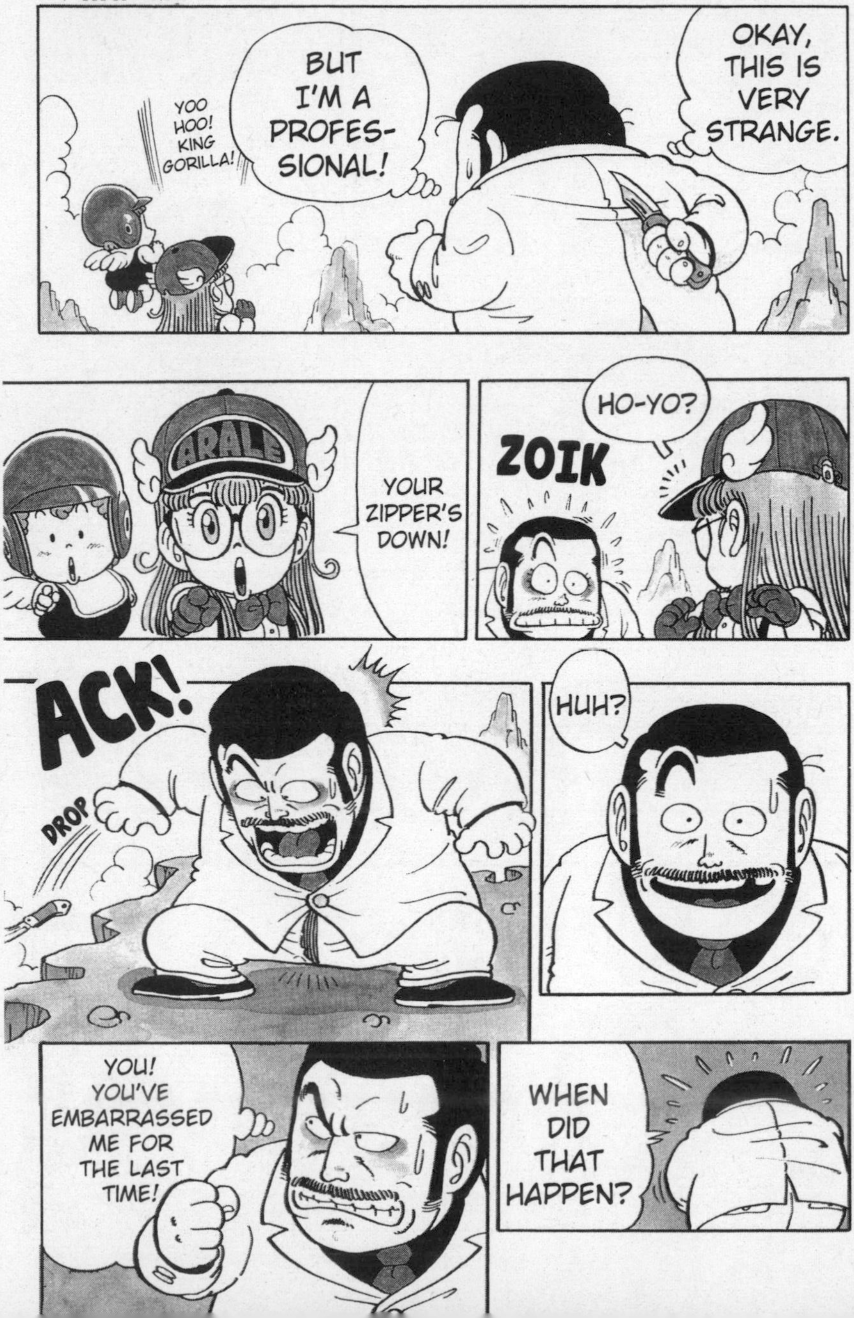
OKAY, THIS IS VERY STRANGE.
BUT I'M A PROFES-SIONAL!
YOO HOO! KING GORILLA!
HO-YO?
ZOIK
YOUR ZIPPER'S DOWN!
HUH?
ACK!
DROP
WHEN DID THAT HAPPEN?
YOU! YOU'VE EMBARRASSED ME FOR THE LAST TIME!

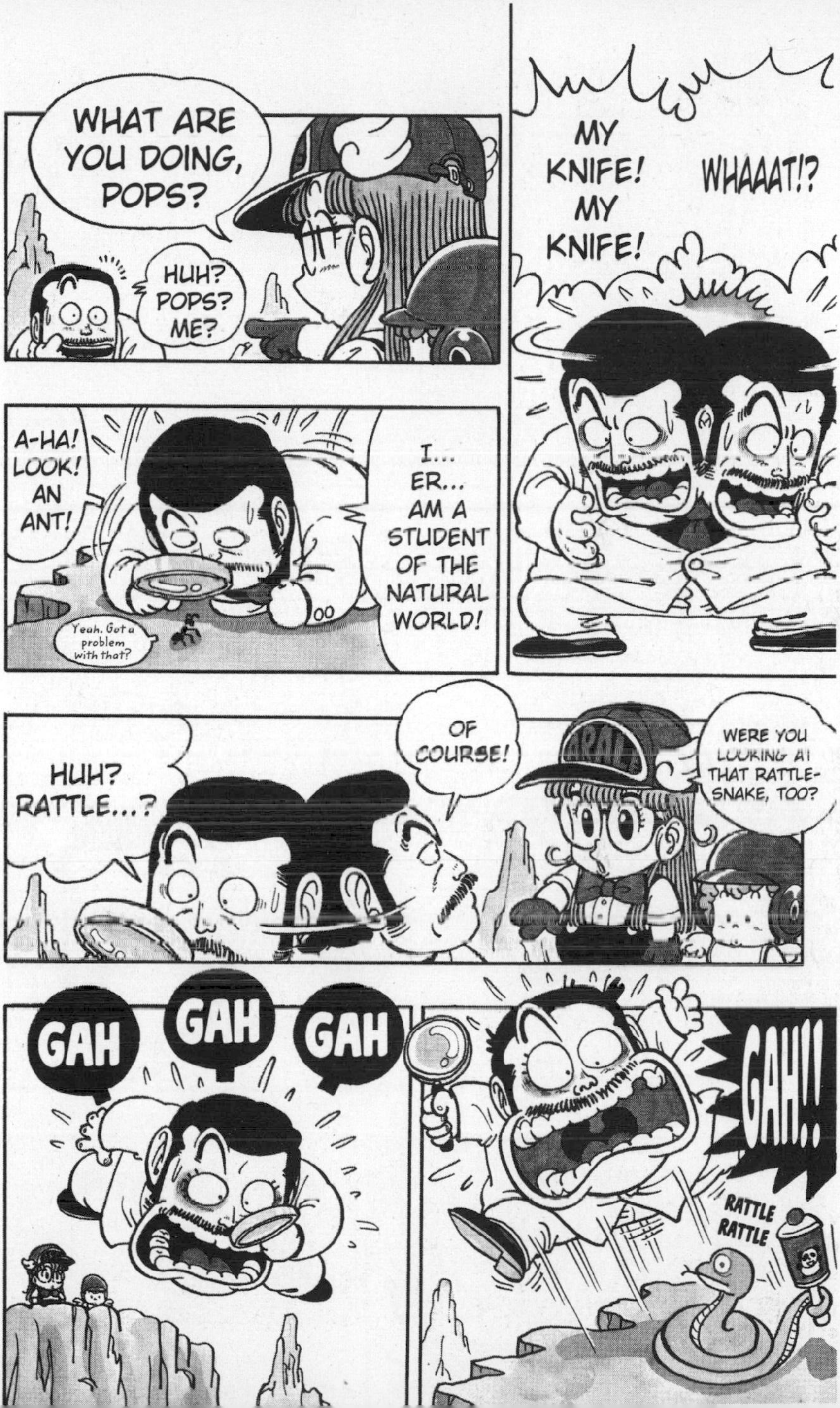
WHAAAT!?
MY KNIFE! MY KNIFE!
WHAT ARE YOU DOING, POPS?
HUH? POPS? ME?
I... ER... AM A STUDENT OF THE NATURAL WORLD!
A-HA! LOOK! AN ANT!
Yeah. Got a problem with that?
WERE YOU LOOKING AT THAT RATTLE-SNAKE, TOO?
OF COURSE!
HUH? RATTLE...?
GAH!!
RATTLE RATTLE
GAH
GAH
GAH

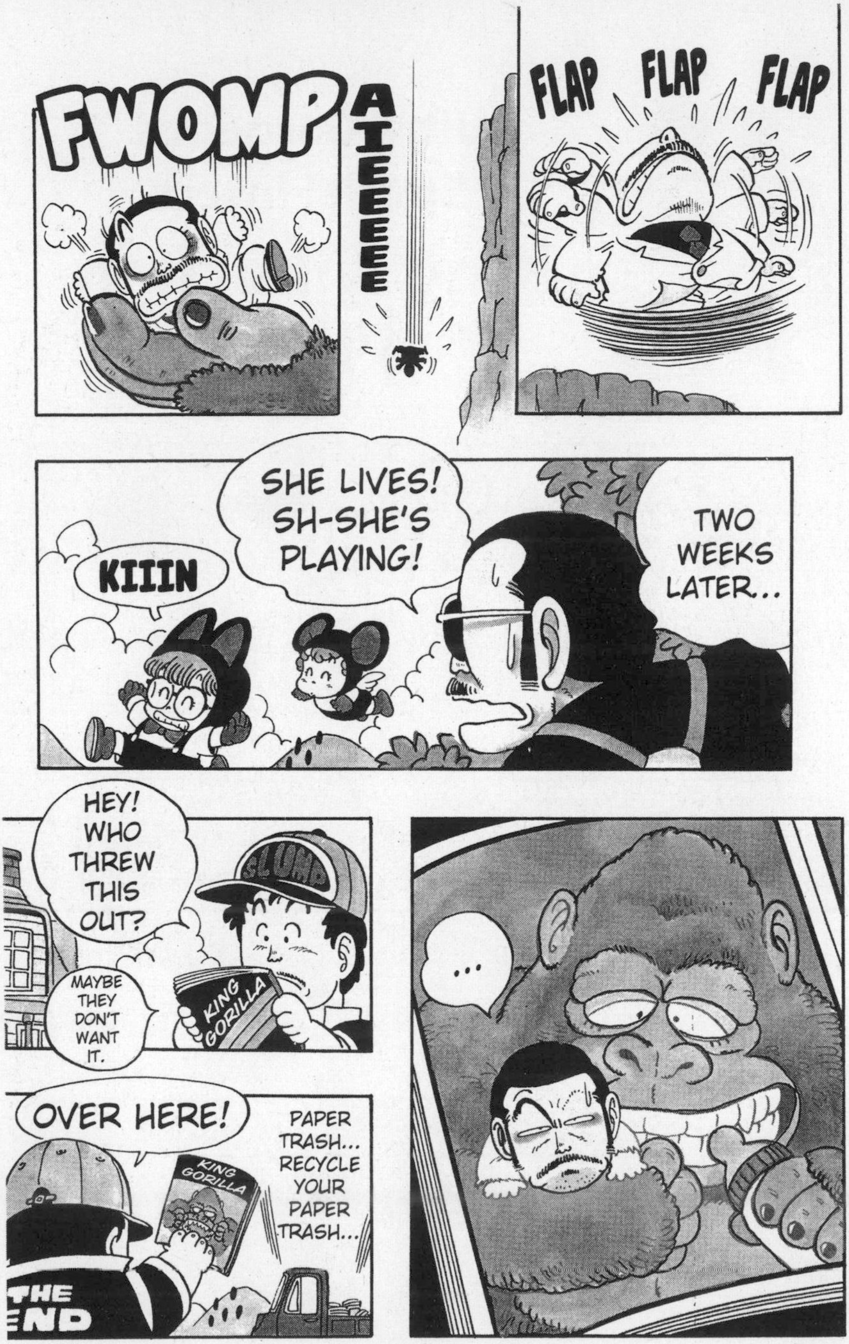
FLAP FLAP FLAP
AIEEEEEE
FWOMP
TWO WEEKS LATER...
SHE LIVES! SH-SHE'S PLAYING!
KIIN
...
HEY! WHO THREW THIS OUT?
MAYBE THEY DON'T WANT IT.
KING GORILLA
PAPER TRASH... RECYCLE YOUR PAPER TRASH...
OVER HERE!
KING GORILLA
THE END

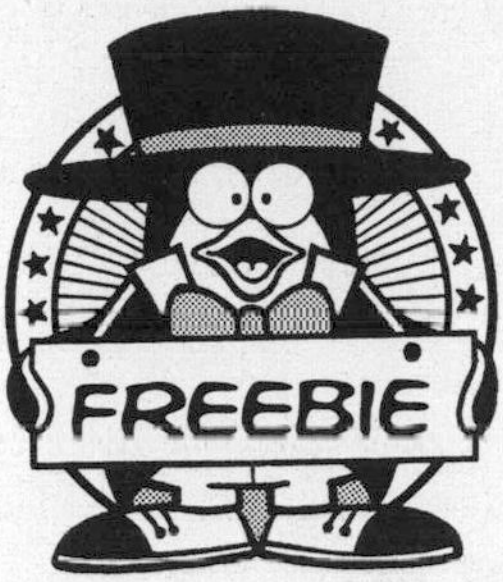
FREEBIE

Ultra Gorgeous Special Insert
King Nikochan Pinup

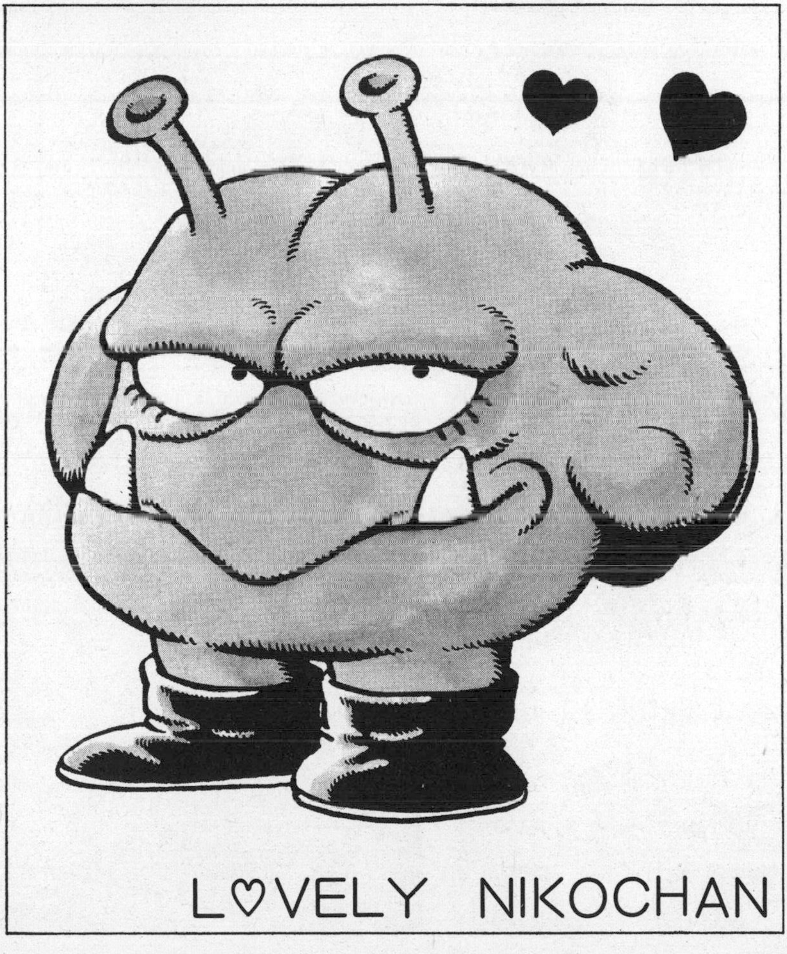
L♡VELY NIKOCHAN

Peasuke's First Love

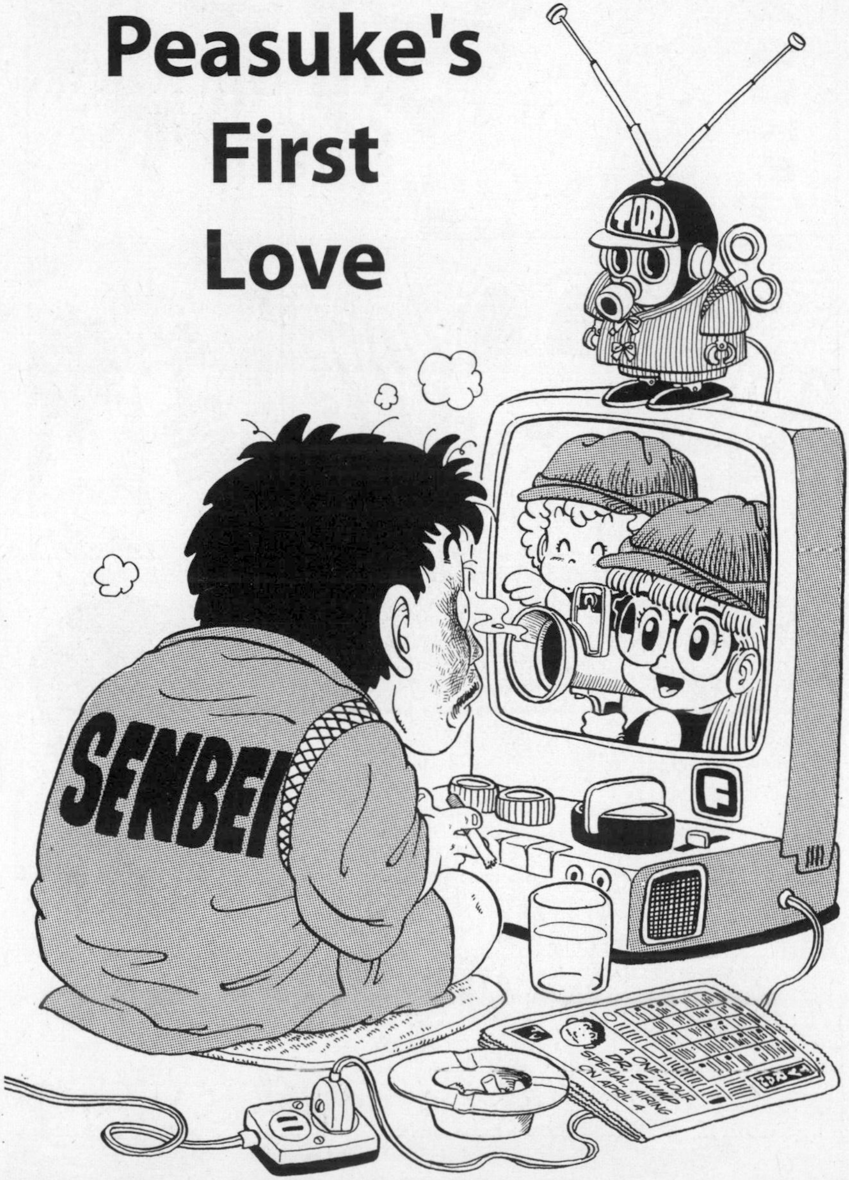
TORI
SENBEI
A ONE-HOUR DR. SLUMP SPECIAL AIRING ON APRIL 4

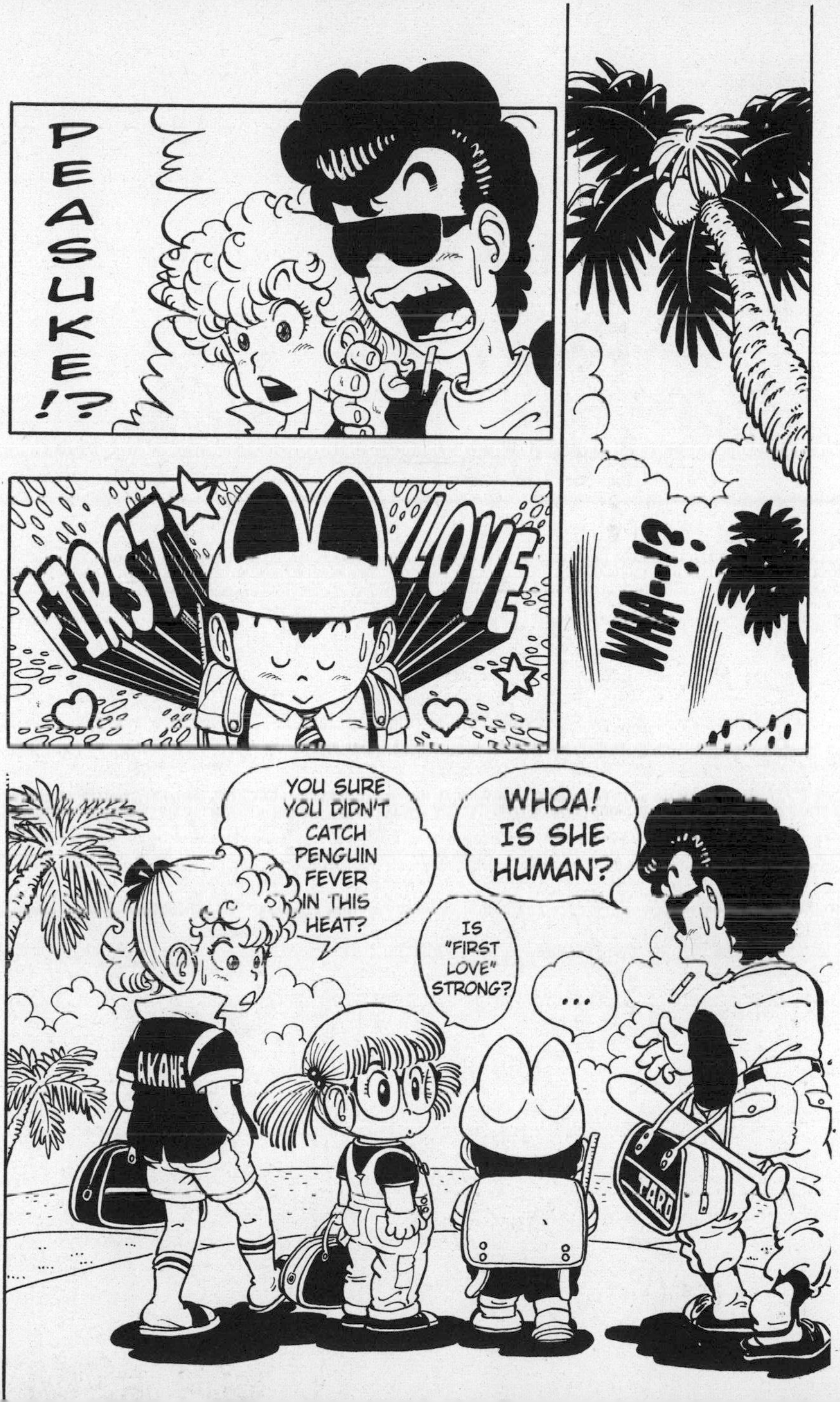
WHA--!?
PEASUKE!?
FIRST LOVE
WHOA! IS SHE HUMAN?
YOU SURE YOU DIDN'T CATCH PENGUIN FEVER IN THIS HEAT?
IS "FIRST LOVE" STRONG?
...
AKAHE
TARO

READ THIS WAY

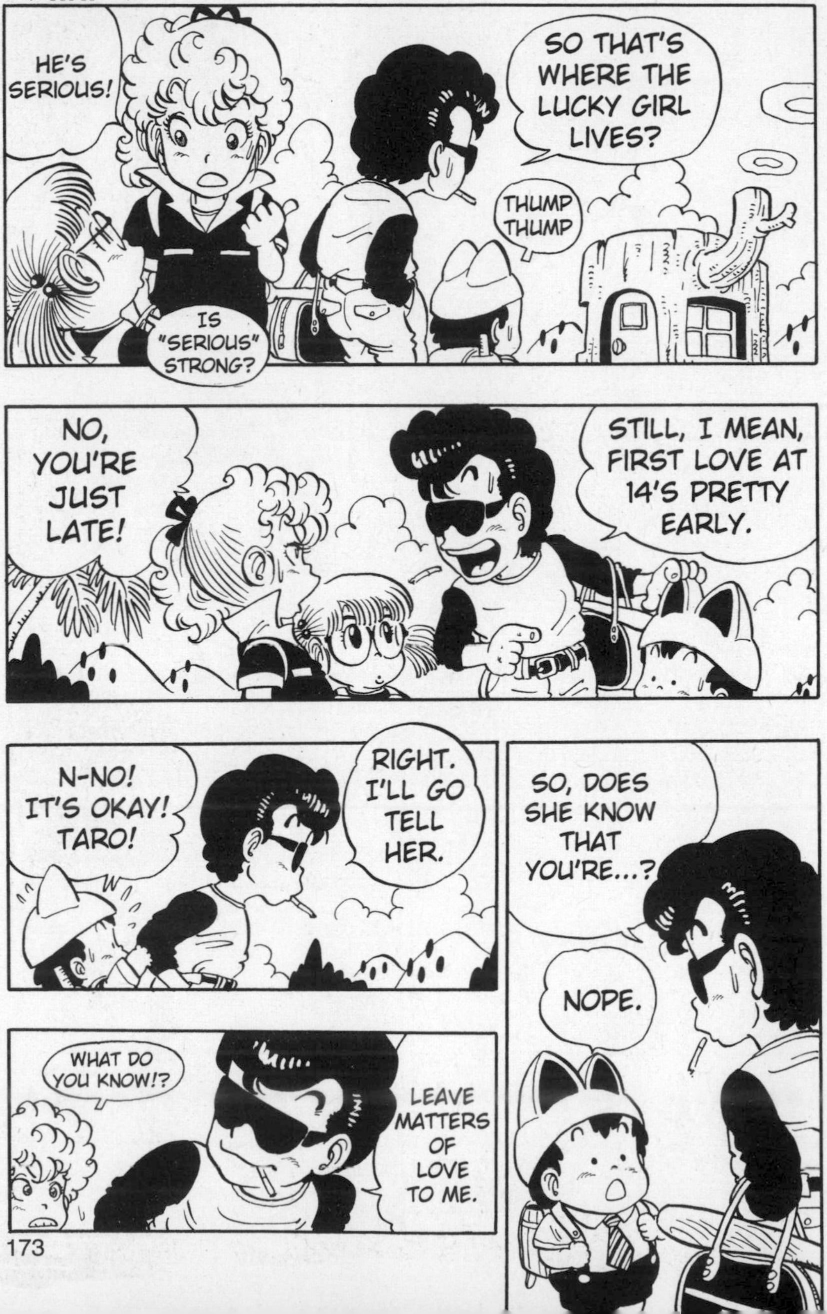
SO THAT'S WHERE THE LUCKY GIRL LIVES?
THUMP THUMP
HE'S SERIOUS!
IS "SERIOUS" STRONG?
STILL, I MEAN, FIRST LOVE AT 14'S PRETTY EARLY.
NO, YOU'RE JUST LATE!
SO, DOES SHE KNOW THAT YOU'RE...?
NOPE.
RIGHT. I'LL GO TELL HER.
N-NO! IT'S OKAY! TARO!
LEAVE MATTERS OF LOVE TO ME.
WHAT DO YOU KNOW!?

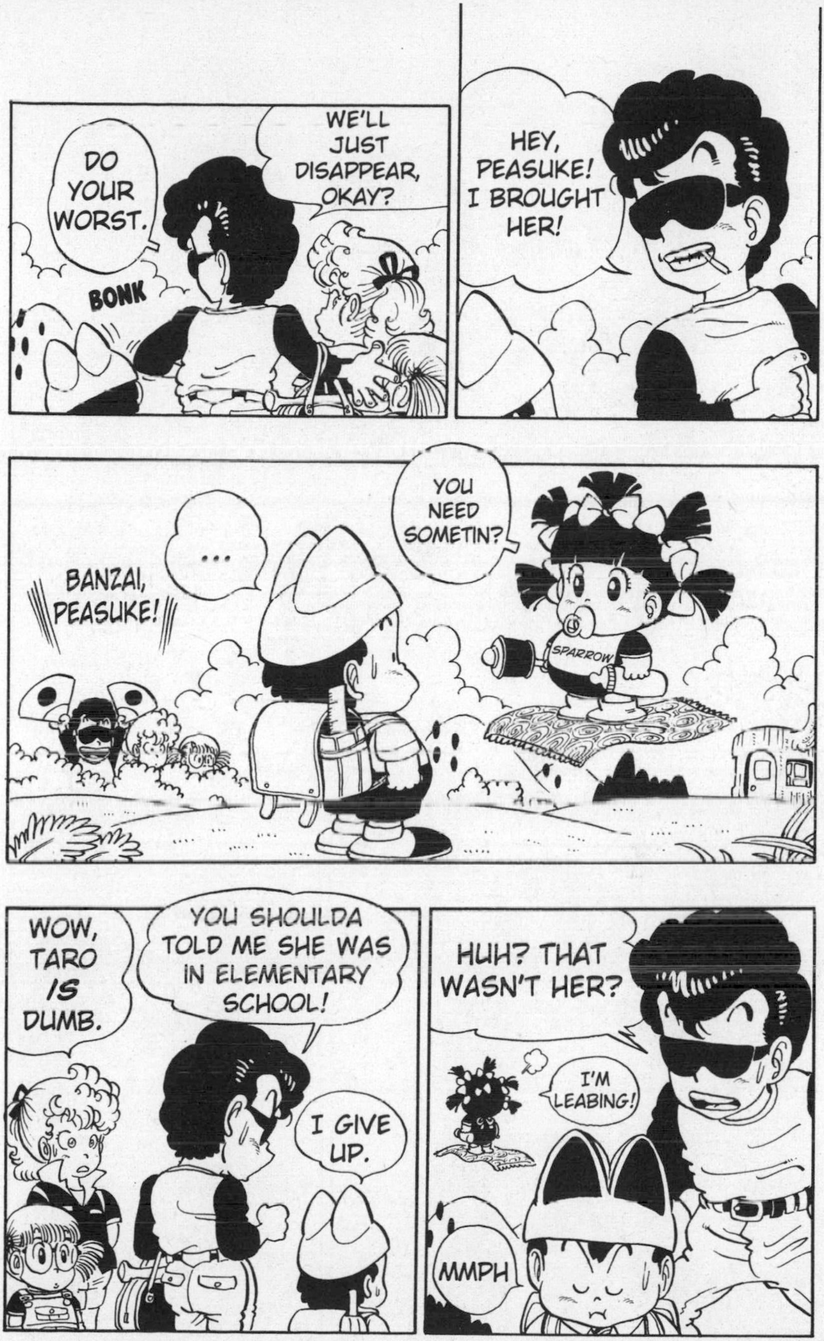
HEY, PEASUKE! I BROUGHT HER!
WE'LL JUST DISAPPEAR, OKAY?
DO YOUR WORST.
BONK
YOU NEED SOMETIN?
...
SPARROW
BANZAI, PEASUKE!
HUH? THAT WASN'T HER?
I'M LEABING!
MMPH
YOU SHOULDA TOLD ME SHE WAS IN ELEMENTARY SCHOOL!
WOW, TARO *IS* DUMB.
I GIVE UP.

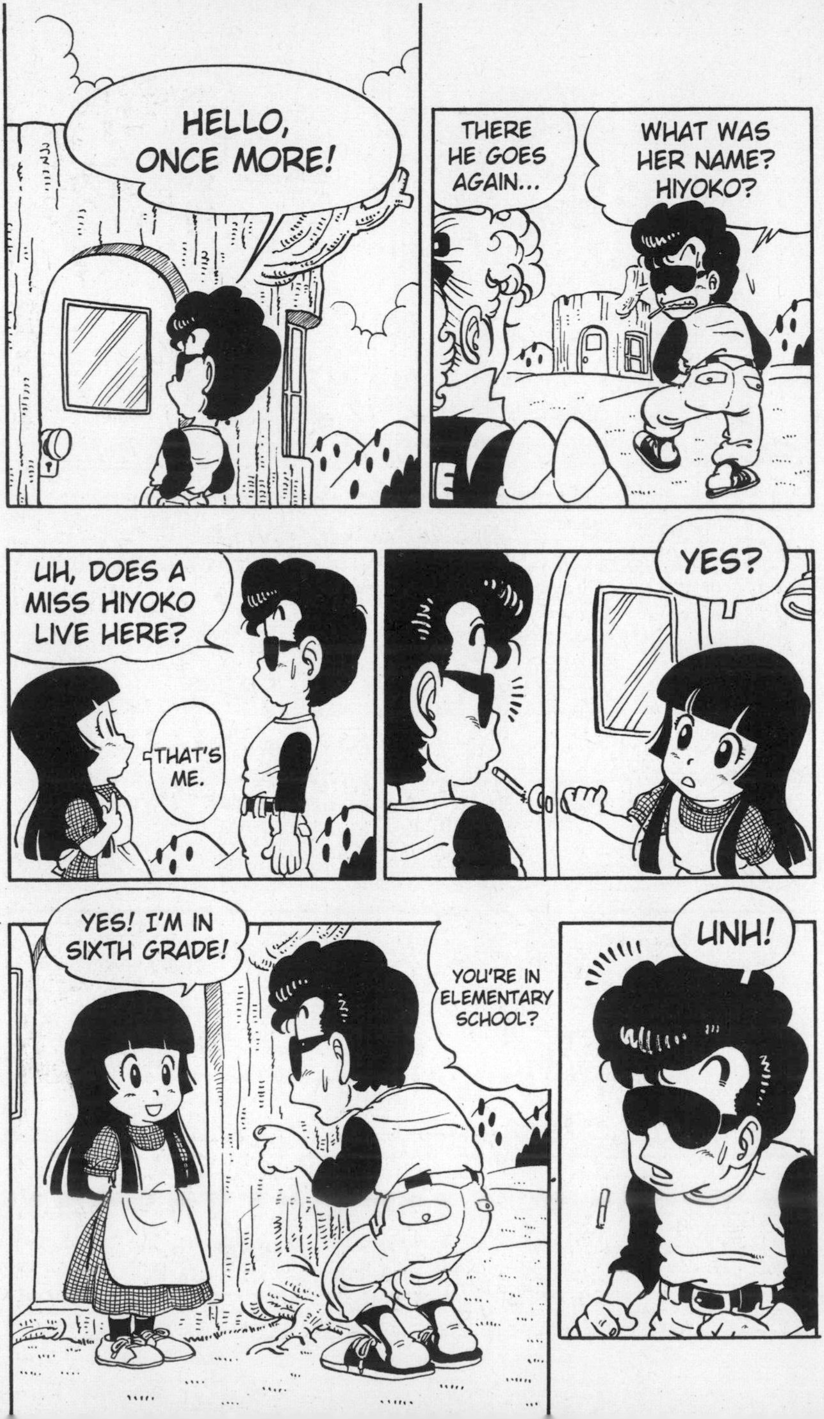
WHAT WAS HER NAME? HIYOKO?
THERE HE GOES AGAIN...
HELLO, ONCE MORE!
YES?
UH, DOES A MISS HIYOKO LIVE HERE?
THAT'S ME.
UNH!
YOU'RE IN ELEMENTARY SCHOOL?
YES! I'M IN SIXTH GRADE!

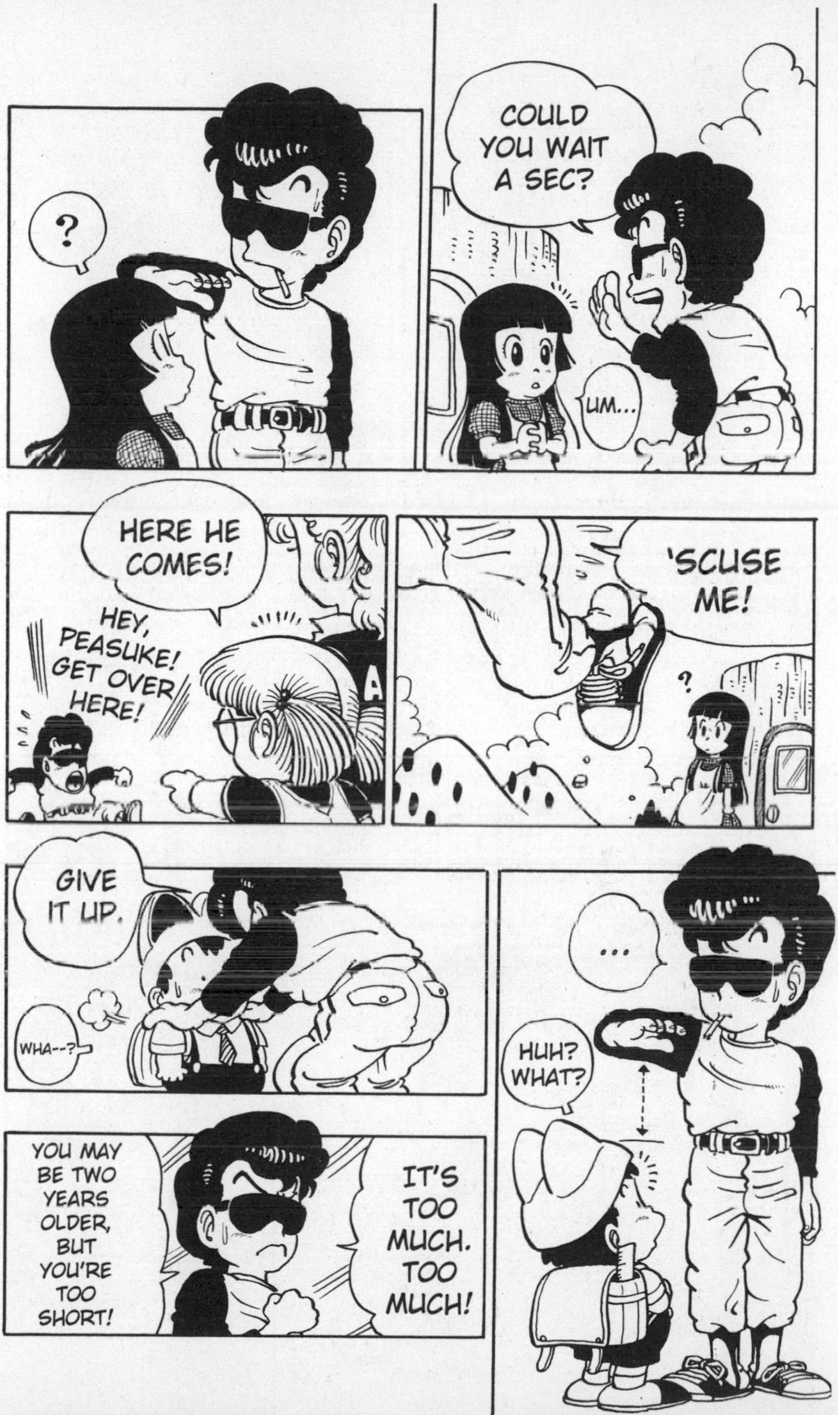
COULD YOU WAIT A SEC?
UM...
?
'SCUSE ME!
?
HERE HE COMES!
HEY, PEASUKE! GET OVER HERE!
...
HUH? WHAT?
GIVE IT UP.
WHA--?
IT'S TOO MUCH. TOO MUCH!
YOU MAY BE TWO YEARS OLDER, BUT YOU'RE TOO SHORT!

READ THIS WAY

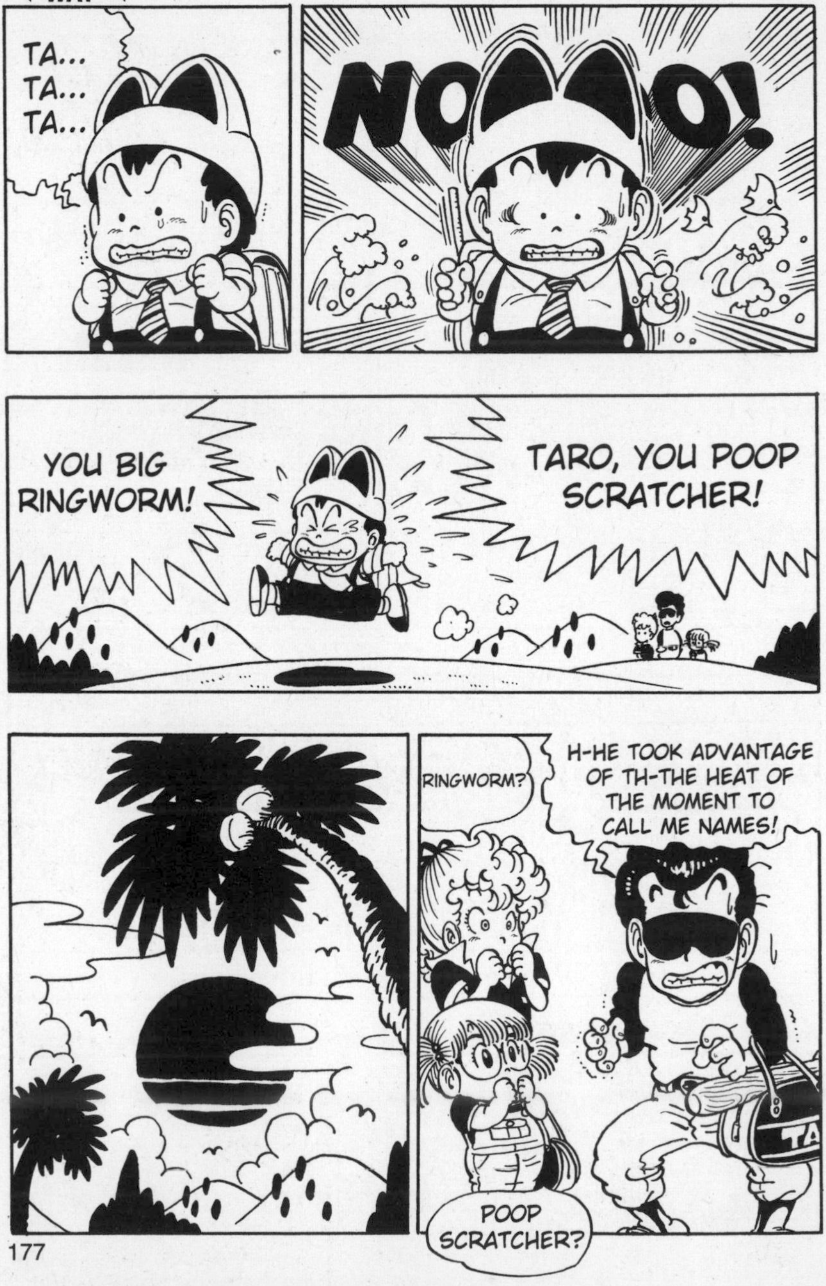
NOOOO!
TA...
TA...
TA...
TARO, YOU POOP SCRATCHER!
YOU BIG RINGWORM!
H-HE TOOK ADVANTAGE OF TH-THE HEAT OF THE MOMENT TO CALL ME NAMES!
RINGWORM?
POOP SCRATCHER?

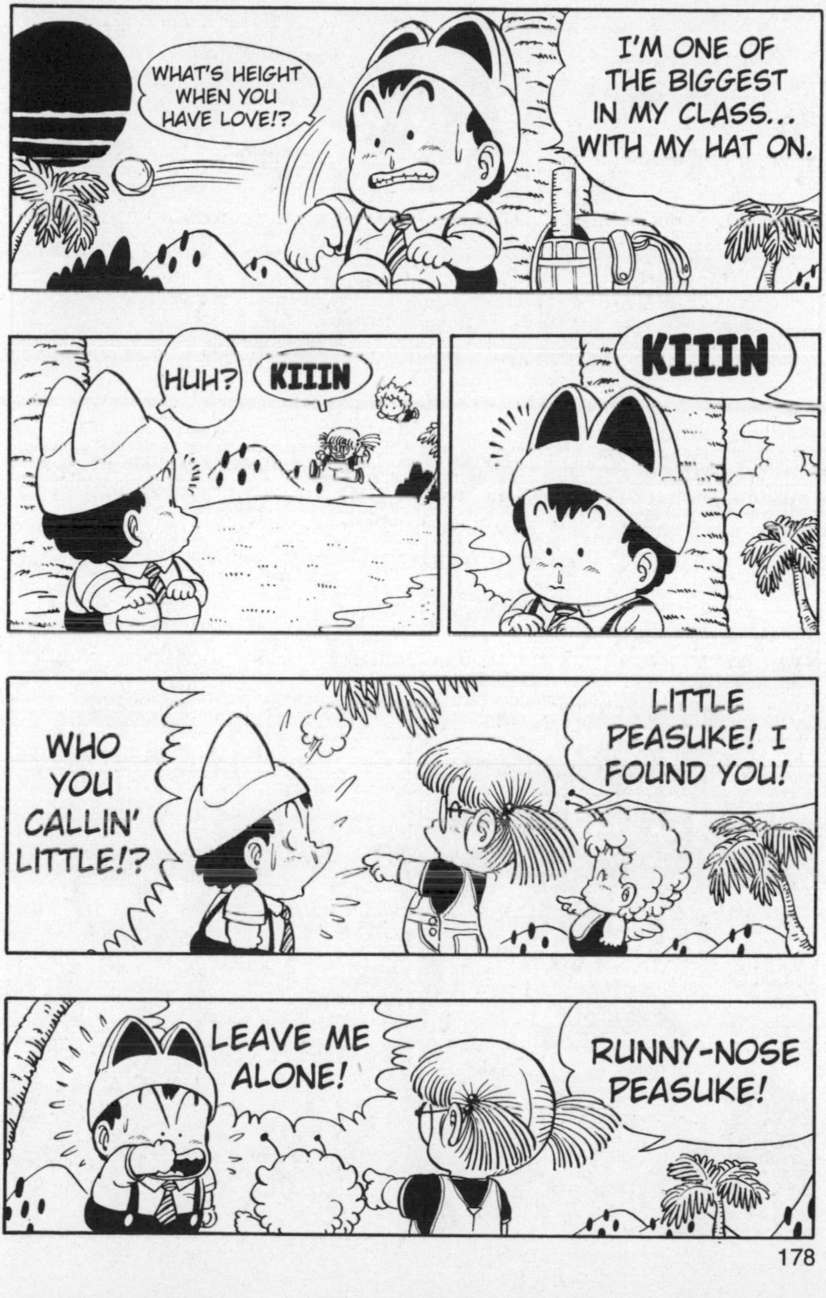
I'M ONE OF THE BIGGEST IN MY CLASS... WITH MY HAT ON.
WHAT'S HEIGHT WHEN YOU HAVE LOVE!?
KIIIN
KIIIN
HUH?
LITTLE PEASUKE! I FOUND YOU!
WHO YOU CALLIN' LITTLE!?
RUNNY-NOSE PEASUKE!
LEAVE ME ALONE!

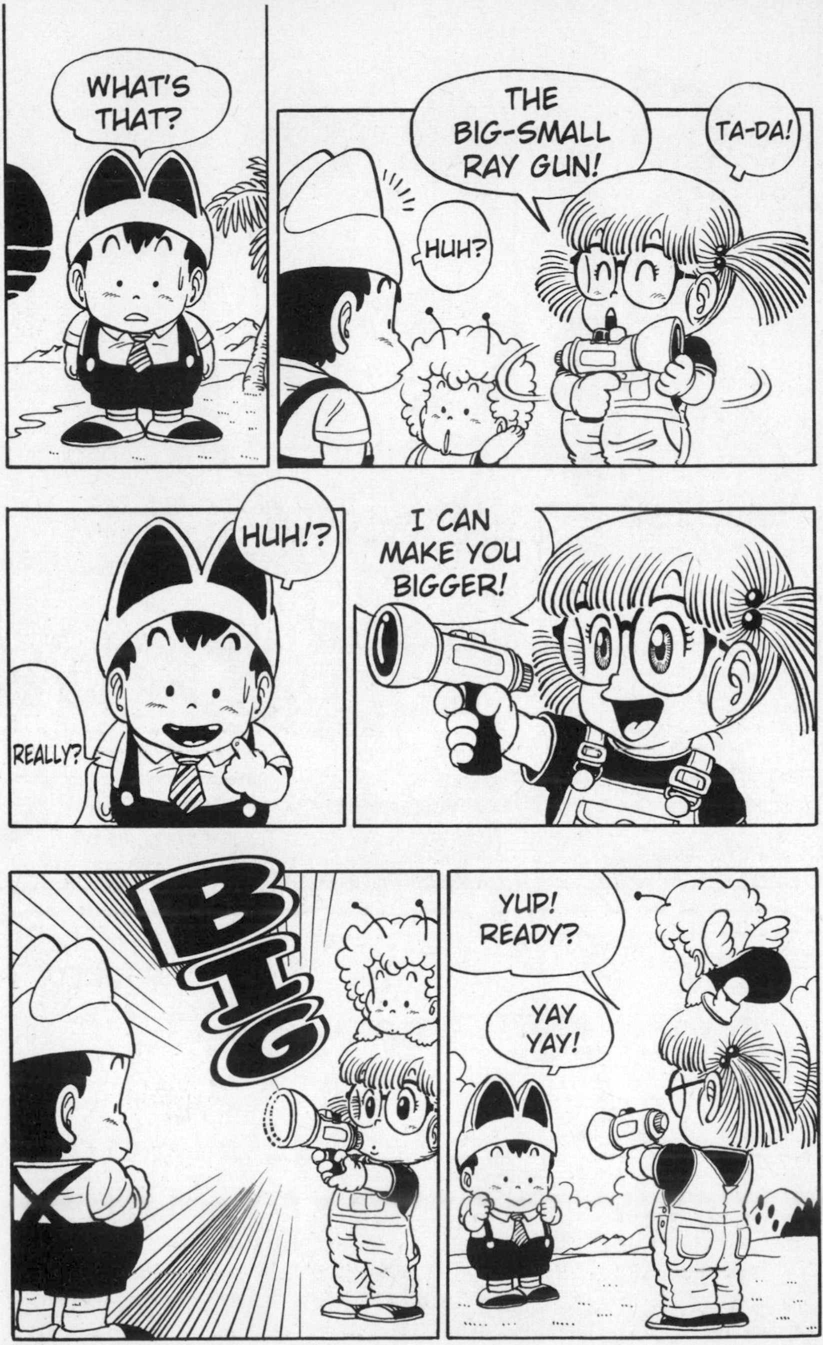
TA-DA!
THE BIG-SMALL RAY GUN!
HUH?
WHAT'S THAT?
I CAN MAKE YOU BIGGER!
HUH!?
REALLY?
YUP! READY?
YAY YAY!
BIG

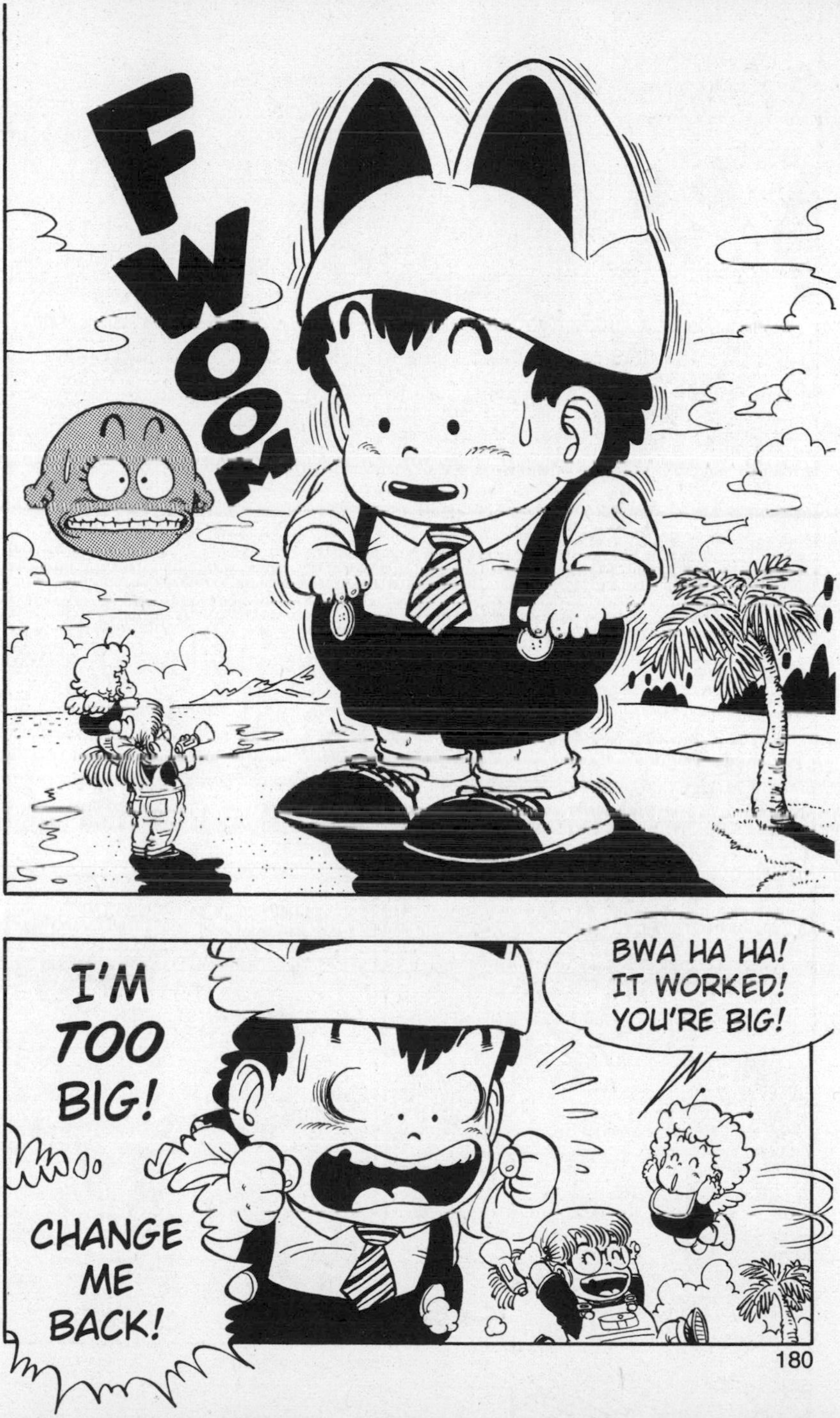
FWOOM
BWA HA HA! IT WORKED! YOU'RE BIG!
I'M TOO BIG!
CHANGE ME BACK!

READ THIS WAY

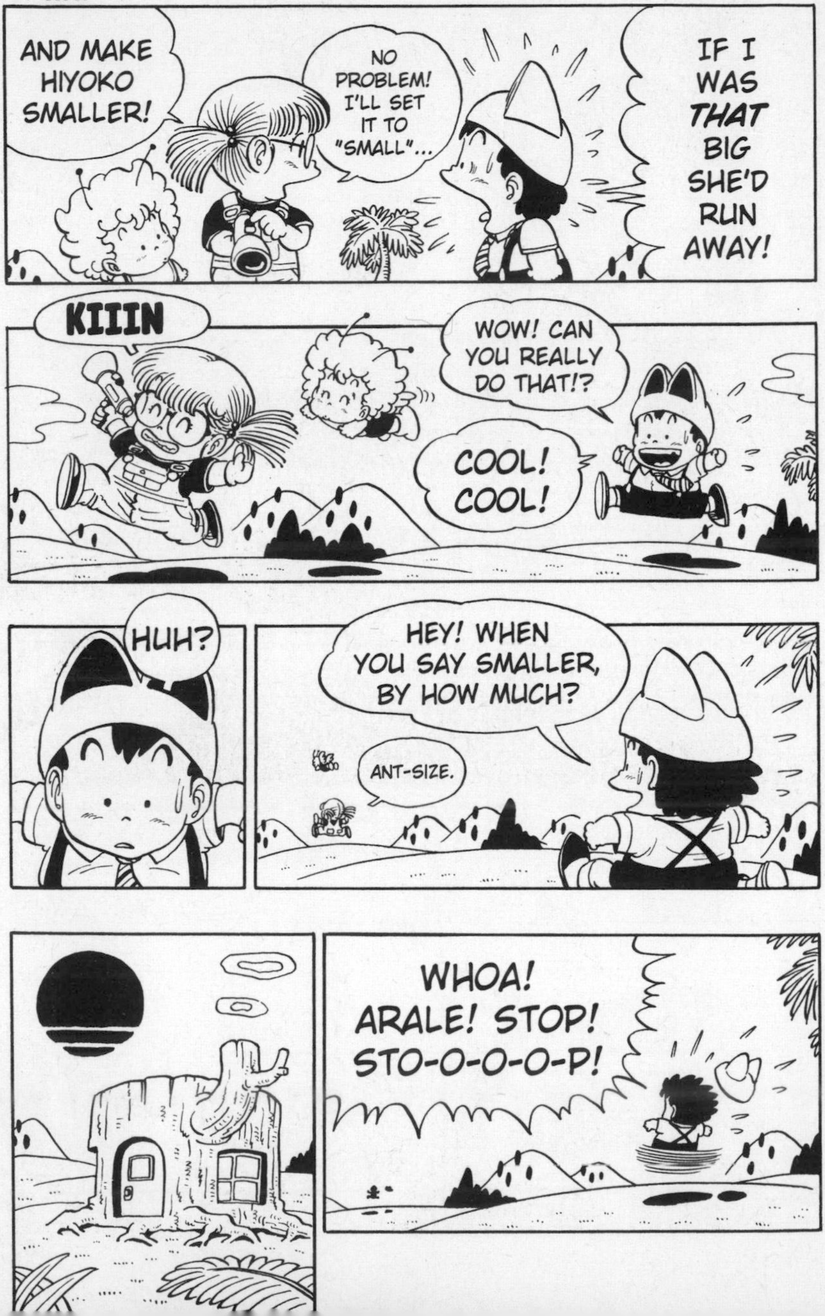
IF I WAS THAT BIG SHE'D RUN AWAY!
NO PROBLEM! I'LL SET IT TO "SMALL"...
AND MAKE HIYOKO SMALLER!
WOW! CAN YOU REALLY DO THAT!?
COOL! COOL!
KIIIN
HEY! WHEN YOU SAY SMALLER, BY HOW MUCH?
ANT-SIZE.
HUH?
WHOA! ARALE! STOP! STO-O-O-O-P!

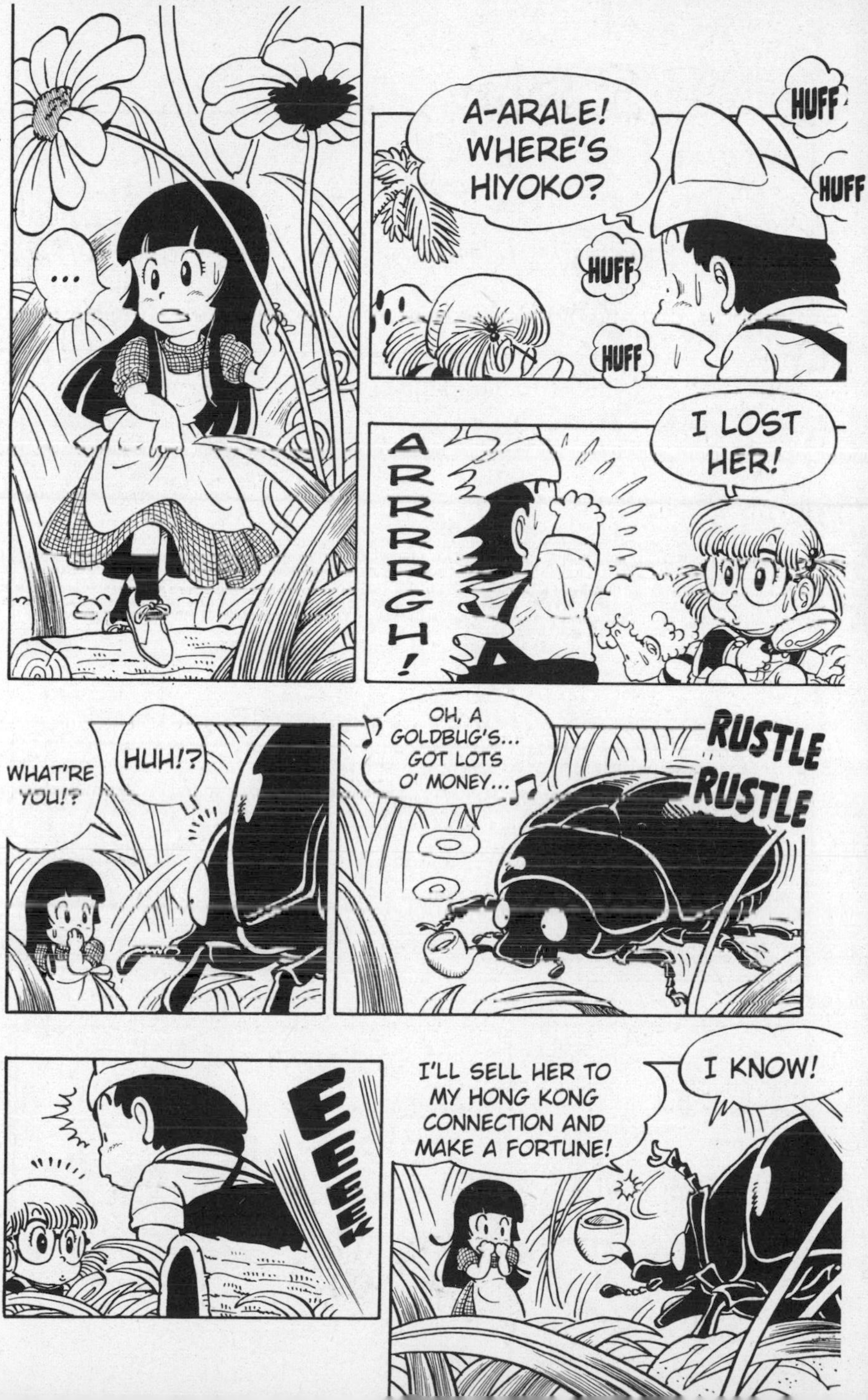
HUFF
HUFF
A-ARALE! WHERE'S HIYOKO?
HUFF
HUFF
I LOST HER!
ARRRRGH!
...
RUSTLE
RUSTLE
OH, A GOLDBUG'S... GOT LOTS O' MONEY...
HUH!?
WHAT'RE YOU!?
I KNOW!
I'LL SELL HER TO MY HONG KONG CONNECTION AND MAKE A FORTUNE!
EEEEEK

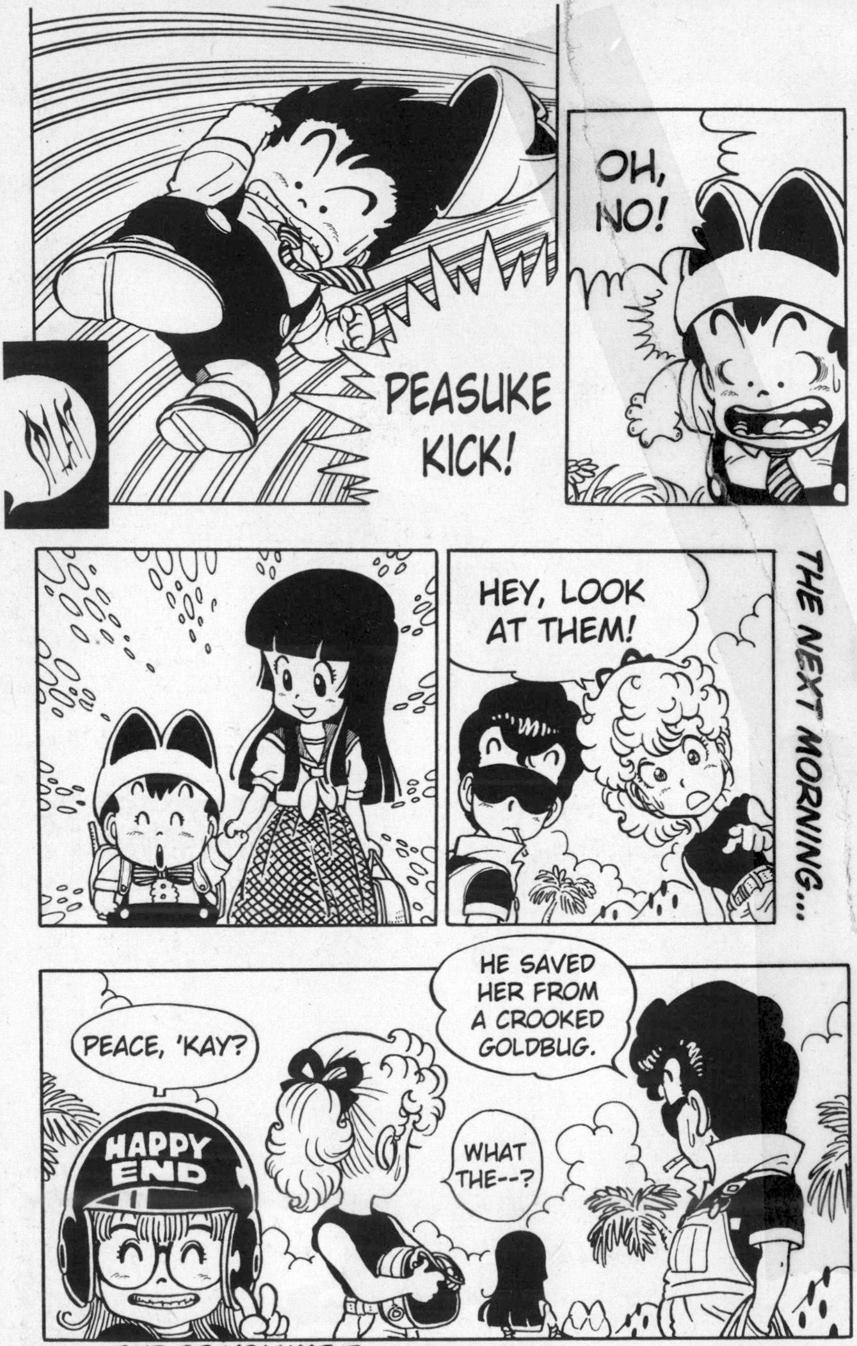
OH, NO!
PEASUKE KICK!
SPLAT
THE NEXT MORNING...
HEY, LOOK AT THEM!
HE SAVED HER FROM A CROOKED GOLDBUG.
PEACE, 'KAY?
WHAT THE--?
HAPPY END

END OF VOLUME 5

In The Next Volume

The dark side comes to **Dr. Slump**. First, the underworld pays Penguin Village a visit to snatch a few souls. Then, the nefarious Dr. Mashirito vows to destroy Arale and make his creation, Caramel Man, the strongest robot in the world. And, finally, Senbei is forced to relive a terrible moment from his childhood, one that will condemn him to an afterlife without dirty magazines...

Available Now!

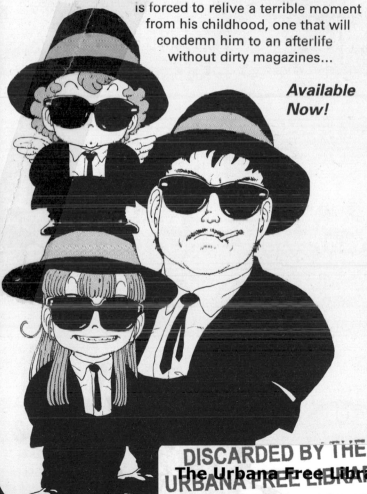